BEST ANCHORAGES of the INSIDE PASSAGE

ANNE VIPOND

WILLIAM KELLY

BRITISH COLUMBIA'S SOUTH COAST
FROM THE GULF ISLANDS TO CAPE CAUTION

OCEAN
CRUISE
GUIDES

Published by: Ocean Cruise Guides Ltd.
325 English Bluff Road
Delta, BC V4M 2M9
Phone: (604) 948-0594
Email: info@oceancruiseguides.com
Visit our web site: oceancruiseguides.com
We would like to hear from you. If you have any comments, suggestions or updates regarding the contents of this book, please write or email us.

Editor: Duart Snow
Copy Editor: Katharine Dawe
Contributing Editor: Mike Woodward
Cartography: OCG.
Design: Ocean Cruise Guides Ltd
Production: OCG, Doug Quiring
Publisher: William Kelly

Photos: Front Cover, Copeland Islands. Page III, Teakerne Arm. Page IV, Hemming Bay.

Printed in Korea

Library and Archives Canada Cataloguing in Publication

Vipond, Anne, 1957-

  Best anchorages of the Inside Passage : from the Gulf Islands to Cape Caution / Anne Vipond, William Kelly. -- 1st ed.

Includes index.

ISBN 0-9697991-7-9

  1. Boats and boating--British Columbia--Pacific Coast--Guidebooks. 2. Boats and boating--Inside Passage--Guidebooks. 3. Pacific Coast (B.C.)--Guidebooks. 4. Inside Passage--Guidebooks. I. Kelly, William, 1951- II. Title.

GV776.15.B7V56 2006   797.1'09711'31   C2005-907392-6

Authors' Acknowledgements

We would like to thank the many people who have supported and assisted us over the years. Bill Wolferstan has been an inspiration to us, as boaters and as writers. Bob Hale has been a welcome presence in our boating lives and in the boating community at large. Mike Woodward has generously shared his expertise on piloting the south coast's numerous tidal passes. And Fred Suthern has been a steadfast friend and advisor.

Our boating friends hold a special place in our hearts. They include Ian Beckett, John and Brenda DeJong, Fred Jensen, Frank and Anne Lebel, Raymond Norris-Jones, Gordon Persson, Mike Robichaud, Fred and Rita Vitringa, and Ulrika Wahlstrom. Our former live-aboard neighbours are among our earliest cruising friends. Barry and Norma Stone, John and Hassina Scott, Derek and Val Morrison, Jacques and Laureen Bacon – they form the 'Dock 9' fraternity to which we have the pleasure of belonging.

  We also thank the many boaters we have met at anchorages, marinas, boat shows and elsewhere, for sharing their personal experiences with us and for offering encouragement to keep writing about the B.C. coast. And we thank the various editors who have published our articles, most notably those who have spent time at the helm of *Pacific Yachting* magazine, namely Paul Burkhart, John Shinnick, Duart Snow, Simon Hill and Peter Robson.

Bill Kelly & Anne Vipond
Tsawwassen, B.C.

A Special Mention
I have had the pleasure of working with many talented editors over the years, but there are two in particular I would like to thank – Richard Hazelton of *48° North*, who was the first editor to accept one of my cruising articles for publication, and John Shinnick, who gave me the opportunity to write a regular column for *Pacific Yachting*.

Anne Vipond

This book is dedicated to Reid and John, and to the memory of Tuck.

FOREWORD

The best cruising guides speak from the heart as well as the mind. They present the facts – how to get there, what is there – the vital details about the safety and suitability of different anchorages, and so on. But they also need to convey stories and impressions that help you to decide whether you should visit these places in the first place. Anne Vipond and Bill Kelly have considerable experience in providing both, having explored the Inside Passage on a variety of vessels, from their own 35-foot sloop *Sway* up to the largest cruise ship. They have written countless authoritative articles on coastal cruising since the early 1980s.

Readers of their articles in *Pacific Yachting* and other boating magazines may not be aware however, that at the same time they were writing about their adventures sailing our coast they were busy producing a superb series of guide books focusing on the major attractions of cruise ship routes in the Mediterranean, the Caribbean, the Panama Canal, Hawaii, and the Inside Passage to Alaska.

Their new book *Best Anchorages of the Inside Passage* is designed to assist small boat operators voyaging between Victoria and Cape Caution with 200 carefully selected anchorage locations, many of which are finely detailed through illustrations, maps and summary pros and cons. In a most comprehensive and entertaining manner, they answer the important questions: What is there and how do you get there? And, why go? Their first-hand local knowledge provides valuable insight into the intricacies of navigating a safe course through tidal passes and into a variety of rock-bound anchorages.

Most important, they also have a native-born sympathy for the local history, flora, fauna, culture and geography of the places they describe. Reading through these descriptions I can only repeat what Miles Smeeton said in his foreword to my first cruising guide on the Gulf Islands: "For those who have already experienced their peace, it will bring back memories to be enjoyed and sometimes perhaps they will wonder, why they ever went away."

Bill Wolferstan
www.linquenda.ca

CONTENTS

Tenedos Bay

There are many scenic waterways in this world, but there is only one Inside Passage. Stretching northward from Puget Sound in Washington State to Skagway in Southeast Alaska, this vast and intricate coastline of winding channels and forested islands is unsurpassed in both beauty and accessibility for boaters. The Canadian portion of the Inside Passage spans 500 nautical miles, from the southern tip of Vancouver Island to the exposed waters of Dixon Entrance where the border runs between British Columbia and Alaska.

This cruising guide, Volume I, covers the southern half of B.C.'s inside waters, the area that lies between Vancouver Island and the mainland coast. Its southern boundary is marked by Juan de Fuca Strait and its northern boundary by Queen Charlotte Sound. Included in this guide is information on the marinas and ports we have pulled into while wandering up and down this section of coast, but the emphasis is on anchorages.

It is the anchorages that inspire us. We have been exploring the coastal waters of B.C. for more than two decades, yet it seems we would need several lifetimes to visit every potential anchorage along the way. Some areas in fact have only recently been charted and many anchorages remain unnamed.

Finding new anchorages is relatively easy when cruising the Inside Passage's myriad of islands and inlets. More difficult was choosing, for this guidebook, our favourite anchorages from the many beautiful and sheltered spots we have called home for the night. Fluctuating factors can colour a person's perception of an anchorage – the weather, the people you meet while there, your own state of mind at the time. Yet, some anchorages provide the haven we all seek and these become, however briefly, the places we enjoy revisiting, even if only in our memories.

Whether tucked into a craggy cove or hidden at the head of a glassy fjord, there are so many fine anchorages along our coast that, whatever your vessel, you will be sure to find one or two that are special. It may be small and unnamed, or a place unremarkable except that it provided shelter in a storm. Or perhaps it was an anchorage that offered a clear view onto the nature and wildness of our coast. Remoteness and seclusion certainly help make an anchorage special, but this guidebook covers the popular destinations as well. We never tire of returning to our old favourites or of discovering new places. This, for us, is the joy of boating.

Anne Vipond and Bill Kelly

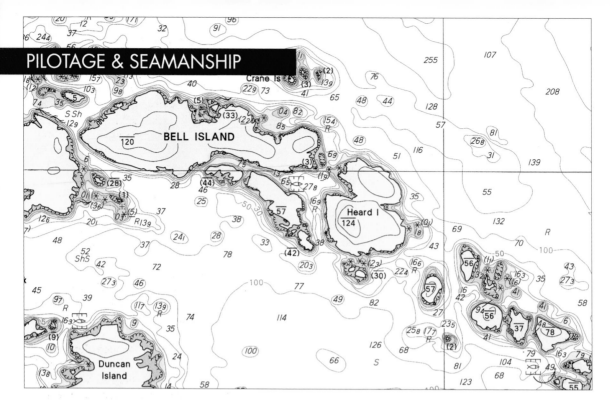

Numerous islands shelter the waters of the Inside Passage from the open Pacific Ocean, but piloting a vessel successfully through the Inside Passage remains a challenge. Unlike freshwater cruising grounds, the coastal waters of British Columbia are swept by significant tides which can produce strong currents in passes and channels. These waters demand an understanding of the elements that make up weather and sea conditions. While some factors are more predictable than others, the ever-changing nature of weather and the sea is what makes cruising along the Inside Passage a fascinating adventure – one that excites the spirit long after the voyage is over.

To us, seamanship means being prepared for any contingency. You are not ready to go anywhere in a boat if you haven't checked that every item on your vessel is in good working order. Detailed charts and Canadian Hydrographic Service publications are, of course, crucial and only a fool would venture from their berth without these stowed aboard. Learning to interpret charts is a lifelong endeavour and very much a part of gaining 'local knowledge.' The nature of the bottom, the topography of the surrounding land, sometimes even the shoreside vegetation and nearby structures, are included on CHS charts and all have a bearing on the quality of an anchorage.

Things can go wrong for even the most experienced skipper and keeping this in mind helps. Halyards jam, bad fuel gets onboard and deadheads find you. Perhaps the most important thing to con-

Canadian Hydrographic Service charts are superb – well inked with definitive colours and text.

trol during an out-of-control situation is yourself. Panicked thinking is common during a crisis on the water and is not easy to suppress. We've found there is usually more time to respond during a critical situation than there appears to be and that most boats (those over 26 feet anyway) can handle even the worst summer conditions of the Inside Passage. The test, as always, is the response of the crew.

Weather and Sea Conditions

Weather systems flow in a west to east direction in the northern hemisphere, so the west coast of North America enjoys the moderating effects of the Pacific Ocean throughout the year. In winter, wet and windy weather prevails along the Pacific coast, its mountainous shoreline a catch-basin for offshore storms flowing into the Gulf of Alaska. Precipitation that falls as snow on mountain slopes rarely remains more than a few days in low-lying areas of B.C.'s south coast.

Summer weather in the North Pacific is dominated by a subtropical high which brings reduced precipitation and increased sunshine. Autumn is a transitional season when the North Pacific High gradually shrinks and the relatively light breezes of summer are replaced with winter storms generated by the Aleutian Low. At any time of year, winds along the sheltered Inside Passage are less intense than those on the open Pacific.

Summer winds are generally light to moderate and seas range from calm to choppy. Wind conditions are highly localized due to the mountainous topography and twisting channels, with acceleration off capes and headlands, and strong outflow winds near large inlets. Generally speaking, winds blow strongest on the north coast and lose their velocity as they move south until they reach Juan de Fuca Strait, where strong westerlies are common.

The waterways of the Inside Passage are sheltered from ocean swells, but local hazards include steep, choppy seas, fog and tidal currents. One of most challenging bodies of water of the Inside Passage is the Strait of Georgia, where very steep seas can be encountered during large tides along the eastern side of the strait south of Vancouver. This results from one of the largest rivers in North America, the Fraser River, emptying its waters into the strait. Johnstone Strait has also gained notoriety for its strong afternoon westerlies which, when opposing an ebbing tide, can whip up large, steep seas. There have been times when afternoon westerlies have persisted for weeks in this strait, and if you are determined to make progress north, a good strategy is to get underway before dawn, or travel in the evening or at night.

In summer, sea fog occurs anywhere there are upwellings of cold water. This dense fog is frequently encountered in Juan de Fuca Strait and Queen Charlotte Strait. Also called advection fog, sea fog occurs when warm, moist maritime air blows onshore across colder coastal water that has been brought to the surface by upwellings. These upwellings are caused either by tidal currents being deflected upward from an irregular sea bottom or by wind pushing away the surface water to allow deeper, colder water to rise to the surface. Sea fog drifts inland on onshore breezes and will drift to the head of even the longest inlets, lingering through the day.

Radiation-type fog occurs on clear cold nights when the land cools, causing water droplets to condense onto fine particles suspended in the warmer air. This type of fog is most dense at sunrise and slowly burns off with daytime heating. Radiation fog begins in September and lasts through February, occurring throughout the Strait of Georgia and adjacent waterways where visibility is reduced to a half-mile on about 20 days per year. In specific areas, such as the Fraser River estuary, where the river's relatively low temperature contributes to the cooling process, up to 60 days per year can be fog-ridden.

The Canadian Coast Guard issues a continuous marine weather broadcast on the VHF weather channel and this should be monitored before leaving port. If you are travelling in poor visibility, it is a good idea to contact the traffic channels maintained by the Coast Guard along the Strait of Georgia and Johnstone Strait. This excellent service alerts commercial vessels of your presence and is very helpful in areas of large-vessel activity, such as Active Pass and the traffic lanes of the Strait of Georgia. See this book's 'Cruising Essentials' for VHF channels for Coast Guard traffic.

Other Hazards

Drifting logs and other debris are a common hazard in B.C. waters, especially following a spring tide or a storm. Seaborne material tends to collect along tide lines and is easy to spot. Harder to avoid are logs lying in the troughs of large waves and deadheads – which are logs standing upright in the water with just a few inches protruding above the surface. Keep a constant lookout for debris while underway and make it a habit to scan the water well ahead with the use of binoculars.

A sailboat heads out into the morning fog of Queen Charlotte Strait in mid-July.

Looking back at notorious Hopetown Passage.

Tides, Currents and Passes

The waters of the Inside Passage are greatly affected by tides, and current from tides is encountered in the many passes, channels and straits. It is also common for anchorages to have remnant current, although not usually more than one or 2 knots. Tides rise and fall twice a day (referred to as semidiurnal or mixed) with one a higher high water and one a lower low water variation as shown in the tide tables. Tides, caused by the gravitational pull on the earth's water by the sun and moon, moves water from the Pacific Ocean to mainland inlets and back again, forcing current to flow around both ends of Vancouver Island. The ocean current enters southern waters through Juan de Fuca Strait, and northern waters through Queen Charlotte Strait, which results in tides flooding north in the Strait of Georgia and south in Johnstone Strait.

The size of tides is related to the phases of the moon and its position with the sun. Every month the lunar cycle results in the difference between the height of high tide and depth of low tide becoming greater. For a period of one or two days (during new and full moons), the difference will be at its greatest (usually about 12 to 15 feet at Point Atkinson) and this is referred to as a spring tide. The cycle then reverses itself and each day for two weeks the tide range becomes smaller until the difference between high and low water can be as little as 3 feet. The region's complex topography of islands and channels creates localized tide and current conditions, and makes the annual Canadian Hydrographic Service's Tide and Current Tables an indispensable reference for boaters cruising the Inside Passage.

Safely transiting any tidal pass is simple if done at or near slack, which is the time span when the tide turns from one direction to another. The CHS Tide and Current Tables contain the times of turn to flood and to ebb, and maximum rates of current, for all the major passes. Local weather conditions and the amount of land drainage can sometimes cause a discrepancy in the predicted time versus actual time of slack water, but generally speaking the CHS Tide and Current Tables are very reliable. When calculating slack water, be sure to add an hour in summer for daylight saving time.

Missing slack water is a reality when cruising the Inside Passage, and transiting a pass before or after slack – when current and turbulence will be encountered – becomes less daunting with experience. Smaller passes with no obstructions or fast currents can be taken with a wider window, and an example of this is Chatham Channel near Johnstone Strait. A wide-open pass without obstructions (such as Seymour Narrows or Hole in the Wall) can be navigated safely on some amount of pulling current during the beginning or very end of a tide. A narrow or intricate pass with hazards (such as Whiterock Passage or Booker Lagoon Passage) is best transited against current or at slack and not when the current is pulling you. Going with the current in large passes saves time and, if done carefully, can work well in improving distance for the day.

Sometimes, whether in the mother ship or in a dinghy, you may find yourself entering inextricably into a passage with more current than expected. If such is the case, stay away from whirlpools or areas of heavy turbulence and steer toward the tongue (the flat, quiet part) of the current where there is usually deeper water.

Detailed information on all the passes is contained in applicable chapters of this book.

Anchoring

Anchoring is often a source of anxiety for people new to boating, and it is open to discussion whether anchoring is an art or a science. As wryly noted in *Oceanography and Seamanship* by William Van Dorn, anchoring is not ordinarily regarded as an emergency procedure but perhaps it should be. Few subjects inspire more opinions with boaters than anchors and how best to set them. After some 25 years of cruising the Inside Passage and the Gulf of Alaska, we've seen there are many ways to stay safely anchored, but the common thread with experienced skippers is to install the largest (heaviest) ground tackle practical and make sure the bitter end is attached to the boat.

CHS team measuring current with an inflatable at Hole in the Wall pass.

Measuring Tides & Currents

The harmonic nature of tides and currents wasn't fully understood until the late 19th century when Dr. A.T. Doodson at the Tidal Institute of Liverpool completed years of study involving complex calculus and algebra. Doodson's method of harmonic analysis, based on a long series of measurements of the tide or current at a particular location, was a remarkable improvement over previous methods and still stands as the accepted principle of tidal prediction to this day.

More recently, and much closer to home, a research scientist at the Institute of Ocean Sciences in Sidney, Mike Foreman, introduced digital computation to the process of harmonic analysis. Modern predictions by the Canadian Hydrographic Society are based on Foreman's routines, but the quality of the predictions are only as good as the series of measurements necessary to derive the local tidal constituents. Typically, a tide station or pass needs a complete year of measurements at one-hour intervals to give oceanographers a complete picture on which to base predictions.

British Columbia's first tide-recording stations were established in the 1890s, and the first tide tables for B.C.'s southwest coast were published in 1901, but attempts to improve predictions of the passes really got underway after World War II. CHS field workers would often set up a fixed transit and float poles with flags through the pass to determine current speed. On one occasion, baby bottles with lights inside were used to gauge Gabriola Passage during night observations.

CHS also uses submerged buoys to measure the current over the long periods needed for harmonic analysis, as well as boats, which were first used in the late 1970s.

In the 1980s, rigid-bottom inflatables became the workhorse of CHS field workers. Their design – based on U.K. rescue vessels – provided a stable platform for CHS workers to maneuver in the passes without losing control in the strong eddies. Working in pairs, the coxswain's job is to hold position while the other team member keeps track of speed and judges the quality of the measurement. According to oceanographer Mike Woodward, "We'd often just sit in a pass – seemingly stuck in one place for a long time. I've wondered how many other vessels have given up after seeing what appears to be our failure to get through the contrary current."

Michael Woodward,
a pioneer of tide & current research

Mariners plying the many passes along the British Columbia coast have detailed information at their fingertips on tides and currents, thanks to research conducted by the Canadian Hydrographic Service (CHS). Many of the passes were thoroughly researched in the 1980s and much of the key data was assembled by Mike Woodward of Victoria. Mike learned sailing from his father Jack who also taught him some of the competitive advantages of playing the currents off Cadboro Bay. Years later, after completing a degree in physics (Toronto, 1974), he found a job with CHS in Current Surveys where he was involved in all aspects of currents to assist the navigation of the various passes.

Mike spent some 20 years studying tidal streams in the narrow passes of the B.C. coast. He developed a unique methodology, spanning measurement technology, field surveys, and computer models, to produce year-long continuous data records of currents in many of our turbulent tidal rapids. This data was then analyzed to establish current predictions for ten key locations that are now included in the Tide and Current Tables: Porlier Pass, Gabriola Pass, Dodd Narrows, Sechelt Rapids, Beazley Pass, Hole-in-the-Wall, Gillard Passage, Arran Rapids, Quatsino Narrows and Nakwakto Rapids. He also used current meters (see photo page 188) to study and analyze tidal streams in Race Passage, Weynton Passage and Scott Channel that resulted in daily predictions for these locations in the Current Tables. Mike retired from CHS in 2001.

Mike Woodward when he worked at CHS.

CQR shows its holding power – with only partial burial into a rocky bottom, the 45-pound anchor was able to kedge off our grounded 6-ton boat.

The debate of all-chain versus chain-and-rope continues unabated. Many mariners swear by an all-chain rode and it seems an equal number stand by a rope-and-chain combination. It really depends on boat size, with larger vessels having the stronger case for an all-chain rode where the weight of the tackle (and winch) at the bow of the vessel has less impact on its sea handling and trim. For our 35-foot

Take your time before picking a spot to set the anchor in a crowded anchorage.

sailboat, we use a 45-pound CQR with 24 feet of 3/8-inch BBB chain shackled to 500 feet of 5/8-inch abrasion-resistant nylon line. We've had consistently good results with this tackle for many years and would not change anything. We have used various types of anchors and keep four on board, but we believe the CQR plow-type anchor or the Bruce anchor are best for our coast because of their ability to penetrate well into the variety of local sea beds and stay set.

The bottom of each anchorage offers holding ability of varying degrees. Although some bottoms are rocky or pebbled and others have kelp or eel grass, almost all are a mud-based mix of material. South of Campbell River, where there is less kelp the bottom is invariably mud mixed with sand, crushed shell or, occasionally, clay. Ganges Harbour and Long Harbour on Saltspring Island have such a mix of mud and clay, which can make anchor retrieval a game of grunt and heave. Some anchorages north of Discovery Passage have thickets of bull kelp which can be difficult or impossible for some anchors to penetrate. Anchorages with rocks or stones and those with heavy kelp bottoms are usually not great for holding but there are exceptions. Port Neville's west shore is notorious for kelp yet, once past the stuff, we've found the holding ground to be quite good. Many anchorages have been home to recent logging operations and debris is often scattered about the seabed. The worst leftovers are lengths of steel cable which, if hooked onto, can be the, last many skippers see of their anchors.

Decaying branches, stumps, abandoned crab pots and other matter can foul any anchor and turn an otherwise good anchorage into a bad memory.

One way you can obtain a feel of the bottom is by snubbing the rode on a short scope (2 or 2.5 to 1) as the anchor drags along the seabed. If the hook is bouncing, the ground may have a mix of large stones or rock. If the anchor line swings back and forth and the anchor is not sure if it wants to hold, the bottom could be soft mud and needs more scope. If the rode has a jerking and sliding feel, like the anchor is trying to set on a conveyor belt, it might in a kelp bed or perhaps hard sand and rock. For most mud bottoms, if the hook is having trouble setting, letting out a few feet more of line (to a minimum of 3 to 1) will usually help it set properly. You can check the set by slowly applying more engine power in reverse.

There are occasions, in soft mud for example, where the holding may start out poor but improve as the anchor worries its way down into a thicker bottom. This is the case in the anchorage at Walker Island Group in Queen Charlotte Strait where the top strata of soft mud and kelp lies over a thicker mix of mud and shell. If you have concerns about the set or the bottom, be extra vigilant for an overnight stay. Check land bearings regularly and keep in mind there is no honour lost in simply re-anchoring.

The surrounding terrain (gentle shoreline vs. steep shoreline; heavily forested vs. bare land) will affect local wind speed and direction, and what might appear to be a well protected bay could turn out to be a wind tunnel under certain conditions. An example of this is Boot Cove on Saturna Island, where the steep cliff-like northwest side of the cove can accelerate southerlies forcefully.

Boaters should also keep in mind that when winds are gale force or stronger almost all anchorages will get some gusts. If wind strength is going to

Bull Kelp

Bull kelp, which thrives in shallow areas of strong tidal current, tells boaters many things. A type of seaweed, its long, rubbery stem is rooted to the sea bottom in depths reaching 30 feet (HW) and its long fronds float at the surface, held there by a ball-shaped float that is kept inflated by trapped gases, the result of rapid photosynthesis. Bull kelp grows rapidly during the summer and alerts boaters to the presence of underwater shoals and reefs. Also, if there is current, the direction and speed are indicated by the plant's fronds flowing with the current away from the inflated float.

If current is pushing the float underwater, the stream is likely flowing faster than 3 knots. If the float remains above the water but the blades are flowing straight out, then the current will be about 2 knots or less. If the blades appear to be gently flowing in opposite directions or are at an angle to the orientation of the pass, you know you are at or near slack. In narrow passes, a distinct open channel clear of kelp usually indicates deeper water. Bull kelp should always be seen as a sign of danger and be given a wide berth. Bull kelp sometimes comes adrift during storms and collects in large clumps with other debris (logs, branches, etc.) along the edges of tidelines and should also be avoided.

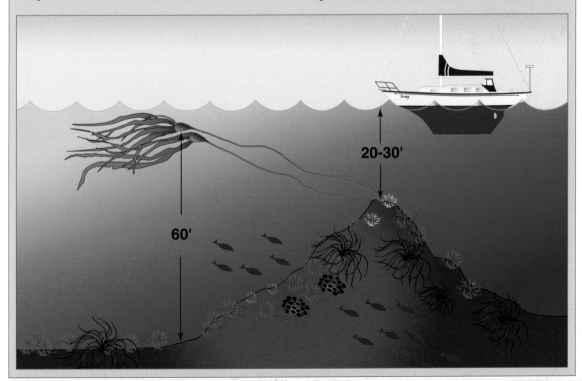

BOTTOMS UP

An anchorage's bottom material has varying ability to hold an anchor and is an important consideration when setting the hook. Mud is the medium which makes up most anchorages and its mix with other material will determine holding power. CHS charts indicate the type of bottom for most anchorages but sometimes there is some guesswork involved for the skipper. The foreshore may give some idea of the type of bottom below or a sample from the bottom might be obtained using a small anchor with the tip smeared in grease. Here in descending order is our view of the best mix for holding bottom:

Mud with clay – sets like wet cement. Can be difficult to retrieve anchor, with large chunks sticking to the anchor.

Sticky mud with sand – grit of sand helps lock

anchor, streaks of mud remain on anchor as it comes up. All anchors set very well in this.

Thick mud with sand or broken shell – anchor sinks well into this and buries deep. Great holding.

Mud / mud sand – most burying anchors do well in this bottom. Generally good holding.

Sand with mud – an all-sand anchorage is rare along the Inside Passage and most sandy bottoms (such as Sidney spit) still have some mud and broken shell mixed in. Holding usually is good. Hard sand will be difficult to penetrate for some anchors.

Soft mud – a good burying anchor will hold here, but not the best medium for many hooks.

Mud and kelp – can be good although the sharp point of a CQR (or a fishman's anchor) may be only anchor able to penetrate well.

Sand and gravel – not easy to penetrate and not usually good holding.

Soft mud and rock – anchors may have a tough time staying set, rocks can foul anchor and holding often fair at best.

Gravel and rock – tough to penetrate and holding usually only fair.

Soft mud over a hard layer – not uncommon along Inside Passage. Holding fair at best.

Oozy mud and rock – one of the poorest bottoms. A good burying anchor such as a Bruce or CQR will be only hope here.

---

be severe, consider a line to a windward shore and pull yourself in as close to the lee of the land as is safely possible. Also, remember that an anchorage which might be well protected from wind on one point of the compass but may be quite breezy should the wind shift by just a few degrees, which is often the case when an anchorage is angular or narrow, such as Princess Cove on Wallace Island.

In a crowded anchorage, there are many factors to consider when deciding the 'anchoring circle' of your vessel. Finding a spot to anchor in tight situations can be intimidating, especially under the territorial glares of other boaters. Study the chart before entering an unfamiliar anchorage and take your time deciding where you want to drop the hook. Inexperienced boaters tend to cluster with other boats and sometimes miss a better anchoring opportunity in another part of the bay. Tying a line to shore in a crowded anchorage is a prudent solution when current or crosswind is not an issue.

Our anchoring routine begins with a slow approach through the anchorage, checking the depth with the chart as we make our way to a clear spot. We bring the boat slowly to the position where we want to be once the anchor has set and take visual bearings while we drift forward to the point where the anchor is finally lowered. If we are anchoring

with the engine running, we'll begin lowering the anchor after the reverse gear has started pulling the boat slowly back to ensure the chain is lying clear of the anchor and the anchor shank is in line with the bow of the boat. Once the anchor has touched bottom, we keep slight tension on the rode and normally snub the anchor on a short scope of about 2:1 to feel how it is biting. Once we feel it wants to set, we let out more rode to at least 3:1 scope and then securely set the anchor by running the engine at half-speed.

When calculating the amount of line to let out, be sure to include the rise and fall of the tide and the height of your vessel's freeboard. Also, be aware of the swinging circles of nearby boats. Set your anchor in line with vessels already at anchor and be sure you have enough water underneath your vessel for your entire swinging circle! More than once we have seen vessels swing into shallow water and end up on the hard (which happened to us at Deep Bay near Chrome Island).

Although some experts extol the benefits of anchoring with large scopes of 6:1 or 7:1, this is rarely practical in most of the tight anchorages of the Inside Passage. We almost always anchor at 3:1 and occasionally, if we have room, let out 4:1 or 5:1 if the wind is picking up. However, in a roadstead anchorage or a large bay where your vessel is exposed to swell or wave action, letting out more scope in windy conditions is the wise course.

If we're in an unfamiliar anchorage, we usually set the hook in the middle of the cove or bay unless a hazard would suggest otherwise. Although the urge is to go to the shallow part of a bay closer to shore, it's usually better to drop the hook in deeper water to give yourself more room if you need to let out line. Deeper water also provides better shock absorption for the ground tackle because the longer rode presents greater resistance to being straightened in deep water. Three-to-one scope in 45 feet (15 m) is better than 3:1 in 15 feet (5 m). Another benefit of deeper water is that wave action is less pronounced in bad conditions and the surge strain on the anchor will be reduced. Most anchorages south of Cape Caution will be in depths less than 50 feet (16 m).

Although a sheltered and deep anchorage with lots of room is perhaps the ideal, sometimes the anchoring conditions in a specific cove call for a stern anchor to create a secure and comfortable mooring closer to shore. Some northern inlets have few good anchorages, but offer numerous bights where one can lie for the night with a fisherman's mooring by tying bow and stern lines to shore. At some popular marine park anchorages, where space is limited, the usual practice is for boaters to tie a stern line to one of the ring bolts installed along the shore. Tying a stern line ashore might seem like a simple operation and for many people, it probably is. For us, though, it often seems that just as one of us jumps into the dinghy a cross-current suddenly appears or a breeze begins pushing the boat away. Our method is to secure the stern line first, then power the boat slowly forward to the point where we want to drop the anchor, while we pay out the stern

line. Once the anchor is down, we pull back on the stern line and using the boat's inertia to set the hook.

Some anchorages have foul bottoms, such as where logging operations have taken place, and a tripline is a prudent step to ensure successful retrieval of the anchor. Most anchors allow a line to be attached at the fluke end of the shank which, when pulled, easily disengages the anchor.

In summer, when the weather is settled, boaters have a natural desire to raft with other boats. The problem with rafts is that if something goes wrong, like a strong wind coming up in the night, each boat tugs and strains to its own rhythm, putting strain on the ground tackle. More prudent, but less fun, is to anchor off and visit friends' vessels by dinghy.

Mooring overnight to a log boom is always a little risky as one is never sure when a tug may arrive to move the logs elsewhere. We rarely tie to log booms for overnight stays, but if we do, we'll thread our lines to the boom stick chains and double these back to *Sway* to allow for a quiet release and departure. The only time we might use rafting dogs or log dogs (which are pounded into a log to provide an anchoring point) is to secure a line to a very large beached log when nothing else is available to us.

Note: Throughout 'The Anchorages' section of this book, any reference to a numbered island means the island is thus marked on the relevant chart. The number refers to the height, in metres, the island is above high water.

The anchorage that nightmares are made of. We were trapped here for 2 days along the Alaska Peninsula in 40- to 50-knot winds. With 400 feet of line out, the CQR held but, through the fault of the skipper, the anchor rode was badly chafed.

HMS Plumper in Port Harvey during a British surveying expedition in May 1860.

A Look Back at Pilotage

Explorers of the 18th century were constantly expanding the frontiers of ocean and coastal navigation. A knack for pilotage meant a successful career in the navy, as was proven by James Cook, whose three Pacific voyages earned him lasting acclaim as the Great Navigator.

George Vancouver, who served on Cook's last two voyages, proved himself a worthy successor to his famous mentor. While Cook often made running surveys of the coastlines he was sweeping past, Vancouver was sent to the Pacific Northwest to conduct a detailed survey of the coastal mainland from Juan de Fuca Strait to Cook Inlet in Alaska. Vancouver's painstaking delineation of our intricate coastline is considered one of the most demanding surveys ever undertaken. He and his men spent three summers (1792-94) on the B.C. and Alaska coasts, departing each fall for the Sandwich Islands (Hawaii), then returning the following spring to resume the survey. This lengthy voyage, which began and ended in England, took four and a half years to complete and covered 65,000 nautical miles, making it the longest continuous sailing expedition in history.

Aids to coastal navigation in the 18th century lagged behind those being developed for ocean navigation. Deviation of the magnetic compass was by then understood and the sextant, a refinement of the quadrant, was an accurate measuring instrument at sea. The most recent breakthrough was the chronometer, which allowed ocean navigators to determine longitude without making complex calculations based on lunar observations. But this state-of-the-art equipment was of limited use when a ship entered uncharted coastal waters. This was when pilotage skills became critical.

The term 'pilotage' derives from the Dutch word *peillood* which means 'sounding lead', the measuring device of Vancouver's day. Attached to a hemp line was a 7-lb lead weight, its lower end cap-shaped to hold a pressed lump of tallow, which, when dragged across the bottom, picked up whatever was down there – sand, mud, shell or, if the tallow came up clean, rock. A 25-fathom line was marked at standard intervals with pieces of leather, cord or cloth, their different textures allowing the leadsman to feel the marks in the dark. Experience and skill were needed to take sounding with this hand line. The leadsman, hanging from the forechains by a bight of line, would swing the lead over and over, then heave it far ahead of the ship so that it was straight below when the bow glided over it.

For deeper waters, a 100-fathom line with a heavier lead was used. With the ship hove to, a 14-lb weight was carried forward, its line leading aft along the weather side and held in coils at regular intervals by seamen. The heavy lead was cast at the order "heave." When the leadsman was sure the weight hadn't touched bottom, he would release his section of line and call to the next man abaft who in turn would release his coil once he was sure the lead had not yet touched, and so on down the line until the lead hit bottom. A sounding rod was used in shallow water when the bottom could be poked.

Vancouver made running surveys of the California, Oregon and Washington coastlines. However, upon reaching Juan de Fuca Strait, he realized he would have to continue the survey in the ships' boats because of the labyrinth of islands and inlets facing him. This meant finding safe anchorages for the two ships, then setting off in open boats for two or three weeks of shoreline surveying. Vancouver and his officers headed the survey teams, sailing or rowing up the many inlets in search of an inland waterway. On shore they took angles of headlands and drew sketches, these findings later plotted on a master chart.

Vancouver's disciplined approach saw him and his officers take frequent and multiple sets of lunar observations to determine the longitude, and the chronometers were constantly monitored. Even so, Vancouver's longitudinal readings were slightly east of actual bearings – a situation he became aware of when he reached Nootka Sound at the end of his first survey season. He decided to carry on with this slightly-to-the-east orientation rather than alter all of his surveying to this point.

Vancouver's search for an inland waterway was of course futile but his survey laid the groundwork for further detailed charting in the 19th century, when Britain extensively surveyed all of her Empire's distant coastlines. The seminal charts produced by Captain Vancouver and his officers were, at the time, unequalled in detail and accuracy, and

Although Captain George Vancouver brought a number of chronometers (one shown above left) for his survey of the Inside Passage, he preferred lunar observations to determine longitude.

are the basis for today's charts of coastal British Columbia and Alaska. For Vancouver and his men, their daunting survey was a nervewracking test of seamanship and pilotage skills. One can't help but marvel at their accomplishment.

Place Names

The natives who first inhabited the B.C. coast had their own names in place when European explorers began filling their charts with new ones. Politicians, naval heroes, winning racehorses and faraway women have all been honoured with place names, not to mention Captain Pender's Skye Terrier, Connis, for whom a point of land was named.

We used to cruise with a Scottish terrier, and even though Tuck cruised extensively along the B.C. coast, spending most of his 14 years living aboard and travelling by boat, we would no doubt have a hard time convincing the Canadian Permanent Committee on Geographic Names to officially name a cove after him. The criteria for bestowing new place names have changed since pioneer days, but anyone can submit a name proposal by first contacting the Geographical Names Office in Victoria for guidelines.

Even sea captains of the Royal Navy can be thwarted in their attempts to bestow place names. Captain Richards tried to honour Rear Admiral Baynes by changing Saltspring Island's name to Admiral Island in 1859. The earlier name, bestowed when some Hudson's Bay Company officers found springs of brine on the island, remained in common use however. So, in 1905, the Geographic Board of Canada adopted Saltspring Island as its official name.

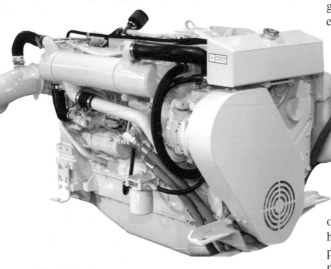

give you a picture of the state of your engine – for example, copper in the oil might indicate the connecting rod bearings are wearing out. If you use an outboard engine, have a mechanic service it before your trip. Fuel supply and consumption should be a subject of keen interest for all boaters with some marinas no longer supplying fuel. It is critical to know, on a daily basis, fuel consumption and fuel levels to plan each leg of your trip. This is especially true north of Campbell River, where fuel supply is limited.

Batteries and Electrical Wiring

Although we like to get out in the wilderness in our boat, we also like to drag along an assortment of household conveniences – all of which consume power. From refrigeration to televisions and computers, every item drains batteries and makes the recharging ceremony a daily ritual on most boats.

On cruises up north, when you may not be near a marina for days or weeks, keep an eye on your vessel's voltage and power consumption. We have four 6-volt golf-cart type batteries on board which store a total of about 450 amps and, despite conservative electrical power use, we rarely can go beyond two days without having to recharge the bank of batteries. The main culprit is the refrigerator. Its significant power draw is hard to avoid because buying ice along the British Columbia coast is not always easy.

The key is always to keep batteries properly charged – not always easy either when the distances to many anchorages in prime cruising grounds can be short and may limit engine running time. Using a 'smart' regulator (such as Balmar's Max Charge or similar) will quickly put a bulk charge into the batteries and keep charging time to a minimum. Larger vessels with onboard diesel generators may not have the above concerns but when you are anchored in a beautiful spot, it seems a sin to shatter the peace with a generator running.

The Engine

North of Campbell River, there are few opportunities to repair boats and obtain parts until you reach Port Hardy or Port McNeill. Because of this, whether your boat is power or sail, maintaining a reliable engine is critical when powering against the currents and wind of the Inside Passage.

We have always followed the manual for our engine's maintenance schedule, religiously changing the oil and filter (usually every 50 to 100 hours of running) and keeping the fuel clean with regular fuel filter changes. When cruising we wipe down the engine every day or two and inspect all wiring and hoses around the engine to ensure nothing has been jarred loose by a bumpy passage.

If you suspect something is amiss with your engine, a sample of its oil can be tested at an oil analysis laboratory. The results of this analysis will

Above, modern diesels are lighter and more powerful than predecessors. Below, all engines benefit greatly from regular maintenance.

Fires on boats often result from a short circuit in the engine area where heavy current is needed for the starter. This is such an important aspect of maintenance that it is worth making a log entry any time you do work on starters, battery cables or main switches, and it is very important that any work in this area is done competently.

Electrical wiring should be secured to a bulkhead, terminated with a proper fitting (such as an eye terminal), securely fastened to the appropriate breaker on the electrical panel and sprayed with a protective coating. The heavy cables to and from the engine should be as large in diameter as possible (we use 1/0 welding cable) and professionally terminated

with a crimped fitting. These high-current cables should be inspected every few months, which includes ensuring the insulation is not being worn away by engine vibration.

Sails and Running Gear

Sailboat owners should check the integrity of their sails, halyards and all running rigging on a regular basis. Seas and winds, especially in open water, can really test the rigging, and the time to ensure everything works is before setting out. One standard practice we follow is to carefully run our fingers along halyards, stays and shrouds near fittings. This is the most likely location for broken strands of wire to occur. A broken strand will jut out slightly from the lay. Chronic rusting of the stay around a swaged fitting is also an indication of needed attention and sometimes indicates the fitting has cracked and should be replaced.

Halyard sheaves at the top of the mast can be a more serious problem. Many sailboats have masts with misaligned sheave boxes and over time the halyard will wear away at the sheave. The only way to get around this is to have the sheave box cocked slightly so the main and jib halyard line up with the head of the sail when fully raised, or to simply replace the sheaves every few years to prevent a halyard from jumping its sheave.

Keeping sails clean is not a simple task. It is a good practice to remove the sails at least once a season and give the sail a good rinse with water and a small amount of detergent. The entire sail should be given an inspection before any big trip, and any frayed or questionable-looking stitching should be repaired. Look closely for wear in the reinforced

Inspection of all rigging is essential on sailboats before setting out for a cruise along the Inside Passage. Top, cotter pins and sheaves at top of mast should be checked. Right, rigging being tuned before cotter pins (or rings) are replaced.

areas and spots where the sail contacts the spreaders. We take our sails to a sail loft every three or four years for maintenance.

Although modern Dacron and nylon lines seem to last forever, it's a good idea to throw them in the washing machine each spring – they come out looking great and will be far more supple without the salt. Important lines, such as the anchor rode, halyards or sheets, should be inspected before setting off on your trip.

Ground Tackle

Most anchor manufacturers supply recommended anchor weights for boat length and offer a variation of anchor weights for uses such as lunch anchor, working anchor and storm anchor. Cruisers should take the storm-anchor weight to be the standard for cruising in B.C. which, depending on the anchor, is about one to two pounds for every foot of waterline.

Every type of anchor has advantages and disad-

Above, our 45-pound CQR lets us sleep soundly at night. Below, today's GPS units can show charted position and depth. In colour yet!

vantages. We've used all the major types of anchors and have relied on a heavy CQR as our main anchor for 20 years. We have a Bruce as a backup and a small high-tensile Danforth as a lunch hook which is mounted on the stern. We use the largest tested shackles possible (the safe working load will be stamped on tested shackles) to connect our 45-pound CQR with 3/8" BBB chain (this short-link chain is also stamped) and we make sure the shackles are wired shut with brass or stainless wire. If using line as a rode, ask for abrasive-resistant nylon. We use braid – although triple-strand nylon has better elasticity, it can be a little harder to stow over time.

Bow cleats are another area where serious cruisers should be extra vigilant. In addition to taking the strain of anchor and dock lines, bow cleats are often called upon for other tasks such as securing a tow line. If you lack confidence in your bow cleats and decide to replace them, choose large, heavy stainless steel or solid bronze cleats with a high saddle. The Herreshoff cleat is an excellent example of a strong fitting that allows numerous lines to be attached. All docking and securing cleats should be through-bolted to a stainless backing plate.

Last, but not least, always make sure the bitter end of your anchor line is secured to an eye bolt or something similar within your anchor well.

As we get older, our interest in anchor winches increases proportionally. There are some very advanced and efficient winches being manufactured which operate electrically or hydraulically. On sailboats, mast-mounted winches can be used and offer the advantage of being at waist-height when manually cranking up the anchor.

Electronics and Navigation

Having the proper charts for your intended cruising area is so fundamental it seems pedantic to raise the subject. Yet sometimes boaters can get caught up with electronic navigation aids (some of which display virtual charts) that paper charts – those low-tech things of wonder – can get overlooked.

Charts are like books. There is much to be seen at a glance and even more upon closer examination. Soundings show more than mere shoals or trenches – they indicate where the current will speed up, where tide lines are likely to align, and where you can seek shelter from the worst waves. Large-scale charts will reveal secret coves, sandy beaches and hidden anchorages to those who take the time to read the detail. No matter where we are, we always have the relevant chart in front of us or handy to look at in an instant. Constant reference to a chart will give you a feel for translating the two dimensions of a chart to the dimensions of reality. Notations and course lines can also be made on paper charts for future reference which can be very handy when trying to remember a course line or bearings which may be important.

Global Positioning System has become a standard navigational aid for many recreational boaters and there is no questioning its usefulness. It helps boaters save fuel and time by staying on course during long transits. In poor visibility, it can help affirm your position. Most skippers regularly check their GPS readings with their chart and other nav aids and do not rely solely on one instrument. Far more important than a GPS, of course, is a boater's ability to take bearings, fix a position on a chart and calculate speed. These skills remain the foundation of safe boating along the Inside Passage and should be in place before relying on the miracle of GPS.

Reliable depth finders or sounders are also imperative for cruising north and many boaters have at least two on board in the event one packs up. (We also keep a lead line on board in the event of an electrical failure.) The main sounder, with its small screen, shows the lay of the bottom and gives some idea of shelving in anchorages. We leave this sounder on almost constantly while underway.

Over time, experienced boaters develop an intuitive feel for exactly where they are by making it a habit to compare soundings from the depth finder with those on the chart. You may be cruising merrily along on a compass course but keeping an eye on charted depths keeps you on a low-level alert should the sounder start showing wonky depths.

Installing a radar is justified if you are planning extensive voyages north, where rain, mist and fog are common. The use of radar helps boaters extend their cruising range by being able to use days of poor visibility for travel. It also helps when the crew is looking for the entrance to an anchorage or picking up landmarks for fixes. And in areas of high traffic, radar performs its most important task of collision avoidance in poor visibility.

One of radar's recent improvements is the interfacing ability most new radars have with GPS or other electronics. Now one screen can display all the information on position, waypoints and, of course, the radar image of landforms. Some radars come with the option of integrating with a chart reader so the operator can toggle between digital charts and the radar screen.

Radar is an expensive instrument, and it certainly needs a good power source to operate. But a vessel with radar onboard has extended capability which, for boaters determined to cover a lot of ground in a

Above, installation of radar antenna on stern is easier but a higher mount provides better reception and improvement in range. Below, radar screen near helmsperson helps when navigating in fog.

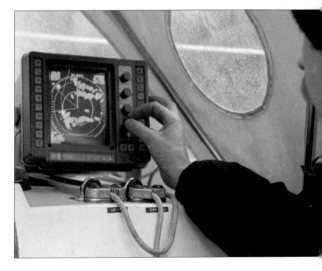

day, can be very handy. However, if you have the time and flexibility to wait out fog or other similar conditions of poor visibility, a radar is not crucial in waters south of Cape Caution.

Canada Customs can be cleared in summer at Bedwell Harbour, site of Poets Cove Resort.

Customs Clearance / Ports of Entry

American boaters arriving in Canadian waters can clear customs at one of several Designated Reporting Stations, including the customs dock in Victoria's Inner Harbour. In the Sidney area, customs can be cleared at Port Sidney Marina, Van Isle Marina (Tsehum Harbour) and Canoe Cove Marina. In summer, Bedwell Harbour on South Pender Island is a popular port of entry where boats can clear Canadian Customs from May 1 through September 30. Bedwell Harbour has the added advantage of being the location of one of the newest upscale marina resorts in the Gulf Islands.

CANPASS holders can clear Canada Customs in Ganges, Saltspring Island (at the public float); Port Browning, Pender Island; Cabbage Island; Horton Bay and Miners Bay, Mayne Island; and Montague Harbour Marina, Galiano Island. Canada Customs Telephone Reporting Centre is contacted at 1-888-CANPASS (226-7277) toll-free. CANPASS permit holders must call this number up to four hours before arriving in Canada and inform a customs officer of their estimated arrival time and destination.

For more information on applying for a CAN-PASS, visit the Canada Border Services Agency website at cbsa-asfc.gc.ca (to view the CANPASS application form, enter form #E672) or write to the Customs Processing Centre, 28 – 176 Street, Surrey BC V3S 9R9, telephone 604-535-9346.

American boaters returning stateside should check with current customs regulations to ensure re-entry guidelines are followed. Reporting in person at the designated customs dock at Friday Harbor on San Juan Island (or Roche Harbor, if it's open) remains the favoured procedure for most boaters, and a passport remains the best identification to carry. New regulations for clearing by telephone are expected to be enforced by 2006, requiring boaters entering the United States to have completed the I-68 (or Nexus) pre-clearance form.

Holding Tanks / No-Discharge Zones

A number of popular anchorages along B.C.'s inner south coast now fall within the Canada Shipping Act's Pleasure Craft Sewage Pollution Prevention Regulations. In accordance with these regulations, pleasure craft visiting these anchorages are required to be fitted with a holding tank if their vessel has a built-in toilet. Vessels without fitted toilets can use portable toilets, which can be emptied via suction wand at a pump-out station or emptied ashore if a pump-out facility is not available. Details regarding holding tanks and approved piping systems can be viewed on Transport Canada's website at www.tc.gc.ca. Pump-out stations are concentrated in southern waters, at marinas and harbour authorities in and around Sidney, Ganges, Nanaimo, Vancouver, Howe Sound, Pender Harbour, Comox and Campbell River.

The sewage pollution prevention regulations require zero discharge overboard in the following anchorages:

Montague Harbour, Galiano Island;

Pilot Bay and Gabriola Sands Provincial Park, Garbriola Island;

Smuggler Cove;

Prideaux Haven;

Roscoe Bay, West Redonda Island;

Squirrel Cove, Cortes Bay, Mansons Landing, Gorge Harbour and Carrington Bay, Cortes Island.

It makes good sense not to pump sewage overboard in popular coves or harbours, especially if a beach or swimming area fringes the anchorage. Many boaters wait until they are in a strait or large channel, well away from shore, before discharging effluent.

Insects

In summer, flies and mosquitoes can be a nuisance. Porthole screens are recommended, as is mosquito netting placed over opened hatch covers on hot summer nights to allow air ventilation while keeping the bugs out. Mosquito coils are a good way to keep insects away while you lounge outside in the cockpit, and sprigs of fresh lavender or mint are also effective. Dark-coloured dodgers attract bugs more than do light-coloured dodgers.

When hiking ashore, your best defense against mosquitoes is to wear long pants and a light-coloured top with long sleeves. Apply insect repellent to your face, neck and hands. Small children and pregnant women should use non-DEET repellent or one containing a low concentration of DEET. Upon returning to the boat, wash off all repellents with soap and water. Also, avoid wearing cologne or any scent that will attract bees and other insects. If you don't want to wear repellent, another option is to wear a sheet of fabric softener under your cap, letting it drape over the back of your neck, or to simply pull a sheet of fabric softener through your belt loop.

Long pants and a hat will also protect you from wood ticks, which are small, spider-like insects that bite into the skin and feed on blood, possibly passing on one of many diseases they can carry, including Lyme disease. After a hike in a forest, check any exposed part of your body, such as the back of your neck, for ticks. Prompt removal of a tick will prevent any infection and is best done with tweezers, gently pulling the parasite straight out and taking care not to crush it. Afterwards, wash the area with soap and water, then apply an antiseptic.

VHF Channels to Cape Caution

During times of poor visibility, or when approaching busy passes, you may alert Vessel Traffic Services of your presence and intentions. In Victoria use Channel 11, which covers the waters between Juan de Fuca Strait in the south, and Ballenas Island to the north. Victoria Traffic also uses Channel 74 east of Sand Heads. Near the entrance to Burrard Inlet and north of Iona Island, use Channel 12 for Vancouver Traffic. North of Ballenas Island, contact Comox Traffic on Channel 71. To communicate with the Coast Guard in a non-life-threatening situation, use Channel 22A. Use Channel 16 for distress or as a calling channel only. To communicate with other recreational vessels use channels 06, 67, 68, 69, 72 and 73. Contact marinas using Channel 66A.

Mobile Phone Coverage

The B.C. coast is served by two cell phone services, Telus and Rogers AT&T Wireless. Both systems provide good coverage of the Strait of Georgia up to Campbell River and parts of Desolation Sound. North of Desolation Sound the service is spotty until Port Neville, where the reception along Johnstone Strait becomes fairly consistent. Queen Charlotte Strait and the western Knight Inlet area generally have good service. Reception is fairly good in Queen Charlotte Strait right up to Cape Caution. As usual with cell phones, try to make your calls out in the open, away from hills and mountainsides.

Telus has two cell towers, one at Alert Bay and one at Port Hardy, each located near the local airport. The best reception will be near the airports which are marked on the charts. The Alert Bay tower covers much of Johnstone Strait and Knight Inlet, and the entrances to the Broughtons at Fife Sound and Wells Passage.

Rogers AT&T Wireless has recently added another signal tower at Alert Bay. This is in addition to the signal tower between Port Hardy and Coal Harbour, a few miles south of Port Hardy. Reception should be good anywhere around Queen Charlotte Strait that is not blocked by mountains. Service should be good in Johnstone Strait and Knight Inlet.

Sidney Spit Marine Park, now administered by Parks Canada, has extensive visitor facilities.

Marine Parks

Marine Parks dot the B.C. coastline and are generally more concentrated in southern waters. Facilities vary from park to park and can include floats, mooring buoys, dinghy docks, campsites, hiking trails, picnic shelters and freshwater pumps. Many others remain, for the most part, undeveloped.

There is no fee for anchoring a boat in a provincial marine park but there is an overnight fee for tying to a buoy and for mooring at a float. (There is no charge for using a dinghy dock.) In Pirates Cove there is a charge for mooring to a stern tie ring. Although marine parks are open year round, user fees are collected only from May 1 through September 30. (www.env.gov.bc.ca/bcparks/)

A number of former provincial marine parks are now administered by Parks Canada (see page 62) but their facilities and fees are generally unchanged. (www.pc.gc.ca).

Pets on Board

For years we cruised with a Scottish terrier and his needs included daily walks ashore. Most healthy dogs are quite happy with two visits ashore – one in the morning, the other in the late afternoon or evening. This routine melds nicely with coastal cruising and we appreciated the fact that Tuck's urgings prompted us to head ashore at every anchorage we visited, come rain or shine, and discover things we might otherwise have missed. The downside, however, were the pests he sometimes picked up on shore and brought back to the boat, including fleas.

Fleas are not fun, and we took daily measures to prevent the arrival of these uninvited guests. Each

morning Tuck's bedding was shaken and aired, his coat was brushed out on deck, and the teak cabin sole was wiped with vinegar. At dinnertime, a clove of raw garlic was diced into his canned food.

Dogs should always be inspected for ticks immediately after a walk in the forest. Run your hands over your dog's back and if you feel a hard little bump, part the fur to see if it's a tick embedded in the skin. Removal can be done with tweezers, gently pulling the tick straight out. (See 'Insects' entry in this section.)

U.S. boaters entering Canada with a dog or cat are required to carry written confirmation from a veterinarian that the pet has been vaccinated against rabies during the previous 36 months.

Provisioning

Most communities of the south coast are well served by local stores situated near the marinas. In the major ports, local supermarkets will usually provide complimentary taxi service back to the docks. At marina resorts, a general store is often part of the facilities, and its selection will vary. Some are well stocked with fresh produce and dairy products, and a liquor off-licence, while others are not. Credit cards are widely accepted at coastal resorts and in all the large centres.

When cruising the Gulf Islands, Sidney, Ganges and Nanaimo are ideal places to stock up on groceries, liquor and other items. In Vancouver, Granville Island is a great place to shop for fresh fish, produce and baked goods. Along the Sunshine Coast, one of the best reprovisioning ports is Pender Harbour, at Madeira Park. For boaters venturing north of the passes, Campbell River is a good place to shop when taking the 'main route' of Discovery Passage, while the 'back route' is serviced by several small ports, including Blind Channel where the resort's general store sells freshly baked bread. At the north end of Vancouver Island, several ports are excellent for reprovisioning, including Port McNeill, Alert Bay and Port Hardy.

Public Docks and Shore Access

What used to be called government docks, easily recognizable by their red railings and maintained by the federal Government of Canada, are now community docks run by local authorities. The public is still welcome at these docks, but the moorage rates and services provided (traditionally, fresh water on the docks and garbage disposal at the top of the ramp) vary from harbour to harbour. In Canada, foreshore up to the high water mark is, with rare exceptions, public property.

Reference Materials

The best investment any boater can make is the purchase of up-to-date nautical charts – the larger the scale, the better. The **Canadian Hydrographic Service** produces beautiful charts, each of which is like a book with good detail and adds to the adventure of boating. U.S. boaters should be aware Canadian charts are drawn to more conservative standards and minimum depths are shown relative to 'lowest normal tides' as compared with U.S. charts which define lower low water as an averaged value of low water. To calculate water depth using CHS charts and tide tables, add the predicted tide height for the time in the area you are cruising to the datum shown on the local chart.

In addition to carrying the appropriate charts, boaters should have CHS's annual Tide and Current Tables (Volume 5 and Volume 6 apply to the area covered in this book) as well as the Sailing Directions for the British Columbia Coast (South Portion). Equipped with the tide tables, the Sailing Directions (SD) and charts, you can explore every mile of our coast and find your own special anchorages. The SD, in addition to offering excellent information on currents, regional weather and local hazards, also provides good advice on approaches to sounds and passes as well as suggestions for anchoring. The SD also has distance tables and weather statistics for many ports along the Inside Passage.

To supplement these essential reference materials are the numerous cruising guides which you can purchase at most chandleries. All are helpful and often complement one another with their varying approaches on how to cruise this complex coastline.

Bill Wolferstan set the standard for cruising guides in the 1970s and '80s with his *Cruising Guides* in three volumes covering the *Gulf Islands, Sunshine Coast* and *Desolation Sound*. His seminal guides remain highly informative and capture the atmosphere of each destination. John Chappell's *Cruising Beyond Desolation Sound*, published in the late 1970s, contained his first-hand insight into anchorages north of Campbell River but is, alas, out of print. *North of Desolation Sound* by Peter Vassilopoulos now covers this area from Stuart Island to the Broughton Islands.

Robert Hale's popular *Waggoner Cruising Guide* is a single-volume pilot companion with comprehensive coverage of marinas and anchorages from Seattle to Prince Rupert which is thoroughly updated annually. The Waggoner also has handy conversion tables for metric and imperial measurements, border crossing information and listings of all fuel docks with phone numbers. **Pacific Yachting** magazine publishes an annual boating services directory called *Boaters' Blue Pages/Marina Guide* which is inserted in the February issue and is especially useful along the remote parts of the coast. Richard E. Thomson's *Oceanography of the British Columbia Coast* is a fascinating reference book for mariners, with chapters devoted to subjects such as tidal flow and currents, and detailed information on specific straits, sounds and passes.

Safety on the Water

If you are new to boating, it is prudent to take a few courses. The Competency of Operators of Pleasure Craft Regulations, enforced by the Canadian Coast Guard, require operators of motorized pleasure craft to have proof of competency on board at all times. These requirements are being phased in over ten years and the requirement of the card varies with the age of the vessel operator. However, cruising boaters should have experience and knowledge far beyond this basic competency, and the best-known supplier of these courses is the Power Squadron, in both Canada and the United States. The Power Squadron's basic Boating Course provides in-depth boat operation and safety training, and teaches you the challenges of plotting and navigation. This course also delves into weather, tides, currents and anchoring.

Sportfishing Licences

B.C. is well known for its excellent sportfishing. Before catching finfish or harvesting shellfish in local waters, all recreational fishermen must obtain an annual B.C. Tidal Waters Sports Fishing Licence, available at marinas and sporting goods stores. The accompanying B.C. Tidal Waters Sport Fishing Guide contains details on species, openings, restricted fishing areas and possession limits. For more information, visit the Department of Fisheries and Oceans website at www-comm.pac.dfo-mpo.gc.ca.

A humble rock cod holds a fascination for kids.

The Prehistoric Coast

Boaters who explore the remote corners of British Columbia's Inside Passage can likely envision this immense coastline as it would have looked long before the arrival of European explorers. The overwhelming aspect of these meandering, mountain-bounded waterways is the dominance of nature – the restless force that creates, destroys and rejuvenates, measuring time in millennia while pockets of human habitation come and go like wisps of fog in the grand scale of Earth's history.

The west coast of North America was formed over hundreds of millions of years by the ongoing collision of two large tectonic plates of the earth's crust. As the Pacific (oceanic) plate rubbed against the North American (continental) plate, pieces chipped off and became terranes. It is thought that part of Vancouver Island was once an island situated near the present-day Philippines, which made its way across the Pacific Ocean to lie off Canada's West Coast.

Over the last few hundred million years, terranes off the Pacific Plate have been pushed, as if on a conveyor belt, up the west side of the North American Plate where they eventually docked against ancestral Alaska at the top of the Gulf of Alaska. If the terrane upon which Los Angeles sits continues moving north at its rate of two inches per year, it will reach the northern Gulf of Alaska in 76 million years. Two small tectonic plates – the Juan de Fuca and Explorer plates – lie between the Pacific and North American plates, and they too are sub-ducting under the outer edge of the North American continent.

The inside waterways of B.C. occupy a coastal trough known as the Georgia-Hecate Depression. It is part of a larger depression extending from Alaska to the Gulf of California that began to form 150 million years ago. Over the millennia the Georgia Depression underwent many ups and downs as landforms to the east and west were uplifted and folded into mountain ranges.

The age of glaciers – the Pleistocene era – came next and it contained four or five separate periods of major glacial advance and retreat. When the last great ice age drew to a close some 15,000 years ago and the glaciers began staging their retreat, these giant bulldozers of ice left behind U-shaped valleys that would eventually become the channels and fjords of the Inside Passage.

Until recently, it was widely believed that the first human inhabitants came to North America by land, crossing from Siberia to Alaska and into the continent's interior via an ice-free corridor called the Bering land bridge, or Beringia. New evidence suggests the first arrivals may have come not by land, but by sea, working their way around the Pacific Rim and using as stepping stones the ice-free coastal refuges that had been exposed by retreating glaciers.

The raw coastal landscape left by the retreating glaciers would initially have been one of freshly exposed rock and soil. Lichens and mosses are the first forms of vegetation to reclaim deglaciated land, breaking down the rock and enriching the soil so that small flowering plants and low bushes can grow.

Thickets of alder and willow are the next to take hold. They build up the soil and are eventually replaced by conifers.

The early inhabitants established village sites near the food-rich shorelines, where lush lowlands and intertidal zones were a habitat for waterfowl and edible greens, such as fireweeds and sea asparagus. Clams were gathered from shellfish beds and sea lions were hunted in local waters. Salmon, caught in traps and weirs, were a major food source, their life cycles and migration patterns an important part of native lore and ritual.

When coastal lands were first relieved of the massive weight of the ice fields, widescale uplifting took place and sea levels dropped. Today's underwater banks in Hecate Strait and Queen Charlotte Sound became exposed as islands and points of land, and the Queen Charlotte archipelago – parts of which remained free of ice throughout the last ice age – became a single land mass, twice as large as it is today.

Over time, growing torrents of glacial meltwater from further inland swelled the oceans and turned valleys into waterways. This rise in sea level brought the "great flood" referred to in Haida mythology, when sea levels rose as much as 50 feet (15 m) above today's levels. Entire villages were submerged, including one at Montague Harbour in the Gulf Islands where scuba divers have performed an undersea archaeological excavation and retrieved artifacts over 6,000 years old.

Sea levels eventually stablilized, and permanent villages began to dot the coastline as it exists today. Evidence of prehistoric habitation can be seen along the foreshore of many anchorages in the form of stone boat skids and fish traps (such as those at the head of Bond Sound). Most obvious, however, are the patches of clamshell beach – ancient kitchen middens – that are found throughout south coastal waters. These are kitchen middens and they began forming during the Middle Period, 5,500 to 1,500 years ago.

A midden is an ancient refuse dump of shells and bones which, over time, is crushed and compressed into a beach several yards deep. The shell in a midden neutralizes the acid in the soil, preserving ancient tools and artifacts such as antler carvings and stone bowls engraved with human and animal figures. Archaeological digs have revealed a prehis-

Above right, a deglaciated valley is slowly reclaimed by vegetation. Middle, fjords were formed by glacial action. Bottom, a prehistoric midden at the head of Echo Bay on Gilford Island.

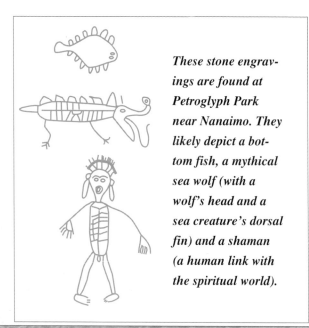

These stone engravings are found at Petroglyph Park near Nanaimo. They likely depict a bottom fish, a mythical sea wolf (with a wolf's head and a sea creature's dorsal fin) and a shaman (a human link with the spiritual world).

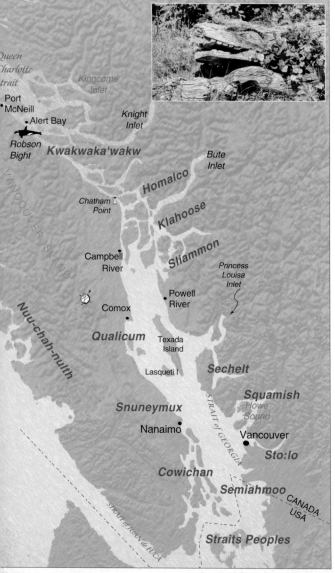

toric society with masters at weaving, woodworking and sculpting. Personal adornments were miniature works of art depicting human, animal and supernatural figures carved from stone, bone, antler and tooth. Weapons for hunting and warfare have also been found in middens, as well as skeletal remains and the caches of warrior chiefs.

The aboriginal people of British Columbia were once called Indians. Today, they refer to themselves collectively as First Nations. It is also appropriate to refer to these peoples as aboriginal, native or indigenous. The lands they occupy are called Indian Reserves ('IR' on CHS charts).

The First Nations' traditional languages were oral, not written, which is why there is often a variation in the spelling of words and names. Early explorers, attempting to phonetically record what they were hearing, gave certain groups erroneous names. For instance, the Nootka were called such by Captain Cook, but they prefer to be known as the Nuu-chah-nulth or simply the West Coast peoples. The Southern Kwakiutl are now called Kwakwaka'wakw – 'those who speak Kwakwala.' Groups living in the Strait of Georgia basin no longer collectively refer to themselves as Coast Salish (the language family to which they belong) but have reverted to traditional names for specific groups within the area.

The natives living on the southern Gulf Islands and south end of Vancouver Island are collectively referred to as the 'People of the Straits,' i.e. Juan de Fuca Strait and Strait of Georgia. These straits were their 'rivers' and migrating salmon were caught in shallow reefs near shore. Nets were anchored by lashing them with twine to beached boulders, and the fishermen would return to specific salmon sites year after year, century upon century.

The northern Gulf Islands were inhabited by the Hul'qumi'num, 'Those Who Speak the Same Language', with individual groups including the Malahat, Cowichan and Snuneymux (Nanaimo). These peoples fished salmon in the Cowichan, Chemainus and Nanaimo rivers of Vancouver Island, using fish weirs stretched from bank to bank where the salmon, crowded into enclosures, would be scooped or speared. In Cowichan Gap (Porlier Pass), the Chemainus hunted the Steller sea lion. Each summer entire villages travelled by canoe across the Strait of Georgia to fish for salmon in the lower reaches of the Fraser River.

While salmon was a major food source for coastal settlements up and down the coast, the inhabitants of Kingcome Inlet were known as the

Tsawatainuk, 'People with Eulachon.' This long, silvery fish, also called oolichan, was valued as a food source and for its oil, which could be used as a condiment, preservative and medicine.

An artistically productive civilization evolved during the late Middle Period (3,500 to 1,500 years ago). With the establishment of permanent coastal villages, the various groups began marking out their territories and protecting them through warfare. The northern tribes would travel hundreds of miles in their canoes to conduct raids on southern villages and capture residents, who became the lowest rank in a social hierarchy consisting of nobility, commoners and slaves. Warrior chiefs were the village leaders, their family crests displayed on totem poles carved from logs of red cedar and erected as frontal and interior poles of their post-and-beam houses.

Sometimes serving as territory markers were petroglyphs, which were pecked or scratched into foreshore rocks, and pictographs, which were drawn with ochre on rock walls. These images depicted animals, humans and supernatural beings. Shamans, who could foretell events and cure sickness, were important members of these prehistoric societies. Also respected were the souls of other living creatures, for it was believed that animals had the ability to transform themselves into humans.

Native mythology explains the creation of the universe and the evolution of humanity in terms of transformation. Raven was a supernatural trickster and transformer who accidentally released the sun and stars and who, upon opening a clamshell, released the first humans. Anthropologists and archaeologists take a more scientific approach to evolution, but all agree that however the early inhabitants may have arrived at our shores, their modern descendants can claim ancestral ties rooted in antiquity, when stands of cedar and spruce first appeared along the water's edge.

Top, family crests displayed on the New Vancouver big house. Above, canoes were carved from huge cedar logs, then steamed to soften the wood and allow the sides to be spread. Separate prow and stern pieces were added and the hull torched to harden the wood before sanding. Below, artist Alan Nakano's depiction of Haida seafarers.

The Discovered Coast

The legend of Juan de Fuca Strait was once a source of great speculation among European cartographers, who referred to it as the **Strait of Anian** – a possible northwest passage. The entrance to this mysterious waterway reputedly was first sighted by the Greek mariner Juan de Fuca while he explored the North Pacific for Spain in 1592. When the English sea captain Charles W. Barkley, accompanied by his young bride Francis, arrived on a trading expedition in 1787, he named the strait for Juan de Fuca. But it wasn't until the summer of 1792, when British and Spanish survey expeditions made a thorough exploration of the waters lying beyond Juan de Fuca Strait, that the Strait of Anian legend was finally laid to rest and the Inside Passage was revealed to the outside world.

The 18th century was a great era of naval exploration. Russian explorers – led by Vitus Bering – set off from Siberia to find out what lay to the east, while Spanish, French and British ships ventured into the Pacific's northern waters in search of the elusive Northwest Passage. They were also pursuing knowledge during this Age of Enlightenment, with naval commanders such as Britain's Cook, France's La Perouse and Spain's Malaspina all leading scientific expeditions to the New World. The logbooks of these and other commanders provide a wealth of information on the native cultures that thrived at this time of First Contact. The natives were truly impressed with the white-winged sailing ships that magically appeared on the horizon. Captains were honoured guests at the homes of village chiefs and, in a show of reciprocal hospitality, ship's tours were often held for high-ranking members of a village.

The Spanish explored much of the Pacific Northwest in the mid-to-late 1700s but were secretive about their discoveries. When the journals of Captain Cook's final voyage (1776-79) were published in 1783, merchant ships began flocking to these northern waters in pursuit of sea otter pelts, which fetched a phenomenal price in China. As more and more ships frequented the coast, many of the natives became wary and, at times, openly hostile. Captain Vancouver's men reported incidents in which they were approached, while in open boats, by canoes filled with armed natives intent on pillage. A few shots fired over their heads would prompt them to unstring their bows and arrows, and offer them in trade. The British sailors gladly exchanged items of barter for weapons, since this was the easiest way to disarm the natives.

Spain, whose colonial empire had long encompassed the Pacific coastlines of the Americas, was aware of the steady increase in fur trade traffic and grew worried about its holdings in the Pacific Northwest. Nootka Sound, Spain's northernmost outpost on the west side of Vancouver Island, had become alarmingly busy with the comings and going of British and American fur-trading ships. As a result, Alejandro Malaspina was sent north from Acapulco in 1791 to investigate the situation and check out the persistent rumours regarding Juan de Fuca Strait and the Northwest Passage.

Several Spanish expeditions had preceded Malaspina's, including one led by Juan Perez in 1774 in which he sighted the northern end of the Queen Charlottes and another in 1789 when Esteban Jose Martinez led an expedition to Nootka Sound and sparking a dispute with Great Britain over terri-

Left, marine artist John Horton's well-known painting of Captain Vancouver's ships in Desolation Sound called 'I Name This Place Desolation Sound.'

torial rights. In 1790, the Spanish sent more soldiers to Nootka Sound to build a permanent fort and settlement while Manuel Quimper explored Juan de Fuca Strait. After wintering in Nootka Sound, the Spanish continued their explorations the next summer, with Francisco Eliza and Jose Maria Narvaez becoming the first Europeans to enter the Strait of Georgia aboard the small schooner *Santa Saturnina*.

Upon returning to Acapulco, Malaspina recommended a continuation of these surveys, and in the spring of 1792 two small schooners commanded by Dionisio Galiano and Cayetano Valdes headed up the coast from Acapulco. A British expedition of two ships, commanded by George Vancouver, had left England the previous spring, wintered in Hawaii, and was now on its way to the Pacific Northwest. All were in the hunt for the elusive Northwest Passage.

Captain Vancouver was also on a diplomatic mission, with instructions to stop at Nootka Sound to take possession of the harbour, as agreed upon in a treaty signed by England and Spain. For the first time in almost 300 years, Spain had formally acknowledged another nation's trading rights in the North Pacific. Vancouver's first goal, however, was to explore the legendary Juan de Fuca Strait and disprove, once and for all, the existence of a Northwest Passage.

When Vancouver arrived on our coast in April 1792 few, explorers had ventured into the twisting and treacherous channels of the Inside Passage, with fur-trading ships preferring to call at native villages that bordered the open Pacific. Vancouver's task was to explore and map every mainland inlet as far north as Cook Inlet at the top of the Gulf of Alaska.

Much of Vancouver's surveying work was done in open boats, with crewmen drawing on the oars from dawn until dusk and sometimes well into the night. They pitched tents on shore and the men on watch cooked the next day's food over open fires. If the forest above the high-water mark was impenetrable, they were forced to sleep in the boats – something the men detested. A few preferred taking their chances on shore, where a rising tide swamped them more than once. On one occasion an oarsman was so tired he didn't wake up and was floating away when roused by his companions.

The men dined on such mainstays as portable soup (similar to today's bouillon cubes), peas, wheat and oatmeal. To add variety to their fare, they hunted ducks, crows and cormorants. They also shot deer whenever they sighted them. While enjoying a picnic lunch of venison pasty in Puget Sound, Vancouver's men were approached by some Coast Salish natives who thought these strange white men

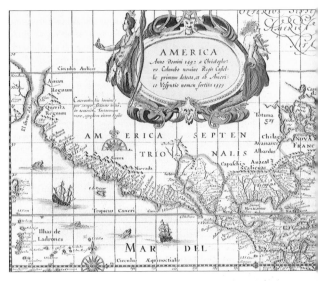

Above, early 17th-century map clearly showing 'El Streto d'Anian' – The Strait of Anian – in top left corner. Below, Captain Vancouver's overview chart showing 'Quadra and Vancouver Island.'

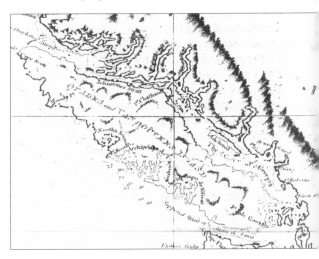

were eating human flesh. The natives conveyed their repugnance by throwing the offered venison on the ground. Vancouver's officers had to show them the deer carcass before the natives were convinced they weren't in the company of cannibals.

When the ships lay at anchor for a few weeks, a brewery was set up on shore to make beer by boiling pine sprouts or spruce sprigs in water and molasses, then fermenting this mixture with dried yeast. The men also collected oysters, clams, berries and nettles on shore, but they soon discovered it was easier to obtain fresh salmon by bartering with the region's residents than trying to catch these elusive fish with their seine nets. Copper was a popular item of trade, highly valued by the Kwakwaka'wakw (Kwakiutl),

Discovery aground in Queen Charlotte Strait.

whose territory extended from Quadra Island to Cape Caution. Kwakwaka'wakw artisans would shape this malleable metal into elaborately decorated shields which became the ultimate symbol of wealth at potlatch feasts and were often broken into pieces to distribute among the guests as a "non-perishable representation of perishable wealth."

Captain Vancouver made only a brief visit to the harbour that would one day be the site of a major city bearing his name. Settlements of the Squamish Nation were located here when Vancouver sailed his ship's boats past the future site of Stanley Park into Burrard Inlet to survey the surrounding shores. In seamanlike fashion, he ordered that the boats proceed "under an easy sail" as a welcoming party of natives paddled out to greet these strange-looking visitors. An exchange of goods (salmon for iron) took place on the run as the British survey boats sailed toward the head of the mountain-enclosed inlet in search of an inland waterway. It was not to be found so, after spending a night camped on shore, the British sailors left at dawn.

In his journals Captain Vancouver frequently mentions the lofty barrier of mountains and snow that frustrated his efforts at finding an inland waterway. The coastal mountains weren't his only source of frustration. He did not realize Spain had also dispatched ships to explore these waters and thought he was the first European to venture into the Inside Passage. However, Galiano and Valdes had been exploring the Gulf Islands while Vancouver and his officers were exploring the mainland inlets, and when Vancouver returned from a survey of Jervis Inlet to see the Mexicana and Sutil anchored off Point Grey, it was an unwelcome surprise. His orders were to be cordial to the Spanish, and the

names English Bay and Spanish Banks commemorate this encounter.

Together, the four ships proceeded up the Strait of Georgia (initially called Gulf of Georgia by Vancouver upon entering it) to Desolation Sound – a name Vancouver bestowed on the area because of its gloomy weather, poor fishing and few inhabitants. The ships anchored in Teakerne Arm and Vancouver's officers set off in boats to explore the mainland shore. Lieutenant James Johnstone led a party of men through the 'back route' of the Inside Passage, where the natives helped with ropes when the men had to haul their boats through the rapids. While Johnstone's party was exploring Frederick Arm and Phillips Arm, some natives fled into the forest at the sight of these strange-looking white men, who left some trinkets – a token of friendliness – in the canoes left abandoned on shore.

Johnstone's first clue to the existence of Vancouver Island came while he and his men were camped on shore in Loughborough Inlet. During the night they were unexpectedly swamped by a tide that was rising several hours earlier than in the Strait of Georgia. This meant the tide was coming in through a northern entrance and this revelation diverted Johnstone's attention from tracing the continental shoreline to locating a seaward passage at the top of Vancouver Island.

He followed Sunderland Channel into the strait that would bear his name and rowed all the way to Pine Island for an unobstructed view of the open waters of the Pacific Ocean. Johnstone and his men were exhausted and hungry by the time they backtracked 130 miles to the ships at anchor in Desolation Sound, but they had found a navigable channel to the ocean.

Upon Johnstone's return, Captain Vancouver bid adieu to Galiano and Valdes and headed for Discovery Passage where they observed the currents from Menzies Bay before proceeding through Seymour Narrows.

It took Captain Vancouver and his officers three summers to survey the entire Inside Passage. His search for an inland waterway was of course futile, but his painstaking exploration of nearly every mainland inlet produced marine charts of remarkable accuracy and laid the groundwork for further detailed charting in the 19th century when Great Britain extensively surveyed all of her empire's distant coastlines.

The lucrative trade in sea otter pelts thrived until the 1820s, and during its peak years, from 1790 to 1812, as many as two dozen merchant ships were on the coast, obtaining tens of thousands of pelts from

the natives in exchange for European goods, including iron tools with which they enhanced their woodworking and carving. As their artistry flowered, so too did their ceremonial traditions, which became ever more elaborate. Kwakwaka'wakw potlatch events were the most flamboyant of all the native groups, their theatrical dances performed with elaborate props and costumes, especially masks. All of the First Nations societies and their existing territories would soon be threatened, however, by the arrival of European settlers drawn to the rich resources of the B.C. coast.

The Working Coast

The Inside Passage has always been a land of plenty. Its maritime climate and abundance of salmon supported a large concentration of native inhabitants long before European seafarers began venturing into these waters in search of sea otters.

The Russians called it 'soft gold' – the thick, lustrous fur coat that keeps these marine mammals warm and buoyant in frigid waters. Once inhabiting coastal kelp beds from Alaska to California, the sea otter was hunted ruthlessly by fur traders who could sell these pelts on world markets for 10 times the price of a beaver skin. After the sea otter was hunted to near-extinction, the merchant ships plying coastal waters turned their sights on beaver pelts.

The Hudson's Bay Company of Great Britain had been working its way westward across the continent in pursuit of beaver pelts when, in 1821, it merged with the competing Northwest Company's opera-

Top, John Horton's painting of Vancouver's ship Discovery undergoing repairs in Restoration Bay. Above, theatrical dances were performed at ceremonial potlatch gatherings.

tions west of the Rockies. The HBC began building trading posts on the banks of strategic rivers to intercept the beaver skins being brought by natives from the interior. Fort Vancouver was built in 1825 on the Columbia, Fort Langley in 1827 on the Fraser, Fort Simpson in 1831 near the mouth of the Nass, and Fort McLoughlin (Bella Bella) in 1833 on the edge of Queen Charlotte Sound. In 1836, the Beaver – the first steamship to work the Inside Passage – arrived at Fort Vancouver and was used by the HBC to supply its posts, collect furs and explore the coast. (The vessel was sold in 1874 and operated as a coastal freighter and towboat until it was wrecked off Stanley Park's Prospect Point in 1888.)

To counter encroachment of the fur trade by the 'Boston Men' – American traders from the east coast – the Hudson's Bay Company sought to regain their monopoly by forming a naval department that hired American skippers (veterans of the coastal trade) to shadow the Boston ships and outbid American traders. As their profits dwindled, the Boston men gradually withdrew from the fur trade and turned to whaling.

Meanwhile, an influx of American settlers into Oregon Territory (which included the modern state of Washington) was pressuring Great Britain to withdraw from this jointly occupied region. In anticipation of an impending border settlement, the HBC built Fort Victoria in 1843 to replace Fort Vancouver on the Columbia River as its trading headquarters on the west coast. Three years later, the Oregon Treaty fixed the boundary between B.C. and the U.S. to lie along the 49th parallel before it dipped south of Vancouver Island. (The line that wove through the Gulf Islands and the San Juans remained in dispute until it was resolved by international arbitration in 1872.)

To encourage colonization of its territory, Great Britain issued the HBC proprietary rights to Vancouver Island (declared a crown colony in 1849) and chief factor James Douglas, who had overseen construction of Fort Victoria, took charge of company operations. Appointed governor of Vancouver Island in 1851, Douglas soon purchased the Saanich Peninsula (with the exception of village sites and potato patches) from the local natives in exchange for 371 blankets. A town sprang up south of Fort Victoria around James Bay, and the outlying area became farmland as white settlers arrived. A natural meadow where the Coast Salish had traditionally harvested camas was set aside as a park reserve that would eventually become Beacon Hill Park, named for the navigational range markers atop its hill.

The HBC also established Fort Rupert in Beaver Harbour in 1849 after coal deposits were discovered there. Mining ceased a few years later, when the HBC found coal deposits more conveniently situated at Nanaimo. There a wooden military bastion was built in 1853 to protect the white settlers who came from England and Scotland to work in the local coal mines. They called their new home Colville Town, but the native name was Nanaimo, which means 'big strong tribe' in reference to the five First Nations villages located in the area. Acting on information provided by the natives, the HBC soon opened another mine on Newcastle Island across the harbour from Nanaimo. But it was gold, not coal, that caused a sudden surge in the region's white population.

When word leaked out of gold deposits on the upper Fraser, a stampede of prospectors converged on the area in the spring of 1858. Most were Americans, numbering some 30,000, and they arrived at Victoria by steamboat, then caught a boat across the Strait of Georgia to the mouth of the Fraser River, where gold was found on the gravel bars below Hope and all the way up the Fraser

Below, a replica of Lady Washington, a ship that played a major role in the fur trade.

Canyon. To protect its lumber and mining interests and prevent any land grabbing, Great Britain declared the mainland a separate colony with New Westminster the point of entry. This new colony was later merged with Vancouver Island to form British Columbia and, in 1868, Victoria became the capital.

The Fraser gold rush was short-lived but other newcomers – many of whom hailed from the British Isles – began exploiting the region's natural resources. Small steam- or water-powered sawmills were soon operating up and down the coast, and in 1861 a British sea captain named Edward Stamp built B.C.'s first export sawmill in Alberni Inlet. He briefly operated another mill in Port Neville before opening Hastings Mill in 1867 on the south shore of Burrard Inlet, around which grew the settlement of Granville (now the City of Vancouver). A. P. Allison, a London-born logger who worked at a sawmill in Chemainus before starting his own logging company, opened a shingle mill at Greene Point Rapids in 1908 and sent the first cargo of B.C. shingles through the Panama Canal in 1914.

Salmon canning became another thriving industry, thanks to a new industrial process that could produce very thin, uniform sheets of metal for making cans. By 1881 there were 10 salmon canneries on the Fraser River, concentrated in Steveston and Ladner. Others opened on the north coast, at Rivers Inlet, Namu and on the Skeena and Nass rivers. Initially the bulk of the salmon was supplied by native fishermen, but by 1900 the salmon fishing fleet was dominated by Japanese and Europeans. Inside the canneries, the processing lines were manned by Chinese workers and aboriginal women.

In 1889, the Union Steamship Company was established to service remote coastal settlements, many of which were built on floats and could move from one sheltered cove to another. Initially these logging camps were collections of bunkhouses, cook shacks and equipment sheds, but with the growing number of women in the camps – hired to cook or accompanying their husbands – tidy floathomes became a common sight. Picket fences, split from

Top right, cannon firing ceremonies take place daily in summer beside Nanaimo's historic Bastion. Middle right, Fisgard Lighthouse at the entrance to Esquimalt Harbour is a National Historic site. Built in 1860, it was the first lighthouse on the B.C. coast. Bottom right, a steamship docks at Knox Bay on West Thurlow Island, where a major logging camp once operated.

The Pig War

When the Oregon Treaty of 1846 fixed the border between the United States and the colony of British Columbia, its exact placement in the waters between the mainland and Vancouver Island remained a contentious issue, with both sides claiming the San Juan Islands.

This dispute came to a head in June 1859 when Lyman Cutler, an American settler on San Juan Island, shot a pig belonging to an HBC farmer named Charles Griffin, who represented British claims to the island. When Griffin demanded $100 in compensation, Cutler responded "I think there is a better chance for lightning to strike you than for you to get a hundred dollars for that hog . . ."

Both sides promptly mobilized. The Americans landed a troop of soldiers and Governor Douglas sent two British warships in a show of force. Fortunately, no military action was taken by either side and joint occupation of the island was agreed to, a situation that prevailed until the German emperor decided the border should run along Haro Strait, making the San Juan Islands an American possession. As for Cutler, he received a small fine for the incident that nearly sparked a war.

cedar, would prevent small children from falling in the water, and some floats were large enough to hold a garden. The logging camp at Simoon Sound evolved into a floating village with a store, community hall, post office and school.

Settlements built on land included Blind Channel on West Thurlow Island, where a sawmill was built in 1910. The surrounding forest was hand-logged by nine lumbermen who would fell a tree with axes while standing on springboards wedged into tree trunks. The timber was hauled out by oxen along skid trails to the mill. The community became a centre for nearby logging camps, with a hotel and dock built to accommodate the Union Steamship boats that called regularly with freight and passengers. A one-room schoolhouse at Blind Channel served the area and children not living on West Thurlow Island were rowed to school by their mothers.

By 1918 the population at Blind Channel had soared to 120, with a cannery and shingle mill in operation. The mill's boiler usually had enough steam left at the end of the day to power a generator that lit everyone's home with a recent invention called the light bulb. A gas engine provided auxiliary power on Saturday nights when the dance hall was lit. Loggers from nearby camps would descend on Blind Channel and forget their worries as they kicked up their heels and "skidded the ladies across the floor."

Other vessels plying coastal waters were the mission boats of the Methodist and Anglican churches, which travelled to these isolated camps and villages to provide medical care and assistance. Some missionaries focused on the aboriginal people, whose local populations were decimated by diseases such as influenza and smallpox, to which they had no immunity. As early as 1782, ten years before George Vancouver arrived to conduct a coastal survey, a smallpox epidemic

Above left, a cannery once operated at Blind Channel. Left, an Alan Nakano painting of a fish-buying boat on the Fraser River.

swept through the villages bordering the Strait of Georgia, killing thousands and sparing few, with nine out of 10 people dying of the disease. By 1890, newcomers outnumbered the aboriginal population, and native villages were being abandoned as the survivors of epidemics moved to central locations to be closer to commercial fishing.

In the summer of 1898, Emily Carr visited her missionary sister in Ucluelet and her fascination with aboriginal subjects began. While sketching scenes of the local Nuu-Chah-Nulth (Nootka), she was given the name Klee Wyck ('the one who laughs'). In pursuit of her art, Carr travelled up and down the coast, visiting remote villages with the aid of native guides, and her paintings captured both a disappearing way of life and the primeval power of a northern rainforest.

While the native population continued to decline through the 1920s, the city of Vancouver was steadily growing. Bowen Island was transformed from a logging and farming community into a holiday resort in 1920 when the Union Steamship Company bought property at Snug Cove, including the local hotel. In summer, day-trippers came by the hundreds from Vancouver to enjoy company picnics and dances in the pavilion.

In 1931 the CPR bought Newcastle Island near Nanaimo and the island, the site of a coal mine, sandstone quarry, saltery and shipyard, was transformed into a holiday resort. An old ship was permanently docked in Mark Bay as a floating hotel and on summer weekends as many as 1,500 steamship passengers would arrive for the day from Vancouver. They came to enjoy such facilities as a dance pavilion, tea house, picnic areas, change houses, soccer field and wading pool. World War II brought an end to these pleasure excursions as ships were diverted by the war effort.

Following Japan's attack on Pearl Harbor, blackouts went into effect and the coast darkened. Lighthouses were covered, vessels travelling at night couldn't use running lights and no weather reports were issued. People of Japanese descent living on the coast were relocated to the interior and their fishing vessels were impounded.

To protect against potential Japanese invasion, flying boat stations (in addition to the existing one at Jericho Beach) were established at Ucluelet, Alliford Bay in Skidegate Inlet, Seal Cove near Prince Rupert, Coal Harbour in Quatsino Sound and Bella Bella. A reserve unit of fishermen within the Royal Canadian Navy was formed to patrol the coast; these 42 boats and 975 men were dubbed the Gumboot Navy. Yorke Island, at the junction of Johnstone Strait and Sunderland Channel, became a military outpost designed to detect and destroy any enemy ships approaching Vancouver from the north with its searchlight and 6" turret guns.

Yorke Island never came under attack and the last firing practice took place on August 10, 1945. The troops were coming home, the Gumboot Navy had disbanded and the B.C. coast, like the rest of the world, was entering a new era.

Above, the old pulpstones on Newcastle Island are a reminder of the coast's past, as is the abandoned steam donkey in Thompson Sound (below).

Montague Harbour Marine Park

The Recreational Coast

At the start of the 20th century, coastal B.C. was a place of abundance with seemingly unlimited raw resources. Thick stands of high-grade timber covered the mountain slopes and pristine rivers swelled with spawning salmon. Lumber and coal barons grew rich logging and mining the land, while fishing ports thrived along the coast, their canneries busy each summer as boat after boat unloaded its catch.

When Muriel Wylie Blanchett, author of *The Curve of Time*, spent her summers cruising the Inside Passage with her young children in the 1930s, she was ahead of her time. Most vessels then plying these waters were pursuing commerce – fishing, logging, mining or servicing the coastal communities centred around these activities. Recreational boating as we know it didn't burgeon until after World War II, when mass production of fibreglass boats and an increase in leisure time and spending power made yachting a pastime everyone could enjoy.

The war brought other changes. A shortage of skilled tree fallers on the coast during the war years

The docks at historic Minstrel Island.

spurred the development of gasoline-powered saws. Following the war, improved machinery, centralization of sawmilling operations and the use of floatplanes to fly logging crews in and out of camps all contributed to the decline of coastal logging communities. Until the 1960s, Minstrel Island was a popular watering hole and steamer stop with a general store and hotel where hand-loggers gathered to drink beer when they weren't felling trees in 'The Jungle,' as the maze of islands at the mouth of Knight Inlet was called. Minstrel Island became a service stop for recreational boaters, but in 2005 the resort closed, its future status unknown.

Blind Channel was another former logging community that transformed itself into a marine resort, its revival dating to 1969 when the Richter family, cruising the coast in their small boat, pulled up to a lonely dock and noticed a 'For Sale' sign on the store. Within months the family sold their Vancouver home and, with entrepreneurial vision and hard work, created a summertime mecca for recreational boaters. Today, the resort's manicured grounds contain a general store and a fine restaurant with picture windows overlooking Mayne Passage.

Sportfishing also increased in popularity following World War II. April Point Lodge on Quadra Island, established in 1945 by the Peterson family of San Francisco, soon became a popular retreat for celebrities, as did the famous Painter's Lodge near Campbell River. When the latter burned in 1985, it was replaced with a new facility.

Salmon like the cold, swift-flowing currents in Discovery Passage, which is also part of the main route for ships travelling the Inside Passage. These same currents used to generate dangerous turbulence in Seymour Narrows – one of the coast's most challenging passes, where currents reach 16 knots –

when a two-headed pinnacle rock in the middle of the pass lay just nine feet below the water's surface at low tide. Suction around Ripple Rock caused the sinking of more than 100 vessels before its top was blown off in 1958. Explosives were inserted into its core by way of an underwater tunnel from Maude Island and scientists from around the world gathered to watch the massive explosion. (See page 196.)

By the 1970s, floathome communities in and around Vancouver (on False Creek and sloughs of the Fraser River) were replaced with modern structures that hooked up to municipal utilities. False Creek was considered a polluted, industrial eyesore in the 1950s, before a revitalization program was initiated. In remote coastal waters, several original floating villages remain in existence. The one at Claydon Bay was towed to Sullivan Bay in 1945 where the string of buildings included a store and post office servicing what was, until the mid-1950s, the busiest floatplane base on the coast. Several of the original buildings remain as part of the Sullivan Bay Marine Resort, operated for the last three decades by Pat Finnerty and Lynn Whitehead, who have developed the floating village into a popular summer destination. Echo Bay on Gilford Island is one of the area's few year-round floathome communities, where the marinas serve boaters each summer and a marine park is located at the head of the bay.

Float camps also served the commercial fishing industry, as did the more permanent boardwalk communities such as Namu, north of Cape Caution in Fitz Hugh Sound. This historic cannery town once housed hundreds of workers who came here to work each summer. Production of canned salmon, which peaked in the 1920s, began to consolidate during the Depression and the closure of canneries accelerated after the war when freezing technology was introduced. The cannery at Namu remained in operation until 1969. By then, surviving plants had centralized at Prince Rupert and in the Vancouver area.

While industry on the coast was consolidating at major centres following World War II, recreational boaters were venturing farther afield, exploring the coast and marvelling not at the resource potential but at the scenic beauty of our coast. To preserve as much pristine and historic property as possible, the

Top to bottom, early attempts to remove Ripple Rock in Seymour Narrows were futile, and nine men returning from the barge were lost in a whirlpool; Sullivan Bay's heritage buildings; Billy Proctor's museum near Echo Bay; Kwatsi Bay is a friendly upcoast resort.

Above, a summer's afternoon at Hardy Island Marine Park. Below, an aerial view of Rebecca Spit Marine Park on Quadra Island.

provincial government began establishing marine parks. Involved in the selection process was the Council of B.C. Yacht Clubs, which was formed in 1958 to represent the interests of recreational boaters in consultations regarding potential parks. Montague Harbour was designated B.C.'s first marine park in 1959, and since then dozens more have been established, including joint acquisitions by the federal and provincial governments under the Pacific Marine Heritage Legacy program. The diverse list of small craft anchorages now protected by park status is inspiring to any recreational boater intent on exploring the Inside Passage. In the Gulf Islands alone, boaters can enjoy a rich variety of easily accessible destinations that encompass beautiful beaches, forest trails and places of historical interest.

Farther north, the parks increase in size, often encompassing several islands and anchorages within their boundaries. Many are undeveloped, dominated by dense forests that have swallowed signs of previous habitation. North America's Pacific forest belt has the heaviest stands of trees in the world, and about a quarter of this temperate rainforest is found in B.C. The forest industry, the province's largest industrial sector, came under heavy criticism in the final decades of the 20th century for its practice of clear-cut logging, and environmentalists waged a much-publicized war in the woods with the forestry companies.

The province's environmental movement began back in the 1950s when Roderick Haig-Brown and other conservationists protested the building of a hydroelectric dam on Buttle and Campbell Lakes for fear the rising waters would destroy valuable wildlife habitat in Strathcona Park. Since then, the preservation of wilderness areas has propelled a growing environmental movement represented by a variety of organizations. Of direct benefit to boaters is the BC Marine Parks Forever Society, established in 1989 by the Council of B.C. Yacht Clubs to raise money and assist BC Parks in establishing new marine parks.

Other organizations working to preserve the coastal wilderness include the Nature Conservancy of Canada – a private, not-for-profit organization created in 1962 that raises funds to acquire properties across the country and preserve their biodiversity for future generations. Specific plant and animal species have also gained protection through the establishment of ecological reserves.

Boaters transiting Johnstone Strait often sight killer whales in the vicinity of Robson Bight, an ecological reserve where killer whales come to rub against rounded pebbles that cover the sea bottom

Cruising Companions

Peter Byrne and George Kirkwood have known each other since their days of racing Flying Dutchmans off Vancouver's Kitsilano Beach in the 1960s. Peter went on to represent Canada at the 1972 Olympics, racing FD's at Kiel, Germany. It was sometime later when Peter and George traded in their racing boats for cruising boats and began sailing extensively along the Inside Passage.

George and his wife Trish have ventured as far as Sitka, Alaska, but they remain devotees of the anchorages around Broughton Archipelago and Queen Charlotte Strait. "We like Laura Bay and Cullen Harbour for the setting and nearby fishing," Trish says. Her other favourite is the small cove deep inside Nimmo Bay.

Peter and his wife Jane have been cruising the Broughtons for over 20 years. Peter doesn't think too much has changed. "I don't know if there are that many more boats coming to the area. I remember having to stern tie at Laura Bay and Waddington Bay back in the early 1980s. But on our last trip this year it didn't seem all that different. Quieter maybe."

Trish & George Kirkwood, Jane & Peter Byrne

The Byrnes keep their Maple Leaf 45 *Excalibur Rex* at the RVYC in Vancouver and the Kirkwoods moor their Aloha 34 *Ali Baba* in Comox. The four have made cruising and exploring the coast together a much anticipated summer ritual.

near shore. These whales feed on the salmon that have traditionally travelled in huge runs along the strait. The early pioneers would boast that the fishing was so plentiful they could cross a stream on the back of spawning salmon. However, decades of overfishing, along with the destruction of salmon habitat, have contributed to dwindling salmon stocks, with some on the verge of extinction. In the city of Vancouver, where 47 salmon-bearing streams once flowed, there are now three.

The proliferation of fish farms is no solace. These salt-water net pens used for raising Atlantic salmon began appearing on the coast in the mid-1970s, despite concerns by environmentalists and commercial fishers that escaped salmon would transmit diseases and weaken wild salmon stocks. Also of concern are the declining southern populations of killer whales, their dwindling numbers blamed in part on pollutants in the water. Scientists have found between three and six times the level of PCBs in members of the southern pods compared to the more populous northern resident orcas that roam Johnstone Strait. Meanwhile, the Fraser River watershed is being cleaned up through upgrades of sewage-treatment plants and the reduction of toxic discharges by pulp and wood mills. Such measures may allow the southern resident killer-whale population to stabilize and ultimately increase.

Time has proven that threatened species can be saved, as shown by the thriving sea otter population on the west coast of Vancouver Island. After the

species was hunted nearly to extinction in the early 1800s, a mere 89 sea otters from Alaska were relocated to Quatsino Sound's Gillam Islands in the early 1970s. Protected by the B.C. Wildlife Act as a threatened species, they now number at least 1,500 and are increasing by about 15% annually.

Past grievances have also been addressed. In 1988 a formal apology was made by the federal government to the Japanese Canadians who were relocated to internment camps during World War II, with compensation offered to those whose property, including fishing boats, was seized. Amends have also been made to the First Nations people, whose potlatch ceremonies were once banned by the federal government. Many of the seized artifacts were eventually returned and are now displayed at local band museums, such as the U'mista Cultural Centre in Alert Bay, a Kwakwaka'wakw fishing village on Cormorant Island.

Much has changed since the days when our early pioneers travelled the coast by boat. There were no marinas then (the word 'marina' was not even part of the vernacular prior to World War II), let alone marine parks and sportfishing lodges. But the primeval mystique of the Inside Passage endures, drawing boaters to its labyrinth of channels, islands and mountain-bounded inlets. A marine highway travelled by vessels ranging from one-man kayaks to cruise ships carrying 2,000 passengers, the Inside Passage is indisputably one of the most beautiful and storied coastlines in the world.

Prideaux Haven, Desolation Sound Marine Park

Artists, Authors & Adventurers

The first artists to inhabit the B.C. coast were the aboriginal people, whose miniature works of art have been found preserved deep within the compacted layers of shell middens. Less permanent is the art form many of us readily associate with the Pacific Northwest – the totem pole.

Made from the trunks of massive red cedars, totem poles were the most monumental of all native artworks. Master carvers were commissioned to sculpt a pole with crests (totems) representing the clan and family to which the pole owner belonged. The average lifespan of a totem pole exposed to the elements is about 60 years before wood decay causes it to topple. When this happens, according to traditional beliefs, the pole's spirit departs and the fallen pole is left to return to nature. However, anthropologists concerned about their preservation began removing totem poles from abandoned village sites at the turn of the last century, and in the 1950s the Totem Pole Preservation Committee at the University of British Columbia's Museum of Anthropology (MOA) in Vancouver, rescued and restored poles that were slowly rotting.

The MOA is one of the best places to view totem poles; dozens of poles and other large sculptures carved in the 19th and early 20th centuries are housed in an Arthur Erickson-designed building inspired by the traditional post-and-beam construction of native big houses. Modern carvings are also on exhibit, including major works by the acclaimed Haida artist Bill Reid, and standing outside on the grounds are two totem poles carved by the Kwakwaka'wakw artist Mungo Martin. Other good places to view totem poles are the Royal British Columbia Museum in Victoria, Vancouver's Stanley Park and the burial grounds in Alert Bay.

Although the British survey expedition commanded by George Vancouver had no official artist among the crew, some of the officers made "faithful representations of the several headlands, coasts and countries, which we might discover." Many of the drawings by these amateur artists were included in Vancouver's official journals, and while most are strictly illustrative aids to navigation, several reflect considerable artistic ability.

The Irish-born 'Indian painter' Paul Kane was the first professional artist to gather material along the fur trade routes of the West when he travelled overland from Toronto in 1846. After descending the Columbia River, he embarked by canoe the next spring on a sketching trip to southern Vancouver Island and the adjacent Gulf Islands. The sea condi-

A thunderbird crowns one of numerous totem poles on display in Vancouver's Stanley Park.

tions in Juan de Fuca Strait on his 11-hour crossing by canoe from Port Angeles to Fort Victoria are vividly described in his diary:

"The wind increased to a perfect gale, and blowing against an ebb tide caused a heavy swell. We were obliged to keep one man constantly bailing to prevent our being swamped. The Indians on board commenced one of their wild chants, which increased to a perfect yell whenever a wave larger than the rest approached; this was accompanied with blowing and spitting against the wind as if they were in angry contention with the evil spirit of the storm. It was altogether a scene of the most wild and intense excitement: the mountainous waves roaming round our little canoe as if to engulph us every moment, the wind howling over our heads, and the yelling Indians, made it actually terrific...It was with the greatest anxiety that I watched each coming wave as it came thundering down, and I must confess that I felt considerable fear as to the event. However, we arrived safely."

Seasickness was Emily Carr's constant companion when native guides were delivering her to remote villages along the coast. At times the natives were suspicious of her motives, but more often they were her friends and protectors. She observed the way they survived hand in hand with nature as they built fires on damp beaches and skillfully paddled their canoes through steep waves.

Emily Carr confesses in her book *Klee Wyck* that to the natives she was but a child, "ignorant about the wild things which they knew so well." She did, however, master the natural elements in her boldly interpretive paintings, eventually gaining recognition as one of Canada's greatest painters. Among her famous works is a 1912 painting entitled *War Canoes, Alert Bay*, which was placed on auction in the spring of 2000 and sold for more than $1 million. A permanent collection of her paintings is displayed at the Vancouver Art Gallery on Robson Square.

Another west coast artist whose paintings are now highly valued is Edward John Hughes. Born in North Vancouver in 1913 and raised in Nanaimo, E. J. Hughes worked as a war artist during World War II. A reclusive artist whose paintings are held in galleries and private collections around the world, Hughes has lived since 1959 in Duncan on Vancouver Island, where he still paints every day for about two hours, now exclusively in watercolours. His oil paintings include *Echo Bay, Gilford Island* (1963) and *Departure from Nanaimo* (1964).

One of the best-known figures of west coast literature is the late Jim Spilsbury, a gifted raconteur, painter and photographer whose talents have been captured in several books published by Harbour Publishing. *Spilsbury's Coast* is an anecdotal recounting of his life on the coast, co-written with Howard White, the award-winning author and founder of Harbour Publishing. Spilsbury's collection of photographs is featured in *Spilsbury's Album* along with entertaining reminiscences of the people and places he came to know along the coast.

Of all the books written about boating in B.C. waters, one that remains on the bestseller list year after year is *The Curve of Time* by Muriel Wylie Blanchet. This coastal classic, written by Wylie Blanchet in her final years and published after her death in 1961, is found on the bookshelf of many a boater who wanders the same watery channels as the crew of Caprice did in the 1930s.

Time was not measured in minutes and hours for Wylie Blanchet during those long-ago summers she spent on the B.C. coast in her 25-foot cabin cruiser. She and her five children got up with the sun and spent their days exploring secluded anchorages and visiting abandoned native villages. For meals, they caught fish or baked beans and bread. They bathed in lakes and washed their clothes in streams. Their world was small in terms of cabin space and conveniences, but it was a world of their own making, filled with grand scenery and endless adventures.

It is still possible to explore many of the same anchorages and to step ashore at the same remote

Above, 'Indian Houses at Alert Bay' by E.J. Hughes, National Gallery of Canada. Below, Emily Carr's 'Kwakiutl House', Vancouver Art Gallery.

village sites for a look back along the curve of time – back to the days when dugout canoes once lined the clamshell beaches and rows of cedar-planked houses, fronted by totem poles, overlooked the waterfront.

Understanding Native Art

Throughout the early years of the fur trade, native groups flourished and their art continued to evolve. However, when white missionaries and schoolteachers moved into these regions, native customs were discouraged and a unique art form was all but abandoned. Its rebirth came in the late 1960s and gained momentum in the '70s when native artists discovered a new medium – the silkscreen print. The ensuing mass production of native art prompted the general public to take an interest. Each group has its own artistic style but they share basic components. The form line defines the shape of the figure being portrayed. Its flowing outline varies in thickness and is usually painted black, with the figure's secondary features in red.

Black and red are the traditional colors of native art. Red was made from ochre (a clay-like mineral) ground to a powder and turned into a paste with the addition of a binding agent such as oil from salmon eggs. Black came from charcoal, graphite or lignite. With the introduction of commercial paints, artists began experimenting with non-traditional colors; however, much of their work is still done in the original colors. The Kwakwaka'wakw (Kwakiutl) traditionally used more colors than the northern artists, adding green, white and yellow to their palettes.

Another basic component is the ovoid – an oval that is pushed out of shape to fit inside the form lines. An ovoid can represent a face, eyes, major joints or simply fill in empty spaces. The U form is used to help contour the figure, fill in spaces or represent features such as feathers. The S form is also used in a variety of ways, such as joining elements, filling in space or representing part of a leg or arm. The four basic design elements – form lines, ovoids, U forms and S forms – are closely assembled to create other shapes in the spaces between them.

Split figures (mirror images) are also widely used, as are transformation figures (i.e. half human/half animal). The basic elements of a figure are sometimes dismantled and rearranged to fit inside a given shape, such as a blanket, hat or spoon. The key to recognizing the figures portrayed in native art is to learn a few of their dominant features.

For example, a raven has a long, straight beak

Bill Reid's 'Killer Whale' outside the Vancouver Aquarium.

whereas an eagle has a shorter, hooked beak. The legendary Thunderbird – a crest used only by the most powerful and prestigious chiefs – is always portrayed with outstretched wings and a sharply recurved upper beak. A bear will have flared nostrils, clawed paws and sharp teeth, sometimes with its tongue hanging out. The beaver has two large front teeth and a cross-hatched tail. The wolf is often shown standing on all four legs whereas the bear and beaver are usually sitting upright.

One of the easiest motifs to recognize is the killer whale, frequently portrayed in an arched position with a tall dorsal fin protruding from its back and two saw-like rows of teeth in its mouth. The moon, an exclusive crest of high-ranking Haida chiefs, is round with a face in the centre. The sun is similar to the moon but with long rays projecting from the outer circle. Human figures are also part of native art and those wearing high-crowned hats atop a totem pole are watchmen who can see others approaching. In Kwakwaka'wakw (Kwakiutl) art, the eyes of supernatural beings are hollow and those of animals and people protrude.

Haida drawings and sculptures embody Northwest native art's classical purity. The trademarks of Haida art are a fluid, stylized use of well-defined form lines and a complex intertwining of figures. Poles and other objects are minimally altered by shallow carvings that blend with the basic shape. Heads are often large (especially those portrayed on totem poles) and in print works the blank spaces are seldom left unadorned.

Tsimshian artists implement many of the traditional northern elements but with slight variations, such as detaching certain components from the main figure. Kwakwaka'wakw art is recognized by its

The painted facade of the Big House in Alert Bay.

U form

form line

ovoids

S form

split U form

This 19th-century Haida drawing by Johnnie Kit-Elswa represents Raven in the belly of a killer whale.

variety of colors, abundance of small elements and the protruding beaks, fins and wings that are added to totem poles.

Nuu-chah-nulth (Nootka) art is more flexible than classic northern art, with frequent breaks in the form lines or even the complete absence of form lines. Shapes are often geometrical and fewer design elements, such as ovoids, are used.

Coast Salish natives used no crest system, so their art traditionally depicted animal and human figures rather than clan emblems. They are noted for their excellent weaving and basketry as well as their carved spindle whorls. The Cowichans on Vancouver Island still employ traditional methods when making their famous sweaters.

With a renewed interest in preserving the traditions of native art, another concern has arisen – that of authenticity. By definition, anything created by an aboriginal is authentic. However, some of the best native artists are not content to replicate the work of their ancestors but are experimenting with their art's classical components. As the acclaimed Haida artist Robert Davidson says, if an art isn't changing, it's dead. Davidson's professional career as a Haida artist began with his carving miniature totem poles for customers at a Vancouver department store. His work is now displayed in art galleries, and his original prints and sculptures are

A mask on display in Billy Proctor's Museum.

collectors items.

The late Bill Reid, of Haida and Scots-American ancestry, is credited with reviving West Coast native art and reintroducing it to the world. His major works include *The Black Canoe*, which is the centre-piece of the Canadian embassy in Washington, DC.

A second casting, *The Jade Canoe*, stands in the departure hall of Vancouver's International Airport. His *Killer Whale* bronze sits outside the entrance to the Vancouver Aquarium, and his massive yellow cedar carving *The Raven and The First Men* is housed at the University of British Columbia's Museum of Anthropology.

When a Haida embarks on an artistic career, the first step is to become an apprentice – one who copies the art of predecessors. The next stage is that of journeyman – learning the symmetrical and classical forms of Haida art. The next stage is to become a master, which entails experimenting with what has been learned. Finally, those with exceptional talent become artists, their work reflecting both mastery and emotion.

The most recent development in native art is the use of computer graphics. Roy Henry Vickers, a talented Tsimshian artist, has recreated traditional forms on a computer screen. He says that his computer-generated ovoids and U-shapes look no different than those created by his ancestors a thousand years ago. The use of computer technology also provides for long-term storage of totem pole designs on disks.

Winter Point, Saturna Island

P lant and animal life thrives along the Inside Passage, where temperate rainforests flourish in the maritime climate and saltwater wetlands provide a nutrient-rich habitat for waterbirds and other species. Pacific salmon travel these waters, destined to spawn in the streams where they were born unless they are thwarted by one of the region's fish-eating predators – humans, marine mammals, eagles or bears.

Boaters might find themselves escorted unexpectedly by a pod of Dall's porpoises or Pacific white-sided dolphins – nautical daredevils which will dart and dive and leap in the bow wave of any moving vessel, from a small pleasure craft to an 80,000-ton cruise ship. Harbour seals and California sea lions are common sights, fishing in the passes or hauling out on rocky outcroppings.

Conifers dominate the forested coastline. They are perfectly adapted to the region's cool, wet winters, able to gather sunlight and grow almost year-round, whereas deciduous hardwoods grow only when their leaves are out. A notable exception to the dense rainforests dominating the B.C. coast is the rain-shadow belt on southeastern Vancouver Island and the Gulf Islands. Here the habitat is warmer and dryer, and the vegetation more complex.

Wildflowers and Shrubs

Spring, when the world is in bloom, is the best time to enjoy the coastal wildflowers of southern B.C. The air is sweet with the scent of rain-drenched vegetation and shoreside trails lead hikers past the intoxicating scent of new spruce shoots. Uninhabited islets, in particular, are a delight to explore. Pink-hued wildflowers such as nodding onion and sea blush grow in profusion, the latter blanketing grassy bluffs, while bluebells grow from rock crevices.

Other indigenous species include the common camas, identified by its purple-blue star-like flower. Native people of the southern straits traditionally used the region's bulbous plants for food, and the common camas was one of these, although great care had to be taken to distinguish it from the poisonous bulbs and leaves of a similar lily called meadow death-camas. The only way to tell the two types apart is by their flowers – those of the death-camas are cream-coloured. The Salish of southern

Above left, camas is a wildflower that thrives on pristine islets, often alongside sea blush (left).

Vancouver Island would weed death-camas from their cultivated beds of common camas, which they harvested during or soon after flowering so as not to confuse them with the death-camas. Only the large bulbs were dug up, while the smaller ones were left to grow. The harvested bulbs were steamed in large pits for a day or more until they were cooked, then served at feasts or sun-dried for storage.

When Europeans arrived they introduced new plant species, sometimes inadvertently importing their seeds in crop seed or straw packing. Others were purposely cultivated. Scotch broom, which grows in golden-yellow abundance along roadsides, was introduced by a Scottish sea captain in 1850. He acquired some seeds while visiting the British consul in the Sandwich Islands (Hawaii) and brought these to Sooke for planting. An invasive shrub, Scotch broom quickly colonized most of southern Vancouver Island and the Gulf Islands, sometimes to the detriment of local flora. Scotch broom's flowers, pods and seeds (which resemble small peas) are toxic and can be poisonous if eaten by children. The shrub's usefulness was as a source of twigs to be bunched into brooms.

Beach pea grows along the edge of sand-and-gravel beaches, while lupine grows in a variety of habitats, its tall spires thick with pea-like flowers that are usually blue or purple. The large-leaved lupine is commonly seen along southern shores while the Nootka lupine thrives in estuarine marshes of the north coast where grizzly bears feed on their roots. One plant found the entire length of the B.C. coast is fireweed, its bright rosy-pink petals blooming on stalks that grow four feet high. Fireweed grows in thick patches on recently logged or burned land and in meadows, thickets and along river bars.

A Walk in the Forest

The dense and complex forests of coastal B.C. form some of the world's most impressive examples of temperate rainforest. Rarely struck by catastrophic fires, the trees of these coastal rainforests have been slowly replaced on an individual basis, creating a many-canopied forest with a dense shrubby under-storey and an abundance of lichens, mosses and ferns growing at the base of trees, up their trunks and on top of decaying logs. Individual trees may be as old as 1,000 years, and the forests themselves are even older. Species such as the western red cedar found refuge in northern California during the last ice age, then moved northward as the glaciers retreated.

Western red cedar, B.C.'s official tree, was called the 'tree of life' by the Kwakwaka'wakw and is considered the cornerstone of Northwest Coast native culture. The tree's rot-resistant wood is straight-grained and easily split, making it the perfect material for everything from house planks and posts to baskets and bentwood boxes. Thriving in moist-to-wet soil and tolerant of shade, the western red cedar's massive trunk (2 to 8 feet in diameter) reaches heights of 150 to 200 feet and bears soft, shiny needles that grow in splayed clusters from branches that droop slightly then turn upward.

Yellow cedar (also known as cypress) grows at higher elevations and is smaller than the western red cedar, reaching heights of 60 to 130 feet, with flattened branches that hang downward. Its inner bark is yellowish and its tough, straight-grained wood was used by Northwest Coast peoples to make a variety of implements, including paddles and bows.

The forest trails at Blind Channel.

Above, the massive trunk of a Western red cedar.
Below, the peeling bark of an arbutus.

The Sitka spruce grows quickly (up to 3 feet per year), reaches an average height of 160 feet, and has a trunk of 3 to 5 feet in diameter. Its branches project at an upward angle from its straight trunk, giving the tree a conical crown, and its spiky green needles are a deep green. In B.C., the Sitka spruce grows at low to middle elevations with the oldest forests occurring in low terraces of river floodplains.

The Western hemlock is a tall, slender tree with branches that droop slightly and twigs that contain two rows of needles which are flat and soft. With an average height of 100 to 150 feet and a trunk diameter of two to four feet, this tree is tolerant of shade and often sprouts up among the faster-growing Sitka spruce. The Western hemlock is more prevalent on B.C.'s north coast than the south coast, and will grow only in soil with significant organic content. Few plants can grow beneath the thick canopy of the Western hemlock, which forms the densest forest canopy of any tree species in this region.

Douglas fir is one of the tallest trees known (over 200 feet) and can live for over 1,000 years. The tree's slightly drooping branches bear flat needles that grow in two rows, and its extremely thick bark provides protection from moderate surface fires. Douglas fir naturally establishes on moist sites following a fire, but also grows in dry, open forests and is found throughout the south coast region, predominantly on the east side of Vancouver Island and the mainland opposite.

The Douglas fir began appearing in our region about 7,000 years ago, and was first described by Dr. Archibald Menzies, the naturalist with Captain George Vancouver's expedition to our coast in the 1790s. The species is named for the Scottish botanist David Douglas, who explored the Pacific Northwest in the 1820s. Douglas was called 'the Grass Man' by the aboriginal people who respected him for his knowledge of the wilderness. The tall cylindrical trunk of the Douglas fir made it a favourite with loggers, and the wood is used extensively in construction. The popularity of the tree has been its downfall, with few of the giant specimens still standing.

Shore pine is common along the immediate coast, its trunk often crooked and its crown irregular. Its branches bear needles that grow in pairs, and hanging from the tip of each branch is a cluster of small pollen cones and an egg-shaped seed cone. This highly adaptable tree is tolerant of sea spray and low-nutrient soil.

The arbutus (madrona) is a broadleaf evergreen found in the south coast's rain-shadow forests. It grows on dry, sunny sites at low to middle elevations, and often shares its habitat with the Douglas fir and Garry oak. Arbutus trees are easy to identify with their smooth, twisting limbs covered in red bark which begins to peel off in August. The broad leaves are a dark shiny green, and in spring the branches are adorned with sprays of white blossoms.

Garry oak is a deciduous tree, with stout branches and a rounded crown. Its bark is light grey with thick furrows and its light-green leaves are round and deeply lobed. Providing splashes of colour in fall is the bigleaf maple, its deeply lobed leaves turning brilliant yellow before falling to the ground. The trunk and main branches of the bigleaf maple are often covered with a moss layer so thick that other tree roots can sprout and grow as 'canopy roots'.

Carpeting the forest floors are over 700 mosses and about 40 species of ferns, the latter needing abundant moisture for reproduction. Skunk cabbage is also found in wet areas, near streams and bogs, and is easy to spot, with its yellow, tulip-shaped inner leaf and large outer leaves. These leaves are eaten by deer and geese, and were widely used by First Nations people to wrap salmon for baking and for lining berry baskets. Slugs, often seen lying on a trail, feed at night on roots and plants. The largest in B.C. (and second-largest in the world) is the banana slug, so named for its yellow-green colour with brown or black spots.

Salal is plentiful, growing in thickets, its branches of waxy evergreen leaves shipped to florists worldwide for use in cut-flower bouquets. The salal's small purple berries appear in mid- to late summer and have long been a common part of the native people's diet. Devil's club, a broadleaf plant related to ginseng, was used as a medicine and protective agent by the area's aboriginal people. The inner bark of the roots and stems was boiled in water, making a tea used to treat various ailments. The plant's bright red berries are a favourite food for bears, but its tough, prickly spines can inflict bad scratches on bare-legged hikers.

Bears

Coastal forests are home to a variety of animals, including bears. Black bears live on the mainland, Vancouver Island and the Discovery Islands, while grizzlies roam the mountainous backcountry, appearing at a few mainland inlets, including Knight Inlet and Mackenzie Sound, when salmon are returning to the streams and rivers.

Most bears avoid humans but not all are timid – some lose their natural fear if they learn to associate humans with food. Small dogs are 'bear bait' so pet owners must be extra careful. If you decide to hike inland, remember that salmon streams and berry

Above, a black bear feeds on spawning salmon.
Top, skunk cabbage. Middle, Devil's club.

Above, grizzly bear soaking in Knight Inlet's Glendale Creek . Below, the shells of an oyster, cockle and butter clam.

sea asparagus

sea urchins

patches attract bears. Watch for bear scat and if you come across a decaying animal carcass, it's probably some bear's food cache and you should leave the area immediately or risk becoming part of the picnic.

The best way to avoid encountering a bear is by being noisy. Talking, singing and jingling bells are better than silence, but the most effective warning is an air horn. Any bear in the area is sure to hear its piercing blast, ensuring you won't come face to face with a surprised and therefore dangerous bear. When surprised, black bears usually behave differently than grizzly bears, which are more likely to charge, especially sows with cubs. A grizzly (a sub-species of brown bear) can be identified by its large size and distinctive shoulder hump. Its fur can range in colour from blond to black with varying shades of brown and gray in between. At 200 to 600 pounds, black bears are smaller than grizzlies (300 to 1,500 pounds) and are usually jet-black or brown with a brown-yellow muzzle.

Should you encounter a grizzly, back away very slowly without making eye contact, which the bear perceives as aggression. If you are charged by a grizzly, play dead and try to protect your face and vital organs from the bear's powerful jaws by curling into a ball on the ground. Should it be a black bear charging you, stand your ground by shouting and defending yourself with a stick or rock. Very few people suffer bear attacks and most can be avoided by taking a few sensible precautions.

Another forest predator to be aware of is the cougar, a solitary predator that hunts deer and small game. Also called mountain lion, this large member of the cat family will rarely attack humans, but when it does, small children are most vulnerable. Cougars are known to stalk and attack from behind and if one is approaching, you are better off acting aggressively using rocks or a large stick to defend yourself. Maintain eye contact, try to make yourself appear as large as possible and do not run or turn your back.

The Intertidal Zone

There is much to explore along the foreshore of an anchorage where tidal pools contain a microcosm of marine life, including tiny shore crabs. Sea stars, which prey on crabs, barnacles, clams and mussels, are often found high and dry, clinging to foreshore rocks with stiff arms that contain rows of feet on their undersides. Brightly coloured sea anemones attach themselves to rocks and look like rounded lumps of jelly when the tide recedes and they retract into themselves to conserve moisture.

The native people harvested much of their food from the foreshore, where clams feed on microscopic plants and animals that they filter from the water through their siphons (necks). These bivalve filter-feeders, along with cockles, oysters, scallops and mussels, are susceptible to harmful blooms of algae, commonly called red tide. When shellfish ingest large quantities of this toxic algae, the poison becomes concentrated. When it is ingested by seabirds and mammals (including humans), this toxin will cause paralytic shellfish poisoning.

Eelgrass, a ribbon-like vascular plant, grows in the lowest intertidal zone and the sub-tidal zone, usually along sheltered shores where Dungeness crab can be found hiding in beds of eelgrass. Eelgrass was traditionally eaten fresh or dried into cakes for winter food; the Kwakwaka'wakw dined on eelgrass at special feasts, while the Haida preferred eelgrass with herring spawn attached to the leaves.

Sea asparagus, or pickleweed, grows along the foreshore and is harvested commercially just before summer flowering for use in salads. If you pick sea asparagus in summer, the plant's excessive saltiness can be diminished by boiling it several times in fresh water with a pinch of sugar until tender.

Bull kelp, a type of seaweed, grows throughout the summer in thick beds from the sea bottom. Its long, hollow, rubbery stem ends at the water's surface with a cylindrical float and long brown fronds that trail across the water, their direction an indicator of any tidal current (see page 13 for more on kelp and current). A variety of marine life finds shelter in kelp beds, including sea urchins, which feed on this iodine-rich plant. Sea urchins consumed vast kelp forests along the Inside Passage after the sea otter, which feeds on sea urchins, was hunted nearly to extinction in the early 1800s.

Jellyfish are not a fish but, like sea anemones, an invertebrate. They swim by pulsing their bodies and they absorb oxygen from the water. Suspended from the edges of its saucer-shaped body are tentacles. The jellyfish protects itself with small stinging cells which can cause discomfort if touched. (A drop or two of alcohol will soothe a jellyfish sting – bar scotch works well.)

At night, water disturbed by the oars of a dinghy will sometimes produce tiny sparkles that look like phosphorescence. They are, however, caused by bioluminescence which is the production of light by living organisms. Certain marine algae, called dinoflagellates, produce light only when disturbed, triggering the change of chemical energy to light.

Right, a bald eagle swoops down to snatch a salmon near the surface with its powerful talons.

Birds

Sooner or later most boaters become casual birders. With so many opportunities to see birds while out on the water, it's a fairly effortless hobby. Who hasn't awoken in an anchorage to a medley of bird calls – eagles chittering, kingfishers chattering, gulls mewing. To hear the haunting laugh of a loon in a northern anchorage is one of those moments that make boating such a rewarding pastime.

Coastal B.C. is part of the Pacific Flyway, a migratory route for millions of birds, and the region's river estuaries and tidal passes provide a rich habitat for the many waterbirds that winter in local waters. The Fraser River Delta is one of the largest and most important estuaries on North America's west coast, its marshes and mud flats supporting more waterfowl, shorebirds and gulls than anywhere else in Canada. Birds congregate near food sources, and the mouth of the Fraser River is a prime feeding area due to upwelling caused by the mixing of saltwater and fresh water. Upwellings of cold water bring plankton and small fish to the surface, and this phenomenon also occurs in channels and passes, such as Active Pass, where strong tidal currents are deflected over underwater ridges.

Bald eagles are often seen fishing in passes, using their keen eyesight, speed and sharp talons to pluck salmon from the water. A high-soaring eagle, with a wingspan of 6 to 8 feet, can spot a fish from over a mile away and can dive from the sky at 100 miles per hour. Eagles, which mate for life, build their nests in the tallest trees of their territory and close to the water. Juvenile eagles retain their ragged plumage until the age of five, when they attain the distinctive markings of a mature bald eagle, including the snowy white head feathers for which the bird is named.

Although they are birds of prey, eagles are also scavengers and each winter, from October through February, they gather by the thousands at the head of

Howe Sound to feed on spawning salmon along the Lower Squamish River. Eagles also gather each December along the shores of Northumberland Channel near Nanaimo in anticipation of the Pacific herring spawn in February and March.

The coast is home to many species of duck. These include **dabbling ducks**, who feed at the water's surface or by dipping their heads and bodies until only their tail is protruding from the water. Dabblers include the well-known mallard, the drake (male) sporting an emerald green head and chestnut chest. Other dabbler species are the teal, northern pintail, widgeon and wood duck.

Diving ducks, as the name implies, completely submerge when feeding. Scoters, goldeneye and bufflehead are diving ducks, as are scaup and harle-

quin. Mergansers are nicknamed 'sawbills' due to their long, tapering bills lined with sharp 'teeth' for grabbing fish. A mother merganser will carry her brood of newborn chicks on her back as she swims near shore.

Shorebirds include the black oystercatcher, which has a long orange beak with which it pries open shellfish. The feet of the pigeon guillemot, an alcid, are also bright orange and quite a sight when this black seabird runs across the surface of the water, gaining speed for take-off.

Gulls are buoyant swimmers and strong fliers. Their long, pointed wings allow them to glide and soar and set down lightly upon the water. Cormorants, which enter the water only to feed, are often seen perched on rocks or buoys, their wings spread out to dry. **Loons**, on the other hand, remain mostly in the water and come ashore only to nest, for they cannot walk on land and they cannot fly during moult. Swimming is their specialty and their heavy bodies are designed for diving.

The largest seabird colony in the Strait of Georgia is on Mandarte Island, known locally as Bare Island, which lies off the northeast side of Sidney Island and is private property, owned by the East Saanich First Nation. More than 8,000 birds nest on this barren island, their numbers building over the summer, with a sizeable flock remaining throughout the winter. Scientists have been studying birds here since the 1950s and have identified more than 100 species. It is the largest seabird breeding colony in B.C. for double-crested and pelagic cormorants, glaucous-winged gulls and pigeon guillemots. It is also a major nesting site for rhinoceros auklets and tufted puffins. The lagoon at the south end of Sidney Spit Marine Park is a productive feeding ground for these birds and others, including great blue herons.

Pacific Salmon

The life cycle of a Pacific salmon makes a fascinating tale. Salmon spawn in fresh water, usually streams, where they spend varying lengths of time depending on the species. Some juveniles migrate directly to saltwater while others linger in river estuaries where they grow and adapt to the mix of fresh and saltwater habitats. Depending on the species,

Top left, oystercatchers can be seen on reefs and outcroppings at low tide. Middle left, juvenile gulls are often mottled with brown. Bottom left, coho salmon is a favourite catch of sportsfishermen but fishing for this species is now restricted.

salmon will spend one to 7 years in the open ocean before returning to their natal streams to spawn.

Salmon struggle against incredible odds to return to the stream of their birth. If a fish makes it past the sport and commercial fisheries, there will be other predators, such as bears and eagles, waiting along stream banks to make a meal of these weary fish. Salmon often have to leap up waterfalls and swim against rushing currents to return to their spawning grounds. Once there, the females dig nests in the gravel and lay their eggs while their male partners release milt which fertilizes the eggs. All Pacific salmon spawn only once, then die. Most salmon spawn in late summer or fall.

There are five species of salmon: king (chinook) is the largest; silver (coho) is prized by sportfishermen; red (sockeye), with its rich red meat, is the highest-priced commercial salmon; pink (humpy) is the most common and an important commercial fish for the canneries; and chum (dog) salmon, when smoked, is a tasty delicacy.

A specific salmon stock – often identified by the name of its spawning stream – is lost forever once its spawning stream is destroyed, and this loss of biodiversity means there are fewer genetic types to deal successfully with future vagaries of the environment. Hatcheries, which recreate a spawning habitat of gravel covered with clear, still, shallow water, have become a substitute for rejuvenating salmon stocks but the survival rate of hatchery fish has been declining.

One of the biggest threats to salmon survival appears to be global warming. A rise of just a few degrees in water temperature causes a salmon's metabolic rate to increase and forces it to expend valuable energy needed to swim upstream. Fish and other cold-blooded animals can't regulate their body temperatures like mammals, and salmon are particularly susceptible because they spend most of their lives near the ocean surface.

Marine Mammals

One of the most thrilling sights while cruising is the sudden surfacing of a whale off your bow. Several species of whale thrived in considerable numbers along the B.C. coast until commercial whaling depleted their populations between 1830 and 1967. Whaling boats have been replaced by whale-watching boats, and killer whales are the big draw, especially in the waters off Victoria and near Robson Bight in Johnstone Strait.

Called cetaceans and found in all the world's oceans, whales vary greatly in size. The smallest are dolphins and porpoises. **Killer whales** (orcas) are the largest member of the *Delphinidae* family of toothed whales. Male orcas, which can reach 30 feet in length, live for about 30 years, while females, who average 23 feet in length, live for about 50 years, sometimes longer. The male is distinguished from the female by his tall, straight dorsal fin (up to 6 feet high on mature males). Females give birth to single calves following a gestation period of 15 months.

A killer whale's most distinctive features are its prominent dorsal fin and the white marking just behind it, called a saddle patch. Scientists who observe killer whales in B.C. waters have developed a database in which regularly sighted pods and their members – identified by individual markings – are given reference names. Every killer whale belongs

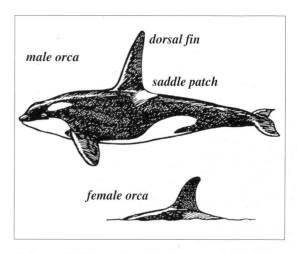

Below, a Dall porpoise skims the water's surface.

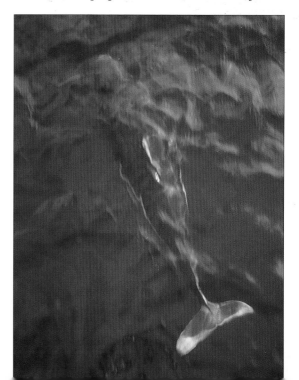

to a pod – the extended family group into which it was born. Each sub-group within a pod consists of a mature cow and her progeny of all ages. Mature males likely mate with females of other pods, but they always return to their own pod and remain with it until death.

Resident pods, with up to 50 members, form the largest groups, remaining near established salmon runs along inshore waters. Transient pods form smaller groups and travel a wider area in search for food, preying primarily on marine mammals such as seals and sea lions. It was because of their swift, ferocious attacks on their warm-blooded prey that killer whales, whose mouths hold more than four dozen sharp teeth, were once feared by humans.

Killer whales can swim for long distances at a cruising speed of about 7 knots, but can accelerate dramatically when attacking prey or leaping from the water. Resident pods communicate with high-pitched sounds that can be heard on hydrophones. These vocalizations include sonar-like clicks, squeaks and whistles. Transient pods remain silent, so as not to alert potential prey of their presence.

Orca Behaviour:

spyhopping – the whale lifts its head vertically out of the water to look around;

slapping – the whale strikes the water's surface with its tail flukes or flippers;

lobtailing – an aggressive move in which the whale uses its tail flukes to club a seal or seal lion, or to warn whale-watching vessels to back off;

breaching – the whale leaps right out of the water and lands with a huge splash.

Dall porpoises are sometimes confused with killer whales because their black-and-white colouring is similar. However, Dall porpoises are much shorter (about 7 feet long) and stockier in shape, and their dorsal fin is topped with white. They are the world's fastest marine mammals, reaching speeds of 30 miles per hour. Travelling in groups of a half-dozen or more, they swim just beneath the surface of the water, kicking up splashes, called rooster tails, when they leap partially out of the water. These social creatures love to ride the bow wave of a moving vessel and will perform dazzling, crisscross maneuvers in which two pairs race toward the bow, one from either side, only to veer off at the last moment to prevent a collision. Their split-second reflexes and swiftness allow them to dart through the water and turn quickly.

Also playful and sociable is the **Pacific white-sided dolphin**, which travels in large groups (115 members on average). Like the Dall porpoise, white-sided dolphins are attracted to the bow waves of moving vessels. Slightly longer than the Dall porpoise, these dolphins are black with a white belly and a hooked dorsal fin. During the fall mating season, they indulge in wild acrobatics, leaping with abandon in front of large vessels and cruise ships.

Baleen whales are also sighted along B.C.'s Inside Passage. These toothless whales feed on schooling fish, plankton and other small organisms, which they catch by swimming with their mouths wide open. When the whale closes its mouth, it raises its tongue to force the scooped water out the sides where the bristles of its baleen plates trap the food. The **humpback whale** is a filter feeder and, although large in size, is an acrobatic whale that performs breaches, flipper-slaps and deep dives. This surface activity and close-to-shore feeding by the humpback made it an easy target for commercial whalers in the 19th century.

By the time humpbacks in the Pacific were protected in 1966, their numbers had dwindled to a few thousand from an estimated high of 125,000. However, their numbers are rebounding and sightings outside coastal Alaska, the summer feeding

Pacific white-sided dolphins in Knight Inlet.

grounds of Pacific humpbacks, are increasing. In recent years, humpbacks have been sighted in the Strait of Georgia and northern Johnstone Strait, although the largest numbers have been sighted southeast of Moresby Island in the Queen Charlottes where scientists have reported more than 100 congregating in spring. Adult humpbacks are, on average, 45 feet long and weight up to 40 tons. Their large flippers provide maneuverability and the pleats on the sides of their mouths can create a pouch large enough to hold six adult humans.

The **minke**, another filter feeder that frequents inshore waters, also has a pouch-like throat but is considerably smaller than the humpback. Measuring 20 to 30 feet in length and weighing up to 10 tons, minkes travel alone and are much more elusive than the humpback, surfacing to breathe but only occasionally to breach or lunge-feed through schools of fish. (See photo, page 292.)

Seals and **sea lions** (which are a type of seal) are widespread in B.C. coastal waters. These fin-footed marine mammals have a thick layer of fat beneath their hair-covered skin and spend much of their time in the water. Unlike whales, however, who never leave the water, seals and sea lions will haul out onto rocky islets, sandbars and mudflats to rest, breed and give birth. In most instances, a seal pup lying alone on a beach has not been abandoned but is waiting for its mother to return, so it should be left alone. Sea lions gather in colonies to breed, with mature males assembling harems. Seals and sea lions live for about 30 years and feed on fish.

Most common in southern waters is the Pacific harbour seal, recognized by its mottled white-black-brown colouring, with males approaching 6 feet in length. California sea lions breed in B.C.'s southern waters in fall and winter. They appear black when wet and are smaller than the tawny-coloured Steller sea lion; male Steller sea lions weigh up to 2,400 pounds and their main rookeries are found in northern waters.

Otters belong to the weasel family and are kept warm not by blubber but by a thick coat of fur. The endangered sea otter is not found in the inside waters of B.C., but the smaller river otter is often seen scampering along the foreshore of an anchorage or swimming near shore. Not considered a marine mammal because it is also found in lakes and rivers, the river otter makes its home on land and, with webbed feet, is agile on land and in the water. Males reach 4 feet in length and weigh up to 25 pounds. River otters are very sociable and playful, and have been observed sliding headfirst on their bellies down mudbanks into the water.

Top, a humpback whale displays its fluked tail before doing a deep dive. Above, the sea otter has the densest fur coat of any mammal. Below, sea lions haul out on the Fraser River jetty near Steveston.

Tribune Bay

When the sun shines, the beach beckons. Boaters cruising B.C.'s south coast can enjoy a variety of beaches, ranging from stretches of fine sand to half-moon slivers of white shell. Those made of sand originated some 10,000 years ago when glaciers retreated from the Strait of Georgia and left behind drift deposits of ground-up sand, gravel and clay. Remnants of these glacial outwash plains are the beaches into which we now like to sink our toes.

More abundant are the white-shell beaches. These were not naturally formed but created in prehistoric times by the area's early inhabitants. The empty clam and mussel shells they would toss into heaps were, over time, crushed and compressed into beaches several yards deep. Archaeological digs have taken place at a number of these middens but the general public is not allowed to disturb them. We can, however, enjoy them as foreshore beaches on which to picnic or go for a swim.

Some of the best swimming spots are found in the northern Strait of Georgia, where currents are generally weak and variable, resulting in relatively warm water. Good spots for swimming can be found in protected bays and coves where the surface water isn't disrupted by vigorous tidal mixing and may be further warmed by a sandy beach or rock foreshore during a rising tide.

And then, of course, there are the lakes. Mariners have, for centuries, delighted in the discovery of a freshwater lake near the head of an anchorage. The early explorers washed their clothes and bathed in this clean water, but modern mariners are more likely to head ashore with pure pleasure in mind as they hike to the nearest lake for a swim. (The use of soap and shampoo is not allowed in marine park lakes.) Numerous anchorages in and around Desolation Sound and the Discovery Islands have trails leading inland to a lake in which you can take a dip.

These are some of the beaches and lakes we have enjoyed along B.C.'s southern Inside Passage.

Sandy Beaches:
Sidney Spit, Sidney Island
Buccaneer Bay, Thormanby Islands
Sandy Island Marine Park
Tribune Bay, Hornby Island
Spilsbury Point, Hernando Island

Middens:
Princess Margaret Marine Park, Portland Island
Russell Island Marine Park
Cabbage Island Marine Park
Hawkins Island
Montague Harbour Marine Park
Matilpi
Burdwood Group
Insect Island
Blunden Harbour

Freshwater Lakes:
Tenedos Bay (Unwin Lake)
Roscoe Bay (Black Lake)
Waiatt Bay/Small Inlet (Newton Lake)
Teakerne Arm (Cassel Lake)

Above, Burdwood Group. Right,
Buccaneer Bay. Below, Russell Island.
Bottom left, Cassel Lake. Bottom right,
Sandy Island.

CHAPTER ONE

SOUTHERN GULF ISLANDS

A shell midden overlooks the Russell Island anchorage at the entrance to Fulford Harbour.

Bordered by dark green conifers, the golden hilltops of the Gulf Islands roll down to a sheltered sea. When heaving a dinghy onto a clamshell beach – for the first time or the hundredth – a boater can't help but be struck by the subtle beauty of these islands, where deer wander freely and narrow roads weave past fenced pastures and country inns on their way to the water's edge. The final bend of a leafy lane often reveals yet another snug cove or secure harbour where boaters can find refuge, recreation and, perhaps, a moment of reflection.

Nestled in the lee of Vancouver Island and named the Gulf Islands when the Strait of Georgia was referred to as a 'gulf', these sheltered islands enjoy an ideal climate – warm and dry in summer, cool and wet in winter. With a decent heater on board, you can cruise these islands year-round and each season brings refreshing changes – from the bright bustle of

Charts and Publications:

Use charts 3440, 3441 and 3442. Large-scale charts include 3412 (Victoria Harbour, replaces 3415), 3476, 3477, 3478 and 3473 (Active Pass). Chartbook 3313 has good detail and covers Gulf Islands to Nanaimo. Use Volume One of the CHS Sailing Directions for the BC Coast, South Portion, and the Canadian Tide and Current Tables, Vol. 5.

summer to the solitude of winter when shorebirds are your only company in an otherwise deserted cove.

The shoulder seasons of spring and fall are ideal times to cruise the Gulf Islands – the weather is changeable but the anchorages are quiet. In spring the arbutus trees are in blossom and tiny wildflowers blanket the green meadows. By mid-summer, drought conditions often exist on the islands, with green fields turned to flaxen gold. Fall brings cool nights and morning fog, but this is when the islands are their most beautiful, the shorelines warmed by the coppery tones of berried arbutus and maple leaves that have turned mustard yellow and plum red.

A cruising paradise, the Gulf Islands are ideal for recreational boating with a network of protected anchorages, marine parks, full-service marinas and meandering channels waiting to be explored. The islands' relatively calm waters appeal to power-boaters, while sailors can take advantage of breezes that funnel up or down the various channels, including a summertime thermal wind that often pipes up in the afternoon, allowing for a leisurely sail from one anchorage to the next.

Gulf Islands National Park Reserve

In May 2003 Canada's 40th national park was established in the Gulf Islands. This new park reserve encompasses various islands and numerous islets within its boundary, which extends southeastward from Active Pass and the southern shores of Saltspring Island to the Canada/U.S. border that runs along Boundary Pass and Haro Strait.

Forming much of this new national park were existing provincial parks – Beaumont, Cabbage Island, Princess Margaret, Winter Cove, Sidney Spit, D'Arcy Island and Isle De Lis – along with additional waterfront properties acquired by the Pacific Marine Heritage Legacy, a federal/provincial partnership program established to protect a network of marine and coastal areas along the B.C. coast. As well, the park features a great deal of Saturna Island – the least developed of the large Gulf Islands –

Winter Cove Marine Park on Saturna Island is now part of the Gulf Islands National Park.

where PMHL acquisitions, ecological reserves and Crown land combine to form the largest parcel of land within the park reserve. In addition, all Crown islets lying within the park boundaries are part of the Gulf Islands National Park Reserve. Until a management plan is in place, existing marine park policies and moorage fees remain in place.

The southern Gulf Islands were considered a candidate for national park status for a variety of reasons, including their natural beauty and a mild year-round climate, unique in Canada, which allows a variety of plants and animals to flourish. The mix of vegetation includes arbutus, Garry oak, western red cedar and broadleaf maple, while animals living in this habitat include the Bendires shrew, Townsend's chipmunk, Douglas squirrel and black-tailed deer.

Boaters have long appreciated the gentle nature of these islands, where a walk ashore poses no risk of encountering a hungry bear or cougar, although a western spotted skunk could be lurking in the bushes. Despite their location within easy cruising distance of three large urban centres – Vancouver, Victoria and Seattle – the Gulf Islands have retained much of their pastoral charm. This was another reason for establishing a national park before the islands succumbed to population and development pressures.

For more information:
Gulf Islands National Park Reserve of Canada
2220 Harbour Road
Sidney, BC V8L 2P6
Phone: 250-654-4000
Website: www.pc.gc.ca

Cruising the Gulf Islands

Prevailing winds in the Strait of Georgia and Juan de Fuca Strait are moderated in the Gulf Islands by the buffer provided by various islands. Most important, these anchorages are not subject to the large seas generated by wind blowing across long stretches of open water. Once you are in the Gulf Islands, you are never far from a safe anchorage.

The holding ground is invariably mud with either sand or a mix of sand and shell. Most anchors set well in this combination, although we did have one unusual experience in Selby Cove when our 45-pound CQR was actually bouncing over the mud-and-shell bottom. Perplexed, we hauled the brute up to discover a large clam shell had been neatly pierced in the centre by the point of the plough, defeating the anchor's burying action.

Many anchorages in the Gulf Islands will have some current but this is rarely a problem. Anchorages with noticeable current include Winter Cove, Sidney Spit, Horton Bay and Russell Island – all in the one- to 2-knot range. Be sure to consult the tide tables when anchoring and allow for variations in depth when you drop the hook.

Prevailing summertime winds in the Gulf Islands follow two general patterns. Up to South Pender Island, a southwest breeze blowing in from Juan de Fuca Strait is the norm during the day and usually dies down in the evening. North of the Penders, northwesterlies prevail as winds adhere to the orientation of Trincomali Channel.

Tides and Currents

For many recreational boaters, the Gulf Islands offer an introduction to the numerous tidal passes you will encounter throughout B.C. waters. A flood tide rushes around both ends of Vancouver Island, pouring into the Strait of Juan de Fuca and the constricted channels of the Gulf Islands on its way to Georgia Strait. Conversely, an ebb tide brings the water rushing back through the Gulf Islands on its way seaward through the Strait of Juan de Fuca.

Boundary Pass

This eastern entrance to Haro Strait separates the Gulf Islands from the American San Juan Islands to the south and is not an especially tricky pass as long as the wind is not too strong against the current. The international border between Canada and the United States lies along Boundary Pass, which is part of the main shipping route, so it's prudent to cross at right angles and make the transit as quickly as possible. Westbound ships rounding East Point can very quickly be on a collision course with you.

This is a wide pass – over 2 1/2 miles – but currents can exceed 5 knots. On large floods, tide rips and overfalls form off the north end of Patos Island, and tremendous turbulence also forms in the reefs and shoal water extending from Tumbo Island and East Point on Saturna Island, the main turning point for flood currents entering the Strait of Georgia via Haro Strait. When wind is against tide, large, steep

The automated lighthouse at East Point.

Bluffs Park on Galiano Island provides an eagle's eye view of the western entrance to Active Pass.

seas will form south and east of East Point. During an ebb, the current sets onto this reef, as the captain of the barque *Rosenfeld* discovered in 1886 when his vessel, in tow from Nanaimo, ran on the rock now bearing the ship's name.

East Point on Saturna Island was widely considered the most dangerous point on the shipping route between Vancouver and Victoria until a fog horn was installed in 1939. The original lighthouse, erected in 1888, was replaced in 1967 with a modern house and skeleton tower. Killer whales (orcas) are frequently sighted in the waters off East Point from May to November, and we have been accompanied by Pacific white-sided dolphins when crossing Boundary Pass.

John Passage

John Passage, lying between Coal and Goudge Islands, is the recommended pass when departing Sidney for points north. Currents through here can run at up to 4 knots but the hazards are obvious – the shallow shelf in the middle of the pass is marked with a day beacon and the reef at the S end is either visible or has wash breaking over the top.

Active Pass

This is the main pass for commercial and recreational vessels heading in and out of the Gulf Islands. It is an 'S'-shaped channel complicated by the regular transits of large, wave-generating car ferries. These ferries, often travelling at speeds of 10 knots or more in the pass, can kick up a lot of wash and must be

given the right of way. Some pleasure boaters avoid Active Pass because of this ferry traffic, but they are missing a beautiful channel abundant with wildlife, towering bluffs and impressive hydraulics. It is also a forgiving pass in the sense that currents aren't usually excessive for small boats and there are ways to work the back eddies if you have missed slack.

That aside, Active Pass is a very challenging stretch of water and requires a skipper to be on full alert from beginning to end. The ferry traffic is almost constant and the recreational boater should never obstruct or impede the course of a ferry in these restricted waters. Remain alert for approaching ferries, both visually and on VHF. Ferries normally announce their arrival at Active Pass on Channel 16 but you can also contact Victoria Traffic on Channel 11 to receive details on ferries or other large vessels approaching the pass.

Although your arrival should be at slack for this pass, we have found ourselves arriving at the Georgia Strait entrance when a flood is already well

---

PASS TIP SHEET – ACTIVE PASS
Location: (48°52'N, 123°20'W) Between Mayne and Galiano Islands.
Maximum Flow: Flood, 8 knots. Ebb, 7 knots.
Slack: 15 minutes on large tides.
Anchorages: Westbound, Whaler Bay and Sturdies Bay. Eastbound, Village Bay.
Hazards: Ferry traffic. Heavy tide-rips near Gossip Island, Fairway Bank and near Lion Islets on flood with a NW wind. Whirlpools and tide rips south of Mary Anne Point.
Key to safe transit: Arrive at or close to slack, be alert for ferry traffic, monitor channel 11 or 16 and keep to the starboard side of channel.

underway. Over the years we've watched fish boats and other craft use the back eddies to get through and we too have employed this method. When inbound, we motor between Fairway Bank and the green can buoy at the S end of Gossip Shoals. We stay within a cable of the buoy, keeping close to it and the Galiano Island shoreline as we make our way toward Mary Anne Point. Once around this point, we normally are able to make our way through the pass, keeping to the Galiano Island side. However, during strong floods the current is strong at Matthews Point and we sometimes have to cross over to Lord Point on Mayne Island. We work close along that shore until arriving at the large kelp bed E of Helen Point where we cross back over to the Galiano Island side to continue through the pass.

The area from Helen Point to Collinson Point is where the current is strongest on a flood (up to 7 knots on the Mayne Island side) and where you may be tempted to turn up the engine revs to get free. If it looks dicey or the current appears too strong, you can turn around and drift back into Georgeson Bay to wait for the current to slacken. In our 20 years of transiting this pass, we've only had to do this once.

Stream direction in the pass: From Enterprise Reef in Trincomali Channel, flood currents rapidly gain speed near Helen Point. The stream makes a beeline to the bluffs on the opposite Galiano shore where it turns 90 degrees to starboard. When this stream combines with ferry wash, there can be tremendous overfalls and rips in the area west of Matthews Point.

A Spirit Class BC Ferry heads for Helen Point.

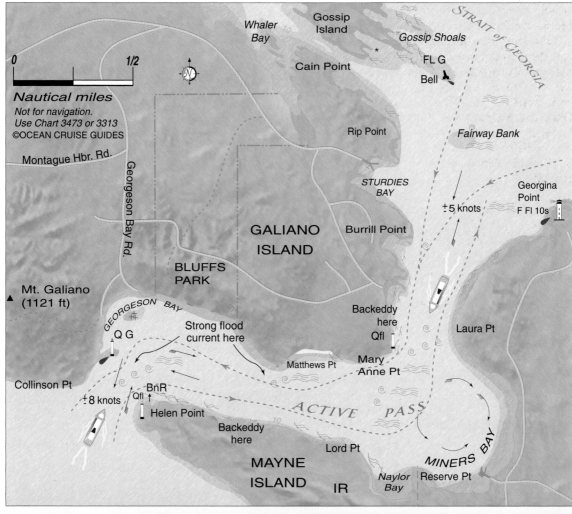

This main stream sets close to Matthews Point (a dangerous area during strong flood tides) and races to Reserve Point, where it makes another course change toward Laura Point. As it approaches Laura Point, the current splits, with some of the stream turning right into Miners Bay while most of the water goes out into Georgia Strait. The stream that turns into Miners Bay creates a clockwise flow of water – a flywheel – which continues well after the flood has ended and often slows the onset of the ebb. This flywheel can cause severe rips where it meets the main stream in the area SE of Mary Anne Point. The spinning direction changes with the ebb to become counterclockwise.

The flood current generates a large back eddy on both sides of the pass from Mary Anne Point into the Strait of Georgia. If you're bucking a flood, the Galiano Island side of the pass should be favoured, for it has less turbulence than the Mayne Island side, and the back eddy can be taken up to and around Mary Anne Point. If the current is too strong here, you can cross over to the Mayne Island side and wait in Naylor Bay or Miners Bay for slack.

An ebb current is generally less turbulent, although ferry wash will continue to be a problem for small recreational boats throughout the pass. Generally speaking, rips are not as bad during ebbs.

If you don't want to transit Active Pass after a late-evening crossing of Georgia Strait or need a spot to wait for slack water, there is a useable anchorage in Whaler Bay just inside the reefs at Cain Point. Further into the bay is a public dock which may or may not have space but be aware that the water is very shallow near the dock. Miners Bay is another possible overnight location, either at anchor or at the government dock (both of which will be bumpy). *See map for detail.*

For information on Porlier Pass, Dodd Narrows and Gabriola Passage, please see Chapter 2.

THE ANCHORAGES

Sidney Spit 1   Marine Park

Some of the best swimming beaches in the Gulf Islands are found at this marine park. Shaped like a South Seas atoll, but consisting of fine sand rather than crushed coral, Sidney Spit extends nearly a mile from the north end of Sidney Island. Understandably popular with boaters, kayakers and campers, the park is also serviced by a summertime passenger ferry from Sidney.

The beach on the SW side of the bay is especially pretty with clean fine sand, and the anchorage here is usually less crowded than the anchorage near the dinghy dock. However, this side of the bay is popular with locals from Sidney and occasionally can be an unpleasantly noisy anchorage with speed boats

Main dock at Sidney Spit Marine Park.

roaring up to the beach for an evening beach party. One option for overnight visits is to anchor or moor in the buoy area of the park and visit this beach by dinghy.

Unlike most of the Gulf Islands, which are formed from hard rock outcropping, Sidney Island is made of glacial till. Back in the 1970s, in an effort to prevent erosion of its sandy spit, B.C. Parks workers drove log pilings into the spit to act as anchors for logs. These efforts have had no effect on stabilizing the spit, but the good news is the spit hasn't eroded from winter storms as quickly as first feared. The spit seems to be holding well. However, the main anchorage area where the mooring buoys are located, will likely fill in over the next 50 to 100 years.

Entering the anchorage at Sidney Spit can be confusing, for it is shallow in the middle and filled with eel grass. The two anchoring areas should be approached separately. The northern approach is along the one-fathom line, which runs almost parallel with the spit starting near the beacon light and terminating at the buoy area where the depths open up. The other approach is just off the south beach staying within the one-and-a-half fathom line (see map). In both spots, the holding ground is generally quite good with a mix of mud and sand that's agreeable to all anchors.

A shallow lagoon lies at the head of the bay and is a great place to observe a variety of waterbirds, especially during the spring and fall migration seasons. Mandarte Island, which lies off the NE side of Sidney Island, is the largest breeding colony in B.C. for double-crested and pelagic cormorants, glaucous-winged gulls and pigeon guillemots. Known locally as Bare Island, this private island is also a major nesting site for seabirds such as rhinoceros auklets and tufted puffins. More than 8,000 birds nest on this island, their numbers building over the summer, with a sizable flock remaining in the area throughout the winter. The lagoon at the south end of Sidney Spit Marine Park is a productive feeding ground for these birds and others, including great blue herons. When venturing into the lagoon, be sure to row as motorized vessels are not allowed to enter this sensitive habitat.

The park trails wind past the head of this lagoon, where a dinghy dock is located. The main dinghy dock is at the park floats (where overnight moorage is available for a fee, as are the nearby mooring buoys). This is the entrance to the park and a good place to begin a hike of the park's forest trails.

The natural attractions of Sidney Island were not always highly valued. Back in 1860, when the Hudson's Bay Company tried selling lots on the island at 6 shillings an acre, there were few takers. The island was called Sallas by the early settlers, possibly for the thick salal that covered the forest floor, but was renamed 'Sidney' by Captain Richards for the son of his friend Captain William Franklyn. Arriving in Nanaimo from England with his family in 1851, eight-year-old Sidney was brought up to the sea service and was the pilot

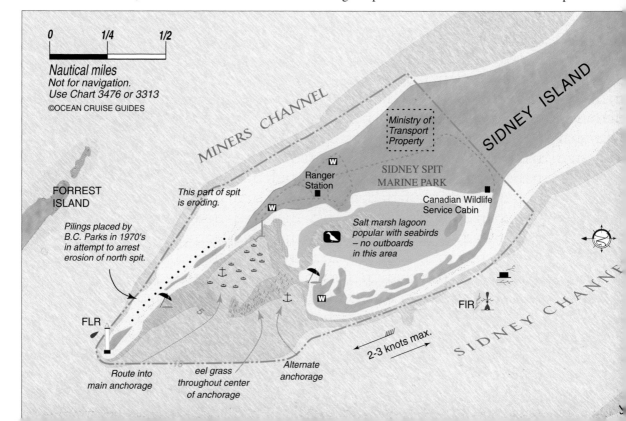

0   1/4   1/2

Nautical miles
Not for navigation.
Use Chart 3476 or 3313
©OCEAN CRUISE GUIDES

MINERS CHANNEL

SIDNEY ISLAND

Ministry of Transport Property

Ranger Station

SIDNEY SPIT MARINE PARK

Canadian Wildlife Service Cabin

Salt marsh lagoon popular with seabirds – no outboards in this area

FORREST ISLAND

This part of spit is eroding.

Pilings placed by B.C. Parks in 1970's in attempt to arrest erosion of north spit.

FLR

FIR

SIDNEY CHANNEL

2-3 knots max.

Route into main anchorage

eel grass throughout center of anchorage

Alternate anchorage

Sidney Spit Marine Park. Below, beach at southwest side of park.

SIDNEY SPIT AT A GLANCE
CHARTS: 3476, 3313, 3441 3462
LAT, LONG: 48°39.00'N 123°21.00'W
PROS: Marine park, good trails, fine sand beaches, swimming, long sunsets, good holding ground, lots of room. Town with marinas nearby.
CONS: Often busy in summer. Comings and goings of small power craft and attendant wake. Anchorage open to NW to SW winds. Mooring buoys have a mixed reputation – check holding if tied up to one.
MUST DO: Swim off beautiful sands of south beach. Have a beach barbecue. Walk the trails.

aboard the *Grappler* when, on the night of April 29, 1883, the northbound steamer lost control after catching fire near Seymour Narrows. Seventy two people – including Sidney Franklyn – lost their lives.

In 1902, George Courtney, a freight and passenger agent for the Canadian Pacific Railway in Victoria, bought Sidney Island for $25,000. He imported pheasants from China and held shooting parties on his island until he discovered a large clay deposit at the island's north end. This prompted his establishing the Sidney Island Brick and Tile Company, its bricks used in the building of Victoria's Empress Hotel and the Hotel Vancouver.

The brickyard, which operated for several years and employed about 70 men, ultimately foundered and the island was sold to a syndicate of Victoria businessmen in 1909 for $150,000, with Courtney retaining 200 acres, including his brickyard. In 1921,

Above, beautiful sunsets are enjoyed at Sidney Spit, where low hills lend a tropical backdrop. Below, a fine beach lies on the bay's SW side.

Above, Sidney Spit Marine Park has excellent hiking trails. Below, an eight metre sloop beats into a southwesterly near Dock Island.

Courtney's property was acquired by the provincial government and it became, 40 years later, Sidney Spit Marine Park. Remains of the brickyard can be seen along the park's 1.2-mile (2 km) loop trail which leads past a portion of beach strewn with broken red bricks.

At night the bright lights of Sidney twinkle across the channel. A quick visit to the town of Sidney can be made in summer by hopping on the passenger ferry at the park's small float and disembarking at Sidney's public pier, located at the foot of Beacon Avenue.

Other Nearby Anchorages

Sidney Spit is near other interesting anchorages which are worth a visit if conditions are agreeable.

D'Arcy Island, once the location of a leper colony, is now a marine park and offers temporary daytime anchorages in settled weather. The most commonly used anchorage is at the north side of D'Arcy near the one fathom (2 m) line but is open to north winds and to chop from Hughes Passage. There are some trails on the island and some fine shell-and-sand beaches on the east side of the island. The east side is excellent for exploring by dinghy but watch for afternoon southwesterlies building in Haro Strait.

Rum Island, which obtained its name from its proximity to the United States during prohibition days, is the location of Isle-de-Lis Marine Park. Just 3 miles from Sidney Spit, the island makes for an interesting afternoon stop with fair protection from south winds behind the shell isthmus connecting Rum with Gooch Island, and affords a fine view to Haro Strait. The anchorage is open to swell from the strait and north winds. There is a loop trail around the island. Nearby, just SE of Comet Island and marked by white buoys, is the diving wreck of HMCS *Mackenzie*.

Sidney

Sidney is the boating hub of the southern Gulf Islands. It has numerous marinas, charter operators, sailing schools, chandlers and boatyards, many of these situated in Tsehum Harbour (also called Shoal Harbour). Van Isle Marina is the harbour's largest facility for transient moorage and can accommodate vessels from 20 to 300 feet in length. (call 250-656-1138 or VHF 66A to arrange for moorage). From Van Isle Marina, you can stroll along Harbour Road toward Armstrong Point to the Latch Country Inn, built of timber and stone in 1920 as a summer retreat for B.C.'s lieutenant governor and now a restaurant. You can also walk in the other direction to Resthaven Drive and from there catch a bus to the main part of town or into Victoria. Across the water, marking the N entrance to Tsehum Harbour, is Curteis Point where Muriel Wylie Blanchet (1891-1961), author of *The Curve of Time*, lived with her five children and set off on upcoast adventures each summer in a 25-foot cabin cruiser. North of Curteis Point is Canoe Cove, where visitor moorage is limited but repair facilities for vessels are excellent. Just up the hill is the cozy Stonehouse Pub.

The Port Sidney Marina is just a short walk from the town. This modern marina and nearby waterfront restaurants are joined by a seaside promenade that leads to the public pier, used by commercial fishing boats and the summer passenger ferry to Sidney Spit Marine Park. Beacon Avenue leads from the public pier into the centre of town where a variety of shops, including supermarkets and a liquor store, are located. The local whale museum has been torn down and will be replaced with a new facility as part of a waterfront hotel complex. Three resident pods of killer whales frequent the waters off Sidney, making this a prime whale-watching area.

Sidney is a convenient place to rent a car or take a bus to Victoria which is a 30-minute drive away.

Above, aerial view of Sidney looking north to Saltspring Island. Below, Port Sidney Marina.

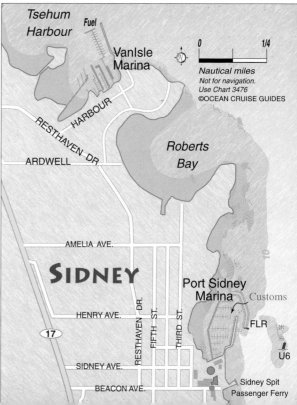

Above, provincial legislative buildings designed by Rattenbury. Below, Victoria's Empress Hotel and Inner Harbour.

Victoria

For visitors arriving in Victoria by boat, moorage is available in the heart of the city in its famous Inner Harbour. The city floats are located right in front of the Empress Hotel. Other marinas for visitors include the Coast Harbourside Hotel and Marina, which offers its hotel facilities to marina guests.

Victoria, the capital of B.C., began as a fur trading post when the Hudson's Bay Company built a fort here in 1843. British immigrants soon arrived by sailing ship, having rounded Cape Horn with their fine English china and Victorian ideals, ready to carve a new home in the rugged wilderness. No other Canadian city more openly displays a British colonial heritage, with its double-decker buses, English-style pubs and hundreds of flower baskets hanging from ornate street lamps.

The city was named in honour of Queen Victoria, Empress of India, whose statue graces the lawns leading to the Legislative Buildings. These were designed by British architect Francis Rattenbury and completed in 1898. Rattenbury also designed The Empress, a grand hotel built by the Canadian Pacific Railway. Restored to its Edwardian opulence, The Empress offers afternoon tea daily in the elegant Tea Lobby or expansive front veranda.

A **Visitor InfoCentre** is located north of the city floats. From here it's a short stroll north along Wharf Street, past the original Customs House (1876) at the foot of Broughton, to historic Bastion Square. Site of

the original fur trading fort, Bastion Square's narrow streets and restored brick buildings include the original courthouse, which now houses the **B.C. Maritime Museum**, its ornate elevator built in 1900 for an elderly judge. Exhibits include Captain Voss's dugout canoe *Tilikum* which he sailed from Victoria to England in 1901. Across the street is the Garrick's Head Pub, which opened for business in 1867. Government Street, between Bastion Square and the harbour, is lined with restored heritage buildings now housing bookstores, chocolate shops and specialty stores selling, among other items, native art and crafts.

South of the harbour, Government Street leads past the Royal British Columbia Museum, rated one of the best museums in North America with its outstanding natural and native history exhibits. Next door is Helmcken House, the oldest house in B.C., built in 1852 by Dr. John Helmcken for his bride, a daughter of Governor Douglas. An island in Johnstone Strait is named for Helmcken, who came from England as a shipboard medical officer.

A few blocks south of Helmcken House, on Government Street, is Carr House – the birthplace of Emily Carr, one of Canada's most acclaimed artists, who was born here in 1871. One block east of Carr House is Beacon Hill Park, the city's oldest municipal park which is named for the navigational range markers that once sat atop its hill overlooking Juan de Fuca Strait. Today's visitors can enjoy the park's classic English landscape garden while in the strait

below a modern beacon (flashing green light) marks the position of Brotchie Ledge which lies on the approach to Victoria Harbour.

Victoria has numerous British-style pubs offering a good selection of local brews.

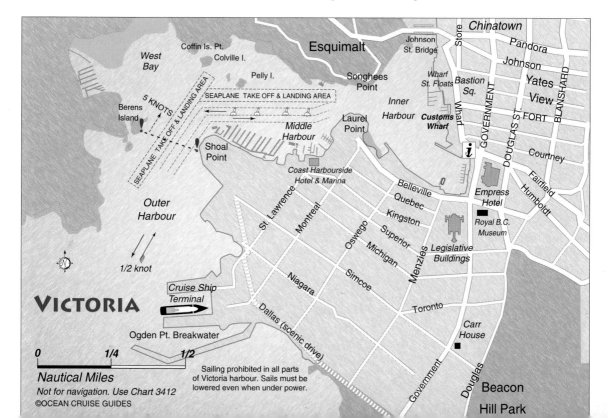

Princess Margaret Marine Park (Portland Island) 2

By the time Portland Island became a marine park in the 1960s, it had been sold, swapped, bought and bestowed several times over. Its owners have included the Hudson's Bay Company, a group of Hawaiians, an eccentric Englishman and a British princess. The island's most lasting legacy, however, was left by its original inhabitants – the Coast Salish natives. Their kitchen middens, created over time from heaps of crushed clamshells, remain as brilliant white beaches which once guided canoe-paddling natives safely back to shore after dark.

Designated Princess Margaret Marine Park in 1967 and now part of the Gulf Islands National Park Reserve, Portland Island is one of the few marine parks where a boater can check out all its anchorages on foot, for an extensive trail system allows visitors to hike from one anchorage to the next.

The most popular cove, Princess Bay, is at the island's SE end, behind the Tortoise Islets. A fair-weather anchorage open to south winds, this spot is popular in summer during settled conditions. Princess Bay is shallow and the holding is only fair in eel grass, soft mud and shell. If south winds come

Aerial view of Princess Bay looking north. South winds can bring uncomfortable swell into the bay.

PORTLAND ISLAND AT A GLANCE
CHARTS: 3476, 3313, 3441, 3462
LAT LONG: 48°43.02'N 123°22.03'W
PROS: Marine park with excellent trails, shell beaches and swimming. Variety of anchorages around the island. Excellent for dinghy exploring.
CONS: Princess Bay is open to S winds and the holding is only fair. Royal Cove (Chads Island) anchorage has better holding but has some ferry wake. Both anchorages can be busy and often require a stern tie.
MUST DO: Enjoy the island trails. Explore beaches at SE and NE sides of island.

up in the night, the anchorage will also be lumpy. However, in sunny, calm conditions it's a great anchorage and will probably be busy, so plan to arrive by noon to find a good spot.

The better overnight anchorage lies at the north end of the island in Royal Cove, located behind Chads Island. In this pretty cove, it's best to tie a stern line to shore and try to keep your bow pointed into the remnant ferry swells that roll in during the latter stages of a high tide. Holding here is good and the cove is fairly well protected from almost all wind. Although depths close to shore vary, up to a dozen boats can anchor here quite comfortably along the E and W shores. Use of outboards is eschewed in this small cove and most people row the short distance to the dinghy dock to access the park trails.

Royal Cove anchorage can accommodate plenty of boats moored with a stern line to shore.

There are several temporary anchorages at Portland Island. These include the anchoring areas north and south of Pellow Islets, which are frequented by dive vessels exploring B.C.'s first artificial reef, the wreck of the sunken freighter *G.B. Church*. Entering the narrow anchorage north of the islets requires careful pilotage to avoid numerous rocks and reefs. This is an excellent area to explore by dinghy or on foot along the shore. Other day stops can be found along the island's west shore, either in a nook SW of Royal Cove or in a bight south of Kanaka Bluff where a lovely shell beach stretches along the SW shore opposite Brackman Island, an off-limits ecological reserve. While anchored here, our boat bobbing in the ferry swells off Satellite Channel, we have enjoyed many a pleasant afternoon hiking the numerous trails of the island. Tree species include some beautiful stands of arbutus and Garry oak on the NW side of the island. In early spring there is plenty of birdlife, especially along the south and east sides of the island, including bufflehead, mergansers, surf scoters and other sea ducks. River otters and seals also frequent this side of the island.

The shoreside trail encircles most of the island while others cut across the middle, past the old fruit orchard planted in the 1920s by Frank 'One Arm' Sutton, who lost an arm while fighting in

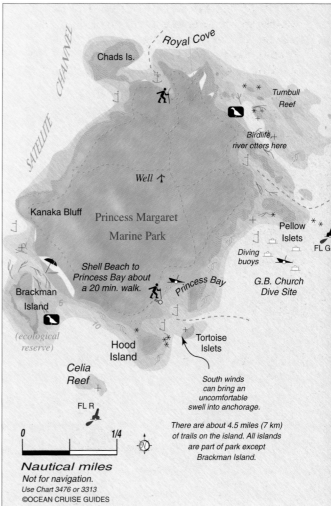

the Gallipoli campaign of World War I. Sutton, who bought the island with funds he won betting on horse races while living in China, planned to raise and train thoroughbred race horses on Portland Island. However, the stock market crash of 1929 wiped out his fortune and brought an end to his aspirations.

The island's next owner was Saltspring entrepreneur Gavin Mouat, who later traded Portland Island to the provincial government in exchange for timber rights elsewhere. When Queen Elizabeth's younger sister Margaret paid the province a visit during its centennial year, 1958, the government decided the island was fit for a princess and presented it to her as a gift. Princess Margaret returned the island when the province decided to designate it a marine park, naming it in her honour.

The island itself was named, in 1858, for the *HMS Portland*, commanded by Captain Henry Chads. The following year, the Hudson's Bay Company gave the island to a group of Hawaiians, known as Kanakas, who had been employed to act as interpreters between the coastal natives and the English-speaking fur traders. Sheep once roamed Portland, but were herded up in 1989 to prevent damage to the island's grassland and wild flowers. Park visitors are now more likely to encounter indigenous species, such as a river otter swimming near shore or, seen from the whiteshell beaches overlooking Satellite Channel, a pod of killer whales.

Top, a boardwalk trail leads across the swampy central part of Portland Island. Middle, huge arbutus trees thrive on Portland Island. Bottom, a fine midden beach along the southwest shoreline.

Russell Island 3

Russell Island, lying at the entrance to Fulford Harbour on Saltspring Island, became protected park land under the Pacific Marine Heritage Legacy and is now part of the Gulf Islands National Park Reserve. Boats anchor in the lee of Russell Island, where the vista is one of mountains rising above Fulford Harbour. The anchorage is protected from most winds, with Saltspring Island providing good shelter from northwesterlies and Russell Island providing good protection from south winds which deflect away from the anchorage. Other than occasional ferry wake from Fulford Harbour, the anchorage is very quiet. Local boaters often tie a line ashore, pulling themselves out of the way of most current and the worst of errant chop.

Settled by Hawaiians (known as Kanakas) in the late 1800s, Russell Island is easy to explore. A trail leads round the west end of the island, past the original homestead, to a charming small shell beach at its

The anchorage at Russell Island is scenic and sheltered, with a shell beach and trails to explore.

western end. There, set among the arbutus and Garry oak which grow on the island, along with Douglas fir and lodgepole pine, are several picnic tables and wooden benches. The Hawaiian children who once lived on Russell Island would attend, by boat, the one-room schoolhouse at Beaver Point on Saltspring Island. Their ancestors had come to the region as employees of the Hudson's Bay Company, many of them eventually settling on nearby Portland Island and southern Saltspring Island.

RUSSELL ISLAND AT A GLANCE

CHARTS: 3313, 3478, 3441, 3462
LAT LONG: 48°45.00N 123°24.75W
PROS: Large anchoring area. Usually uncrowded. Pretty trail around west end of island, beautiful small shell beach good for swimming. Very good holding ground. Good protection from S winds.
CONS: Somewhat exposed to NW and E winds. Open to some ferry wake and current.
MUST DO: Visit clean shell beach and go for a swim. Take 30-minute hike around island.

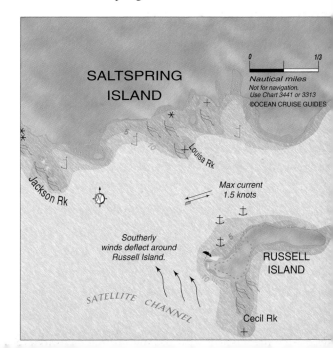

Tod Inlet 4

Boaters visiting fjord-like Saanich Inlet have the opportunity to visit one of B.C.'s most popular tourist attractions – the Butchart Gardens. Anchorage can be gained in adjacent Butchart Cove at the entrance to Tod Inlet, where a dinghy dock provides summer access to the gardens' back entrance. The cove also has 4 mooring buoys for visitor use. Anchoring near the mooring buoys is not recommended because of submerged cables.

Butchart Cove can be crowded in summer, but the head of Tod Inlet provides good alternative anchorage and is surrounded by park land. The main anchorage near the head of Tod Inlet is reached via a narrow, cliff-sided entrance. A sheltered anchorage, it is bounded by steep slopes on the south side and gentle hillsides on the other where wild flowers flourish in summer. A trail leads to the gardens from the inlet's north shore. Keep to the left at any forks as you head north out of the park. Upon reaching the parking lot, take the road to the main gates.

Jennie Butchart began cultivating her idyllic gardens in 1904, shortly after a summer home was built adjacent to her husband's cement factory near Tod Inlet. An inexperienced gardener at the outset, she soon developed an eye for colour and form and, with dazzling speed, a variety of gardens surrounded what eventually became the family's permanent residence. Assisted by a Japanese landscape artist, a Scottish gardener and workers from the cement plant, Mrs. Butchart next oversaw the completion of the Japanese Garden, the property's first formal garden, which sloped from the house's lawn to Butchart Cove where Mr. Butchart kept a boat moored.

Above, the Sunken Garden is just one of several beautiful sites within the Butchart Gardens. Below, Tod Inlet is well sheltered and peaceful.

TOD INLET AT A GLANCE

CHARTS: 3313, 3441
LAT LONG: 48°34.26'N 123°28.48W
PROS: Quiet and pretty anchorage. Access to famous Butchart Gardens. Good holding, sheltered from all winds.
CONS: Occasionally busy. Long detour from main channels.
MUST DO: Well, visit Butchart Gardens of course! Also, explore Bamberton Provincial Park just across inlet, with its fine beach.

The Japanese Garden was soon joined by the Sunken Garden – a challenge Mrs. Butchart couldn't resist after her husband's cement company had exhausted the site's limestone quarry. Hanging over the sides of the quarry in a bosun's chair, Mrs. Butchart spent hours tucking ivy into the rock walls' pockets and crevices. Water from a natural spring was allowed to fill the deepest part of the quarry, transforming it into a shimmering lake, and a massive outcropping became a towering rock garden with stone stairs leading up to a viewpoint.

In winter, the Butcharts would embark on foreign voyages, collecting exotic flowers and Italian sculptures for their gardens. They named their home 'Benvenuto', Italian for 'Welcome', and warmly welcomed all visitors to their estate. Summer houses were scattered about the property where afternoon tea was served to all who came to view the gardens. This tradition continued until the sheer number of visitors made it impossible, although the gardens remained open to all.

Today more than a million visitors annually view the Butchart Gardens, which feature a Saturday night fireworks display in July and August. The summer season is the Gardens' busiest and boaters with flexible schedules are well advised to visit the grounds in late afternoon or early evening to avoid the crowds. At night the gardens are transformed with hundreds of tiny lights.

Sansum Narrows

The most direct route north from Saanich Inlet is via scenic, steep-sided Sansum Narrows, where the wind – fed by mountain valleys – often funnels its length. Currents flow N on a flood tide, south on an ebb, and rarely exceed 3 knots, although whirlpools and tide-rips can occur around Burial Islet, and between Sansum and Bold Bluff Points. The famous sailing couple Miles and Beryl Smeeton once owned a farmhouse at Musgrave Landing on a bluff overlooking the narrows. Cowichan Bay, Genoa Bay and Maple Bay offer nearby sheltered anchorage and marina facilities for boaters transiting the narrows.

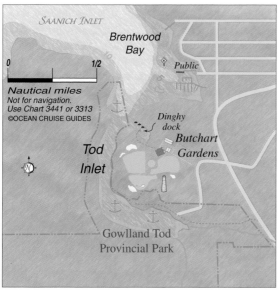

Panoramic view from Mount Maxwell on Saltspring Island looking to Sansum Narrows.

Bedwell Harbour, 5  South Pender Island

Bedwell Harbour has long been a popular summer-time port of entry for boaters entering Canadian waters from the American San Juans. After clearing Canada Customs, boaters stay at the adjacent resort facilities or head over to the anchorage between the marina and Beaumont Marine Park which has 15 mooring buoys. There is also room to anchor in this wide bight, on a good holding ground of mud and sand, where some shelter is provided from the SE winds to which Bedwell Harbour is exposed.

Boats can clear customs here from May through September. The Poets Cove Resort, Spa and Marina is located beside the government float. Its facilities include a fuel dock, swimming pool, dining room

and pub (VHF channel 66A). The resort sits on a site once occupied by a tiny shack of a post office built in 1902. Back then, the coal-fired *SS Otter* would dock twice a week in Bedwell Harbour, bringing mail and supplies to local residents.

An important archaeological site is located along the shores of the canal that joins Bedwell Harbour with Port Browning. Excavated in the mid-1980's the Helisen site contained artifacts dating back 3,500 years. It's located on the North Pender Island side of the bridge joining the two islands.

South Pender Island is the more rugged and sparsely populated of the two Penders, and Beaumont Marine Park was established here back in 1962 on land donated by the philanthropist Ernest Godfrey Beaumont. He had purchased this property in 1918 from Gilbert Ainslie, an Englishman who had his log cabin on Saturna Island dismantled and moved to Bedwell Harbour in 1905 with the aid of the crew of *HMS Egeria*'s who were doing survey work in the area.

The boundary between Canadian and American waters had been established in 1872, but the islanders who lived on either side of Boundary Pass treated this international border as an opportunity to pursue a profitable form of free trade, also known as

The bridge spanning Pender Canal and connecting the Pender Islands has a clearance of 28 feet (8.5 m). The canal leads to Shark Cove.

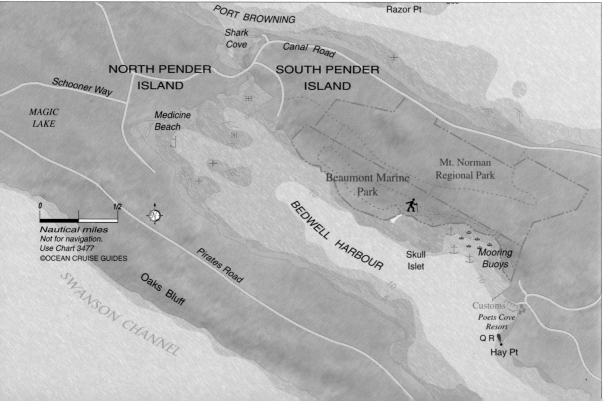

smuggling. Pender Island residents would sail or row across Boundary Pass to Friday Harbor to buy cheaper groceries, and residents of the San Juans would buy wool from sheep farmers on Pender and other Gulf Islands, then sell this commodity at twice the price back home. In the early days of American prohibition, rum-runners would pay local farmers to hide sacks of bottled booze in their sheds, but the islanders opted out of this illicit and increasingly dangerous activity as hardened criminals became attracted to its high stakes.

Logging was another early industry on South Pender, and in the 1890s large schooners would arrive to take on their cargoes of small logs, called props, that were destined for Mexico and South America for shoring up mine tunnels. Decades later, when the provincial government was establishing Beaumont Marine Park, additional acreage was donated by the Crown Zellerbach forestry company.

The park's shoreside path, dotted with benches, provides splendid views overlooking the harbour. This trail, set atop a bluff, is accessed by a set of wooden stairs located near the park's westernmost mooring buoys, which lie east of Skull Islet.

Reefs extend westward from Skull Islet toward an islet connected to shore by an isthmus. This shallow, beach-lined cove is suitable for exploration by dinghy and offers good spots for picnicking. For hiking enthusiasts, the shoreside trail continues inland where it eventually leads into adjoining Mount Norman Regional Park. An hour-long climb to a viewing platform at the top of Mount Norman rewards hikers with a panoramic look at neighbouring islands and surrounding channels, where international boundaries dissolve into the seascape.

Above, beach near Skull Island, Bedwell Harbour.
Below, looking south across the anchorage.

BEDWELL HARBOUR AT A GLANCE:
CHARTS: 3477, 3313, 3441, 3462
LAT LONG: 48°45.10'N 123°14.00'W
PROS: Marine park, trails, beach. Large anchorage with very good holding. Pubs, resorts and marinas nearby. Good dinghy exploring. Handy spot after clearing customs for U.S. boaters.
CONS: Open to S wind, sometimes busy.
MUST DO: Hike trails of Beaumont Marine Park and Mount Norman Regional Park. Explore the pass to Shark Cove by dinghy.

Boat Passage, between Saturna and Samuel Islands, is a tight fit for most vessels.

Saturna Island

Saturna Island promises peace and solitude for residents and boaters alike. Sparsely populated and not directly linked by ferry to Vancouver, this scenic island has retained its rural atmosphere and small-town friendliness. Passing motorists wave to you when you're hiking the quiet roads of Saturna, and most of the island's summer visitors are boaters because there is no overnight campground on the island and only a handful of bed-and-breakfast inns.

We have enjoyed Saturna in every season and celebrated many a holiday in the embrace of her

shoreline, including a peaceful Christmas in Winter Cove. We have hiked her quiet roads under a warm September sun and been blown out of Boot Cove during an Easter gale. Year after year we enjoy returning to Saturna where change comes slowly and our favourite anchorages are like familiar faces.

Nearly half of the Gulf Islands National Park Preserve is situated on Saturna Island, where BC Crown Lands, ecological reserves and recent land acquisitions interconnect to form a tract of mountainous parkland dominating the island's interior and stretching eastward to the shores of Narvaez Bay. Boaters can cycle or hike to Saturna's interior parkland from either Winter Cove or Lyall Harbour (the latter is closer) by taking East Point Road to the head of Lyall Harbour where the Saturna General Store is situated at the crossroads.

From here take Harris Road into the park area, turning left onto Staples Road. This gravel road loops through forest toward the summit of Mount Warburton Pike, Saturna's highest mountain at 1,425 feet (430 m). The distance from Saturna General Store to Mount Warburton Pike is about 1 1/2 miles (2.5 km). Nearby is the Brown Ridge Nature Trail, overlooking Plumper Sound and Boundary Pass. Mount Warburton Pike was named in honour of an settler who arrived in 1884 to pursue sheep farming. Not only was Pike widely travelled and Oxford educated, he was an astute businessman who soon owned much of Saturna Island. On the other side of the island, a long, straight section of East Point Road

Left, the view of Strait of Georgia and Mt. Baker from Winter Cove Marine Park trail. Opposite, view from road leading to head of Lyall Harbour.

use this pass at HW slack

Georgeson I

Bennett Bay

use this pass at LW slack when reefs are visible

Aerial view of Winter Cove.

STRAIT OF GEORGIA

Curlew Island

Georgeson Passage

Belle Chain Islets

Max current 4 knots

HORTON BAY

Robson Channel

Public

MAYNE ISLAND

SAMUEL ISLAND

Northerly winds can come thru low point here:

Anniversary I

Lizard I

IRISH BAY

Ralph Grey Pt

BOAT PASSAGE
Max current 8 knots

Russell Reef

St. John Pt

Minx Reef

WINTER COVE

WINTER COVE MARINE PARK

0   1/2

Nautical miles
Not for navigation.
Use Chart 3477 or 3313
©OCEAN CRUISE GUIDES

Veruna Bay

Winter Cove Rd

East Pt. Rd

East Point Rd

MT. DAV

Winter Cove's picnic area.

King Islets

SATURNA ISLAND

Fl(2+1)R   *Crispin Rk*

B.C. Ferries

U58

Store/Pub

Fuel / public

LYALL HARBOUR

School (tennis courts)

East Pt. Rd

Payne Pt

Boot Cove

Saturna General Store / LCB

Narvaez Bay Rd

To Mt Warburton Pike

Payne Rd

Harris Rd.

Staples Road

ELLIOT BLUFF

runs from Winter Cove Marine Park to East Point Lighthouse, affording splendid views of the Strait of Georgia with some flat foreshore areas that are ideal for a picnic lunch. To make it to East Point and back in a few hours, a bicycle is recommended.

Saturna Island anchorages (and Samuel Island) are open to NW winds, although it does have to be blowing fairly strong before it is a problem in Winter Cove. If a really bad NW wind is forecast, consider Horton Bay or Port Browning.

Winter Cove 6

A circular-shaped cove lying between Saturna and Samuel Islands, this marine park anchorage provides good holding ground and shelter from all but strong northwesterlies. One October weekend we comfortably rode out a 38-knot southerly in this cove, which we had all to ourselves, in contrast to summer weekends when the anchorage fills up with boats, especially when the popular Lamb Barbecue is held here on Canada Day, July 1st. We usually anchor west of the marine park's launch ramp, between shore and a shallow spot in the middle of the cove. See photo page 62.

On shore, a broad sand-and-mud beach for landing dinghies is situated beside the boat launch, adjacent to a grassy picnic area with some wooden tables and a freshwater pump. From here a trail loops through the woods and along the Strait of Georgia shoreline to Winter Point where you can watch the tide rushing through Boat Passage. During prohibition, rumrunners used this narrow, reef-strewn pass to dodge government revenue boats patrolling the Strait of Georgia.

Today the pass is used as a shortcut by small boats heading to Cabbage Island and can be transited at HW slack. Currents in Boat Passage can reach 6 knots or more, with dangerous whirlpools during spring tides, and there is a set onto the rocks extending from Ralph Grey Point on Samuel Island. Should you decide to attempt it, do so at HW slack (when the pass will have about 15 feet of depth) and, if eastbound, proceed slowly in the centre of the channel. Remain parallel with the stream (and the Saturna shoreline) until you are about 100 yards (90 m) E of the entrance, then turn to port to clear the S end of Anniversary Island. Chart 3313, page 12, gives good detail of Winter Cove and this pass.

Should valour give way to caution, another shortcut is through Georgeson Passage, between Curlew and Samuel Islands. Upon clearing Samuel Island, turn to starboard and navigate between the islands (see map) south of the Belle Chain Islets and continue past Russell Reef to Cabbage Island. Vessels pro-

ceeding north into Georgia Strait can take the small pass between Georgeson Island and the reef extending from Mayne Island, being careful to transit at HW when there is ample depth. Current throughout Georgeson Passage can reach 5 knots.

Lyall Harbour 7

When other Gulf Island anchorages are chock-a-block with boats at the height of summer, Lyall Harbour can be surprisingly quiet. The inter-island car ferry docks at the mouth of this harbour and pleasure craft can tie to an adjacent public float, but the anchorage itself is often ignored. We avoid the area just to the east of the public dock where we once snagged our anchor on some debris and prefer instead to anchor near the head in about 30' of water. The anchorage is exposed to NW winds but the holding ground is very good in thick mud and there is plenty of room to let out scope.

A pub and general store are at Lyall Harbour.

> ### WINTER COVE AT A GLANCE
> **CHARTS:** 3477, 3313, 3442
> **LAT LONG:** 48°48.74'N 123°12.60'W
> **PROS:** Beautiful setting, large area for anchoring. Good holding ground in mud. Marine park with excellent trails. Store and fuel nearby. Good dinghy exploring nearby. Views out to Georgia Strait.
> **CONS:** Occasionally busy. Somewhat open to NW wind. Shallow in parts, with several drying reefs and submerged rocks.
> **MUST DO:** Walk the trail to Boat Pass when current is running at full flood. Explore the Belle Chain Islets by dinghy.

Lyall Harbour's steep slopes are thickly treed and dotted with hillside homes, and a private small-craft marina lies along the south side. We have disembarked by dinghy at this marina and hiked up to East Point Road which, if taken in its westerly direction, leads to Saturna's main general store (at the Narvaez Bay Road junction) where you can purchase groceries, fresh produce, liquor and locally baked bread and cookies. A smaller selection of these items can also be bought at the store beside the government float, where the Lighthouse Pub is open year-round and in summer serves patrons on a sun deck overlooking the water.

At the head of Lyall Harbour, where rubber boots are recommended for hauling your dinghy across the muddy foreshore, a waterfront village lies on the floor of a small valley. Sunset Boulevard leads through the centre of this hamlet, past the schoolhouse, playground and adjacent tennis courts. We have often headed ashore for a leisurely game of tennis, enjoying the early morning coolness on a hot summer's day or, better yet, the bright afternoons of autumn when the falling leaves of surrounding maple trees drift lazily onto the courts.

Nearby **Boot Cove** is not attractive as an anchorage. It has numerous small buoys and an aquaculture operation is located along the west side. The cove can also be surprisingly gusty in SE winds.

Irish Bay, Samuel Island 8

Situated on the S side of Samuel Island is the excellent anchorage of Irish Bay. We tend to anchor here in bad weather, when shelter from the wind is more critical than shoreside activities, for privately owned Samuel Island offers no opportunities for exploration above the HW mark. However, the anchorage is lovely in fair weather, when sunlight sparkles on the water and the shoreside trails of Winter Cove Marine Park are a short dinghy ride away. When seeking shelter from northerlies, we anchor beneath the treed cliffs at the NW end of the bay. The S part of the bay is sheltered from southeasterlies.

Samuel Island has been owned by various prominent people, including a relative of Earl Grey, who was Governor General of Canada from 1904 to 1911, and A.J.P. Taylor, the Vancouver engineer who developed British Properties and the Lions Gate Bridge. Taylor had a lodge built overlooking Winter Cove where he entertained whenever he and guests visited the island, their luxury yachts anchored in Irish Bay. He eventually sold Samuel Island to food-store magnate Garfield Weston.

On our last visit to Samuel Island, we noticed the current owner had posted signs warning visitors not to trespass and to 'watch for rattlesnakes' (which lurk, presumably, just above the HW mark). A security guard was patrolling by 4X4 the road that runs between the buildings at the island's south end and the pocket beach lying at the NW end of Irish Bay.

During World War II, the Belle Chain Islets were used for target practice by fighters and bombers, much to the dismay of the resident caretaker on Samuel Island. Not only did he and his family have to endure the incessant drone of aircraft and their dropping of cartridge cases, in one instance the lodge overlooking Winter Cove was mistakenly fired at, with a bullet narrowly missing one of the caretaker's daughters. A complaint was filed and the training pilots were told to be more careful about hitting their target.

Nearby **Horton Bay** on Mayne Island offers good shelter in NW winds. The anchorage does, however, experience tidal current, which should be taken into account when anchoring.

Samuel Island's Irish Bay is wide, deep and a good alternative anchorage to Winter Cove.

Cabbage Island
Marine Park 9

There's an exotic, isolated feel to Cabbage Island, lying as it does on the outer edge of the Gulf Islands with the Strait of Georgia stretching into the distance. When approaching the anchorage of Reef Harbour, the island appears almost tropical with its green foliage and fringe of white sand. The park's 10 mooring buoys are located in Reef Harbour (not really a harbour) where the reef regularly disappears at HW. The buoys are well utilized in summer, and you'll be lucky to find one empty if you arrive late in the day. However, the holding ground is good in mud and broken shell and, in settled conditions, the anchorage is more than adequate.

In addition to the beautiful beach overlooking the anchorage, there are also camping and picnicking facilities on shore. At LW, you can take an interesting half-hour hike around Cabbage Island, where conglomerate rock extends from its eastern shore toward Tumbo Island. Only 11 acres in size, tiny Cabbage Island reportedly sold for a dollar an acre in 1888. A coal mine briefly operated on adjacent Tumbo Island in the 1890s, and in the early 1900s a

Above, aerial view (looking north) of Cabbage Island and Reef Harbour with mooring buoys. Below, fine beach makes for good swimming.

hermit lived on the island's west side until he was shot dead one night while exchanging gunfire with an unwelcome visitor.

Tumbo Island was purchased by the Pacific Marine Heritage Legacy program in 1997, and is now part of the Gulf Islands National Park. The island's natural vegetation includes groves of Garry oak, arbutus and old-growth Douglas fir, and its freshwater marsh is a habitat for waterfowl.

CABBAGE ISLAND AT A GLANCE
CHARTS: 3313, 3441, 3462
LAT LONG: 48˚47.92'N 123˚05.86'W
PROS: Marine park with good trails and swimming beaches. Fairly large area for anchoring with good holding ground.
CONS: A fair-weather anchorage, shallow in places. Open to winds coming off Georgia Strait. Attracts revellers on summer long weekends.
MUST DO: Walk Cabbage Island, relax on the beach, explore the tidal pools.

Otter Bay, North Pender Island 10

Otter Bay is best known for its marina (located in Hyashi Cove), an ideal family destination with excellent facilities. These include a heated swimming pool, playground, general store, showers, laundry and washrooms. Bicycles can be hired at the marina for a tour of North Pender, its hilly and winding roads leading past leafy lanes and country craft shops. (Call VHF channel 66A for reservations.)

A breakwater protects the floats from most of the wash generated by the car ferry that docks at the small terminal around the corner from Otter Bay. Keep the green spar buoy to port when approaching the marina. If the marina is full, the anchorage at the head of Otter Bay (to the east) provides shelter from SE weather and the mud bottom is very good. Setting a stern anchor will keep your bow pointed into the occasional ferry wave coming into the bay.

An alternative anchorage, also good, is in Hyashi Cove east of the marina, riding parallel with the outside dock. With a stern anchor or a line ashore the rolling action from the ground swell of the ferry traffic will be reduced.

Nearby attractions include the island's nine-hole golf course, which is a 15-minute walk or a quick shuttle ride from Otter Bay Marina. Further afield is the Malahat Properties parkland, about a 1.2 mile (2 km) hike from the marina, heading east then south along Otter Bay Road. Purchased in 1998 by the Pacific Marine Heritage Legacy and now part of the Gulf Islands National Park Preserve, this parcel of mostly second-growth forest has numerous trails, a small lake and some waterfrontage bordering the NE shore of Shingle Bay, a temporary anchorage.

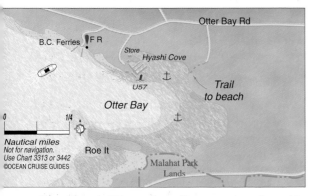

Otter Bay and its marina offer a pretty setting with good hikes and golfing nearby.

Prevost Island 11

One of our perennial favourite destinations of the entire coast is Prevost Island. Situated in the hub of the southern Gulf Islands, surrounded by ferry routes and marine traffic heading to and from Active

Pass, this island has miraculously maintained an aura of isolation. Accessible only by private craft, pastoral Prevost Island remains relatively unchanged by the waves of development that have washed over many of the Gulf Islands.

Prevost Island was named by Captain Richards in 1859 for Captain James Charles Prevost, commander of the *HMS Satellite* and the commissioner appointed to settle the San Juan boundary dispute between B.C. and the United States. However, it was Digby de Burgh, an Irish nobleman from County Limerick, who determined the fate of Prevost when he bought the island in the 1920s for raising sheep, goats and cattle. De Burgh's son Hubert and daughter-in-law Jean eventually took over the island farm, where they raised four daughters – one of whom became a concert pianist.

Much of the island remains in the family's hands, although waterfront houses began appearing in the 1980s along the northwest side. When one was built at our favourite nook in Selby Cove, we gloomily speculated that Prevost's days as a destination providing pristine anchorages were numbered. Then, in 1996, the Pacific Marine Heritage Legacy came to the rescue. This federal/provincial program, estab-lished to protect a network of marine areas along the B.C. coast, bought portions of waterfront in James Bay and Selby Cove. Private property became parkland and sheep trails became public footpaths. This parkland has since become part of the Gulf Islands National Park (see map page 92).

The channels and currents around Prevost provide interesting cruising and a few challenges. Although currents rarely exceed 2 or 3 knots in Captain Passage, it would be easy, with a lapse of concentration, to be swept toward Horda Reef (named after the Norwegian steamer that ran aground here in 1901) off the west side of Prevost. This is especially hazardous if you are southbound with an ebb current, as the set to the reef is quite pronounced. Otherwise, the currents follow the channel. The only cross eddy we've noticed is in the narrowest part of the passage near Nose Point, where some of the current splits off into Long Harbour with a set to Nose Point.

Prevost is deeply indented with an abundance of anchorages, and it seems everyone has a favourite among the four facing Captain Passage. **Glenthorne Passage** provides good shelter in most winds but is the most developed, with private docks lining the anchorage's SW side along Secret Island. The next anchorage over is **Annette Inlet**, a long narrow inlet which provides good shelter, but is shallow in parts and has limited swinging room, so is suited for tying

Looking north over Prevost Island to Glenthorne Passage and Annette Inlet.

Above, spring wildflowers blanket the islet beside Owl Island on the southwest side of Prevost Island.
Below, Selby Cove on Prevost Island provides a tranquil retreat from the busier marine parks.

a stern line ashore. The entrance should be approached with caution for there is a drying rock lying off its mouth and shoal depths on the north side. Hiking in Annette Inlet is limited to the foreshore and, with an extensive mud flat at the head, heading ashore at LW means wearing a pair of rubber boots. At HW it's possible to see right across the lowland at the head of Annette Inlet to Ellen Bay on the other side of the island.

Selby Cove, on the island's NW side, is our favourite for its peaceful setting, with sheep often seen grazing in the pasture at its head. River otters frequent the foreshore, and surf scoters, mergansers

and other sea ducks gather here in winter. Selby Cove is fairly well sheltered and most westerlies die out about halfway into the cove. The worst winds seem to come from the south. There is an intriguing blind spot in strong S winds, about 150 yards S of the islet that is joined to shore by a drying tombolo near Annette Point. We once noticed that a boat anchored in this spot didn't receive a breath of wind even with 25 knots gusting through the cove.

What appears to be a derelict float lies about two-thirds of the way into the cove with a sign telling boaters to keep off. Fortunately, the main anchoring area remains unencumbered, and the holding ground

is good in mud and shell in about 20 feet. We normally anchor between the derelict float and a private dock extending from the west shore which serves a solitary house perched dramatically atop the cliff.

The opposite shoreline is only slightly less rugged, with a hillside house situated in a bight near the entrance. Further into the cove is another, broader bight where we have anchored with a stern line ashore. Its small beach is backed by a grass clearing bordered by young spruce trees that provides a good picnic spot with views overlooking the anchorage and passing boat traffic in Captain Passage. This property is part of the island's parkland, and a trail can be followed from here to James Bay.

Although exposed to northwesterlies, **James Bay** has good holding ground and the water is fairly deep, making it a safe anchorage in most conditions. We once rode out a winter gale here with SE winds of 49 knots reported at East Point on Saturna Island. Although a few strong gusts did find us in James Bay, the thickly treed shoreline acted as a buffer and our anchor easily held in 50 feet of water near the head of the bay.

James Bay is now almost completely surrounded by park property, from its NE entrance point to the head and halfway along its SW shoreline, where a small orchard has always been an attraction with its springtime apple blossoms and fall fruit. The reef extending from the W shore makes for interesting exploring at low tide. Boaters can head ashore to the broad gravel beach at the bay's head (called O'Reilly Beach) where a valley leads inland and a sheep trail can be hiked to Peile Point. The entire Peile Point peninsula, with views overlooking Trincomali Channel, is part of the park.

Exposed to southeasterlies and ferry wash off Swanson Channel, **Ellen Bay** is nonetheless an adequate anchorage with its deep water and mud holding ground. Depths here reach 90 feet (27 m) in the middle of the bay and are 55 feet (17 m) near the head, so the ferry swells are long and gentle. Where the foreshore of Ellen Bay ends, private farmland

Above, the James Bay shoreline includes an old orchard. Below, vessels can tuck well into the bay.

PREVOST ISLAND AT A GLANCE

CHARTS: 3478 or 3313

PROS: The four anchorages facing NW all have their charms with, generally, good holding ground. Good dinghy exploring. Annette Inlet is safest in a NW wind. James Bay is best in S winds.

CONS: James Bay and Selby Cove are open to NW winds, Annette Inlet has a tricky entrance and Glenthorne Passage anchorage is usually busy.

MUST DO: Walk trails from James Bay. Explore tidal pools at Owl Island. Visit Hawkins Island.

begins. When a friend of ours anchored in Ellen Bay one spring to avoid a northwesterly forecast for overnight, he said he hardly noticed the ferry swells but he could hear the sound of a tractor on shore.

Hawkins Island 12

These tiny islands tucked against the east shore of Prevost Island are one of our secret getaway spots in the Gulf Islands. A good place to picnic or spend an afternoon lounging, the islands have an atoll feel with a small crescent beach encircling a lagoon of

Hawkins Island is a good place to enjoy a picnic.

turquoise water. These uninhabited islets also host several species of birds, including oystercatchers and migrating surf scoters. After anchoring in the channel between Prevost and Hawkins Islands, we like to row ashore to the clamshell midden at the NW end of the largest of the three islets. An aqua-culture operation for scallops currently occupies a strip of the channel between Hawkins and Prevost, but the little beach has retained its appeal and on a

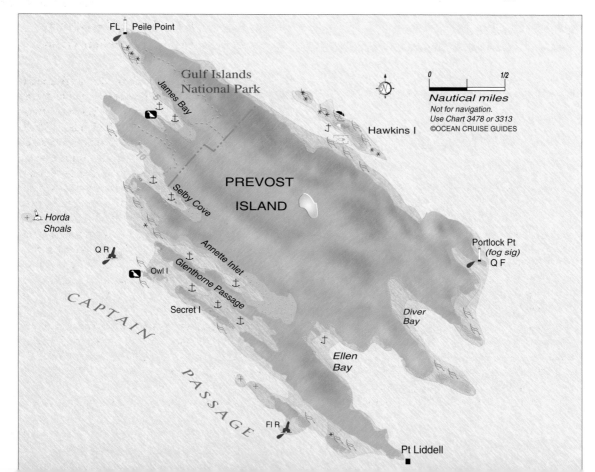

sunny summer afternoon it provides a splendid view of boats lazily sailing up and down Trincomali Channel. Above the beach is a shady knoll, reached by scrambling over some boulders, past clusters of purple camas and pink sea blush which bloom in spring. We leave Hawkins Island when the tide is rising and all that remains of the beach is a strip of crushed clamshells.

There can be impressive current (over 2 knots) between Hawkins Island and Prevost Island, which can make anchoring a challenge. The best place to drop the hook is in the area between the islands and the shellfish farm. Holding is good but the anchorage gets regular ferry swell and is not suitable for an overnight stay.

Ganges Harbour 13

Ganges Harbour on Saltspring Island is a fine if sometimes busy anchorage with excellent holding ground. Summer winds often funnel up the harbour from Captain Passage, providing sailing yachts with a downwind sail into Ganges and a tacking duel with other sailboats upon departure (dodging the numerous crab pots that line the entrance to the harbour). The wind, in summer, usually dies down by early evening. Moorage is available at the government floats or at two full-service marinas, where scooters and bikes can be rented. Local services include two banks and a credit union (all with bank machines), a post office, supermarket and liquor store.

Ganges is an good place to reprovision, fuel up and enjoy a meal ashore while cruising the area.

With a population of about 10,000, Saltspring is the largest and most populated of the Gulf Islands, and the seaside village of Ganges is the island's commercial hub. Pedestrian-oriented Ganges is perfect for boaters setting off on foot along boardwalks leading past restaurants, shops and a waterfront park. For provisions, Thrifty Foods is located right on the waterfront. For chocolate delicacies, Harlan's on Lower Ganges Road is highly recommended. And boaters seeking a gourmet meal can make dinner reservations at Hastings House, located a short walk east of Salt Spring Marina along Upper Ganges Road. A *Relais et Chateaux* property, this luxury inn, set on manicured grounds atop a bluff, was the former home of Warren Hastings, an English naval architect who moved to Saltspring in 1937 and modelled his new manor on his 11th-century country estate back in Sussex.

From April to October, a Saturday food-and-crafts market is held at Centennial Park, and throughout the summer ArtCraft is held at Mahon Hall where locally hand-crafted jewellery, clothing and folk art are sold. Saltspring has long been an artists' haven and the island's art galleries are con-centrated in Ganges, including the well-known Pegasus Gallery, located in Mouat's Mall which was built in 1912 by the Mouat brothers. Thomas Mouat was the first to arrive from the Shetlands in 1895, but this entrepreneurial family's most successful businessman was Gavin Mouat, who once owned Portland Island before trading it to the provincial government in exchange for timber rights elsewhere. The Embe Bakery is housed in the island's first creamery, built by the Mouats in 1903 and a thriving business until 1957, when farmers throughout the Gulf Islands shipped their fresh milk here for processing. The Salt Spring Island Chamber of Commerce and Tourist Information Centre, located beside the Fire Hall, provides walking maps of the town and its heritage buildings.

Saltspring Island was named for the springs of brine discovered there by some Hudson's Bay Company officers, and Ganges was named for *HMS Ganges,* the flagship of Rear Admiral Baynes who served in local waters from 1857 to 1860. Saltspring's early pioneers were a hardy lot and

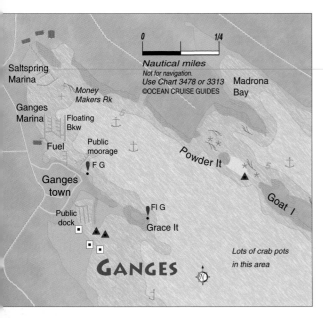

GANGES

Harbour. We have threaded our way past these islands and dropped anchor in the NE arm of the harbour, away from the hustle and bustle of Ganges. Although exposed to southeasterlies, the holding ground here is good in mud and clay, and the numerous islets and islands dispel some of the wave action coming off Captain Passage. This is, however, a fair-weather anchorage.

The two main marinas, Salt Spring Marina and Ganges Marina, can be contacted on VHF channel 66A. Both have good dock facilities, showers and laundry.

Long Harbour 14

Long Harbour on Saltspring Island is protected from most winds, although strong northwesterlies can gust through the central area of the anchorage. Southeasterlies can be felt near the entrance but you can dodge these if you pull in close to the N shore behind a number of bights or in the lee of a cluster of islands near the entrance. South winds tend to weaken as they travel the length of the inlet, which is over 2 miles long. There are several nooks in which to anchor along the harbour's NE shore but we invariably pick one of the bights near the southeast end.

The anchorage closest to Nose Point lies between a reef on the N side of a small cove and the rock outcropping to the south. This spot is fairly shallow and requires a line ashore below HW to keep your boat away from the dangerous N reef – we saw a raft of boats land on this in a January gale and it was not a pretty sight. The anchorage north of the small group of islands (the largest of which is known locally as Fisherman Island) provides superb holding and lots of swinging room between the red buoy and Athol Peninsula. A small house and private dock occupy Fisherman Island, which is owned, naturally, by a local fisherman. The nearby islets and rocky shoreline are ideal for exploring by dinghy or kayak, and the bight's two beaches are lovely for picnics. Walks ashore are limited, however, for the adjacent land is privately owned by a consortium of home owners. Fortunately this has not diminished the privacy of the anchorage, for the development's waterfrontage has been set aside as a communal park for its residents and the foreshore is usually very quiet.

As noted, there are several bights along the NE shore to drop the hook, several with midden shell beaches. Be sure to stay well away from Clamshell Island for the BC Ferry turns around the N side of

included Australians who had failed to strike it rich in the Fraser River gold rush. The island's first house was built in 1859 by a handful of settlers at Ganges Harbour, near the site of the present Harbour House Hotel. The local Cowichans, who had for centuries picked berries and hunted on the island, continued to gather clams in the harbour, and intermarriage took place among the natives and settlers, who were of various races and nationalities, including Hawaiian, Scottish and African American. Peace and harmony did not always prevail, however, and the first farmers faced numerous hardships, including long winters without mail service, wolf attacks on their farm animals, and raids by local Cowichans, not all of whom took kindly to the newcomers.

The Cowichans also had a long-simmering dispute with the northern tribe of Bella Bella natives, and in the summer of 1860 they massacred a number of them at Ganges Harbour. The Deadman Islands were used as a mass burial site and they form part of the Chain Islands, which run the length of Ganges

Left, midden beaches dotting Long Harbour's N shore testify to centuries-old occupation of the harbour. Opposite, a quiet nook in Long Harbour.

Long Harbour, looking southeast.

LONG HARBOUR AT A GLANCE
CHARTS: 3478, 3313, 3442, 3462
LAT LONG: 48˚50.50'N 123˚25.33'W
PROS: Interesting harbour with numerous spots to anchor. Good to excellent holding ground in soft or sticky mud. Generally provides good shelter.
CONS: Some wake from the ferry which usually comes twice a day. No access to north shore.
MUST DO: Explore by dinghy the lagoon at head of harbour. Go swimming.

this island when departing Long Harbour. At the very head of Long Harbour is a fairly sheltered spot to anchor in about 10 feet (3 m) opposite a private marina. Although there are many boats moored here on buoys, there is usually space for visiting yachts to anchor. Holding, in soft mud, is good and this end of the bay is usually well sheltered from wind. Be sure to take a dinghy ride to the head of the slough at HW. This half-mile sojourn takes you past low banks, small wooden docks and pretty waterfront cottages.

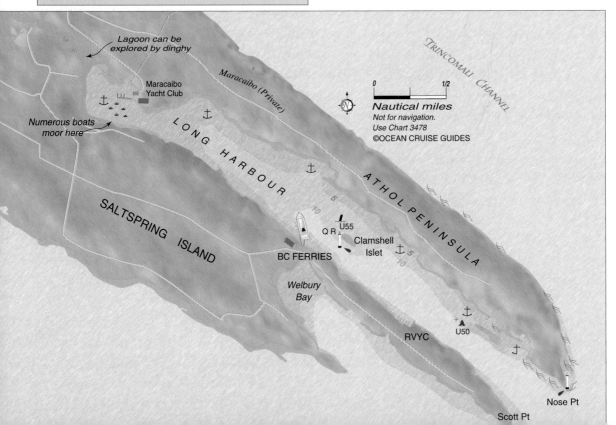

Montague Harbour & Marine Park, Galiano Island 15

It's only fitting that this beautiful anchorage contains the first marine park established in B.C. in 1959. A favourite destination with just about everybody, the park's mooring buoys and small boat dock are busy throughout the summer, as is the tent-filled campground, but there's always room to anchor in this large harbour which can easily handle dozens of vessels. The marine park occupies the NW end of the harbour and is the busier side of the bay, but there are excellent anchoring possibilities at the SE side of the harbour, a good spot to be if south winds pipe up in the night. Northwesterlies can also blast over the gut of the lagoon into the anchorage, and the holding ground SE of the lagoon is only fair with a layer of ooze over mud and sand. The holding east of the dinghy dock is better, as is the bottom in the south part of the harbour.

The park's shoreside trails can be enjoyed year-round and in summer the adjacent white shell beaches are dotted with sunbathers. These extensive mid-

B.C.'s first marine park, Montague Harbour is a very popular destination for boaters.

dens of crushed clamshell are evidence of a large settlement of Coast Salish natives which thrived at Montague Harbour for thousands of years. Various archaeological digs have unearthed artifacts (stone and bone implements) from three distinct cultures, the oldest dating back 6,000 years.

A store and marina, located beside the public dock and old ferry wharf, are open during summer

MONTAGUE HARBOUR AT A GLANCE

CHARTS: 3473, 3313, 3442
LAT LONG: 48°53.50'N 123°24.00'W
PROS: Popular marine park with lots of mooring buoys and plenty of room to anchor. Store and restaurants nearby. Fair to good holding.
CONS: Be careful where to anchor if winds are forecast. Some parts are less protected than others and holding is poor south of lagoon.
MUST DO: Walk around Gray Peninsula and enjoy the beautiful beaches.

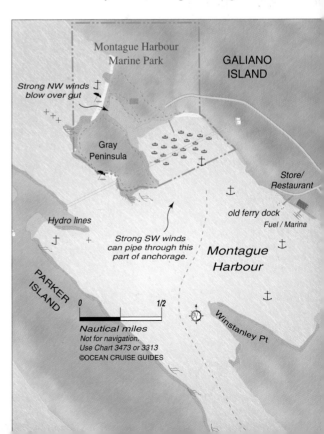

Montague Harbour Marine Park

GALIANO ISLAND

Strong NW winds blow over gut

Gray Peninsula

Store/ Restaurant

Hydro lines

old ferry dock
Fuel / Marina

Strong SW winds can pipe through this part of anchorage.

Montague Harbour

PARKER ISLAND

0   1/2

Nautical miles
Not for navigation.
Use Chart 3473 or 3313
©OCEAN CRUISE GUIDES

Winstanley Pt

months. A recommended hike from the public floats is the 4-mile (6.5 km) walk to Bluffs Park overlooking Active Pass. Starting at the public docks, follow Montague Harbour Road to Georgeson Bay Road, then turn right onto Georgeson and take it to Bluff Drive which leads to the park entrance. The distance is about 4 miles (6.5 km) over hilly terrain. Montague Harbour Road can sometimes be busy with ferry traffic from Sturdies Bay, but once you turn onto Georgeson Bay Road the pastoral scenery will draw you toward wooded Bluffs Park. A short distance within the park entrance is a path that leads to the edge of a bluff overlooking the western entrance to Active Pass, and this eagle's eye view is well worth the effort of getting here. A lofty picnic can be enjoyed while watching vessel traffic below and eagles soaring above the pass.

In winter, Montague Harbour is reclaimed by shorebirds and the park trails are all but deserted. One year, over the Christmas holidays, we tied to a mooring buoy and awoke the next morning to a strong southeasterly and blowing snow. At midday we moved our sailboat to the empty dock and that night we all slept in the saloon to be close to the

Top left, a rare winter snowfall blankets the beaches of Montague Harbour Marine Park. Left, the park's beaches in summer. Below, view of west beach and main anchorage.

diesel stove. The snow stopped sometime in the night and by morning the wind had shifted to a northeasterly with gusts to 35 knots at East Point. When the winds finally subsided and the sun made a brief appearance, we ventured ashore in the knee-deep snow. The marine park we knew so well had been transformed into a winter wonderland and we happily trudged through the deserted campground in our rubber boots.

Walker Hook 16

This summertime lunch stop is situated on the west side of Trincomali Channel, about three and a half miles west of Montague Harbour. Anchor on the SE side of the isthmus connecting Walker Hook – a narrow, wooded peninsula – with Saltspring Island. The sand-and-crushed-shell beach lying along this isthmus is popular with island residents and used to attract nude sunbathers to its remote location.

The anchorage's sand-and-mud bottom provides good holding but because of its exposure to both northwesterlies and southeasterlies, is not always a comfortable place to spend the night at anchor. Northwesterlies can send a bad swell around the corner of the hook, making for a rolly and sleepless night. If you have decided to chance it, go as far into the crux of the anchorage as possible where the swell is moderate. Tying a line to shore is not viable because of the constant current which flows parallel with the foreshore. Entry can be made through a nar-

Above, Walker Hook's fine sand beach is ideal for kids. Below, an aerial view of Walker Hook.

row gap between the two rocks lying off the SE point of Walker Hook and Atkins Reef, which parallels the shoreline. For afternoon stops, we usually anchor close to the beach to avoid any wash from traffic in Trincomali Channel. The bottom shelves gradually to about 3 fathoms (6 m), then rises more steeply. The swimming here is good, with warm water and a fairly clean beach. Views to the south, toward Active Pass, are spectacular.

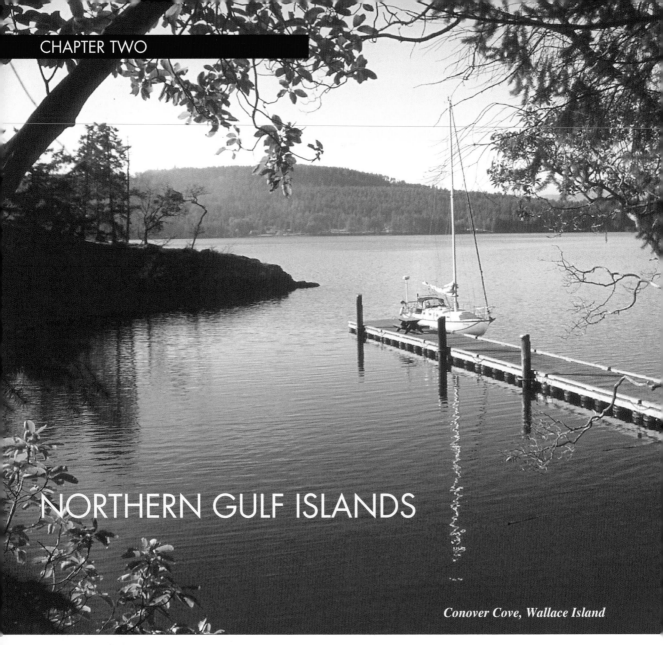

CHAPTER TWO

NORTHERN GULF ISLANDS

Conover Cove, Wallace Island

For an overview of the Gulf Islands, please see pages 60 to 63.

Trincomali Channel, stretching from Active Pass to Pylades Channel, is the main channel connecting the southern Gulf Islands to their northern neighbours. Tidal streams are generally weak (up to 1.5 knots) except in the vicinity of Porlier Pass where rates in Trincomali can reach 3 knots. Tidal reference for most anchorages within Trincomali will be on Fulford Harbour and for locations on the Strait of Georgia side are on Point Atkinson. A handful of anchorages lie near the junction of Trincomali Channel and Porlier Pass, and boaters seeking solitude can still find a few surprises in this area.

TIDES AND CURRENTS
Porlier Pass

The largest gate pass south of Campbell River, with currents reaching 10 knots, Porlier Pass can generate impressive whirlpools and overfalls from Race Point to the reef opposite Dionisio Point. This is especially dangerous if the current is flowing against strong easterly winds. The flood current, which piles up on the Trincomali Channel side of the pass, can be seen spilling into the Strait on large tides and is especially impressive along the rocky west shore of Race Point. In addition to fast currents, it is the degree of turbulence due to numerous shoals and reefs that makes Porlier Pass potentially the most dangerous of all the Gulf Islands passes.

Comox •

22 Sandy Island

DENMAN ISLAND

HORNBY ISLAND

20 Tribune Bay

VANCOUVER ISLAND

21 Deep Bay

Strait of GEORGIA

TEXADA ISLAND

Scotty Bay

17

False Bay 18

LASQUETI ISLAND

Boho Bay 15

Jedediah Island 14

Anderson Bay 19

Squitty Bay 16

0   2.5   5
Nautical miles
©OCEAN CRUISE GUIDES

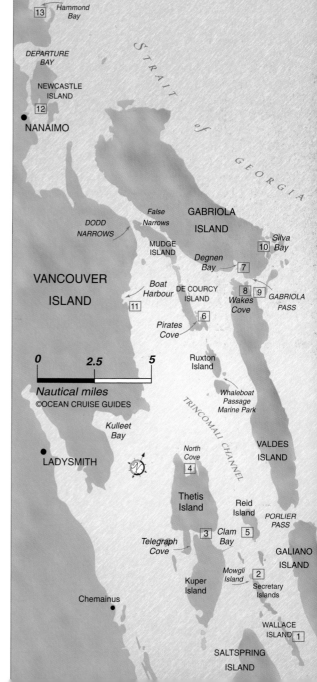

13 Hammond Bay

DEPARTURE BAY

NEWCASTLE ISLAND

12

• NANAIMO

Strait of GEORGIA

DODD NARROWS

False Narrows

GABRIOLA ISLAND

MUDGE ISLAND

Degnen Bay

Silva Bay 10

7

VANCOUVER ISLAND

Boat Harbour

11

DE COURCY ISLAND

Pirates Cove

6

8 9

Wakes Cove

GABRIOLA PASS

Ruxton Island

Whaleboat Passage Marine Park

VALDES ISLAND

0   2.5   5
Nautical miles
©OCEAN CRUISE GUIDES

Kulleet Bay

North Cove 4

TRINCOMALI CHANNEL

• LADYSMITH

Thetis Island

Reid Island

PORLIER PASS

Telegraph Cove

3 Clam Bay 5

GALIANO ISLAND

Kuper Island

Mowgli Island

2 Secretary Islands

Chemainus •

WALLACE ISLAND 1

SALTSPRING ISLAND

Charts and Publications:

Use: CHS Charts 3442, 3443, 3458, 3473, 3475, 3477, 3512 and 3527. Also, the book of charts 3313, which covers the Gulf Islands in detail up to Nanaimo; Sailing Directions for the BC Coast, South Portion; and the Canadian Tide and Current Tables, Volume 5.

Because of strong currents in this pass, try to arrive at or near slack. If slack water has been missed, and the tide is not too large, you can usually work your way through Porlier by staying parallel with the current, clear of the heavy water, while steering as close to the centre of the pass as possible. The stream is a fairly straight and short run through

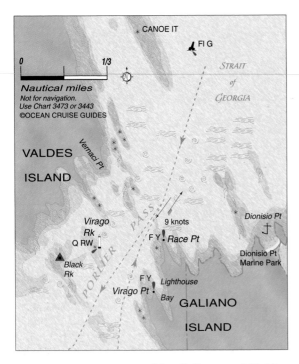

Nautical miles
Not for navigation.
Use Chart 3473 or 3443
©OCEAN CRUISE GUIDES

PASS TIP SHEET – PORLIER PASS
Location: (49°01'N 123°35'W) Between Galiano and Valdes Islands, 11 miles NW of Montague Harbour. Pass is less than a quarter mile wide.
Maximum Flow: Flood, 10 knots, Ebb, 7 knots.
Slack: 15 minutes on large tides.
Nearby Anchorages: In calm, Dionisio Bay if westbound. If eastbound Clam Bay, Reid Island and small bight on W side of Hall Island.
Direction of Flood: North
Key to safe transits: Arrive at or close to slack. Give reef N of Dionisio Point a wide berth and be aware of the set near Virago Rock and Black Rock. Set your course using U41 buoy.

the restrictions presented by Galiano and Valdes Islands, with two major deflections, a result of the island topography and numerous reefs. The main danger when transiting Porlier is being swept onto reefs at the E and W ends of the pass. Boaters sometimes steer a little too close to Galiano Island and

Anchorage in pretty Dionisio Bay, at the east end of Porlier Pass. Race Point is in background.

find they are being set onto the reef extending from Dionisio Bay where depths at LW can be just a few feet. The area NE of this shoal water can be very dangerous in gale conditions and is where some of Georgia Strait's roughest and largest seas can occur.

Over the years a number of vessels have gone down in and around this pass, including the 190-foot sidewheel steamer *Del Norte* which sank after striking the reefs south of Canoe Islets after trying to back out of the pass in 1868. This wreck is still noted near these reefs in the current edition (2004) of the CHS Sailing Directions. The tug *Peggy McNeil* sank in the pass in 1923 and only one of her crew of 6 survived. Of note for tidal pool explorers, Canoe Islets is now an Ecological Reserve and landing is not permitted without a permit.

In our westbound transits of Porlier, we arrive within a quarter-to-a-half mile off the green flashing buoy at the N entrance. Lining up this buoy with the light at Race Point allows us a course through the deep water of the pass and out of danger of the rocks off Valdes Island. Once we are a half mile from Race Point, we turn to a middle route through the pass between Virago Rock and Virago Point. There is a Q RW sector light on Virago Rock for night transits. Sometimes there can be strong turbulence off Romulus Reef and a N set towards the reef extending from Black Rock. It is essential to maintain your bearings, especially at night, to ensure you are clearing these dangers.

The only times we've had engine problems in a pass have been in Porlier. Both times, fortunately, we were east of Race Point, travelling with the current along the axis of the pass, and our boat easily drifted to the inside waters. The ebb is, generally, a smoother and less-turbulent flow because the seaward side contains fewer obstructions.

One of the main drawbacks of Porlier Pass is, during strong N winds, the lack of shelter on the Strait of Georgia side for vessels waiting for slack.

Dionisio Bay, a marine park at the N end of Galiano Island, provides some shelter in S winds but is quite open to the north. This bay makes for a good temporary stop in settled weather with good holding in sand and mud. The marine park has a rich history as evidenced in the shell middens which make up the beach and date back more than 3,000 years. Archaeologists conclude this beach has been used extensively by the Penelakut First Nation.

Tugs and barges often use Porlier Pass and you can obtain information on their movements by listening to Channel 11, Victoria Traffic. Tug operators can usually be contacted directly on Channel 16.

Gabriola Passage

Few passes along the entire B.C. coast are as straightforward as Gabriola Passage. This pass is a yes/no situation and either your boat has the guts to buck the current or it doesn't because, in a slower moving sailboat at least, there is no chance to wiggle through if arriving too late.

In the 1950s, CHS field workers were using baby bottles with flashlights inside to measure nighttime currents at Gabriola Passage. The bottles were cast out by fishing rods from shore and as they gained speed and were swept through the pass, the workers would take transits on the lights and reel the bottles back to shore. By the 1970s, field workers were experimenting with fixed pods on boats to measure current. As a result of study and analysis done in 1979, daily tables were introduced for Gabriola Passage starting with the 1987 edition of the Tide and Current Tables. (Prior to this, predictions for Gabriola were based on Active Pass.)

Gabriola Passage is basically a straight-line stream with the main turbulence occurring with the flood, beginning at the pass and extending to Rogers Reef. Some turbulence can also be expected around the reef near Dibuxante Point. Current in this pass can attain over 8 knots on both flood and ebb. The danger at the W end is near the light beacon off Dibuxante Point where a vessel can get swept onto this reef in either tide direction. You can wait out the tide behind Kendrick Island if bucking a flood or in Wakes Cove if fighting an ebb. The reefs at the south end of Degnen Bay can generate impressive whirlpools and should be given plenty of room.

Cowichan Gap:

Cowichan Gap is what the local natives called Porlier Pass long before the Spanish explorer Jose Narvaez named it in 1791 for an official in Madrid. The following summer two more Spanish explorers, Galiano and Valdes, decided to transit Porlier Pass in search of sheltered anchorage. A fresh easterly was blowing in the Strait of Georgia as they sailed their schooners into the pass. They soon regretted this decision, for a current was running and they "saw at once how risky it was to entangle ourselves among these islands." So they spent two hours rowing their ships back through the pass, dodging reefs and taking soundings as they struggled "in constant labour and danger."

Above, Porlier Pass, looking toward the Strait of Georgia. Below, Dionisio Bay, on the SE side of Porlier Pass, is a good spot to wait for slack tide.

Dodd Narrows

This short pass, with no submerged hazards and a straight-line stream, presents few problems except those created by other boaters. Because this pass is very narrow, often with fast streams and no room to work back eddies, it is susceptible to wash from fast-moving power boats which, when bucking the current, can trigger large standing waves capable of swamping smaller craft. When the pass is busy, as it often is in summer, slower vessels may want to stand-off a short distance to check for oncoming powerboat traffic.

A flood current pushing into Northumberland Channel against a strong summer northwester can result in a significant chop for a few miles beyond the pass. Also, there can be strong turbulence on ebbs just east of Joan Point.

Nearby lies one of the great temptations in passes – **False Narrows**. This is a pretty pass, in a dinghy. We haven't mustered the courage to go through in our Spencer 35. With streams easily 4 knots, shoal water, kelp and numerous reefs, this is obviously not a safe pass and best left to the locals who know it well.

THE ANCHORAGES

Wallace Island [1]
Marine Park

Every island has a story, and Wallace Island is no exception. Over the last century this island has been a hermit's haven, a youth camp, a summer resort, a potential subdivision and, since 1990, a provincial marine park. In some ways, the island has come full circle, its park status preserving the natural beauty and peacefulness that so appealed to its first full-time resident, a Scotsman named Jeremiah Chivers

Looking south, Dodd Narrows at full flood.

who lived alone on the island from 1889 until his death at the age of 92 in 1927. A long, low-lying island, it was called Narrow Island until renamed in 1905 by Captain Perry of the Royal Navy to honour Captain Wallace Houston, HMS *Trincomali*, who served in local waters in the 1850s.

Following the death of Chivers, Wallace Island became a summer camp for boys. One of the respondents to an American newspaper ad seeking youth counselors for an island retreat in the Canadian wilderness was a young man named David Conover, who was then living in Los Angeles. After two summers spent working at the camp on Wallace Island, Conover returned with his wife Jeanne and, although having little experience living in the bush, they bought the island and moved there in 1946.

The next summer they opened a resort at Conover Cove, which they operated until the mid-60s. Summers were idyllic days for young Davey, the Conovers' only child, who grew up on Wallace Island. On his website (www.dconover.com), David Conover Jr. recalls that his summers were a boyhood dream of outdoor activities centred around the holiday resort where he played with the children of families staying in the rental cabins. Winters were decidedly different, however. An only child living on a private island, Davey saw other children only when he commuted by boat to school on Saltspring Island, and "those long, cold, isolated winters seemed to stretch into eternity."

WALLACE ISLAND AT A GLANCE
CHARTS: 3313, 3442, 3463
LAT LONG: Princess C, 48°56.60'N 123°33.37'W
PROS: An excellent marine park with good hiking trails, summertime swimming, fair-to-good shelter, good holding and stern tie rings allowing for plenty of boats. Good dinghy exploring along its shoreline.
CONS: Often busy in summer. Anchorages vulnerable to strong NW and SW wind.
MUST DO: Hike the entire island, visit Chivers Point at low tide and explore tidal pools.

Above, Conover Cove is protected but shallow.
Right, Princess Cove is sheltered from southerlies.

When the Conovers sold their resort in the 1960s, Jeanne moved to Victoria where Davey attended high school. David Sr. moved to a new home he had built on an unsold waterfront acreage overlooking Princess Cove, which remains in private hands. Jeanne didn't move back to Wallace Island but David Sr. lived there until his death in 1983 at the

Governor Rock

Governor Rock in Trincomali Channel south of Wallace Island was named by Captain Richards after an incident in 1859. His ship had been lying at anchor in Nanaimo Harbour when he received an urgent order from Governor Douglas to return to Victoria. While steaming south down Trincomali Channel, HMS *Plumper* ran full speed into an unknown rock and Richards promptly named it Governor Rock.

James Douglas, who became governor of British Columbia in 1858, came to British North America as a fur trader and was an agent of the Hudson's Bay Company when he oversaw the construction of Fort Victoria in 1843. Douglas married Amelia Connolly, the 16-year-old daughter of a native woman and a white man. She and Douglas had 13 children and although she became Lady Douglas when her husband was knighted, she was never fully accepted by the ladies of Victoria society.

age of 63, writing two books about his life there, namely *Once Upon an Island* and *One Man's Island*.

In the latter Conover states, "For weeks now I have had no inclination to leave the island. If I don't watch out, I'll soon take root like a fir. The prospect, I admit, I find not unpleasant." This is a sentiment easily understood by anyone who has visited Wallace Island for any period of time.

For boaters seeking a bit of peace and solitude, the off-season is the best time to visit Wallace Island and relive its storied past, when the sounds of summer have fallen quiet, the calls of children and dogs now replaced with the twittering of eagles. Apart from two private properties at the mouth of Princess Cove, the entire island is a marine park. Trails run the length of the island, joining the two main anchorages, and these are often deserted, as are the anchorages themselves, in contrast to the bright bustle of summer when anchored boats line up Mediterranean-style with stern lines to shore.

'Chivers Pass'

From Porlier Pass there are several routes to get to the anchorages of Wallace Island but our favourite is through the small pass just N of Chivers Point between Wallace and Secretary Islands and known locally as Chivers Pass. This pass has a minimum of about 6 feet of water at LW, but it must be navigated very carefully because of currents and nearby reefs.

The approach to the pass is made by first locating the large drying reef situated in the middle of the channel. If southbound, approach the pass at right angles to Wallace Island on a course of about 220°. We aim for the reef until about 150 feet away, then turn right about 45° toward the small E point on Secretary Island until we're between the reef and the island. We then turn S in an arc to exit. If the reef cannot be seen, aim for the midway point between Chivers Point and the point on Secretary Island and, proceeding slowly, begin turning toward Secretary Island when you are abeam of Chivers Point. When about 60 feet off the point of Secretary Island, turn S and exit. The pass appears to receive about 2 to 3 knots of current, which would make a transit a little challenging during a strong N wind and ebb tide because of the set to the reef.

Princess Cove

Although the approach to Princess Cove is guarded by an ominous line of reefs, there is plenty of water on either side for pleasure craft. At LW, this reef is a popular haul-out for seals, while oystercatchers and other shore birds can also be spotted here. If entering the cove from the SW, the channel between the outer reef and the point at the entrance to the cove provides an easy route.

The cove with two mooring buoys, has limited swinging room and a stern line to shore is de rigueur

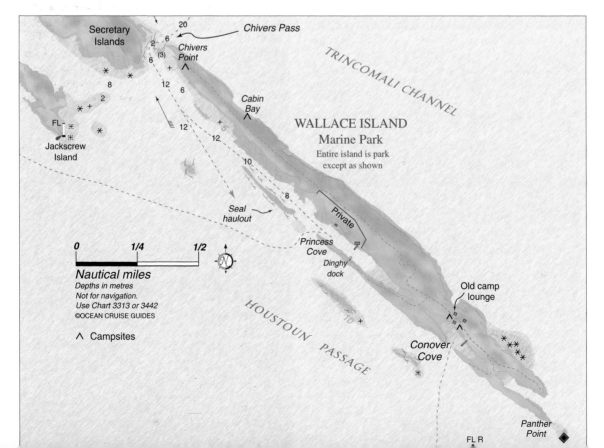

Princess Cove often requires stern-ties in summer.

in summer when the anchorage gets busy and boats line up Mediterranean-style along the cove's west side. Rock ledges lie along the W side of the cove and it's a good idea to check your depth as the tide drops to ensure your vessel doesn't drift back onto one of these. A dinghy float is located on the W side, opposite a private dock.

Princess Cove affords excellent shelter from southeasterlies but is quite open to strong N winds. In a SE wind, Princess Cove is an absolute hurricane hole. During a SE gale you can hear the wind howling overhead and barely receive a gust in this snug anchorage. Winds from the SW, however, do come over the saddle from Conover Cove and vessels lying broadside to strong SW winds will be straining their ground tackle. The cove is also exposed to NW winds which often bring a low swell into the cove. Although the holding is very good, consider moving your boat if a NW gale is in the offing.

Conover Cove

This cove still bustles with life each summer, its small float holding 6 to 10 boats. There's little depth to play with in this tight anchorage and, because of limited swinging room, most boats anchor in the N part of the cove and tie a line to one of the rings anchored to the E or W shore. Minimum depth in this area can be less than a fathom, so it's crucial to consult the tide tables.

The greatest depth, and best spot if anchoring, is N of the dock on the E side of the cove with a stern line ashore. Be sure to bury your anchor well because strong winds can whistle through the anchorage and often vessels are broadside to the wind. If you're tying to the dock, the deeper water, by about a foot, is on the N side of the dock. Northerly winds can also whistle through the cove.

On shore, opposite the dock, is an original signpost pointing to the island's various trails and points of interest. Several heritage buildings, including one of the resort cabins and the main house where young Davey grew up, stand on the edge of a grass clearing that overlooks the anchorage and is bordered by purple pea-like flowers which flourish in summer. As children play along the sandstone foreshore and dogs leap into the water for sticks, a visitor stepping ashore can quite easily envision the island as it would have been a half century ago.

Exploring Wallace Island

Hiking the trails of Wallace Island is one of the great treats of cruising the Gulf Islands. There is a new dinghy dock on the W side of Princess Cove, making it very easy to get ashore and begin the hike. The trail from the dinghy dock leads to the head of the bay where it connects with another trail leading to Conover Cove. Along this trail is a rusting 1950s-style jeep, a reminder of days past when roads were

Above, tidal pools are a major attraction on Wallace Island. Below, Mowgli Island at sunset.

bulldozed and wells drilled in a failed attempt by the Wallace Island Holding Company to sub-divide the island after it was purchased from the Conovers. Today not even bicycles are allowed on the park trails, a measure aimed at protecting the island's sensitive flora and fauna. Black-tailed deer live on the island, amid thickets of salal and the springtime proliferation of lupine, Indian paintbrush and wild peas.

At Conover Cove there is a bomb shelter (built by David Conover), as well as a picnic shelter built when Wallace Island was a summer youth camp. The names of boys from those long-ago summers are carved into the open-air structure's supporting logs. Pieces of driftwood adorn the wall on either side of the stone fireplace with names of boats that have visited Wallace Island since it became a marine park in 1990. Nearby, on the edge of a grassy clearing, are several more heritage buildings, including resort cabins and the main house, built on the foundations of Chivers's cabin.

A trail runs the length of the island, terminating near Chivers Point at its N end where there are several campsites. Campfires are not permitted anywhere on the island, which becomes tinder dry in summer. Back in the 1920s a negligent camper started a fire on the island and burn marks remain on some large firs and cedars. There is a small cove beneath Chivers Point, where erosion has hollowed out puddingstone formations in the rock ledges.

Mowgli Island   2

This small anchorage, sometimes used by fishing boats, is often passed over by pleasure craft but is a pretty overnight stop in settled weather. Its NW shoreline is formed by Mowgli Island (known locally as Spike Island) and to the south are the Secretary Islands. A reef extends from Mowgli Island's SW shore and must be given a wide berth as you come into the anchorage. This same reef deflects much of the wave action created by passing vessels in Houston Passage. Oystercatchers and gulls frequent this reef, their medley of calls punctuated by the chattering of kingfishers.

A few houses have been built on Mowgli Island but the shoreline remains pleasing, its slopes covered with grass and a variety of trees. Along the foreshore, small patches of white shell beach appear as the tide recedes. The channel separating Mowgli Island from the Secretary Islands is shallow and not recommended as an entrance. Skiffs sometimes cut through the anchorage but most boats keep to the main channel and pass right by. Holding is good in mud and sand, and the anchorage is protected from NW winds but somewhat open to S winds.

Clam Bay / Telegraph Harbour, Thetis Island   3

Nestled on the north side of Kuper Island, Clam Bay is a convenient anchorage for boats entering or exiting the Gulf Islands through Porlier Pass. It also is a good spot for northbound boaters to pause and rest before heading into the Strait of Georgia.

Clam Bay is a big bay, allowing for dozens of vessels to find shelter for the night. Entrance is made between the SE end of Centre Reef (marked with a starboard hand buoy) and Penelakut Spit, comprised of a long strip of crushed clamshells. At night, you may have trouble spotting the entrance buoy, but Penelakut Spit can usually be seen and used to navigate into the anchorage.

Once inside Clam Bay, most boats anchor in its southern half, where Penelakut Spit provides shelter from SE seas and the thick mud bottom provides superb holding. In summer, we tend to anchor outside the 2-fathom (4-metre) line to avoid the crowds and allow ourselves plenty of swinging room. In strong N winds, the north half of the bay provides better shelter.

Penelakut Spit is named for the inhabitants of Kuper Island whose village is situated on the hillside overlooking the spit. Their ancestors, who were skilled at hunting sea lions entering the Gulf Islands through Cowichan Gap (Porlier Pass), would paddle their canoes across the Strait of Georgia in summer

CLAM BAY AT A GLANCE

CHARTS: 3477, 3313, 3442, 3463
LAT LONG: 48°59.00'N 123°38.72'W
PROS: Clam Bay is a large, wide anchorage and, although somewhat open to the north, provides good shelter in most winds. Holding in sticky mud is excellent.
CONS: Entrance encumbered with a marked reef. Anchorage somewhat open to strong N winds and even S winds will gust across Penelakut Spit.
MUST DO: Take your dinghy through The Cut to Telegraph Harbour. Explore Penelakut Spit.

Above, The Cut at low tide. Below, a quiet evening in Clam Bay.

Looking east over Telegraph Harbour to Clam Bay and Reid Island. Porlier Pass in background.

to fish for salmon in the lower reaches of the Fraser River near present day Sand Heads.

On the W side of Clam Bay is the entrance to a narrow, dredged channel called **The Cut** – suitable for dinghies – that leads to Telegraph Harbour, cutting between Thetis and Kuper Islands. A narrow strip of land once joined Thetis and Kuper Islands,

until a canal was dug in 1905 to allow the passage of small craft between Clam Bay and Telegraph Harbour. A bridge was built to rejoin the two islands, but this was knocked down in 1945. This did not stop cattle owned by the residents of Kuper Island, which is an Indian Reserve, from crossing over to Thetis at LW and helping themselves to the farmers' crops.

Although we've taken our Spencer 35 through The Cut, that was many years ago and the channel has filled in somewhat since then. Taking a keel boat

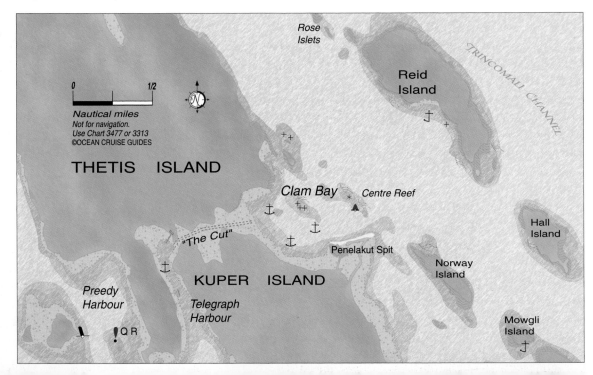

through The Cut should not be attempted during anything less than tides of 12 feet, as the channel dries in two spots to about 6 feet at datum. Chart 3477 and the CHS chart book of the Gulf Islands – 3313 – provide good detail of the pass.

Telegraph Harbour, a popular place in summer with its two marinas, provides snug, although sometimes crowded anchorage north of Thetis Island Marina. There is an inviting pub at the Thetis Island Marina and an old-fashioned soda fountain at Telegraph Harbour Marina. Within walking distance of both marinas are several island crafts shops as well as the ferry terminal at Preedy Harbour. The ferry makes regular crossings of Stuart Channel to Chemainus on Vancouver Island – a pleasant day trip for boaters who travel as foot passengers to take a look at the colourful street murals and enjoy the sidewalk cafes of this former mill town.

North Cove, Thetis Island 4

This lovely bay at the north end of Thetis Island is a pleasant alternative to the often-busy anchorages of the northern Gulf Islands. Although open to north-westerlies, the bay is wide and deep, allowing for plenty of scope in excellent holding ground. Because few boats anchor here, it is a quiet and relaxed spot suitable for a few days of unwinding. The reefs in the area are well marked and close attention to the chart will make your entry and exit easy. A private stone breakwater has been built inside Fraser Point but development around this quiet bay is minimal, with hillside houses nestled unobtrusively among the evergreens and arbutus. We usually drop the hook in about 40 feet (13 m)

near the west side of the bay, opposite the summer youth camp which has a small dock for its sailing dinghies. There are, however, numerous other locations to anchor in the bay.

There are several bible camps on Thetis Island, a tradition that began back in 1904 with the establishment of an Anglican retreat by a retired British major and his sister. The island had become known as an English colony through the efforts of Mr. and Mrs. Henry Burchell who, after losing most of their life savings in a business venture, settled at Preedy Harbour in 1892 where they built a new home, store, farm and orchard. At Christmas they held a children's party and each fall, under the harvest moon, they threw a dance complete with oysters and sparkling white wine, which was attended by guests who would sail or row from the other Gulf Islands. North Cove is wide open to the north and in sum-

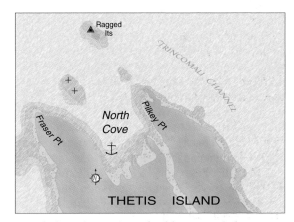

North Cove is scenic and seldom crowded.

mer, when northwesterlies prevail, mariners should keep an ear to the weather. If you do get caught here overnight, the good holding ground should keep you until the dawn. Alternatively, nearby Kulleet Bay provides shelter from N winds. In winter, North Cove offers excellent shelter from SE winds. We've been here in winter gales and nary a puff of wind ran through the rigging.

Reid Island   5

This wide bight on the SW side of the island (see map page 110) is bordered by an attractive pebble beach. This is a quiet spot to anchor when Clam Bay and Telegraph Harbour are busy. Although open to the south, it provides fair shelter from NW winds and, in settled weather, is an excellent spot to watch the sun set while tending the barbecue. This anchorage is also easy to access in darkness if you're concerned about the more difficult entrance to Clam Bay. The holding ground is very good in sticky mud.

Another small temporary anchorage lies at the south end of Reid Island, formed by an islet and some drying rocks. This spot provides some protection from the north but the anchorage's exposure to current from Porlier Pass and the unpleasant proximity of reefs make an overnight stay something to think about carefully. These same reefs mark the spot where we once grounded our blameless Spencer 35. While rounding the corner of Reid Island on our way to Porlier Pass (where a flood was in full stride) we cut the curve too sharply and didn't notice the strong current setting us sideways onto the reef.

Beachcombing along the bight on Reid Island.

After slamming into the submerged rocks, we powered off the reef and continued on our way with the lesson learned to beware of complacency and always know where you are – exactly.

Apart from this incident, our associations with Reid Island have all been positive. The gravel beach is ideal for children to explore and the view, past the decaying wooden pilings of a remaining Japanese saltery, is lovely. Many a sunny afternoon we have picnicked on the foreshore, enjoying this view across the sparkling water to Clam Bay.

Reid Island is privately owned, with cabins clustered along its NW shoreline where pocket beaches of crushed clamshell reveal themselves at low water.

Pirates Cove Marine Park, De Courcy Island   6

Although this picturesque marine park at the SE tip of De Courcy Island is protected in moderate conditions, strong NW winds penetrate the entire cove and can make for an uncomfortable night. Pirates Cove is popular with many boaters for its unique location at the north end of the Gulf Islands and for the excellent trails lacing the park. The park's shoreside also includes two dinghy docks and a decent beach area looking out to Ruxton Passage.

The challenges of Pirates Cove begin with an entrance guarded by a long narrow reef extending 100 yards NW beyond the beacon. There is also a rock that juts out due N of the end of this reef (shown as 03 on the chart) and it is this rock that many boats have grazed when approaching the cove. The other rock that catches vessels is just inside the entrance and is marked by a red buoy. Favour the E

side of the entrance passage to avoid this rock. The holding ground (oozy mud) is mediocre and when a big northwesterly blows through the anchorage, it's not unusual to see large boats dragging anchor. At LW they have no choice but to stay because there's not enough depth at the entrance to get out. Regulars to Pirates Cove are usually seen tying a stern line to shore, but in strong winds they'll anchor in the centre of the cove to point into the wind.

Most boaters are willing to put up with Pirate Cove's deficiencies, for it is a beautiful anchorage. It also has a colourful past. Brother XII – one of Canada's most infamous false prophets – established a communal settlement here in the early 1930s. An itinerant sea captain cum charlatan, Edward Arthur Wilson was a charismatic occult leader who called himself Brother XII and whose Aquarian Foundation headquarters were located at Cedar-by-the-Sea, south of Nanaimo. Using funds donated by followers willing to denounce all of their worldly possessions, Brother XII was able to acquire property at Pirates Cove on DeCourcy Island. He didn't

like outsiders and would curse – and occasionally shoot – from shore anyone who ventured by boat into his harbour. He eventually disappeared with a stash of gold he had collected from members of his cult, and died some years later in Switzerland, but his legend lives on. (See Wakes Cove for more on Brother XII.)

PIRATES COVE AT A GLANCE

CHARTS: 3475, 3313, 3443, 3463
LAT LONG: 49°6.03'N 123°43.94'W
PROS: Marine park, good trails, and generally good shelter from moderate winds and wash from boats in Trincomali Channel.
CONS: Often busy in summer. Holding only fair.
MUST DO: Walk the trails and contemplate the colourful character of Brother Twelve.

Right, good trails at Pirates Cove. Below, entrance to anchorage is tricky.

Above, Pirates Cove anchorage. Right, small beach near Ruxton Island.

Alternative Anchorages: If Pirates Cove is full, an alternative anchorage in settled weather is the marine park's outer bay facing Ruxton Passage. This bay has decent protection from W wind and the holding is good. It does. however, get some swell from boats taking the passage and is open to the SE. Another option is **Herring Bay** at the north end of Ruxton Island where the holding ground is better than Pirates Cove and the bay affords a good view over to Vancouver Island. It is, however, a tight anchorage with some shallow patches including an uncharted rocky ledge that dries one foot (0.3 m) in the middle of the west entrance to the bay. Another good spot, in settled conditions, is **Boat Harbour** on Vancouver Island (see page 118).

We sometimes stop at **Whaleboat Passage Marine Park** at the SE end of Ruxton island, for it is usually quiet. Lying at the eastern entrance to Whaleboat Passage, the anchorage itself can accommodate only a few boats due to a drying rock that limits swinging room. Most boats anchor N of the drying rock. Some caution is required when approaching the anchorage from Pylades Channel, for a reef extends from the NE end of Pylades Island, forcing a northbound vessel to swing wide when entering the anchorage. Whaleboat Passage is navigable only by small craft. The park's islet was known locally as Eagle Island before it was renamed Whaleboat Island in 1981 when the marine park was established. It is completely treed and has a steep sandstone foreshore.

0₃

0₃

■

R
U38

Park Sign

⚓ dinghy dock

⚓ W

Keep well clear
of this reef when
anchoring

Stern-tie
along here

dinghy
dock

Darkwoods Trail

Pylades Trail

Brother XII Trail

**DE COURCY
ISLAND**

Pirates Cove
Marine Park

W 🚶

W ⚓

⚓

0   1/8

Nautical miles
Not for navigation.
Use Chart 3475, 3443 or 3313
©OCEAN CRUISE GUIDES

Degnen Bay, Gabriola Island 7

A good hurricane hole, this bay is well protected from wind – it's the boats swinging on permanent moorings that are the worry. Degnen Bay has become clogged with boats in recent years and the public wharf is now monopolized by local vessels. Occasionally there have been complaints from boaters not being allowed dinghy access to the dock. However, legally, you can tie up here to go ashore for brief periods without charge. Although the holding ground is good, there is mooring debris on the bottom which could foul your anchor.

Despite its drawbacks as an anchorage for visiting boaters, the natural and historical attractions of Degnen Bay endure. A single petroglyph of a killer whale can be found on a foreshore rock near the head of the bay, while a walk ashore heading west on South Road leads to the site of more petroglyphs, located behind the United Church. The land around Degnen Bay was settled in the 1860s by an Irish immigrant named Robert Degnen. He had married the daughter of a local chief and together they farmed the land and raised nine children. They built a wharf and transported their produce to market in Nanaimo using a large dugout canoe, eventually replacing it with a steam launch that could carry passengers as well as freight.

Wakes Cove, Valdes Island 8 🏃

Wakes Cove, a provincial marine park, provides good shelter from SE winds. The cove is a little exposed to the NW, but the fetch is limited. Although the cove is out of the current stream of Gabriola Passage, which can reach 8 knots, it does receive some wake from vessels transiting the pass. The holding in mud here is good, however there are usually large patches of kelp and reports of bottom debris from its years of logging operations.

Created in 2002, the park encompasses the Valdes shoreline from Coal Mine Bay on its Pylades Channel side to a point SE of Kendrick Island on its Georgia Strait side. Several waterfront parcels are excepted from the park, including Kendrick Island and Dibuxante Point, as well as most of the E shoreline of Wakes Cove. Some private floats are situated here and the point of land opposite Cordero Point is also private. The head of the cove is parkland, however, and provides access to a forest of arbutus, Garry oak and old-growth Douglas fir trees. Along the park trail leading west, there are numerous old cars and trucks rusting in the shade.

The park's southern boundary lies adjacent to reserve land owned by the Lyackson First Nation,

Above, Degnen Bay is often crowded with moored boats. Below, the dinghy dock at Wakes Cove.

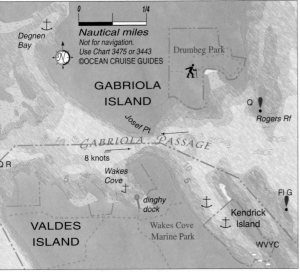

the island's traditional inhabitants. Their village is located south of Coal Mine Bay, where a nook in the rock bluff provided a safe landing place for canoes. The property was acquired in 1876 by a retired British naval officer, Captain Baldwin Wake, who regularly rowed across Gabriola Passage to teach at the local school. Wake died mysteriously while sailing his sloop home from Nanaimo where he had picked up some boxes of personal belongings shipped from England. His body was never found but his dismasted boat and some empty boxes washed ashore on Thetis Island.

Wake's widow moved to Esquimalt with her two daughters but her son Baldwin stayed at Wakes Cove. His widow Amelia was still living there in the late 1920s when much of the surrounding land was purchased by Edward Arthur Wilson, better known as Brother XII, the occult leader whose followers donated money to his foundation headquartered at Cedar-By-The-Sea. Brother XII's plan for Valdes was to establish a secluded retreat where he would train selected disciples. He began landing his workers and supplies in a small cove near Dibuxante Point. However, upon installing his pregnant lover in a newly built cabin, he was suddenly accused of turning the island property into a personal love-nest and the communal settlement was never completed. Brother XII eventually fled to Switzerland with a fortune in gold, leaving only scandal in his wake.

Kendrick Island Anchorage 9

If Silva Bay is too crowded or you are waiting for slack at Gabriola Pass, this anchorage on the W side of Kendrick Island is a good choice. Charts 3475 and 3313 give good detail of this area. Three islands surround this long narrow bay and the holding in thick mud and sand provides secure anchorage. This anchorage is a better overnight stop than nearby Wakes Cove, receiving less wake from vessels transiting Gabriola Pass. There are a few nearby middens including a pretty beach along the anchorage's E side. A short dinghy ride across Gabriola Pass will take you to a good swimming beach in the bay fronting Drumbeg Park on Gabriola Island.

Although strong southerlies and northwesterlies will gust through the cove, the holding ground is excellent, making the anchorage safe for most summer conditions. The best area to anchor is north of the docks and buoys belonging to the West Vancouver Yacht Club. South of these facilities, the water shoals quickly to a rocky kelp-strewn bottom. Anchor in 35 to 40 feet in mud and sand.

Above left, old cars at Wakes Cove Marine Park.

Left, the pocket beach at Kendrick Island.

Silva Bay, Gabriola Island [10]

Silva Bay lies outside of the tidal passes into the Gulf Islands, so it's a popular resting stop for boats approaching the Gulf Islands from the Strait of Georgia. A large bay with room for "one more", its proximity to Vancouver sometimes makes it a hangout for partying charter vessels. But, with a pub nearby and a good location to rendevous with friends, its popularity is justified – especially as a departure point for northbound vessels.

There are, however, a few inherent problems with Silva Bay which need a bit of getting used to. The approach to Silva Bay from Vancouver requires your senses to be on full alert. Starting with Thrasher Rock, there are a numerous reefs to be careful of, especially those ringing Acorn Island.

Many boaters use Thrasher Rock as a way point and aim for the flashing light SE of Tugboat Island before turning north. The final challenge, of course, is wending your way into the anchorage around the reefs of Tugboat and Vance Islands, giving the Tugboat reef a wide berth on the final turn into Silva Bay. Many vessels have ended up on the reef SW of the beacon, but keeping an eye on the depth and favouring Vance Island will get you through.

The narrow channel S of Sear Island, with a minimum depth of about 4 feet, can be used for entering and exiting Silva Bay, depending on the stage and size of tide, but be careful if your boat draws more than 6 feet. In strong southeasterlies, large swells will be breaking at the E end of this channel, which can be dangerous for sailing vessels equipped only with an outboard.

Although we've never had a problem with our CQR holding in Silva Bay, we've seen other boats drag anchor. The holding is only fair, with a thin layer of mud over rock (or something equally hard) which doesn't provide great holding when the wind comes up which it seems to do in the evening. Although the anchorage is well sheltered from seas off the Strait of Georgia, winds blow strongly through the islands ringing the bay. We like to anchor directly north of Sear Island which keeps us out of S winds while giving ourselves room to let out line should a N wind come up. There are marina facilities in Silva Bay for boaters who would prefer to tie to a dock for the night. The Royal Vancouver Yacht Club owns Tugboat Island with its dock facilities located along the west side of the island.

Although Spanish place names dominate Gabriola Island, Silva Bay is named for members of the large Portuguese family that settled here and in other locations around the Strait of Georgia. The family patriarch, Joseph Silvey, had arrived in B.C. in 1852 aboard a whaling ship and, after running the first grocery store in Gastown (Vancouver), he moved to the Sunshine Coast where he founded the fishing port of Egmont.

When anchored in Silva Bay, we like to explore by dinghy the nearby shoreline which includes **Drumbeg Park**, located about a mile south of the bay near the entrance to Gabriola Passage.

The main entrance to Silva Bay is at top centre, between Vance Island and Tugboat Island.

Above, Boat Harbour and marina at Kenary Cove.
Right, Hemer Park trails lead to Holden Lake.

Boat Harbour 11

An uncrowded anchorage, this bay does get some swell and chop from passing boats and is open to the south but is relatively sheltered from northwesterlies. We have spent the night here in settled weather, and we usually anchor opposite Flewett Point in about 50 feet over a mud bottom, although you can anchor closer to the marina to get out a S swell.

A private marina occupies Kenary Cove in the south part of the harbour and a few homes dot the harbour's northern shoreline in a pastoral setting of treed and grassy slopes. The area between the marina and the small peninsula offers limited anchoring but it is shallow and buoys dot the waterline. The peninsula, which is joined to shore by a neck of land, was formerly a railway embankment used when coal was shipped out by steamer in the 1870s and is now owned by an offshore consortium. You can row ashore and quickly find the path used by locals that leads to the edge of Hemer Provincial Park – a gift from John and Violet Hemer. The park itself pro-

vides groomed trails that can be hiked for about a mile and a half to Holden Lake where wood benches overlook the lake.

Back at Boat Harbour, a good picnic site is atop the peninsula on a gentle bluff overlooking the anchorage, its low banks of sandstone eroded into smooth and unusual shapes. The marina in Kenary Cove is known for its woodworking shop where master shipwright Bruce Martyn and his apprentices work on restorations of classic boats.

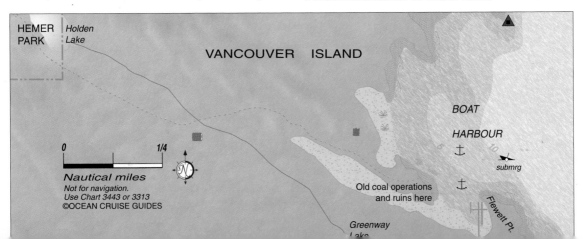

HEMER PARK | Holden Lake

VANCOUVER ISLAND

BOAT HARBOUR

submrg

0 — 1/4
Nautical miles
Not for navigation.
Use Chart 3443 or 3313
©OCEAN CRUISE GUIDES

Old coal operations and ruins here

Greenway Lake

Flewett Pt.

Newcastle Island 12 Marine Park

Newcastle Island is Nanaimo's version of Vancouver's Stanley Park but with no vehicle access, so it is perfectly suited to boaters who can tie at the park floats or anchor nearby in Mark Bay. The holding ground is excellent, which is a good thing because S and E winds can be quite gusty coming off Gallows Point on Protection Island.

If you're approaching Mark Bay from McKay Channel, the only hazard is Satellite Reef which extends close to the 2-fathom (4 m) line around Protection Island. Tugs often moor barges to the buoys east of Satellite Reef. For these reasons, we normally keep the reef to starboard when approaching Mark Bay.

The anchorage can be busy in summer months, but there always seems to be room for one more. We try to stay away from the passenger ferry routes between Nanaimo, Newcastle and Protection Islands. The best area to anchor to avoid wind, and slop from traffic, is just S and W of the public docks. The holding ground is excellent and protection is good from most winds although strong S winds will make it around Protection Island into the bay.

Moorage is available at the park floats, located next to the ferry wharf where foot passengers from Nanaimo disembark, but boaters often anchor and row ashore to the dinghy dock. The visitors pavilion, open during the summer, is located nearby.

Boaters docked in Nanaimo have the option of taking the passenger ferry to Newcastle Island.

Named after the famous coal town in Northern England, Newcastle Island was the site of a coal mine, sandstone quarry, saltery and shipyard before it was bought by the Canadian Pacific Steamship Company in 1931 and transformed into a holiday resort. An old ship was permanently docked in Mark Bay as a floating hotel and on summer weekends as many as 1,500 steamship passengers would arrive for the day from Vancouver. They came to enjoy such facilities as a dance pavilion, tea house, picnic areas, change houses, soccer field and wading pool. World War II brought an end to these excursions as ships were diverted by the war effort, and Japanese residents operating a saltery and shipyard here, were interned. After the war, in 1955, the City of

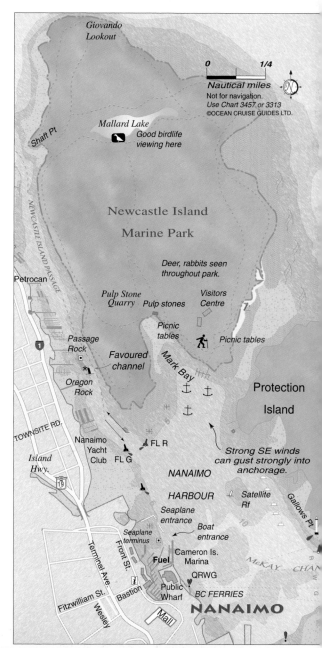

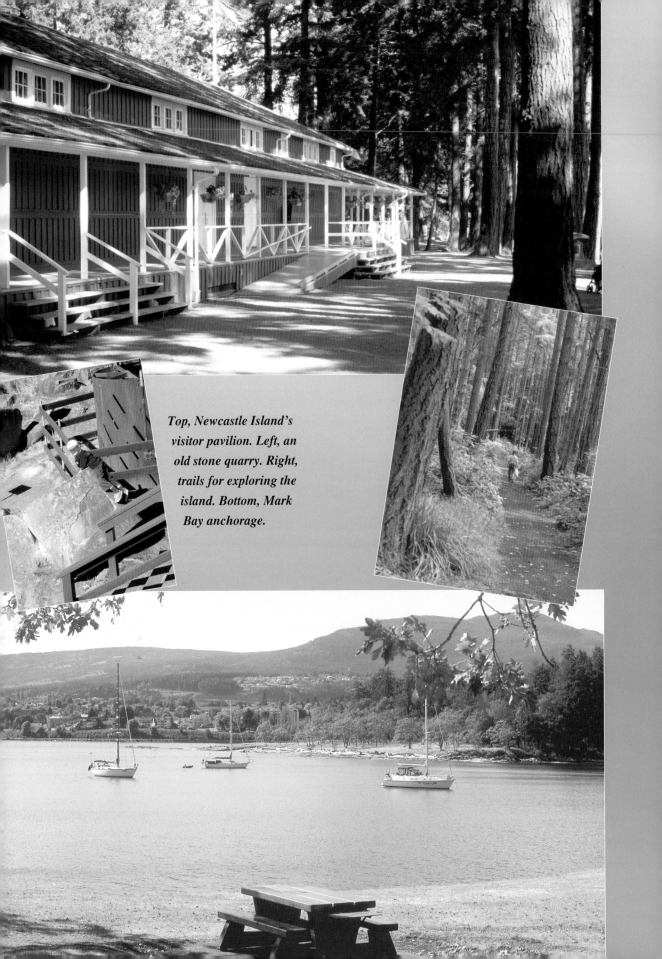

Top, Newcastle Island's visitor pavilion. Left, an old stone quarry. Right, trails for exploring the island. Bottom, Mark Bay anchorage.

Nanaimo acquired the island, turning it over to the Province in 1961 as a marine park. The restored dance pavilion now houses the Visitor Centre, open throughout the summer, where a map of the island's extensive trail system is available.

The trails, covering more than 12.5 miles (20 km) in total, encircle and crisscross the entire island, providing access to many natural attractions such as Mallard Lake. Ringed by steep sandstone cliffs and sandy gravel beaches, the island's interior is gently hilly and forested with Douglas fir, arbutus, Garry Oak and dogwood trees. One of the highlights of a hike on Newcastle is Nares Point at the island's NW tip where Giovando Lookout provides a sweeping view of the Strait of Georgia. The wooded trails give way to open grassy areas at the south end of the island where picnic sites, a playground and the old sandstone quarry are located near the floats.

The animals living on Newcastle know a good thing when they see it. Raccoons, blacktail deer, beavers, river otters and rabbits all thrive here, while Mark Bay is a popular gathering place for Canada geese who like to cruise through the anchorage at happy hour. A short dinghy ride away is neighbouring Protection Island where a floating pub and shoreside store are located.

Above, Mark Bay, Newcastle Island. Below,
Nanaimo's harbourfront looking toward Mark Bay.

Nanaimo

Nanaimo is a great place to reprovision and enjoy some shoreside attractions with the city's public floats conveniently located in the Boat Basin adjacent to downtown. The harbour is the hub of Nanaimo, with floatplanes landing and taking off, and small passenger ferries bobbing across the water to nearby Protection Island and Newcastle Island. In summer, on the fourth Sunday of July, about a hundred vessels gather here for the start of the World Championship Bathtub Race, first launched in 1967. To qualify for this unusual race, which ends on the

other side of the Strait of Georgia in Vancouver's English Bay, an entry "must contain a component which conforms to the general shape and design of an old-style roll edge bathtub", be propelled by a 7.5 horsepower motor and have an escort boat.

Standing guard over Nanaimo Harbour is a wooden military bastion, built by the Hudson's Bay Company in 1853 to protect the white settlers who came from England and Scotland to work in the local coal mines. They called their new home Colville Town, but the native name of Nanaimo, which means 'big strong tribe' in reference to the five villages located in the area, has endured. The area's historic native presence is in evidence at Petroglyph Provincial Park, situated a few miles south of downtown just off the Island Highway on a hill overlooking Nanaimo Harbour. The park contains some of the best petroglyphs in the region, several of these prehistoric sandstone carvings dating back more than a thousand years.

In summer, The Bastion serves as a Tourism Infocentre. The nearby museum, on a hill overlooking the downtown core, displays a replica coal mine and a model of Nanaimo as it would have looked at the turn of the last century. Heritage buildings, many now housing shops and restaurants, can be found on Front Street and along winding Church Street, while a walk up Bastion Street leads to the Old City Quarter of restored brick-and-stone buildings where more shops and eateries await, including

the highly recommended Wesley Street restaurant which serves contemporary west coast cuisine.

Provisions can be purchased at the Harbour Park Mall (situated a few blocks south of the boat basin) which contains a supermarket, pharmacy, liquor store and specialty shops. A pedestrian-only waterfront promenade winds from the Boat Basin to Maffeo Sutton Park, location of an excellent children's playground and a man-made tidal pool called Swy-A-Lana Lagoon, beyond which are the marinas and chandleries lining Newcastle Island Channel.

Hammond Bay 13

Hammond Bay, six miles north of Nanaimo, provides shelter from northwesterlies but is exposed to easterlies. It's a good spot to wait out a strong headwind when proceeding up or down the west side of Georgia Strait and to regroup. During northerlies gusts and swells will snake around Neck Point into the bay, but the sand-and-mud bottom provides good holding ground. Anchorage can be gained at the head of the bay, opposite a Crown islet known locally as Shack Island.

During the Depression of the 1920s, as many as two dozen families squatted on this 4-acre islet, living in makeshift shacks. The men worked in the Nanaimo coal mines and augmented their income by rowboat fishing in local waters. They trolled for salmon with a hand line and for ground fish with a leg line – the latter tied around one of their legs.

Among the rowboat fishers living on Shack Island was the Luoma family from Finland. The father, Matt, and his two sons, Ed and Pat, established a boatyard on Shack Island, building their classic double-ended rowing skiffs with hand- or treadle-powered tools because there was no electricity. Driftwood logs of yellow cedar were their source of softwood lumber, and the hardwood needed for structural pieces came from an oak bar they salvaged from a hotel. With painstaking craftsmanship the Luomas produced lightweight but strong skiffs prized by local fishermen for their speed, handling and seaworthiness.

Many of the original dwellings still stand on Shack Island and descendants of these fishing families can claim inherited squatters' rights. Some of the shacks are used by summer campers who walk out to the islet at LW and set up temporary house in one of them. The nearby tidal lagoon is a protected reserve, and Hammond Bay's laid-back atmosphere is reminiscent of the 1970s, when a back-to-the-land movement saw the B.C. coast dotted with squatters.

Anchorage near Shack Island, Hammond Bay.

Sailing North: The last set of Gulf Islands begins with Lasqueti and Jedediah Islands, which are well worth including in the any sail plan. The two islands are split by **Bull Passage**, which usually has one or 2 knots of current flowing either north or south, depending on the tide. A thoroughfare for recreational boats, this pass is sometimes used by commercial fishboats and tugs with stick booms.

Bull Passage is a good haven if a SE gale is blowing in the Strait of Georgia, providing welcome shelter from the rough seas south of Lasqueti. During a northwesterly however, Bull Passage receives its share of wind but Jervis Island acts as a breakwater and reduces much of the swell coming into the pass. The best place to be in NW conditions is either in Deep Bay or tucked well into Boho Bay.

Whiskey Golf

Exercise Area WG is an underwater test range operated off Nanoose Bay by the Canadian Navy. Whenever Whiskey Golf is being used for testing non-explosive torpedoes, sonobuoys or sonars, vessels are not allowed to pass through the "active" portion of this restricted area, but can pass N of Winchelsea Island and E of South Ballenas Island in the safe transit lane, its location marked on CHS charts 3512 and 3459. The no-trespassing policy is for the public's safety, and even a killer whale passing through will result in a test being cancelled. Tests take place, on average, four days per week, usually Tuesday through Friday from 0800 to 1730, and active times are broadcast on VHF 21B and Weather 3.

The test site, established in 1967, is owned and operated by the Canadian government. It was chosen because its bottom topography is perfectly suited for technical acoustic testings. Most of the tests are conducted by Canadian and American surface ships and submarines. The range is linked to the U.S. Naval Underwater Warfare Centre at Keyport, Washington, and although the U.S. Government has invested heavily in the site, it is owned and operated by the Canadian government on land leased from British Columbia. Two other testing ranges are situated in quiet deepwater areas off Jervis Inlet.

Radio contact with Winchelsea Island Control can be made on VHF CH 10 or 16 for permission to transit WG.

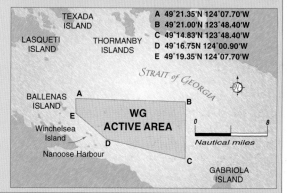

A	49°21.35'N 124°07.70'W
B	49°21.00'N 123°48.40'W
C	49°14.83'N 123°48.40'W
D	49°16.75N 124°00.90'W
E	49°19.35'N 124°07.70'W

Sunset over Whiskey Golf

Beautiful and secluded Sunset Cove gets the sunsets but not a lot of boats.

Jedediah Island 14

Long before Jedediah Island became a marine park in 1995, the anchorage at its north end was used by tugboats and fishing vessels working in local waters. Known locally as **Deep Bay** and protected from NW winds by Paul Island, it is one of the safest anchorages in the area although it can be crowded and, once the sun goes down, gloomy. Swinging room is limited and most boaters tie a stern line to shore, allowing a dozen or so boats to anchor in this sheltered cove. Be sure to set your bow anchor as close to the opposite shore as you can to get a good set and to be able to pull yourself away from your stern shore once the tide drops. We have seen numerous vessels get hung up by the stern and we have come close ourselves. A trail leads from Deep Bay, through an old-growth forest of fir, hemlock, arbutus and pine, to a hilltop meadow and the old homestead overlooking **Home Bay** on the east side of the island.

There are several other anchorages around Jedediah Island, none of which provide the same landlocked security as Deep Bay, but which are worth investigating if you are spending a few days around the island. Our two favourite coves are on opposite sides of the island – one is **Sunset Cove** on the west side opposite Boho Bay; the other is at the SE end and is known as **Codfish Bay**.

Sunset Cove has a reef at its entrance which knocks down wake from other boats and keeps westerly swell from coming into the cove but presents a hazard if trying to enter the cove at night. We keep the reef to starboard coming into the cove and favour the north shore where there is plenty of water (minimum of 12 feet). We set the bow anchor in the middle of the cove and either use a stern anchor or tie off to one of the trees on shore to lie parallel with the north shore, a rocky bluff dotted with evergreens. Holding is good in soft mud and shell, and minimum depth in the centre of the cove is about 12 feet (4 m). This little cove will fit two or three boats, with vessels using shorelines.

The next cove over, known as **Otter Cove**, also

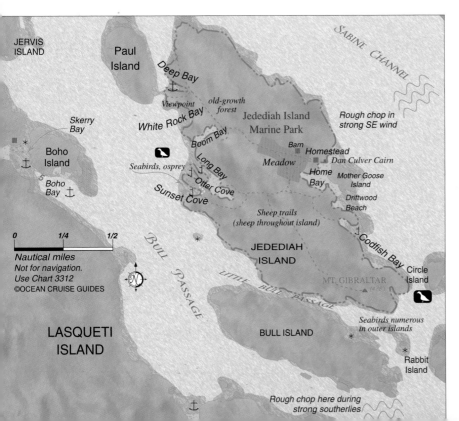

JERVIS ISLAND

Paul Island

Deep Bay

Skerry Bay

Viewpoint   old-growth forest

White Rock Bay

Jedediah Island Marine Park

SABINE CHANNEL

Rough chop in strong SE wind

Boho Island

Boom Bay

Barn

Homestead

Long Bay

Meadow

Dan Culver Cairn

Seabirds, osprey

Home Bay

Mother Goose Island

Boho Bay

Otter Cove

Sunset Cove

Driftwood Beach

Sheep trails (sheep throughout island)

Codfish Bay

Circle Island

JEDEDIAH ISLAND

0   1/4   1/2

Nautical miles
Not for navigation.
Use Chart 3312
©OCEAN CRUISE GUIDES

Bull Passage

Little Bull Passage

MT. GIBRALTAR

LASQUETI ISLAND

BULL ISLAND

Seabirds numerous in outer islands

Rabbit Island

Rough chop here during strong southerlies

fits one or two boats with stern lines. This spot provides similar protection to Sunset Cove with the same steep-sided features. This cove gets a bit more wake and swell however.

Long Bay and **Boom Bay** back onto mud flats which at LW can have that familiar decaying smell. However, we have seen lots of vessels contentedly anchored here when Deep Bay fills up. Part of the problem with these bays is that the bottom shelves steeply and many boaters are reluctant to drop the hook in a hundred feet of water and so they come too close to the shore when heaving the stern line. There is a nasty reef at the north entrance to Boom Bay which seems to regularly catch the unwary, so give your keel lots of room if anchoring in this small bay. **White Rock Bay**, the next over, is another popular spot and gets less swell and chop. This bay also gets the best sunsets. There is a rock reported just off the north outcropping.

Codfish Bay, entered from Sabine Channel, is sheltered from all NW winds and from moderate SE winds and swells off the Strait of Georgia by a cluster of small islands near its entrance. Inside this narrow cove, the setting is starkly beautiful with a cliff-sided islet forming part of the northeast shoreline and grassy bluffs on the opposite shore. A broad beach lies at the head of this narrow cove where a path leads inland and connects with other trails, one leading to the old homestead and fruit orchard at **Home Bay**. This is the former home of Al and Mary Palmer, the last private owners of Jedediah, who were known for their friendliness and hospitality toward visitors. A previous owner, a gentleman farmer from Ireland named Henry Hughes who owned Jedediah Island in the 1920s and '30s, was not so receptive to uninvited guests. Suspecting trespassers of poaching his sheep, the reclusive Hughes once greeted a tugboat captain named Jim Anderson with the pointed barrel of a gun and an order to get off his land. Anderson, who regularly anchored his tug in Deep Bay, was determined to befriend the bearded, bookish Hughes whose eccentricities were widely known and included setting a place at the table for his dog. So the next time he ventured

Above, trails on Jedediah Island are extensive and offer scenic views. Below, unique Codfish Bay has a wall of granite surrounding much of it.

JEDEDIAH ISLAND AT A GLANCE
CHARTS: 3312, 3512
LAT LONG: Deep Bay 49°30.32N 124°12.93W
PROS: Variety of anchorages, lots of room. Great island for walks with many good trails. Fair to good protection offered from most winds. Holding ground generally very good.
CONS: Some anchorages can be crowded. Limited protection from NW winds.
MUST DO: Explore the island, walk the trails. Try more than one anchorage.

Above, sheltered from all winds, Deep Bay attracts the most boats. Below, the view looking south from Home Bay, suitable for small boats only.

ashore he brought a peace offering – some back issues of Vancouver and London newspapers. Anderson later wrote that "folks had told me if he'd spend more time working his place and less time reading he would be better off, so I knew I had the right ammunition." Over time, Anderson befriended both Hughes and his black dog Caesar, inviting them back to his vessel one day for supper where the dog enjoyed dining at the special place set for him next to his master.

Well educated and wealthy enough to bring with him from Ireland a manservant, cook, gardener and shepherd to tend the sheep he planned on raising, Hughes was apparently more suited to the academic world than the farming life. After depleting his financial resources and losing all of his hired help, Hughes lived alone on the island with his faithful dog until meeting his future wife, an English nurse named Jenny, when she arrived one summer by boat with some sailing friends. Her party had ventured ashore to walk the trails when they bumped into Hughes who invited them to his house at the head of Home Bay. When sheep farming didn't pan out for Henry Hughes, he hoped to sell Jedediah Island to the Canadian Pacific Steamship Company for development as a summer resort, one that would compete with the Union Steamship Company's resort on Bowen Island, but the CPR instead purchased Newcastle Island near Nanaimo.

Jedediah Island was eventually bought, in 1949, by Mary Palmer and her first husband. The island, 640 acres in size, has never been subdivided and contains a network of sheep trails that pass through old-growth forest, open fields and a hilltop meadow. Human hikers share the trails with the island's four-footed residents which include deer, sheep and goats whose ancestors were left to graze on Jedediah by 18th-century Spanish explorers. The island's highest point, dubbed Gibraltar, stands at the south end of the island and is reached by a trail that ascends 500 feet above sea level, winding past ferns, salal and dwarf conifers. The summit provides views of nearby islands and Jedediah's rugged shoreline.

Overlooking the water at Home Bay is a plaque dedicated to the memory of Dan Culver – an outdoorsman, yachtsman and mountain climber who fell to his death in 1993 at the age of 41 after ascending K2. His will stipulated that a piece of coastal wilderness be saved, so his brother (the executor of Dan's estate) donated $1.1 million to a highly publicized fund-raising campaign to purchase Jedediah Island from the Palmers for preservation as a provincial marine park. The funds, as visiting boaters will attest, were well spent.

Above, Boho Bay is a good anchorage during a westerly. Below, Squitty Bay Marine Park.

LASQUETI ISLAND
Boho Bay / Skerry Bay 15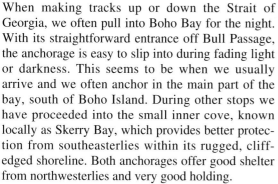

When making tracks up or down the Strait of Georgia, we often pull into Boho Bay for the night. With its straightforward entrance off Bull Passage, the anchorage is easy to slip into during fading light or darkness. This seems to be when we usually arrive and we often anchor in the main part of the bay, south of Boho Island. During other stops we have proceeded into the small inner cove, known locally as Skerry Bay, which provides better protection from southeasterlies within its rugged, cliff-edged shoreline. Both anchorages offer good shelter from northwesterlies and very good holding.

Squitty Bay Marine Park 16

This marine park at the southeast tip of Lasqueti provides shelter and limited dock space, but the anchorage is shallow and its entrance is a bit tricky – a small channel with about 5 feet (1.7 m) of depth at LW. Favour the channel's port side when entering the bay, leaving the mid-channel drying rocks to starboard. The anchorage is picturesque, with picnic tables overlooking the water. A park trail leads to a beautiful juniper reserve on the adjacent peninsula that was bought by the Nature Trust of B.C. – an organization that purchases park land, then hands it over to B.C. Parks for their care.

A quiet road leads out of the park and winds the length of Lasqueti Island to False Bay, the island's main harbour where the foot passenger ferry from French Creek docks. The roads on Lasqueti are pleasant for walking due to their limited car traffic as no car ferry docks at Lasqueti.

Scottie Bay 17

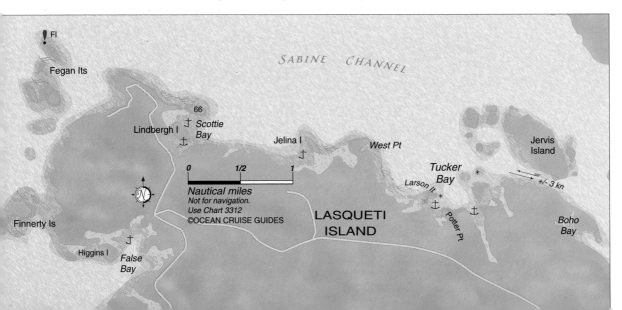

The inner cove of Scottie Bay provides excellent shelter in all winds.

Scottie Bay is an excellent anchorage on the northwest end of Lasqueti. The cove in the SW corner of this bay, south of Lindbergh Island, is sheltered from all winds and although tight, provides excellent anchorage for half a dozen visiting craft. Some small resident vessels are moored further inside at the west end of the bay. Entry is made through a narrow channel, staying close to the Lasqueti Island shore to avoid the reef extending halfway across the channel from Lindbergh Island.

There is a wharf and some buildings for a small fishing operation along the south part of the bay, and fish boats will arrive at almost any time of day and night. The road that connects to other parts of the island can be accessed here.

If the inside bay is busy, north of Lindbergh Island is another, more-open bay where we have anchored many times in settled weather. The holding is good and the bay provides adequate protection from NW winds and a perfect venue for viewing summer sunsets. We usually anchor S of the islet marked '66' on Chart 3312. Other good anchorages on the N side of Lasqueti include two locations in **Tucker Bay** – one just west of Potter Pointer and the other, to the east, in front of a wide creek bed. Both

Fl

Fegan Its

SABINE CHANNEL

66

Lindbergh I   Scottie Bay

Jelina I

West Pt

Jervis Island

Tucker Bay

Larson It

Potter Pt

+/- 3 kn

0   1/2   1

Nautical miles
Not for navigation.
Use Chart 3312
©OCEAN CRUISE GUIDES

LASQUETI ISLAND

Boho Bay

Finnerty Is

Higgins I   False Bay

provide good shelter in most winds. Another spot, sheltered from S winds, is north of **Jelina Island** and, although sheltered from the south and light north winds, it is subject to an uncomfortable swell during northwesterlies.

False Bay 18

When anchoring in False Bay, stay close to the bay's northern shore to avoid a local southwesterly that can send erratic swells into the anchorage. Called the Qualicum, this strong wind blows in from the Pacific Ocean, funnels down the Alberni Canal on Vancouver Island, then sweeps across Qualicum Beach and over the open water into False Bay. The public dock provides access to a store, pub and post office which is just up the road.

Several drying lagoons border the main anchorage which are pleasant to explore by dinghy. One of these secluded lagoons was once home to China Cloud, hand built and launched on Lasqueti Island by the late Alan and Sharie Farrell, legendary west coast sailors. This beautiful wooden vessel is engineless and, with two bilge keels drawing only 2 1/2 feet, the Farrells would pole her into shallow inlets where she sat comfortably on the mud at LW.

China Cloud, built by the Farrells, is shown here at anchor in a lagoon of False Bay.

A beautiful trail lies at the head of Anderson Bay.

Anderson Bay 19

At the SE end of Texada Island is an excellent haven, especially if you're slogging up the Strait of Georgia in a northwesterly. Much of Anderson Bay is a provincial park which encompasses the small island and peninsula, for a total of some 78 acres (35 hectares.) This anchorage can be approached easily from the south or from the east through the small pass between Texada Island and the small island protruding from the point. Minimum depth in the pass is about about 15 feet (4 m). Be sure to stay in the middle of the pass and be careful rounding the peninsula as the reef shown on the chart extends further south than you might guess. Holding is very good in thick mud, but stay well south of the log dump area where debris can be expected. The bay is open to south and SE winds.

A hike can be enjoyed on the old logging road that starts at the dumpsite on the west side of the bay and connects with the Pipeline Trail, which travels the length of the island. This is a fairly easy hike along the natural gas pipeline right-of-way and is a very pleasant way to spend a sunny afternoon beneath the forest canopy. Blacktail deer, birds and intertidal life can all be found in the park.

Tribune Bay Marine Park, Hornby Island 20

In settled weather, this is a splendid summertime anchorage. Its wide and sandy beach is considered one of the best in the Gulf Islands and is ideal for small children, sloping gradually into the water and allowing swimmers to wade a considerable distance from shore. This same shelving bottom forces boats to anchor a fair distance from the head of the bay.

The bay provides good shelter from the prevailing summer northwesterlies but is completely open to the south. The holding ground, however, is good (sand and mud) and most anchors should be able to handle summer breezes from the south. If stronger S winds (over 15 knots) are predicted, think about moving to Ford Cove on the west side of Hornby

Island, or Deep Cove on Vancouver Island or, in very strong SE winds, Comox Harbour. CHS chart 3527 gives good detail of this entire area.

Overlooking the entrance to Tribune Bay is beautiful Helliwell Park, a gift from a private citizen named John Helliwell. We have walked to this park after landing our dinghy along the bay's eastern shoreline where the sandstone bedrock has been eroded into mushroom-shaped outcroppings and honeycomb hollows. Parkland lies at the head of Tribune Bay, where a footpath leads up a grassy slope past windswept clumps of trees which give way to forest as the trail winds through a picnic area to the road. Follow this road for about a mile and a half to Helliwell Provincial Park where a sign-posted trail at the entrance takes you through thick stands of Douglas fir as well as arbutus and oak. At the edge of the forest is a sweeping meadow of golden grass which shimmers in the sea breeze. Beyond the edge of the bluff is a panoramic view of the Strait of Georgia with the mountains of Vancouver Island stretching across the horizon. The park's 3-mile circle walk goes right to St. John Point before looping back to the entrance. The sea cliffs below consist of interbedded sandstone and conglomerate rock, which attracts great numbers of nesting cormorants and gulls.

In 1997, Flora Islet, which lies within Tribune Bay Marine Park, was added to Hornby Island's park land. In spring this treeless islet is carpeted with wildflowers, as are the meadows of Helliwell Park.

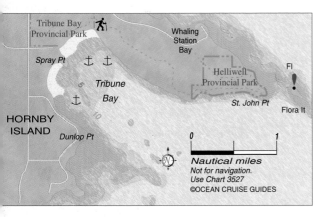

Tribune Bay, below and opposite, is the quintessential summer anchorage with a beautiful, broad beach.

Deep Bay, Vancouver Island 21

Of all places to run aground at anchor, Deep Bay seemed an unlikely spot. Maybe it was the name that lulled us into complacency. Or perhaps it was the scenic setting of this anchorage with its mountainous backdrop and sandy, grass-covered spit extending from the end of Mapleguard Point and once covered with maple trees before some houses were built there. During the 1946 earthquake, a huge wave engulfed this spit which, according to eye witnesses, completely disappeared for a few minutes.

Shoal water extends northward from the spit, jutting into Baynes Sound. After making the wide turn into Deep Bay, we dropped anchor in 24 feet (8 m) over a mud bottom and tucked ourselves close to the SW shore to gain some protection from the S winds that blow with force through this anchorage. It turned out we tucked in a little too close. Early next morning we were aground. Our first clue was the chatter of clam diggers on shore. They sounded uncomfortably close. Bill got up and noticed we were listing slightly to starboard. A glance out the

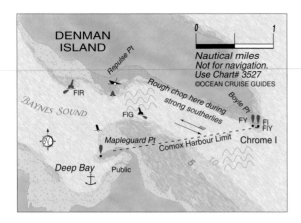

porthole as he turned on the depth sounder confirmed that we had just touched bottom. On a falling tide, our Spencer 35 had swung towards shore and planted her keel in the mud. We rowed out the spare anchor and tried to kedge off, but this didn't work because the tide was still dropping. Fortunately the ebb finished before *Sway* heeled right over. While the clam diggers went about their business, seemingly uninterested in the grounded sailboat lying awkwardly on her keel, we rowed the short distance to the exposed foreshore and plodded across the mud, our Scottish terrier tucked under Bill's arm. Most anchorages look prettier at HW than at LW, and as we gazed at our beached boat, this particular bay definitely looked less scenic, not to mention shallower, than when we had dropped anchor the previous evening. By noon we were afloat on a rising tide and able to depart Deep Bay.

Protection from strong SE winds is generally poor in Deep Bay and reports about the holding are mixed, with some people saying they have dragged in this anchorage. The problem may be that since the anchorage is so deep – anchoring depths start at over 85 feet (26 m) and shelve quickly from there – some boaters may not be putting out enough scope.

Not-so-deep Deep Bay snares another skipper.

Still, Deep Bay has the advantage of being near two great beach locations at Tribune Bay and Sandy Island Marine Park.

The passage leading to Baynes Sound from Chrome Island can be dangerous if a large tide is ebbing against a SE gale; such conditions can produce waves in the 10- to 15-foot range.

Sandy Island Marine Park 22

This island, known locally as Tent Island, is located on White Spit at the N tip of Denman Island and is a great beach stop. At spring LW, this drying spit of sand and mud connects Sandy Island and the adjacent Seal Islets to Longbeak Point on Denman Island, with over 2 miles of beach to stroll along. The area abounds in tidal pools thriving with crabs and other shell fish. When herring are spawning in spring, the beach at LW is often lined with bald eagles and cormorants enjoying the feast. Good temporary anchorage lies off the W end of Sandy Island, in about 50 feet (16 m), where the sand spit drops off sharply and provides protection from SE seas (but not SE winds). If a fresh NW is blowing, anchor in nearby Henry Bay in 50 feet (16 m), which is close enough to visit Sandy Island by dinghy.

Comox Harbour

Boaters heading up or down the west side of Georgia Strait can pull into Comox Harbour for fuel, provisions and some shoreside activity. The Beaufort Mountains and Comox Glacier provide a beautiful backdrop to this harbour, while the extensive breakwater provides shelter for visiting vessels. Crossing the bar into the harbour can be tricky in strong SE conditions during an ebb, when swells will develop at the entrance area and along the bar. Be sure to locate the red entrance buoy (FlR and marked P54) and come within a quarter mile to the south of it, then aim for the last red conical buoy to the west (P50, lighted). The shallowest area of the bar is

immediately east of the cone buoy. Range markers on the Vancouver Island shore are also of assistance in poor visibility. The area south and east of Cape Lazo must be given a wide berth during strong SE winds, when steep falling seas are common near the cardinal buoys. See Chart 3527 for detail.

The Comox Valley Harbour Authority welcomes visiting pleasure craft and monitors VHF Channel 66A. The guest moorage for recreational boats is on the E side of the main breakwater. Services include fuel, fresh water, 20-amp plug-ins and a marine pump-out. Nearby are washrooms, showers, laundry facilities and a hydro-hoist, while within easy walking distance are shops, pubs and restaurants. Anchorage is available between the permanent buoys and the DND wharf area, where the holding is good.

Local attractions include Filberg Heritage Lodge & Park, located a short walk east along the harbourfront. The park grounds feature flower gardens and paths that lead to the stone-and-timber home of the Swedish-born lumber baron and philanthropist Robert Filberg, who arrived as a young man in 1909 and soon became chief engineer of Comox Logging Company. Near the water stands a totem pole depicting the four main family crests of the Comox First Nations – thunderbird, sun man, white whale and bear.

Comox (a native word for 'plenty') was chosen in the 1850s as a training site by Britain's Royal Navy. Settlers soon moved into the area to farm the fertile valley, and Comox became a service centre after a wharf was built in 1874 and steamer traffic began arriving. In 1942, a Canadian Forces Base was opened here, its personnel now specializing in air-sea rescue. The Comox Air Force Museum is beside the airport, and visitors can wander freely among the vintage aircraft on public display at the Heritage Airport.

Above, a Hobie Cat sailing in Comox Harbour. Below, the breakwater provides good protection.

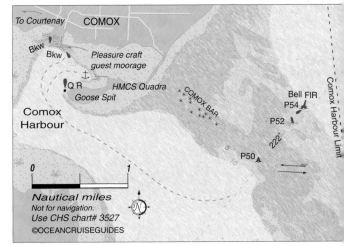

CHAPTER THREE

VANCOUVER & THE SUNSHINE COAST

Hardy Island Marine Park

The mainland side of the Strait of Georgia encompasses one of B.C.'s busiest boating areas, its waters stretching over 100 miles from Boundary Bay in the south to Desolation Sound in the north. In between are the Fraser River estuary, the port city of Vancouver, the glacier-carved fjords and inlets of the Sunshine Coast, and some of the best beaches this coast has to offer.

Strait of Georgia

This major body of water is busy with commercial traffic, including car ferries, freighters, tugs with barges and, from May through September, cruise ships. A vigilant lookout is a must when crossing the ship traffic lanes, which are about 5 miles wide near Sand Heads. In clear weather, freighters can be spotted heading to or from Boundary Pass and Vancouver and we limit our time in these traffic lanes by cutting straight across them. Recreational vessels should always defer to large ships in the strait and in a close situation we make our intentions obvious by making course changes that cannot be misunderstood. Freighters don't always respond to calls on Channel 16 (tugs and cruise ships are better on that score); if you don't get a response, try Victoria Traffic on Channel 11 or Vancouver Traffic on Channel 12 to get details on the movements of freighters and alert them to your sailing plan.

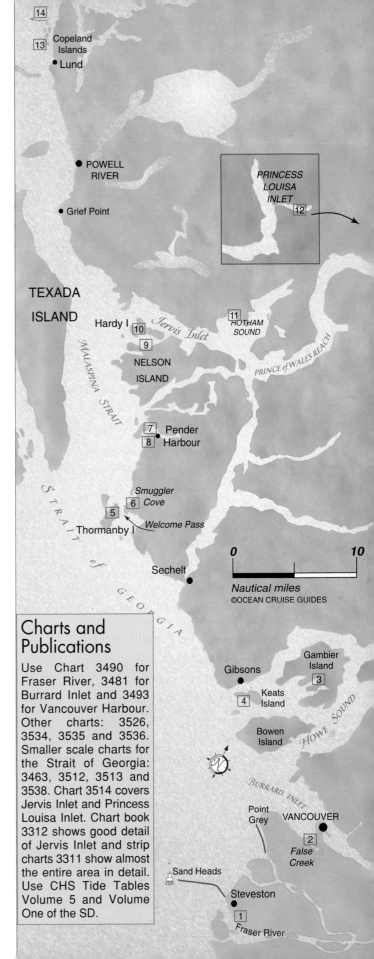

The southern Strait of Georgia is dominated by the Fraser River's outflow, especially from May to early August, when the freshet is running. This freshwater run-off from mainland mountains pushes huge volumes of green, silt-laden freshwater over 12 miles across Georgia Strait to Active Pass and south to Boundary Pass. So, unless you're planning a visit to the village of Steveston on the Fraser River, you should keep to the west side of the strait when northbound. This is especially important if you're bucking an ebb which can reach 5 knots near the river banks stretching from

Charts and Publications

Use Chart 3490 for Fraser River, 3481 for Burrard Inlet and 3493 for Vancouver Harbour. Other charts: 3526, 3534, 3535 and 3536. Smaller scale charts for the Strait of Georgia: 3463, 3512, 3513 and 3538. Chart 3514 covers Jervis Inlet and Princess Louisa Inlet. Chart book 3312 shows good detail of Jervis Inlet and strip charts 3311 show almost the entire area in detail. Use CHS Tide Tables Volume 5 and Volume One of the SD.

Point Grey to Point Roberts. Timing your passage with a flood tide is a good idea, but be aware that during a large flood there is a set onto these banks on the east side of the strait with flood currents often in the range of 2-3 knots. Currents in the middle of the strait are usually about 1-2 knots. The Sailing Directions also notes 'residual currents' can cause water circulation to differ significantly from that expected from the combined action of wind, tides and river runoff, meaning the current you expect to help, can be contrary.

The prevailing summer winds in the Strait of Georgia generally blow NW or SE, with variants to the south and southwest. A northwest breeze will usually start mid-morning and often build to 12-to-16 knots by early afternoon, with a resulting chop of 2 to 3 feet. A SE wind will be foretold by high cirrus clouds and mare's tails. Southwest winds can be transition breezes, indicating a clearing trend, and are otherwise common near the south end of Saturna Island and off Qualicum Beach where they can blow strongly. Winds from this location are renowned in summer, often sending a tedious ground swell into False Bay on Lasqueti Island making the anchorage uncomfortable. Mainland inlets such as Howe Sound often have onshore winds in the day (up the sound) and offshore winds at night (down the sound).

Coast Guard continuous marine weather broadcasts should be monitored throughout the day, as revisions for the Strait of Georgia are common. Luckily, safe havens are never too far away. Boaters arriving from U.S. waters can pull into Point Roberts, where an excellent marina provides transient moorage, before heading north into Canada.

The seas in the Strait of Georgia can quickly develop into a steep, uncomfortable chop in moderate winds. Especially nasty seas can develop within 3 or 4 miles of Roberts and Sturgeon Banks, and also at Halibut Bank and off the major passes when a northwest wind is blowing. The most dangerous seas, however, are those off Sand Heads at the mouth of the Fraser River's south arm.

The Fraser River

All arms of the Fraser River influence the Strait of Georgia but none more so than the main (south) arm, its entrance marked by the imposing structure at Sand Heads. This tower was rebuilt in 2002, when the old white-and-orange building was removed and a new white structure erected 100 feet further west. The light has changed to a flashing green every 6 seconds, visible for 10 miles. Between strong currents, shoal banks and freighters entering the river, the mouth of this arm is one of the most hazardous bodies of water on the B.C. coast. Add NW winds to an ebb current and the ensuing steep chop makes conditions challenging for all small vessels.

A trip up the main arm of the Fraser River is worthwhile, however, and is an opportunity to visit the ports of Steveston and Ladner (5 and 10 miles upstream respectively). Low-powered vessels navigating up the river should arrive well after the flood has started (reference Point Atkinson) and this is especially important during the months of freshet from June to early August when the river is discharging large volumes of water from mountain snowpack. During these months we usually arrive at Sand Heads with an hour or two left in the flood. Currents can be unpredicable around Sand Heads and the buoys should be given lots of room when entering the river mouth. Using chart 3490, small craft often proceed upstream keeping the red buoys to port by a boat length or two where the stream is weaker and where they will be out of the way of commercial traffic. This route can be taken right up to S16 near Garry Point (see page 138 for route).

A sailboat under spinnaker heads north in the Strait of Georgia.

There is a good chance you will encounter freighters or tugs with barges at some point on the river and, as always in tight channels, these vessels have the right of way because of their limited ability to maneuver. The waters around Sand Heads can be nerve-racking when commercial traffic is entering or leaving the river. As mentioned, you can report your vessel's position to Victoria Traffic on Channel 11 if you want clarification or direction entering the river. If you want to speak to a ship entering the river, which we have done, pilots can usually be reached on Channels 16 or 17.

A common sight on the Fraser is the bright-red pilot vessel heading up and down the river. The crew are members of the Fraser River Pilots Association and they guide the comings and goings of large freighters. They also have to know the river like the back or their hand and they receive regular updates of channel depth from the Coast Guard. Silting of the main channels during freshet can be dramatic and depths can change overnight. Mike Van Der Gracht, chairman of the association, says he remembers having to send freighters on the wrong side of the red buoys (between S4 and S6) during a time of severe silting in 1999. "That really confused the yachts coming up the river," he recalls.

The job of keeping the river clear of sediment falls to the Fraser River Port Authority (a federally mandated port authority operating under the Canada Marine Act) which keeps the dredge Fraser Titan stationed near Steveston for most of the winter and early spring months. Patiently dredging away at areas of infill (typically between Steveston and the bend to the west and south to S4), the dredge usually draws silt into its belly and hauls it away to a storage site to be sold for construction purposes. In late spring, when dredging might damage fish stocks during salmon fry migration, the Port Authority relies on the strong current during freshet to take most of the silt out into the strait. Dredging is crucial not only to ensure there is enough depth for freighters, but to keep the river deep enough to handle the additional water volume during freshet. Without dredging, large parts of the river delta could flood during spring freshet.

In late July and August, gillnetters are often fishing the river between Sand Heads and Steveston. Although the openings are fewer and shorter than in the past, boaters cruising the river in this period should monitor weather channels or call the Department of Fisheries at (604) 666-2828 for a 24-hour recording on opening information. Recreational vessels must keep clear of the nets laid across the river by gillnetters.

Top, Sand Heads light station at mouth of Fraser River. Below, tugs, barges and freighters are part of the constant traffic encountered on the river.

Above, Steveston Harbour.

Below, Captain's Cove Marina near Ladner.

Fraser River History

The Fraser River is B.C's most important watershed. It originates in the Rocky Mountains, at Yellowhead Pass, and meanders for 850 miles before emptying into the Strait of Georgia. Along the way, its tributaries drain a watershed of nearly one-third of the province and its basin supports half of the province's agricultural land. Thousands of waterfowl nest annually on the river's delta and migrating salmon return regularly to the mouth of the Fraser, which contains North America's chief spawning grounds for the Pacific salmon. In the 19th century, salmon canning became a thriving industry and by the 1890s there were 45 canneries on the river, concentrated in Steveston and Ladner, the latter founded in 1868 by William and Thomas Ladner, farmers from Cornwall, England.

Steveston 1

Enter Steveston between Garry Point and the QR beacon on Steveston Island, favouring the W side of the entrance where depths are greater. Transient moorage is available on the E side of the main wharf; you can call Steveston Harbour Authority at 604-272-5539 to reserve a berth. The office is at the top of the main wharf. Although anchoring is prohibited in summer in the W end of Cannery Channel, you can anchor east of the Esso dock, with the better overnight anchorage lying at the far east end of Cannery Channel in about 12 feet (3.5 m). This is near the last marina basin. Holding in sand and mud is good but you will experience some current and boat traffic in the channel. The channel's east end is closed by a rock finger.

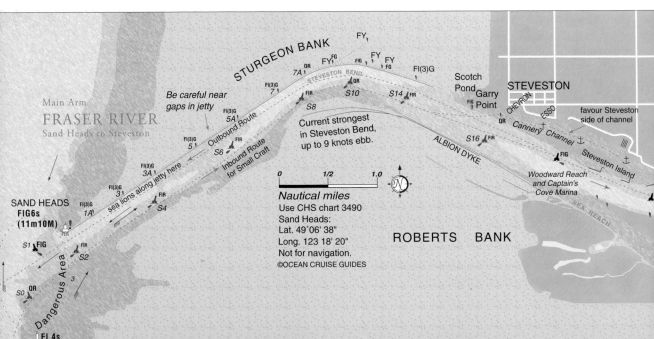

Steveston's townsite was established in 1878 by a dairy farmer named Manoah Steves. The village quickly grew into a bustling harbour, busy with large numbers of fishboats arriving to unload their catches. Local canneries employed hundreds of workers, and sailing ships from around the world pulled into port to take on cargoes of canned salmon. The Gulf of Georgia Cannery, built in 1894, is now a national historic site and since 1994 has operated as a museum, open to visitors throughout the summer.

Steveston is known for its excellent seafood restaurants which overlook the fishboat docks, where fresh fish is sold off the boats. Other nearby attractions include marine stores, gift shops, and a waterfront park with cycling trails.

Ladner

Located upriver from Steveston, the town of Ladner can be reached via Sea Reach (its entry opposite Steveston Island) or by proceeding along the river's main arm to Deas Slough where visitor moorage is available at Captain's Cove Marina, a full-service facility with a fuel dock, pub/restaurant and adjacent golf course. The only drawback to this marina is the shallow depths at the entrance to Deas Slough which are less than 3 feet at zero tides.

The town of Ladner is a half-hour walk (or a 5-minute taxi ride) west of Captain's Cove Marina. The town, centred around the historic village, has shopping centres and several good restaurants, including La Belle Auberge which serves fine cuisine in one of Ladner's many heritage buildings.

Aerial view of the Fraser River and Steveston, with the tall ship Nippon Maru in foreground.

Outbound on the Fraser

When heading downriver, stay on the starboard side of the river to give way for commercial craft. We sometimes come closer to the jetty if we spot sea lions or seals on the rocks. This must be done carefully as the jetty has several gaps through which a strong cross-current flows, creating turbulent water on spring ebbs. Currents during freshet on strong ebbs can be up to 10 knots.

In summer months, NW winds will create very steep seas off Sand Heads for a distance of 2 to 3 miles into the Strait. These seas can be dangerous to small craft if winds reported at Sand Heads are above 16 knots, so be sure to listen to the weather before heading down river. If strong winds are predicted, try to leave early in the morning.

Once your vessel is clear of the last buoys off Sand Heads, a crossing to Active Pass, Porlier Pass or Silva Bay is straightforward. Porlier Pass is 12 miles from Sand Heads, while Active Pass and Thrasher Rock (the entrance to Silva Bay) are just over 13 miles away. Further up the Strait, Lasqueti Island, Smuggler Cove and Bargain Bay (near Pender Harbour) are all about 40 miles distant.

VANCOUVER 2

Set on the scenic shores of English Bay, the city of Vancouver is an exciting destination to approach by boat. Its famous skyline seemingly rises from the waters of English Bay and floats on the horizon. Gradually the shoreside parks appear as a green ruffle on the watery edge of a city flanked to the north by mainland mountains and to the south by sand banks and beaches. If approaching from the south,

be very cautious of the drying and shifting shoals off Spanish Banks, and stay well west of all markers with your depth sounder on at all times.

Upon entering False Creek or Coal Harbour, boaters can obtain moorage at several marinas located right on the downtown's doorstep, within walking distance of the city's major attractions. Visiting boaters can obtain city information and assistance with making slip reservations at the **Boater Welcome Centre**, which is located in a restored boat moored at the False Creek Yacht Club on the north shore of False Creek under the Granville Street Bridge. This centre can be reached by phone at 604-648-2628 or (toll-free) 866-677-2628. The fuel dock at the entrance to False Creek and the fuel barges in Coal Harbour are also sources for temporary moorage information.

False Creek

False Creek is easy to enter by boat and the marinas lying along its south shore offer transient moorage when slips are available. The docks at Granville Island Public Market provide a few hours of free moorage for boaters who want to shop for provi-

> ### FALSE CREEK AT A GLANCE
> **CHARTS:** 3493, 3311, 3463
> **PROS:** False Creek puts you right in the centre of Vancouver. Holding varies, with good sticky mud along the north shore and soft mud along the south shore. Well sheltered with good views of the city.
> **CONS:** Sometimes crowded. Limited places to secure your dinghy for protracted stays on shore. Because of the alignment of False Creek, westerlies and eastlies can whistle through here.
> **MUST DO:** Go shopping at nearby Granville Island and walk the seawall to Vanier Park and the Vancouver Maritime Museum. Take one of the passenger ferries across False Creek to visit Vancouver's West End and downtown attractions, including an array of excellent restaurants. Go for a walk in Stanley Park.

sions or enjoy the restaurants there. There are two excellent marine stores located on Fir Street, a short walk from Granville Island.

Anchorage for small craft is available in False Creek along its south side, between Spruce Harbour Marina and Heather Civic Marina, provided you are not in the way of commercial craft heading to and

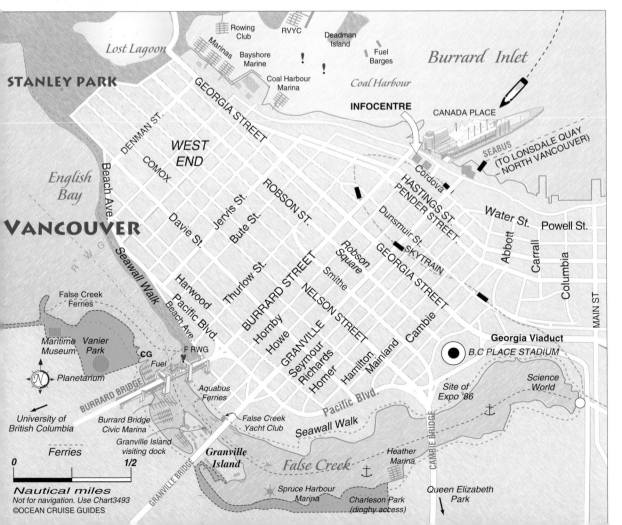

from the head of False Creek. In recent years, the proliferation of boats permanently moored in this area has generated a plethora of complaints by local residents. New regulations allow visiting boaters to anchor here for a maximum of two weeks in summer and three weeks in winter. Permits to do so, which are free, can be obtained at the **Boater Welcome Centre**. Dinghy access from this anchorage can be made at Charleson Park, which is a 5-minute walk to Granville Island. Passenger ferries servicing Granville Island will sometimes pick up passengers from anchored vessels.

False Creek's remarkable transformation from industrial waterway to livable neighborhood began in the early 1980s when its former railyards on the north side became the site of Expo 86, Vancouver's world's fair. Granville Island, on the south shore of False Creek, had already opened in the late '70s, and was soon attracting visitors year-round to its public market, craft boutiques, restaurants and live theatres. The visitor information centre, which provides maps and other information, is opposite the Public Market.

Vanier Park can be reached on foot from Granville Island via the False Creek seawall or by False Creek Ferries. Several museums are located within this park, including the Vancouver Maritime Museum which houses the historic St. Roch, the first vessel to navigate the Northwest Passage. Floating vessels are displayed in the adjacent Heritage Harbour dock.

English Bay, at the foot of Denman Street, is the West End's favourite gathering spot and can be reached by taking a ferry to the north side of the creek and walking along the seawall which runs along Sunset Beach at the entrance to False Creek. The blue-coloured False Creek Ferries, which make

Above, a view of False Creek, showing (from left to right) Granville Island, Burrard Bridge Civic Marina, entrance channel and False Creek Yacht Club (in foreground). Below, Stanley Park's Brockton Point at the entrance to Coal Harbour.

regular summertime runs to the Maritime Museum at Vanier Park, depart from the west end of Granville Island while the multi-coloured Aquabus ferries use the east float of the visitors dock fronting the Public Market. You can access other creekside attractions, including Science World at the head of False Creek, with these ferries.

Above, aerial view of Point Grey and downtown Vancouver with English Bay in centre. Below, a powerboat passes Point Atkinson lighthouse.

Vancouver Shoreside Attractions

Coal Harbour, inside Burrard Inlet, is reached via the First Narrows, which is spanned by the Lions Gate Bridge. Sailing vessels must be under motor power when transiting the narrows, where tidal currents can be strong and commercial traffic heavy. Once inside this scenic harbour, boaters can choose from two large marinas offering guest moorage and immediate access to Stanley Park and the West End. A reservation at any of the city marinas is recommended when planning a visit to Vancouver.

Anchoring is strictly prohibited in Coal Harbour.

A few blocks east of Coal Harbour is the downtown core, where a Travel Info Centre is located at the Waterfront Centre, right across the street from Canada Place Cruise Terminal – a city landmark with huge white sails crowning the waterfront complex which contains a luxury hotel, restaurants, shops and a CN IMAX Theatre. Built for Expo 86, a world's fair celebrating Vancouver's 100th birthday, the terminal is busy throughout the summer with passengers boarding cruise ships bound for Alaska while sightseers stroll the outdoor promenades.

For a bird's eye view of the city, visit The Lookout!, downtown Vancouver's highest viewpoint at the top of the Harbour Centre Tower, located a few blocks east of Canada Place. Nearby is Gastown, Vancouver's original townsite, where visitors can stroll along cobblestoned Water Street and enjoy upscale shops and restaurants housed in refurbished brick buildings. Beyond are the streets of Chinatown, the second largest in North America.

Directly west of Coal Harbour is Stanley Park, the largest urban park in Canada, which originated as a 1,000-acre military reserve in the mid-1800s. A 12-pound muzzle-loader was eventually installed near Brockton Point, but its use became one of a time check for local fishermen when it would fire each Sunday at 6 p.m. Today, it booms across the water each evening at 9 o'clock. A pedestrian seawall encircles Stanley Park, which can also be toured by horse-drawn tram or on a free shuttle bus, both departing from the lower parking lot throughout the summer. Bicycles and rollerblade skates can be rented near the entrance to the park. Among the park's many attractions are a rose garden, a totem pole display and the Vancouver Aquarium.

HOWE SOUND

A popular weekend destination for Vancouver-area boaters, Howe Sound is one of the most developed fjords on the B.C. coast. Its shorelines and islands are edged with waterfront homes and its waters are busy with car ferries transporting passengers between West Vancouver's Horseshoe Bay and the bedroom community of Bowen Island or Langdale at the bottom of the Sunshine Coast. The busy Sea-to-Sky Highway (leading to Whistler) traces Howe Sound's eastern mainland shore, where suburban homes cling to the mountainside, their sun decks providing cliffside views of waters once used only by dugout canoes.

Several villages and fish camps of the Squamish First Nation dotted the shores of Howe Sound when Spanish explorers arrived in 1791. The following year Captain Vancouver's expedition surveyed the sound and named it after Admiral Earl Howe, a British naval hero. Other place names in Howe Sound, such as Bowen Island, recall officers who served under Howe.

Bowen Island was transformed from a logging and farming community into a holiday resort in 1920 when the Union Steamship Company bought property at Snug Cove, including the local hotel. In summer, day-trippers came by the thousands from Vancouver to enjoy company picnics and dances in the pavilion. Snug Cove remains a popular destination for Vancouver-area boaters, while the upper reaches of Howe Sound attract those seeking a bit of off-season seclusion among its steep-sided channels.

In summer, Howe Sound's wind pattern is dominated during sunny weather by daytime sea breezes (southerlies or southwesterlies) and nighttime land breezes (northerlies). This pattern is frequently interrupted by a passing weak front or the prevailing westerly flow of air from the Pacific onto the coast.

Above, regatta sailing in Queen Charlotte Channel in Howe Sound. Below, aerial of Howe Sound showing Gibsons and Keats Island.

In winter, Howe Sound is dominated by inflow and outflow winds. If a southeasterly is blowing, it funnels into strong up-channel winds. If a Squamish is blowing from the north, fed by cold air masses inland, it will cause strong down-channel winds.

Gambier Island 3

The southern bays of this large and mountainous island were once used extensively for storing log booms, to which boaters would moor their vessels with the aid of metal eye hooks (called 'dogs') which they would hammer into an outside log when docking, then remove when leaving. Now that most logs are sorted and stored on dry land, visiting boaters should be prepared to anchor. Because there is some leftover logging debris lying on the bottom of these bays, a trip line is recommended.

Halkett Bay Marine Park

This bay offers sheltered anchorage during summer winds, but is open to southerly winds and wash from passing ferries. A cluster of rocks lies in the NW part of the bay, and a detached rock with less than 6 feet (2 m) over it sits in the middle of the fairway near the head. Log booming continues in Halkett Bay, along its east shore.

The marine park provides one mooring buoy and a dinghy float. On shore are wilderness walk-in campsites and trails leading in several directions. One connects with Centre Bay; another winds through forested uplands to Mt. Artaban, which has a lookout tower at its summit. The last third of this trail is rough and steep, and the 6-mile (10 km) round trip takes about 5 hours. Another trail leads to Brigade Bay on the east side of Gambier.

Port Graves has a wide open entrance with room for lots of boats in good holding.

GAMBIER ISLAND AT A GLANCE
CHARTS: 3311, 3526, 3512
LAT LONG: Port Graves, 49°27.48'N 123°21.79'W
PROS: Gambier Island, with numerous good anchorages remains very popular throughout the year especially with Vancouver boaters. A convenient destination for northbound vessels after visiting the city. Walks beginning from the government dock at Camp Artaban are excellent. Holding ground is generally very good.
CONS: Busy in summer. The south-facing anchorages are somewhat exposed to winds from this direction. Old logging debris in south bays.
MUST DO: Walk the trails from Port Graves.

Port Graves

Also known as 'East Bay' or 'Long Bay,' this is the principal anchorage in Howe Sound, providing shelter in all winds except for southerly gales. Many boaters anchor near the head of the bay near the red public dock in depths ranging from 15 to 45 feet (5 to 15 m) in sticky mud. In summer, moderate afternoon southerlies usually die down by early evening. Occasionally, strong outflow winds blow over the saddle from Bridgade Bay making Centre Bay a better bet in such conditions for overnight.

Leading from the dock is a system of trails, maintained by hikers and members of local yacht clubs, which provide excellent walks on the southest side of Gambier Island. Follow the trail markers that lead visitors around the property belonging to Camp Artaban, which is located above the public dock. Beyond the camp are trails leading to Centre Bay, Lost Lake, Mt. Artaban and Brigade Bay.

Centre Bay

Although recent residential development has lessened its appeal, Centre Bay remains attractive for local boaters with numerous spots along the shoreline to drop anchor. The holding ground is very good but boaters have lost ground tackle that snagged on discarded logging gear, such as cables, near the head of the bay or close along the shoreline. An anchor trip line is a wise precaution here .

The busiest area is on the west side of the bay behind a small point known locally as 'The Hook' with anchorage in 18 to 24 feet (6 to 8 m). This spot provides superb shelter in summer conditions, but approval has been granted for local landowners to build a large dock in this cove, which will diminish its attractiveness and anchoring room. Royal Vancouver Yacht Club has an outstation on the west side of Alexandra Island.

West Bay

Wide and deep, West Bay is often quieter than Gambier's other bays, with a good view out to the Strait of Georgia. However, recent residential developments along the shore of this bay have limited shore access and diminished the bay's feeling of remoteness. On entering West Bay, beware of extensive shoal water on the east side of the entrance; the safest route is along the bay's western shore. Near the head of the bay, rotting remains of the wreck of the ship *Sir Thomas Lipton* can still be seen at LW.

Brigade Bay

Located in the middle reaches of Howe Sound, on the east side of Gambier Island, this bay is fairly well sheltered from S winds and is recommended during summer calms. A treed bluff forms the bay's northern entrance, and it's just inside this point that we have anchored, setting the stern anchor off the broad mud beach at the head of the bay, then powering forward to drop the bow anchor in the steeply shelving bottom.

The anchorage provides sublime views of mainland mountains, including The Lions. On shore, trails lead through the thin forest behind the bay where recent logging has taken place. At the turn of the last century, this land was the site of a homesteader's cabin and fruit orchard. Trails lead from Brigade Bay to the head of Port Graves, and an old logging road leads up the north face of Mt. Artaban.

Top, remains of wreckage of Sir Thomas Lipton in West Bay as seen in late 1980s. Bottom, Brigade Bay provides a view of The Lions.

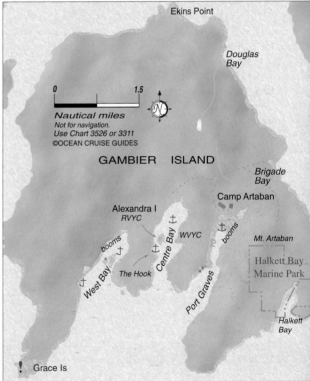

Ekins Point provides good anchorage in most conditions with a view of a pulp mill and mountains.

Ekins Point

On the 'back side' of Gambier Island, this nook lies west of Ekins Point, between a thumb of land and a private marina. We have anchored here in 30 feet (10 m) at LW with a stern line to shore. The down-channel view of the Port Mellon pulp mill is not the prettiest, but the view in the other direction is of snowcapped mountains. A swath of grass graces the water's edge just inside the eastern point of this nook, while the rest of this pristine section of shoreline is treed and hilly, part of a recreation reserve that extends for a half-mile on either side of Ekins Point. Moderate winds dissipate in the vicinity of Ekins Point, allowing for sheltered anchorage inside this small nook. Strong outflow winds will gust through the anchorage and this spot will experience swell from the channels outside.

Plumper Cove Marine Park, Keats Island 4

Located just 3 miles (5 km) east of the town of Gibsons, this popular cove offers good shelter from the Strait of Georgia with marine park facilities including a wharf for boats and dinghies, and mooring buoys. SW of the park is a roomy anchorage with depths of 40 to 50 feet (12 to 15 m). The holding is generally good in soft mud and shell, but due to current running between Keats Island and the Shelter Islets, there are kelp patches which frustrate some anchors. We generally anchor just to the NE of the larger islet to stay out of afternoon westerlies which snake around both sides of this islet.

On shore is a pebble swimming beach and a grassy picnic area which provides access to the park's well-maintained hiking trails. The loop trail takes about 1 hour to hike, while a longer trail leads

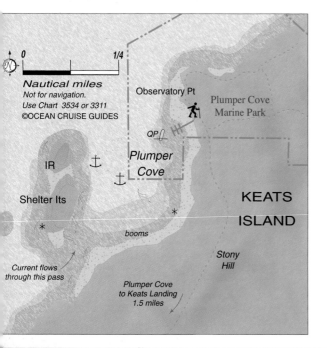

Plumper Cove Marine Park on Keats Island.

to Stony Hill (710 ft) and Lookout Mountain, the highest point on Keats Island at 795 feet.

The shallow gap between Keats Island and the mainland's Steep Bluff can present a hazard at LW when a strong W or S wind is blowing. Often a bad chop develops from the bar out to Gower Point. During such conditions, exiting Howe Sound via Barfleur Passage may be a better tactic. In light winds during mid- to HW, the bar is safe for most vessels. Use charts 3534 or 3311 for good detail.

THE SUNSHINE COAST

The Sunshine Coast, which stretches from Howe Sound to Desolation Sound, has been attracting visitors since the late 1800s when steamships began running excursions to summer resorts along this scenic coastline. The name 'Sunshine Coast' was coined by Harry Roberts, whose grandparents founded Roberts Creek in 1889. The Union Steamship Company adopted the term for its 1925 brochure, touting the region's 'Sunshine and Sea-charm along Holiday Shores on the Gulf Coast.' The Sunshine Coast does receive more sunshine than Vancouver, but less than Victoria. Its appeal for boaters lies more in its variety of anchorages – from beach-lined bays and craggy coves to glacier-carved fjords.

There are also plenty of marinas along the Sunshine Coast, where much of the shoreline is lined with recreational and retirement homes, and where several major towns are located. Gibsons marks the S end of the Sechelt Peninsula and is the former setting of the long-running *Beachcombers* television series. The show's fictitious coffee shop, called Molly's Reach, is now a seafood restaurant located at the head of the wharf in Gibsons. Sechelt is the cultural centre of the Lower Sunshine Coast. The Sechelt natives' House of Hewhiwus (Chiefs) is located here and contains an art gallery, theatre and museum. Each August, the town hosts the Sunshine Coast Festival of the Written Arts, which is held at the heritage Rockwood Centre.

Farther up the coast is **Secret Cove**, another former steamship landing and today the site of several marinas. Farther north still, **Pender Harbour**'s numerous bays contain several marinas and coastal communities, the main one being Madeira Park where a marina, public wharf and shopping mall are located. Madeira Park is also home to Harbour Publishing, founded by Howard and Mary White in 1974 and featuring regional titles by B.C. authors about living and working along the coast.

Powell River, on the Upper Sunshine Coast, is a classic company town (declared an official heritage district in 1995 by the federal government) which grew up around the pulp-and-paper mill that was constructed between 1910 and 1912. A large marina is located south of the city in Westview, a seaside

Malaspina Strait / Welcome Passage

Malaspina Strait, like the Strait of Georgia, is a wonderful place if the wind is with you. For northbound cruisers, however, summer northwesterlies often start blowing in mid-morning and usually increase to 15 to 20 knots. As in the Strait of Georgia, a short steep chop quickly develops and will often be in the 2- to 4-foot (.8 to 1.2 m) range which can make the journey a real slog. Fortunately, there are good anchorages along the southern half of the 30-mile strait in which to pull out if the going becomes too tedious.

The first hurdle to enjoying the delights along Malaspina Strait is getting beyond Merry Island and Welcome Passage, where currents can be 3 or more knots. During spring tides, the current will be felt at the S end of Merry Island and, if you happen to be bucking an ebb, it can make the trek up to Smuggler Cove a long day. If setting out from the W side of Georgia Strait (the Nanaimo area or Silva Bay, for example), following a course to the west of the Thormanby Islands is a good way to approach Smuggler Cove, Bargain Bay or Pender Harbour. You will be free of obstacles and most of the current and tug traffic. Also, if a northwesterly is blowing, Lasqueti and Texada will provide a decent lee right up to Pender Harbour.

A sailboat northbound in Malaspina Strait passes the water tower located near Stillwater Bay.

suburb of Powell River, and has sheltered moorage for transient vessels in the South Harbour which is inside the southern breakwater. A chandler is located at the marina and fuel is available. Groceries and other supplies are a walk up a steep hill and shuttles are sometimes available from the marina.

South of Grief Point, the **Beach Garden Resort and Marina** is undergoing major renovations to its restaurant and hotel but continues to welcome visiting boaters at its substantial 90-berth marina. Showers, fuel in summer and a beer-and-wine store are on site. Restaurants are nearby. This is a good pull-out in strong winds.

Near the north end of the Sunshine Coast, at the end of the Sunshine Coast Highway, is the coastal hamlet of **Lund** – founded in 1889 by Charles and Frederick Thulin, brothers who had recently arrived from Sweden. They named the townsite Lund, which means 'forest grove' in Swedish, and built the historic Lund Hotel. Lund is the termination of Highway 101 which connects, via ferry, with Vancouver. For boaters, Lund operates a public wharf and there is a haulout here also.

Another small settlement was established at **Bliss Landing** during World War I, and today this former steamship stop is home to a private marina.

Anchorage at peaceful and protected Surrey Islands in Buccaneer Bay.

The Sunshine Coast has several sandy beaches, thanks to the glaciers that left behind drift deposits of pulverized sand, gravel and clay when they retreated from the Strait of Georgia some 10,000 years ago. Remnants of these glacial outwash plains are found at Harwood, Savary and Hernando islands, but the area's most extensive beach is at Buccaneer Bay in the Thormanby Islands.

Buccaneer Bay, [5] Thormanby Islands

The unconsolidated sands and gravels on North Thormanby Island have been eroded, over time, from its steep cliffs and washed onto the shores of Buccaneer Bay, forming a sweep of sandy white beach that stretches down the west side of the bay to its head. Part of the beach is actually a drying flat that joins North Thormanby with South Thormanby; the passage between them drying at about 10 feet (3 m). A tiny marine park is located at Grassy Point, at the S tip of North Thormanby, but most boats anchor closer to the head of the bay off Gill Beach or in adjacent **Water Bay**, which offers better protection from northwesterlies.

Another option is to anchor behind the **Surrey Islands** on the east side of Buccaneer Bay, and dinghy over to the beach. This anchorage offers better protection from NW winds and is only exposed to southwesterlies. Using a stern line, we like to pull ourselves close to the South Thormanby Island shore. To minimize wake from the many small powerboats zipping around the bay we anchor with the bow pointed west. Holding ground throughout the bay is very good in mud and sand.

Captain Richards and the officers of H.M.S. *Plumper* apparently had horse racing on their minds while surveying these waters in 1860. They had just received the 'welcome' news that the racehorse Thormanby, owned by Mr. J.C. Merry, had won the

---

BUCCANEER BAY AT A GLANCE
CHARTS: 3535, 3311, 3512
LAT LONG: 49°29.60'N 123°59.06'W
PROS: Great family destination with excellent swimming on the fine sand-and-shell beach. Holding is good in sand and mud. Large bay with many anchoring opportunities. Surrey Islands provide best-sheltered spot. Smuggler Cove is a short distance away for more secure anchoring or for exploring by dinghy.
CONS: Open to NW winds; head of bay also open to S winds. Swells from Malaspina Strait can make their way well into the bay.
MUST DO: Go swimming off this beautiful beach.

Above, aerial view (looking east) of Buccaneer Bay, Welcome Passage, Smuggler Cove and Secret Cove. Bottom right, sand beach at Buccaneer Bay.

Derby back in England and that Buccaneer had placed second. Other area names inspired by the horse races at Epsom include Oaks Point, named for 'The Oaks', an annual race for three-year-old fillies, and Tattenham Ledge, named for 'Tattenham corner', the race course's last turn.

For boaters approaching Buccaneer Bay's entrance, the thrill of the turf gives way to some navigational caution. Both Epsom and Oaks Points should be given a wide berth on rounding due to a continual shifting of the shallows, which could result in less depth than indicated on the chart. When entering Buccaneer Bay from Welcome Passage, between Tattenham Ledge and the drying reef off Derby Point, be aware of tidal streams that could push your vessel sideways onto the rocks. In December 1953, a tug seeking shelter from a SE gale hit a reef here, rolled over and sank, claiming 5 of the 7 crewmen's lives. The captain had been able to radio a Mayday, but two tugs tied up in nearby Secret Cove didn't respond to the distress call because their crews had switched to the broadcast band to listen to a hockey game. This tragedy prompted the Tugboat Owners Association to require all tugboats monitor the emergency channel and the Department of Transport ordered the broadcast band removed from all radiotelephones.

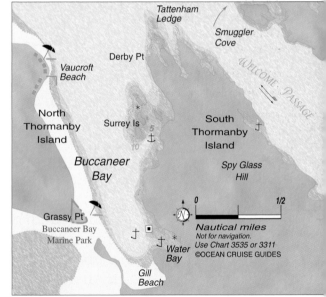

Tattenham Ledge
Smuggler Cove
Derby Pt
Vaucroft Beach
WELCOME PASSAGE
North Thormanby Island
Surrey Is
South Thormanby Island
Buccaneer Bay
Spy Glass Hill
Grassy Pt
Buccaneer Bay Marine Park
Water Bay
Gill Beach

0   1/2

Nautical miles
Not for navigation.
Use Chart 3535 or 3311
©OCEAN CRUISE GUIDES

Top, Sway moored to the 9-metre island during strong NW winds. Above, powerboat enters Smuggler Cove during NW blow. Left, trail through park includes boardwalk sections. Bottom, private cabin on small islet at entrance to inner anchorage.

Smuggler Cove 6

Some anchorages beg to be explored by dinghy, and Smuggler Cove is one of those. This provincial marine park's collection of islets and coves offers an idyllic setting for leisurely rows, especially on clear summer evenings when a setting sun lingers above the treetops and casts its glow across the anchorage. One of the Sunshine Coast's most popular boating destinations, Smuggler Cove manages to retain the charm of a small-craft anchorage even on busy summer weekends when boats are tucked into its every nook and cranny.

Anchoring in Smuggler Cove usually requires vessels to tie a stern line ashore or set a stern anchor in order to make room for other boats. Strong NW winds can make their way through the small islands near the entrance, sending gusts to boats anchored behind the small islet marked '9' on strip chart 3311. There is a least depth of 6.5 feet (2 m) in the small easternmost cove and the channel leading to it. This cove has the best protection from all winds.

Near the entrance to Smuggler Cove, vessels tie to shore with bows pointed first south and then west, following the curve of the shoreline. Although this stretch is fairly protected from NW winds, southerly gusts make themselves keenly felt.

Eight islets lie within the cove and most are connected to shore by drying reefs. Private cottages occupy some of the islets, built before Smuggler Cove was transferred to the Parks Branch in 1971. The cove is completely surrounded by parkland and its trails wind through the surrounding woods to the outer shorelines and inland to a small parking lot used by visitors arriving by road.

Smuggler Cove was once the hideout of Larry 'Pig-Iron' Kelly, a 19th-century seaman of the Royal Navy who, in a career move, turned to smuggling immigrant workers by boat from Canada into the United States. During prohibition, the cove was said to be a storage area for bootleg whiskey that was distilled on Texada Island and smuggled by boat into American waters. Providing shelter from all winds and discouraging casual visitors with its narrow entrance, the cove was a natural choice for clandestine activities.

SMUGGLER COVE AT A GLANCE
CHARTS: 3535, 3311, 3512
LAT LONG: 49˚30.91'N 123˚58.09'W
PROS: Secure and roomy anchorage; good protection from most winds with good holding. Interesting area to explore by dinghy or on foot.
CONS: Often busy, usually requires a stern line.
MUST DO: Hike trails, explore islets and reefs.

One of several inviting nooks in Smuggler Cove.
Most vessels stern-tie for secure overnight moorage.

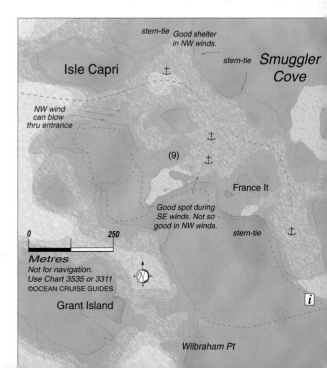

Smuggler Cove's narrow entrance no longer keeps pleasure-seeking boaters away but it still demands careful pilotage and a close eye to Chart 3535 or 3311. When entering, boaters should favour the Isle Capri's shore (which has a provincial park sign). Although entering in strong winds can be intimidating, the wind and chop die quickly once you're just past the park sign.

Pender Harbour 7

Pender Harbour is a major service centre for pleasure craft cruising the Sunshine Coast, its collection of populated bays offering an array of good marinas, repair facilities stores, restaurants and a nearby golf course. The most popular anchorage in Pender Harbour is **Garden Bay** which also has a provincial marine park. This anchorage has good holding in 30 feet (10 m) over mud. Swinging room is limited and your anchor light should be on at night to alert boats heading to and from Madeira Park. NW winds can gust through the anchorage keenly.

The marine park has a dinghy dock connecting to a trail leading inland for a mile to the spectacular views from Mount Daniel, its summit a protected archaeological site in recognition of its importance to the local Sechelt natives. Before a smallpox epidemic in 1782 wiped out 90 percent of the native population in the Strait of Georgia, the shores of Pender Harbour were the location of a major settlement. Its main village, situated at Garden Bay, con-

The dinghy dock and anchorage at Garden Bay, with Madeira Park on the far shore.

sisted of seven huge longhouses – 800' long by 300' wide by 50' high. The native cemetery on the waterfront is now a protected archaeological site.

Other anchoring options for smaller craft in Pender Harbour include Hospital Bay and Gerrans Bay, just south of Dusenbury Island. Gunboat Bay at the head, is a pretty bay which provides good holding in soft mud but entry is along a narrow channel with a least depth of 2 feet (.7 m). Current and a drying rock that lies close to the N shore in the entrance dissuade many cruisers.

Several marinas line the shores of Pender Harbour including the large public wharf at Madeira Park. With over 600 feet of visitor moorage available, this is a good location to reprovision at the nearby grocery stores and liquor store.

Bargain Bay 8

Entered off Malaspina Strait between Edgecombe Island and the east side of Francis Peninsula, this excellent harbour extends south of Pender Harbour

---

PENDER HARBOUR AT A GLANCE
CHARTS: 3535, 3311, 3512
LAT LONG: Garden Bay, 49°37.71'N 124°1.34'W
PROS: Pender Harbour and area has some good anchorages and is generally very well protected. Many good marinas. Fuel, groceries and marine supplies can be purchased here. Good dinghy exploring and hiking at Garden Bay Marine Park.
CONS: Can be a little hectic on weekends with small powerboats and dinghies zooming about. Many rocks and reefs to watch for.
MUST DO: Explore Canoe Pass by dinghy. Go for a walk at Garden Bay.

and is joined to it by a narrows. Vancouver-area boaters heading north like this spot – it is a short drive off the watery highway north and is usually quiet. Two rocks, each with less than 6 feet (2 m) of water over it, lie in the entrance fairway; the SW rock is large and locals have marked it with a makeshift white float. When entering, favour the starboard side of the channel, keeping the makeshift buoy to port for safe passage between the two rocks. If the buoy is not there, favour the east shore and follow the contour of this shoreline into the main anchorage.

The anchorage at the head is well sheltered from most winds (strong southerlies will send gusts into the west side of the bay) and the holding is good in depths of 40 feet (12 m) in sticky mud. Bargain Narrows, sometimes called Canoe Pass, connects this anchorage with Pender Harbour. It leads from Bargain Bay to Gerrans Bay, and is navigable at or near HW in a dinghy only, for it dries over 6 feet (2.1 m). Overhead, a road bridge connects the mainland with Francis Peninsula, formerly known as Beaver Island. Bargain Bay has retained an atmosphere of bygone days, when the Pender Harbour area was

Anchorage at head of Bargain Bay. Nearby narrows connects with Pender Harbour

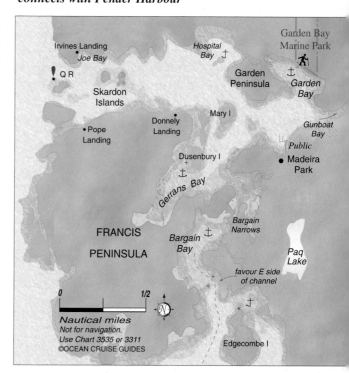

Spilsbury's Coast

Coastal pioneer Jim Spilsbury (1905-2003) spent much of his long life living and working along the Sunshine Coast. When he was nine, his English-born parents moved from a farm in the Fraser Valley to Savary Island where they lived in a large tent for the next 10 years. The tent's platform was made of planks salvaged from the beach and the tent frame supported canvas walls. In 1924, his Cambridge-educated father received an inheritance and the family built themselves a comfortable home beside the wharf. Spilsbury's mother, who had enjoyed roughing it, didn't like being back in a real house and within a year had moved into the shed out back.

As a young man in the 1920s, Spilsbury began selling and servicing radio equipment in remote coastal communities up and down the south coast, travelling by boat and then, in 1944, by floatplane. This single aircraft was the beginning of what would become Queen Charlotte Airlines, a commercial carrier that Spilsbury sold in 1955 to return full-time to exporting radiotelephone equipment.

In his later years, Spilsbury and his second wife owned a cabin at Ballet Bay on Nelson Island, to which they traveled from Vancouver in their cabin cruiser *Blythe Spirit*. His entertaining anecdotes about life on the B.C. coast in the last century are contained in his bestselling books *Spilsbury's Coast* (co-written with Howard White) and *Spilsbury's Album*. His days in the airline industry are retold in *The Accidental Airline*. All three books are published by Harbour Publishing, located at Madeira Park, Pender Harbour.

*The narrows joining Pender Harbour and
Bargain Bay can be traversed by dinghy at HW.*

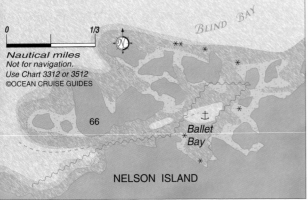

Nautical miles
Not for navigation.
Use Chart 3312 or 3512
©OCEAN CRUISE GUIDES

BLIND BAY

66

Ballet
Bay

NELSON ISLAND

much less developed. The anchorage is quiet compared to Garden Bay, and loons still visit here in summer.

A temporary anchorage lies at the mouth of Bargain Bay. This scenic spot is north of Edgecombe Island and its reefs and rocks are all visible, allowing for straightforward pilotage and making it a good pull-out spot if you're arriving late at night. Although the holding is good, southerly winds can blast through the anchorage.

Ballet Bay, Nelson Island   9

Nestled along the southern shores of Blind Bay behind a cluster of islets, Ballet Bay is well sheltered with good holding ground. There are, however, several reefs and rocks encumbering the entrance into the anchorage, and the Sailing Directions advises mariners without local knowledge to enter at LW, when the reefs reveal themselves. Entry is best made from the west, proceeding with caution, for a rock lies well off the point on Nelson Island that juts into the anchorage. Submarine cables are another hazard to avoid in Ballet Bay, and the location of these are marked on Chart 3312 which has excellent detail.

Once the hook is set, the numerous islets beckon to anyone who enjoys poking around by dinghy or kayak. Waterfront homes surround the anchorage, precluding the possibility of hiking to Hidden Basin. (Hidden Basin is best visited by dinghy because of its treacherous entrance. We know of one boater who was trapped in Hidden Basin for several days waiting for a tug to arrive after his sailboat was wrecked in the shallow, bottleneck entrance.)

Ballet Bay, named for the ballerina Audree Thomas whose parents homesteaded here, is a bit of an anomaly in an area dominated by place names associated with famous officers and battles of the British navy. Horatio Nelson's victory at Copenhagen is recalled in the names of Blind Bay and Telescope Passage. It was at this battle that Nelson claimed not to see his commander-in-chief's signal of recall because he had put his telescope to his blind eye.

Telescope Passage is also a useable exit for small craft wanting to make their way further north into Jervis Inlet and the delights of Hotham Sound and Princess Louisa Inlet. The passage has a least depth of about 23 feet (7 m) but with rocks in mid-channel and on the west side, it must be transited carefully, favouring the Nelson Island shore.

*Ballet Bay offers sheltered anchorage at the
mouth of Jervis Inlet.*

Above, Hardy Island anchorage. Right, adding the finishing touch to rock art on Musket Island.

Hardy Island (Musket Island) Marine Park, 10

First impressions needn't be lasting impressions when it comes to an anchorage. The first time we sought shelter along the southern shores of Hardy Island, at the mouth of Jervis Inlet, the spring weather was wet and dreary, and the area looked uninspiring. We anchored in the 9-fathom cove and spent the night listening to rain pounding on our coachroof. Years later we visited Hardy Island again when the summer weather was hot and sunny, and not a drop of rain had fallen for weeks. It was now the site of a marine park, initially called Musket Island, then changed in 2004 to Hardy Island because this was the name commonly used for the anchorage (the park encompasses Musket Island and the foreshore of Hardy Island, which is private).

The day we arrived at the Hardy Island anchorage, we had taken advantage of favourable winds and made a run from the Copeland Islands down to Jervis Inlet. By early afternoon the seas were building in Malaspina Strait as a northwesterly funneled between Texada Island and the mainland, and we were glad to pull into the lee of Hardy Island. Again we sought shelter along Hardy Island's southern shore, but this time we pulled into the anchorage formed by tiny Musket Island, which at LW is

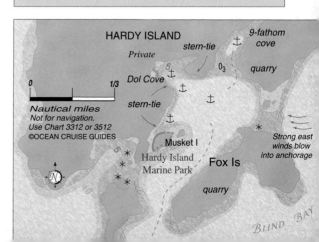

HARDY ISLAND ANCHORAGE AT A GLANCE
CHARTS: 3312, 3311 and 3512
LAT LONG: 49°43.74'N 124°12.62'W
PROS: Marine park; undeveloped; excellent anchorage with room for lots of vessels, large and small. Good holding and well protected. Swimming can be enjoyed from the clean rock foreshores.
CONS: Can be busy at height of season; some exposure to southeasterly winds. Limited hiking.
MUST DO: Swim and explore tidal pools.

HARDY ISLAND
Private
stern-tie
9-fathom cove
0.3
quarry
Dol Cove
stern-tie

0
1/3
Nautical miles
Not for navigation.
Use Chart 3312 or 3512
©OCEAN CRUISE GUIDES

Musket I
Hardy Island Marine Park
Fox Is
Strong east winds blow into anchorage
quarry
BLIND BAY

joined at its western end to Hardy Island by a drying tombolo. A few boats were anchored here with stern lines to the Hardy Island shore, but there was room enough for us to tuck well into this bight and tie off. This is a secure spot with good depths at LW (at least 10 feet). Anchoring depths are greater (50 feet or more) near shore along other parts of this pretty bay. Holding is very good throughout the anchorage.

This T-shaped anchorage is sheltered from most winds, especially northwesterlies. (If a strong SE wind is in the offing, Ballet Bay would be the safer anchorage.) Mediterranean-style mooring allows many vessels to tie along the shoreline thoroughly the anchorage. Large vessels often anchor in the middle of anchorage at the entrance where depths and room allow for two or three big boats.

Musket Island is a pleasant spot to picnic or explore the many tidal pools and there is a short trail around the perimeter of the island. Swimming is good, with wide flat rocks along the shore of Hardy and Musket Island, providing convenient and safe access into the water.

An old granite quarry on Hardy Island, adjacent to this anchorage, has resumed operations but its activities do not spoil the appeal of this marine park. The quarry first operated during World War II, when Hardy Island was owned by a Seattle financier named LeRoy Macomber. He owned the island from 1930 to 1951, during which time his caretaker turned it into a deer sanctuary. The island was later logged extensively by a series of owners and present timber growth is about 20 years old.

Harmony Islands   11

This picturesque cluster of four islets lies along the eastern shores of Hotham Sound, where forest-clad mountains provide a stunning backdrop. A small anchorage known locally as Kipling Cove lies amid the three northernmost islets, one of which is part of **Harmony Islands Marine Park**. (The two other islets are privately owned.) A rock lies at the entrance to this tiny cove with less than 6 feet (2 m), and there is no room to swing, so a stern line to shore is required. If the cove is filled with boats, there is additional anchorage in 15 to 30 feet along the east side of the islands and also opposite, along the mainland shore. In settled conditions there is also anchorage behind the islets near Syren Point in 90' and using a stern line to shore. The pass between the southernmost of the Harmony Islands and the mainland has less than 3 feet (1 m) at LW.

Opposite, aerial view of Hotham Sound and Harmony Islands. Inset, pretty Kipling Cove.

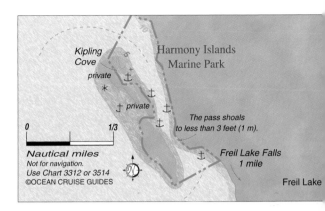

The winds that funnel up and down the reaches leading to Princess Louisa Inlet tend to dissipate in Hotham Sound, and on a calm night at the Harmony Islands, the only sound is the distant roar of Freil Lake Falls, which tumble 1,400' into the still water. Holding in the anchorage is good in mud and shell.

The Harmony Islands were named by Dr. Campbell Balmer, a Vancouver dentist who, with two friends, bought the four islands in 1932 for $248. His son, Jack Balmer, recounted in an article he wrote for *Pacific Yachting* in 1995 that each summer his family would travel to the Harmony Islands aboard their cabin cruiser and tie up to the small dock his father and friends had built out of beach logs. Their nearest neighbour was a hermit living up from the beach on St. Vincent Bay, for whom they would bring fresh bread and pipe tobacco whenever they visited. During World War II, fuel rationing and other restrictions took the pleasure out of boating for Dr. Balmer and he sold both his boat and his island. His two friends also sold their ownership in the other three Harmony Islands.

According to veteran cruiser and writer Sven Donaldson, it is possible to hike up to spectacular Freil Lake. His interesting story on this, in the July 2002 issue of *Pacific Yachting*, describes hiking up forested slopes to the base of the prominent rocky knob that's about 1500 feet north of the falls and from here skirting around its northern flank to follow a 40-degree slope up its backside to the summit. This very challenging hike takes over 2 hours, requires backcountry experience and should only be undertaken in dry conditions.

Princess Louisa Inlet   12

Erle Stanley Gardner, the American writer who created Perry Mason, was deeply moved when he first laid eyes on Princess Louisa Inlet. "One views the scenery with bared head and choking feeling of the throat," he wrote in *Log of a Landlubber*. "It is more than beautiful. It is sacred."

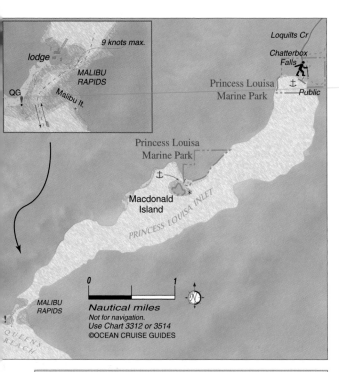

Princess Louisa
Marine Park

Macdonald
Island

PRINCESS LOUISA INLET

0   1

Nautical miles
Not for navigation.
Use Chart 3312 or 3514
©OCEAN CRUISE GUIDES

MALIBU
RAPIDS

QUEENS
REACH

PRINCESS LOUISA AT A GLANCE

CHARTS: 3312, 3514
LAT LONG: Chtbx Falls, 50°12.25'N 123°46.28'W
PROS: This spectacular marine park includes mooring buoys, stern pins, a boat dock and a dinghy dock. For boaters who want to disembark passengers there are a number of campsites, a picnic shelter and toilets. Beautiful scenery, perhaps unsurpassed on the southern B.C. coast. Good (and challenging) hiking.
CONS: Can be busy, dock use limited. Well off the major routes and a long drive each way. Sometimes a battle to get through Malibu Rapids if timed wrong.
MUST DO: Enjoy the sublime setting and go for a hike.

Anyone who has guided a boat to the head of a breathtaking fjord such as Princess Louisa Inlet has no doubt shared Gardner's sense of reverence. Deepwater fjords flanked by mighty peaks are nature's cathedrals, their humbling presence a reminder that we are mere mortals whose time amid these earthly paradises is a gift to be cherished. These are places so serenely beautiful, a person can't help but believe that some omnipotent force had a hand in their creation.

Most B.C. boaters sooner or later make the pilgrimage to Princess Louisa, one of the most stunning fjords on our coast. For sailboats, afternoon inflow winds often help when heading up Prince of Wales Reach, the first of three steep-sided reaches that twist inland from Jervis Inlet. Combined with a flood tide, boaters can make good time travelling the 35 miles to the inlet, passing beneath the cliffs of Marlborough Heights and into Princess Royal Reach. Winds usually die in Queens Reach.

The entrance to Princess Louisa Inlet lies halfway along this reach, where **Malibu Rapids**, with currents up to 9 knots, should be traversed close to slack water. Although there are no obstructions in the pass, there can be impressive turbulence and other boat traffic to deal with – skippers should ensure they keep their vessels on the starboard side of the channel. Malibu Islet presents a blind corner for northbound vessels and in poor visibility it might be a good idea to alert southbound traffic via radio or airhorn of

Sailing up Prince of Wales Reach with an inflow wind of 20 knots.

Top, View of Chatterbox Falls and anchorage at Princess Louisa Inlet. Above, Macdonald Island anchorage. Right, Malibu Rapids.

your approach. Just inside the rapids, on the north shore, is an impressive lodge with an outdoor swimming pool. It was built in the 1930s as an exclusive retreat for Hollywood movie stars and moguls. Today it is a summer youth camp.

Once through the pass, mariners witness one of nature's grandest glories, their vessels dwarfed by the lofty mountains and chalky white waterfalls that plunge into the still water. A narrow gorge carved by glaciers, Princess Louisa Inlet's sheer rock walls rise to heights in excess of 6,000 feet. At its head you will find the Chatterbox Falls tumbling 1,800 feet down tiers of granite into the turquoise water.

It was here, in the 1920s, that a Nevada prospector named James (Mac) Macdonald, obtained land and built a log cabin. After years of welcoming mariners to his own piece of paradise, Mac donated his property in 1953 to the Princess Louisa International Society, and it became a provincial marine park in 1965. He wanted the inlet preserved "as God created it, unspoiled by the hand of man" so that "all may enjoy its peace and beauty." To this end, BC Parks and the Society play a joint role in preserving the inlet in its natural state and maintaining the park's facilities, which include a picnic shelter, a dinghy dock and a large float where boaters can moor for up to three days.

Anchoring is possible on the shelf at the base of Chatterbox Falls, where current from the falls will keep your vessel from swinging into shallow water at LW. Mooring rings for stern lines have been installed a few hundred yards west of Chatterbox Falls. On shore, a loop trail leads to Chatterbox Falls where signs warn visitors to be cautious on the slippery rocks. A much more strenuous hike can be made along a very rough trail that climbs up the mountainside to an old trapper's cabin. This is a hard 2-hour climb but worth it for views of the inlet.

In 1972 a special campaign resulted in the Princess Louisa Society raising sufficient money to build a shelter for boaters – named the James F. Macdonald Memorial Lodge. That same year, the Society acquired Hamilton Island (situated about midway up the inlet) and 30 acres of low land east of the island, as well as a couple of other small islands. The island has been renamed **Macdonald Island** and boaters can tie to one of six mooring buoys installed E of the island or anchor with a stern line to either shore (look for stern rings). A dinghy dock serves the park's mainland shore.

In 2001, the Society secured options to purchase the remaining freehold land in the inlet from Weyerhaeuser Canada over a 10-year period. Two years later, the Society, in partnership with the Nature Conservancy of Canada and with the generous support of the Tula Foundation, Weyerhaeuser and Society members, purchased the 2,221 acres immediately surrounding Mac's original lands and added it to the marine park. The Society is continuing to raise funds to acquire the remainder of the land under option.

Copeland Islands 13

The Copeland Islands have long been a popular roadstead for commercial vessels, and log booms are still regularly secured to concrete abutments on the east side of Thulin Passage, which runs between the mainland and these picturesque islands. Now a popular marine park conveniently situated en route to Desolation Sound, the Copeland Islands are enjoyed by pleasure boaters as both a day stop and, in settled conditions, an overnight anchorage.

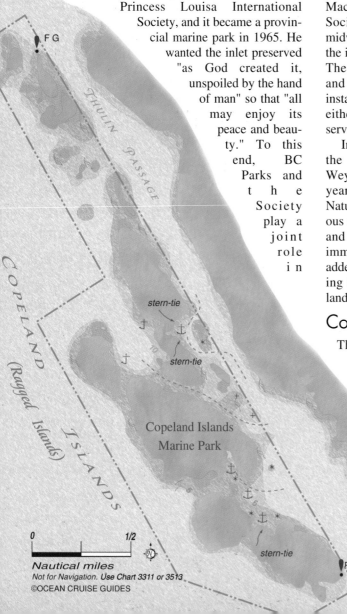

FG

THULIN PASSAGE

COPELAND (Ragged Islands) ISLANDS

stern-tie

stern-tie

Copeland Islands
Marine Park

stern-tie

Fl

0   1/2

Nautical miles
Not for Navigation. Use Chart 3311 or 3513
©OCEAN CRUISE GUIDES

We have anchored in several spots, including the anchorage halfway along the island chain where the marine park sign is posted. This scenic cove, accessed off Thulin Passage, is somewhat protected by an islet from the wash of passing vessels but not from southeasterlies. When these are forecast, we have moved around to the other side of the island where the view of the sunsets are lovely, but swell from the Strait of Georgia can make the anchorage uncomfortable.

One of our favourite spots for anchoring is the passage running between the two southernmost islands. There is good protection along the southern shore of this passage in the lee of the island marked '73'. You can either use a stern line to stay clear of the reefs in the bay or ride freely in the area clear of the rocks to the N. We sometimes anchor inside the nook on the northern shore where we tie a line to a tree on the bluff that rises above the anchorage. The

Above, anchorage off Thulin Passage. Below,
Sway anchored in cove between the two southern
islands. Keep drying rock to port on entry.

COPELAND ISLANDS AT A GLANCE
CHARTS: 3311, 3538 3513
LAT LONG: 50°0.61'N 124°48.56'W
PROS: Marine park; undeveloped; adequate protection from moderate winds with generally good holding. A miniature archipelago which is excellent for dinghy exploring and has several spots for swimming and hiking. Good views on west side of islands.
CONS: Some anchorages open to wind and swell. Can be busy. Anchorage on Thulin Passage side gets some wake from passing vessels. Current throughout.
MUST DO: Explore island chain by dinghy.

channel with deeper water is east of the drying rock. Although this is a good place to anchor, you can expect some swell and gusts will come around the corner of the western point during NW winds. If such winds are predicted, tuck yourself as far as possible into this small cove. At the western entrance to this anchorage is a foreshore of pink granite that forms tiered steps into the water. On sunny summer days, as the rising tide laps across this smooth stone, the water is warmed by the sun-baked rock, making it a lovely place to ease into the water for a swim.

The Copeland Islands are also ideal for exploring by dinghy or by kayak, and the hiking is easy through thin forests of arbutus and spruce. There are a few wilderness campsites on these pristine islands but no facilities except two pit toilets.

Known locally as the Ragged Islands, the islands' name was changed by the Canadian Hydrographic Service in 1945 to honour Joe Copeland, an American trapper and handlogger who came to the area in 1900 and settled at Portage Cove. Copeland was one of several colourful characters living in the vicinity of Desolation Sound in the early 1900s. He served as a Confederate soldier during the American Civil War and afterwards, according to Jim Spilsbury in his book *Spilsbury's Coast*, he became an outlaw, joining a renegade gang that robbed stagecoaches. Upon escaping to Canada and the remote B.C. coast, 'Old Joe' relived his war years by meeting the steamboat dressed in full Confederate army uniform.

The beach at Spilsbury Point.

Hernando Island 14

One of the most beautiful beaches of the Sunshine Coast lies at the north end of Hernando Island, extending in both directions from Spilsbury Point. On several trips north we have dropped anchor either west of the point in about 60 feet or around the corner in Stag Bay, between Spilsbury and Hidalgo Points. It's a short row ashore for lunch from either location to this lovely stretch of tan-coloured sand on the west side of the point.

The views from here are sweeping. To the west is barren Mitlenatch Island, a nesting and breeding site for thousands of birds, especially glaucous-winged gulls. The island, a provincial nature park, receives relatively little rain (the prickly pear cactus grows here) and, because of the long swim, few predatory mammals threaten the young nesting birds.

Directly across from Stag Bay, on the north side of Baker Passage, lie the **Twin Islands** where there is a decent anchorage in settled conditions in Echo Bay. In 1940 a mining engineer named Dick Andrews bought the Twin Islands and had a 14-bedroom log house built on the neck between the two islands. Andrews had become wealthy from his business interests in Japan but could see trouble coming and returned to Canada just weeks before Japanese warplanes bombed Pearl Harbour in December 1941.

In 1961 a German aristocrat (and nephew of Britain's Prince Philip) bought the Twin Islands. The Prince and Queen Elizabeth, accompanied on board the Royal Yacht Britannia by their daughter Princess

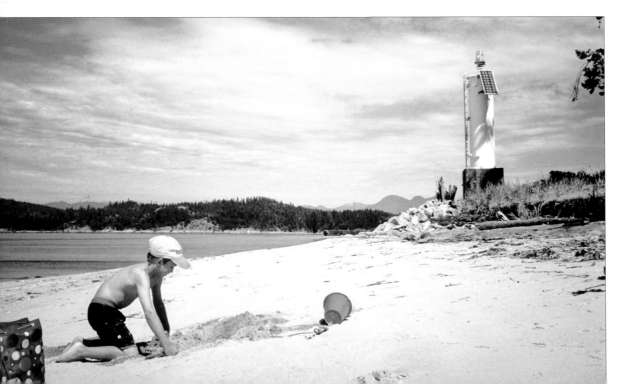

Anne, anchored off these islands in 1971 and spent a day ashore at the log lodge set on manicured grounds and maintained by caretakers.

Hernando and Cortes Islands were named for Hernando Cortes, conqueror of Mexico, by the Spanish explorers Galiano and Valdes while surveying these waters in June 1792. The *Sutil* and *Mexicana* had sailed up the Strait of Georgia with the *Discovery* and *Chatham*, commanded by Captain George Vancouver, after the two survey parties chanced upon one another off Point Grey. Vancouver was himself busy bestowing place names on the islands and channels in the vicinity, including Savary Island which, like Hernando Island, is a remnant of a retreating glacier.

Stag Bay is a fair-weather anchorage, open to the north with shoal water extending well into the bay, but the sandy holding ground is good and there is protection from southerly winds. Keep an eye on the depth sounder to find a spot near the end of Spilsbury Point. There is current between Spilsbury Point and Sutil Point which is fairly constant.

On a couple of occasions we've noticed the weather come up quite suddenly in this area between Vancouver Island and the mainland. If menacing clouds start collecting to the south, it may be time to head for the protection of Cortes Bay or Gorge Harbour on Cortes Island. After a sunny afternoon spent on the beach at Spilsbury Point, it's a quick run to either bay for sheltered overnight moorage.

Above right, anchored west of Spilsbury Point.
Below, the view toward Desolation Sound.

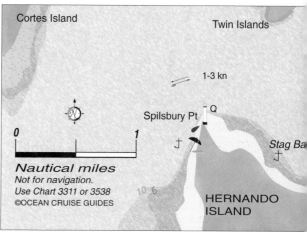

Cortes Island

Twin Islands

1-3 kn

Spilsbury Pt   Q

Stag Ba

0   1

Nautical miles
Not for navigation.
Use Chart 3311 or 3538
©OCEAN CRUISE GUIDES

HERNANDO
ISLAND

CHAPTER FOUR

DESOLATION SOUND

Roffey Island

Desolation Sound is one of the B.C. coast's most scenic cruising areas. There are few sights more thrilling than that which unfolds as you round Sarah Point on Malaspina Peninsula to view Homfray Channel winding its way through the massive green and grey portals of the Coast Mountains. To port looms mile-high Mount Addenbroke on East Redonda Island, its eastern slope plunging into the deep waters of Homfray Channel. To starboard is Mount Denman, rising over 6,590 feet (2,000 m). Perpetual snowfields crown distant mainland mountains and widely different types of vegetation cling to the rugged slopes, from light patches of alpine lichen to dark stands of spruce, fir and cedar. At the base of these mountains lie anchorages of outstanding beauty, their wilderness preserved by their park status but tested each summer when boats arrive by the hundreds.

The unique recreational appeal of this area was recognized in 1973, when the provincial government established Desolation Sound Marine Park. It became British Columbia's largest marine park, with 40 miles of shoreline and over 20,000 acres of upland. As Bill Wolferstan notes in his seminal book *A Cruising Guide to Desolation Sound*, there are so many anchorages in this area that a cruiser could spend over two months here without anchoring more than one night in the same location.

There are many uncrowded spots to be found in the Desolation Sound area, and even the most popular anchorages are relatively quiet in the shoulder seasons of early June and mid-to-late September. However, at the height of summer Desolation Sound is one of busiest cruising grounds on the B.C. coast and many anchorages require stern lines to shore. The topography of the area is such that the anchor-

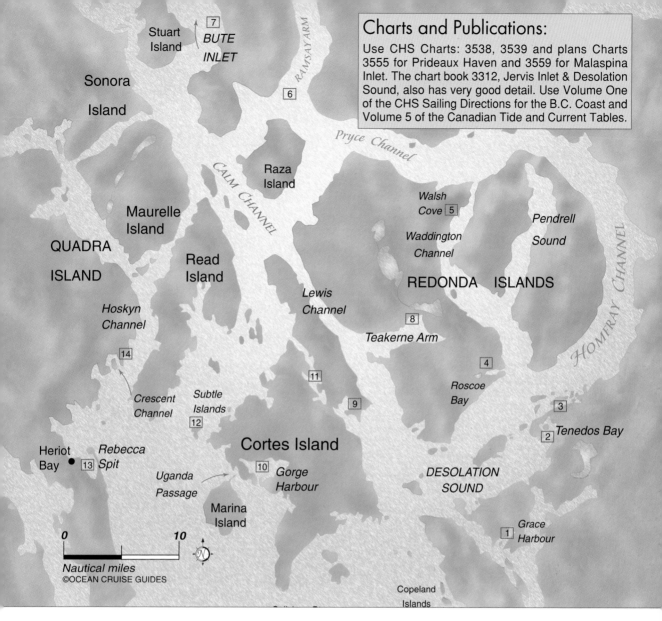

Charts and Publications:

Use CHS Charts: 3538, 3539 and plans Charts 3555 for Prideaux Haven and 3559 for Malaspina Inlet. The chart book 3312, Jervis Inlet & Desolation Sound, also has very good detail. Use Volume One of the CHS Sailing Directions for the B.C. Coast and Volume 5 of the Canadian Tide and Current Tables.

Stuart Island — **BUTE INLET** — 7

Sonora Island

6

RAMSAY ARM

Pryce Channel

Raza Island

Walsh Cove 5

Waddington Channel

Pendrell Sound

Maurelle Island

CALM CHANNEL

REDONDA ISLANDS

QUADRA ISLAND

Read Island

HOMFRAY CHANNEL

Hoskyn Channel

Lewis Channel

8

Teakerne Arm

14

11

4

Roscoe Bay

3

Crescent Channel

Subtle Islands

12

9

2 *Tenedos Bay*

Heriot Bay • 13 Rebecca Spit

Cortes Island

10 Gorge Harbour

DESOLATION SOUND

Uganda Passage

Marina Island

1 Grace Harbour

0 — 10

Nautical miles
©OCEAN CRUISE GUIDES

Copeland Islands

ages run perpendicular to the dominant wind directions in the Strait of Georgia, and most winds are muted by the time they reach anchorages in Desolation Sound.

Some of the best swimming on the B.C. coast is found in the vicinity of Desolation Sound, where tidal currents are weak and the complex topography is ideal for surface waters to rise in temperature. Good swimming spots are usually found in protected bays and coves where surface water isn't disrupted by tidal mixing and may be further warmed by a sandy beach or rock foreshore during a rising tide.

And then, of course, there are the lakes. For centuries, mariners have delighted in the discovery of a freshwater lake at the head of an anchorage. The early explorers washed their clothes and bathed in this clean water, but modern mariners are more likely to head ashore with pure pleasure in mind as they hike to the nearest lake for a swim. Numerous anchorages in and around Desolation Sound have forested uplands offering a shady refuge of trails and small lakes in which you can take a dip.

More marine parks lie immediately north and west of Desolation Sound amid the Discovery Islands – a maze of islands lying between the mainland and Vancouver Island. Those parks located south of the tidal passes are easily accessible and offer scenic anchorages. A few coastal communities are also found in this area, along with an array of marinas that welcome summertime boaters.

Tides and Currents

Flood currents from Johnstone and Georgia Straits meet in this area and result in weak and inconsistent tidal streams in Desolation Sound, seldom exceeding 2 knots. This will vary as a result of wind which

Ample fresh water and a sheltered anchorage kept Captain Vancouver in Teakerne Arm for weeks.

may be noticeable in Homfray and Lewis Channels. The very last vestiges of flood current from the Strait of Georgia flow N past Kinghorn Island, turn east along the north side of the island and flow NE into Desolation Sound where they dissipate.

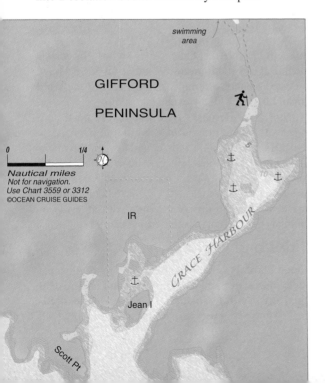

Desolation Sound Marine Park

It's understandable, if somewhat ironic, that Captain George Vancouver chose the name Desolation Sound for what is now one of B.C.'s busiest boating destinations. In 1792, when Vancouver was surveying the Inside Passage, the shores of Desolation Sound probably did seem desolate, their overwhelming impression one of inhospitable wilderness. Arriving on a dark and rainy night in June 1792, unable to gain soundings close to shore, his ship drifting about in light and variable winds as if "it were blindfolded in this labyrinth," Vancouver was finally able to anchor just before midnight on the north side of Kinghorn Island "in company with the *Chatham* and the Spanish vessels, in 32 fathoms."

After dragging anchor the next day in heavy squalls, the ships moved to **Teakerne Arm** and remained there for about two weeks while survey parties set off in the ships' boats. Meanwhile, Vancouver wrote in grim terms of the surrounding countryside – the forests were gloomy, the deep water yielded no fish and the precipitous mountainsides offered little in the way of useable foreshore. There were a few native villages in the vicinity, including one at Prideaux Haven, but this was deserted when visited by one of Vancouver's survey parties. A smallpox epidemic had struck 10 years earlier, devastating the local native population.

By the early 1900s, the quiet solitude of Prideaux Haven made it an appealing place for hermits. Muriel Wylie Blanchet describes in her book *The Curve of Time* the two resident hermits she would visit there – one living in a cabin at Melanie Cove, the other at Laura Cove. The local population took a dramatic upswing whenever Blanchet arrived in her 25-foot cabin cruiser with her five children aboard and a dog in tow. There was no room on board for their Gordon setter, who slept in the dinghy. In wet weather the dog would sleep on shore, under shelter of some sort, and one night she was driven by a cougar into the water where she stood chest deep until morning. Prideaux Haven is now part of Desolation Sound Marine Park, the two other major anchorages within the park being Tenedos Bay and Grace Harbour.

Grace Harbour 1

Located off Malaspina Inlet, this large anchorage is usually less crowded than the other major anchorages in Desolation Sound. It offers excellent shelter and can accommodate several dozen boats. A good spot to anchor is at the harbour's head, where sticky mud provides good holding. Another sheltered spot to drop the hook is north of **Jean Island**. A major

Above, the head of Grace Harbour viewed from the trail head. Below right, a pleasant trail leads to the lake near Grace Harbour. Bottom, summer winds are usually light in Malaspina Inlet.

village of the Sliammon First Nation used to occupy the shores of Grace Harbour and some midden stretches of beach are in this anchorage.

At the head of Grace Harbour is a forest trail that leads to a nearby lake (an easy 15-minute walk). The turn-off to the lake veers left from the main trail and winds a short distance through thin forest to the lake's edge. There's a grassy clearing and some wide flat rocks providing access into the water, slightly murky from a peat and mud bottom. Garter snakes thrive along the trails and shore of the lake where we have seen them slip into the water for a swim.

Several overnight anchorages can be found on the southwest shore of **Malaspina Inlet**, along the approach to Grace Harbour. The anchorage behind the **Cochrane Islands** lies within the boundaries of Desolation Sound Marine Park and provides access to park trails. The anchorage south of the island marked '53' on Charts 3559 and 3312 of the **Josephine Islands** is outside the park but provides good shelter. Around the corner from Grace Harbour are a number of inlets and bays to explore, including Lancelot Inlet and Isabel Bay, which can be very quiet even in summer but does have an aquaculture operation at the south end.

Tenedos Bay 2

This anchorage, when surveyed by Vancouver's officers, was described as 'the deep bay' by Archibald Menzies, the expedition's botanist. Tenedos Bay had everything Vancouver disliked about the area – deep water (over 300 feet/100 metres in the central part of the bay) and steep slopes which provided no extensive foreshore for recreation or the picking of edible vegetation. Recreational boaters, on the other hand, find much to approve of in Tenedos Bay, including its dramatic anchorages, excellent shelter and the lovely hike to Unwin Lake for a freshwater swim.

There are several spots to anchor in Tenedos Bay, including the always-popular bay just west of Unwin Lake which provides shelter from SE winds . The advantage of this spot is its proximity to excellent swimming in the lake. The hike to the lake takes about 15 minutes. Some logs along shore provide a platform for swimmers.

Tenedos Bay's westernmost cove, known locally as **Three Fathom Cove** (for its depth), lies between the large unnamed island and the mainland shore. This cove is avoided by many because of the shallow entrance (a shoal extends from the SW tip of the island) but the holding here is good and the cove offers superb protection. A drying tombolo, connecting the island with the mainland, separates Three Fathom Cove from the more popular spot that lies

Left, looking down from our lofty perch on the west side of Tenedos Bay. Below, the bay's east arm provides good anchorage.

TENEDOS BAY AT A GLANCE

CHARTS: 3312, 3538
LAT LONG: 50°7.26N 124°42.06'W
PROS: All-round great anchorage with many places to safely drop the hook and relax. Good swimming nearby and some hiking.
CONS: Often busy, but with a little searching one can find a quiet spot.
MUST DO: Take a dinghy ride to the tombolo. Go for a swim in Unwin Lake.

along the NW side of the island and opens up to a fairly large bay. This area is also well protected. We often tuck ourselves fairly close to the tombolo end in about 13 feet (4 m) of water with a line to shore. We once anchored here and climbed up the bluff overlooking this nook where we enjoyed an eagle eye's view of our boat at anchor. The sun felt warm that June day, the summer crowds had not yet arrived, and we lingered on our lofty perch, enjoying the surrounding wilderness in all its desolate glory.

Vessels can also anchor with sternlines along the north shore opposite the large island. This is protected from most winds but is exposed to strong southerlies which often brings a chop right into the bay. Another spot that provides good shelter lies south of the island in the area west of a reef and where a stern line will be needed.

Above right, swimming is good at Unwin Lake.
Below, peaceful Three Fathom Cove.

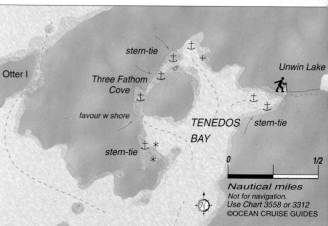

Otter I — stern-tie — Three Fathom Cove — Unwin Lake — favour w shore — TENEDOS BAY — stern-tie — stern-tie

0   1/2

Nautical miles
Not for navigation.
Use Chart 3558 or 3312
©OCEAN CRUISE GUIDES

Prideaux Haven 3

Nestled along the mainland shore is a collection of coves, islands and lagoons referred to as Prideaux Haven – one of the most popular anchoring areas on the B.C. coast. Yet, busy as Prideaux Haven becomes in summer, you can always find a spot to drop the hook. We've often arrived late in the day and always found room. The holding in sticky mud is very good throughout the various anchorages, which are well-protected.

The Prideaux Haven anchorage is the largest and can easily accommodate a dozen boats in depths ranging from 22 to 60 feet (6.7 m to 18 m). Although vessels stern-tie along the north and south shores, this puts them broadside to west winds which occasionally gust through the gap from **Eveleigh Anchorage**. We've seen large boats let go of their stern lines in such winds.

The entrance to Prideaux Haven lies between Eveleigh Island and Oriel Rocks, along a channel less daunting than it looks on a chart. If entering at HW, we maintain a parallel course along Eveleigh Island and into the anchorage. At LW the hazards are visible and easy to navigate around.

Large yachts favour Prideaux Haven for its depth and size, while smaller vessels can be found in Melanie or Laura Coves. **Melanie Cove** seems to be the wallflower anchorage and is often relatively quiet when the other bays are packed. Melanie Cove offers the best protection in strong NW winds; favour the Melanie Point shore when entering. **Laura Cove** is perhaps the prettiest anchorage of the group, with pleasing vistas of islets and mainland mountains. A trail runs between the east end of Laura Cove and the parks information shelter at Melanie Point.

In addition to the main anchorages of Prideaux Haven, Melanie Cove and Laura Cove, boats can tuck into various bights along the outside of **Copplestone Island** and along the north side of Eveleigh Anchorage. Boats also anchor with a stern line along the north shore of the peninsula protecting Melanie Cove. This passage is popular with small powerboats which often raft here in large numbers.

Above, anchorage north of Copplestone Island. Left, aerial view looking across Eveleigh Anchorage to Prideaux Haven. Opposite, aerial view of Prideaux Haven.

'Haystack Bay', east and south of Roffey Island, offers stunning views of mainland mountains.

If the main anchorages are too busy for your liking, a quieter spot can usually be found east or south of **Roffey Island** at the far end of the marine park. Reefs, capped with small islets, extend east from Roffey Island and north from the mainland. They resemble a series of haystacks for which regulars have named this cove. The extent of the reef from Roffey Island can be difficult to identify (we saw a large powerboat go merrily right over it at HW) and the main cove east of the island is more easily entered from the north. There is some current through the anchorage, about a knot at most, so setting a stern line can be a little tricky. Anchoring south of the island affords a better view of Homfray Channel and the mainland mountains.

There are several quiet nooks in which to anchor on both sides of **Homfray Channel**, including a small horseshoe-shaped cove near the southern tip of East Redonda Island which is well sheltered from prevailing summer westerlies. Homfray Channel is named after Robert Homfray, a civil engineer from Worcestershire, who arrived in Victoria in 1860 and worked as a surveyor. In *British Columbia Coast Names, Their Origin and History*, Captain John Walbran states Homfray "was of an eccentric disposition, and for some years before his death had his tombstone erected in Ross Bay cemetery, with all particulars on it with the exception of the date of his decease" which was added after his death in 1902.

When Captain Vancouver was surveying local waters, the expedition's botanist Archibald Menzies and some crewmembers were exploring the entrance to Laura Cove when they came upon a fortified village perched on an islet. The British seamen were fascinated with this small citadel, "built on a rock, whose perpendicular cliffs were nearly inaccessible

---

PRIDEAUX HAVEN AT A GLANCE

CHARTS: 3555, 3312,
LAT LONG: entrance: 50°8.75'N 124°41.04'W
PROS: An outstanding series of anchorages with good protection from wind and good holding ground. Numerous opportunities for swimming, hiking and exploring by dinghy.
CONS: During peak season of July and August it is busy, but with a little exploring you can usually find a quiet spot.
MUST DO: Explore the reefs of Laura Cove and Copplestone Island by dinghy. Find a quiet nook in Homfray Channel to go for a swim.

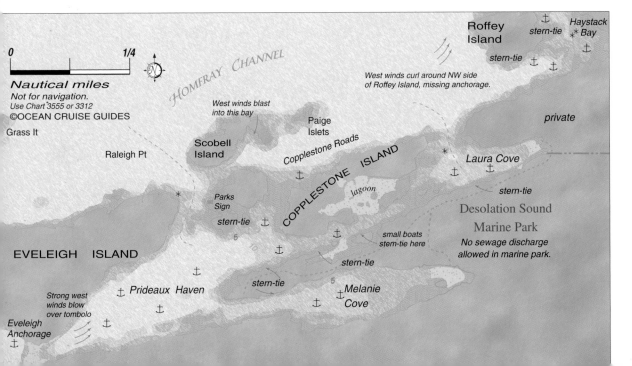

on every side; and connected with the main, by a low narrow neck of land". As Menzies and the others wandered through the recently deserted village, they were suddenly pounced upon by a horde of fleas. The men rushed into the water up to their necks, but the fleas refused to drown, so the men towed their clothes back to the ship and boiled them to get rid of the vermin.

A hermit named Phil Lavine lived in Laura Cove in the early 1930s near another hermit named Mike over at Melanie Cove. Mike was a philosophical fellow, his cabin lined with books, and when he died the old Frenchman Phil, who couldn't read, built shelves around his bed to hold Mike's library.

Roscoe Bay,
West Redonda Island [4]

This marine park is extremely popular in the summer months and tying a line ashore has become standard practice for this long, enclosed anchorage to accommodate the number of boats that squeeze in. And squeeze in, they do, through the narrow entrance where a drying bar can be crossed by keel-boats only at or near HW. At high neap tides, there is about 12 feet (3.5 m) of water. Inside, this well-protected anchorage is usually like a millpond although occasionally NW gales will gust through the bay.

Logging used to take place on the shores of Black Lake, and a channel was dug the short distance between the lake and the head of Roscoe Bay for floating out the logs. Today a trail traces the remnants of this flume and leads to the north side of Black Lake where some smooth rocks are ideal for summer sunbathing and for a freshwater swim. A dinghy or kayak could be portaged to the lake, and it's also possible to hike up a trail overlooking the lake. There is camping near the lake.

The shores of the anchorage itself are also good for exploring. One sunny afternoon in early June we climbed to the knob on its north side, then returned to the water's edge to lounge on the smooth sandstone. Our reverie was broken only briefly when another boat entered the cove, motored around, then left us to our private paradise.

ROSCOE BAY AT A GLANCE
CHARTS: 3312, 3538
LAT LONG: 50°9.65'W 124°45.96'W
PROS: Well sheltered, with freshwater swimming nearby. Good holding.
CONS: Often busy in summer and can resemble a parking lot with everyone tied to shore.
MUST DO: Go for a swim in Black Lake. Investigate the bar at the entrance by dinghy.

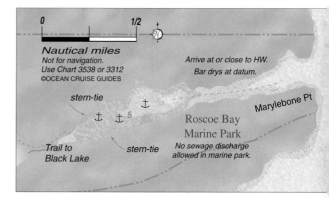

Entering Roscoe Bay requires high water.

Like many marine parks, Roscoe Bay is closed to sewage discharge and vessels are required to keep sewage in holding tanks while at anchor. Because of the restricted entrance, Roscoe Bay has especially poor tidal flushing. The high fecal coliform count measured here each summer is still a concern for BC Parks, which does not recommend swimming in the bay until water quality improves.

Walsh Cove Marine Park, West Redonda Island 5

This small but sheltered anchorage on the east side of West Redonda Island provides a safe and scenic anchorage for boaters looking to get away from the Desolation Sound area. This a good spot to spend the night, with the Gorge Islets acting as a breakwater to wake from vessels passing in Waddington Channel and the surrounding islands blocking most winds. The recommended approach into the anchorage is from the south, west of Bluff Point.

The Gorge Islets, which are part of the park, are very scenic and offer a great spot for picnicking with a view over the anchorage. There is also excellent swimming at mid-to-high tide along the reefs just west of these islets. Good prawn fishing is reported just south of the Gorge Islets and in Toba Inlet, west of Double Island. If you're passing Walsh Cove in the evening and there is room here, it is a good decision to stay the night rather than have to jockey for a spot at Prideaux Haven or Roscoe Bay.

Frances Bay and the Channels 6

The head of this expansive bay off Raza Passage is well sheltered from all winds but strong southeasterlies. Situated at a crossroads of scenic channels, the anchorage's magnificent vista is of Raza Passage flowing eastward into Pryce Channel which disap-

Below, Walsh Cove anchorage provides good shelter from W winds but loses the sun quickly.

pears into the distant folds of forested mountains.

The west end of Raza Passage connects with Calm Channel, which leads north to the mouth of Bute Inlet. Along the way, overlooking Calm Channel on the mainland side, is the tiny village of Church House, established here by the Homalco First Nation after a gale in 1900 destroyed most of their village across the channel on Maurelle Island. By the end of the 20th century, the Homalco had abandoned their villages in Bute Inlet and many were living at the village of Sliammon (north of Powell River) and at Campbell River. Church House was still occupied (now abandoned) when we pulled up to the dock in the mid-1980s and asked if we could look inside the small wooden church, built by missionaries, for which the village was named.

Bute Inlet 7

Flanked by tall mountains, 35-mile long Bute Inlet is one of the longest fjords on the B.C. coast. Its milky colour is the result of glacial meltwater from the Homathko Snowfield which, along with other nearby glaciers, drains into the Homathko River, which empties into the head of Bute Inlet. Strong outflow winds often sweep down from Mt. Waddington (at 13,177 feet [4,016 m] it is the highest peak entirely in B.C.) and funnel past the fjord's steep sides. Temperatures at the head of the inlet are cooler than the Desolation Sound area by about 5° C. Anchorages are limited along the inlet with depths often over 200 feet (65 m) close to shore (see charts 3542 or 3312). Mountain goats can sometimes be seen along the cliffsides lining the inlet and bears are often sighted in the Waddington Harbour area.

Originally occupied by the Homalco Nation, Bute Inlet also became home to a handful of trappers, loggers and fishermen. Bute Inlet was considered as a terminus for the transcontinental railway and, before that, the British entrepreneur Alfred Waddington (for whom the mountain was named) attempted to build a road from the Chilcotin interior

Above, looking up Bute Inlet. Right, Seattle boaters Kris and Bob Ridenour.

to Bute Inlet. However, the Tsilhqot'in who lived there objected to a work crew cutting a road through their territory and a confrontation erupted in violence with 19 people killed and five Tsilhqot'in eventually seized and hanged for murder.

A Honeymoon Cruise to Bute Inlet

For most boaters, cruising beyond Desolation Sound means heading north of Dent Rapids, but Bob and Kris Ridenour of Seattle couldn't resist a special detour which took them north without the rapids. For years they had cruised Desolation Sound. However, in 1994, on their honeymoon, they wanted a destination that was remote yet within the two-week time frame required to get back to their business. They had explored Toba Inlet the previous year, and enjoyed the beauty and tranquility of the inlet and so fixed their sights on the 40-mile-long Bute Inlet for their honeymoon. With their C&C 30 they made it as far as Orford Bay on their first day and anchored in front of Orford River.

"There was almost no wind, it was very still," Kris recalls. "We passed a beautiful waterfall opposite Clipper Point and felt we had got away."

The next day's destination was the head of Waddington Harbour with a lunch stop to explore the foreshore near Bear Bay. All along the inlet, towering mountains dwarfed their small boat as they made their way north.

They tied up to a log boom on the west side of the 3-mile wide bay and headed ashore with their mountain bikes after spotting a nearby logging road. It was to be a short ride.

"After about 15 minutes we came around a bend and saw a small black bear sitting on a stump," says Bob. "We didn't think too much

about it so we continued on for a few more minutes then saw the sow crashing about in the underbrush. It took us just a couple of minutes to get back to the bottom of the hill." They jettisoned the bikes in favour of the dinghy to explore two miles up the Homathko River, enjoying the view of mountains and glaciers.

Horseflies forced their departure the next day but they found another gem of an anchorage at Leask Creek where they hiked to the lake and went swimming." It was a cruise we always remember vividly," Kris says.

They now have a Taswell 43 named *Luna* and cruise extensively along the Inside Passage looking for new inlets.

Homathko R

WADDINGTON HARBOUR

Southgate R

Bear Bay

Purcell Pt

Boyd Pt

Orford Bay

waterfall

Clipper Point

Fawn Bluff

waterfall

Leask Lake

BUTE INLET

0   5

Nautical miles
Not for navigation.
Use Chart 3542 or 3312
©OCEAN CRUISE GUIDES

Teakerne Arm Marine Park, West Redonda Island 8

This popular anchorage, considered one of the best swimming spots in the area, is well known for its 100-feet-high Cassel Falls and the hiking trails to Cassel Lake. A dinghy dock provides access to the half-mile (1 km) park trail which ascends past the falls to the lake, where several good spots can be found along shore for swimming.

Most boats anchor in the bight west of the falls with a stern line to shore where eyebolts have been installed. You may find the water deep here (usually 100 feet or more), but setting a stern line to shore and ensuring the anchor digs into the upslope of the steep bottom will keep you secure in the black thick mud. Further west is another excellent spot in a bight near a small reef outcropping. East of the falls,

> ### TEAKERNE ARM AT A GLANCE
> **CHARTS:** 3312, 3538
> **LAT LONG:** 50 11.30'N 124°51.10'W
> **PROS:** Beautiful location, dramatic scenery and fair to good anchorage in entire arm. Excellent swimming at nearby Cassel Lake. Some hiking.
> **CONS:** Can be a little crowded at lake. SE winds will be a problem for those in N arm.
> **MUST DO:** Go for a swim in warm fresh water!

Above, swimming in the warm water of Cassel Lake. Below, a waterfall flows from Cassel Lake into the head of Teakerne Arm.

Small cove on east side of Teakerne Arm.

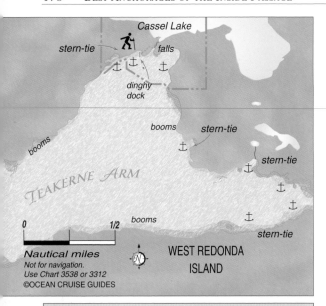

Cassel Lake

stern-tie   falls

dinghy dock

booms   stern-tie

stern-tie

booms

TEAKERNE ARM

booms   stern-tie

0   1/2

Nautical miles
Not for navigation.
Use Chart 3538 or 3312
©OCEAN CRUISE GUIDES

WEST REDONDA
ISLAND

Where the Walrus might be found

In Pendrell Sound, near the mouth of Toba Inlet, the top 15 feet (5 m) of surface water can reach temperatures of 70 degrees F (21 degrees C) in early August. These calm, stable conditions are also required for the Pacific oyster to spawn, and Pendrell Sound is one of the few places on the B.C. coast where the water remains consistently warm enough for this to occur. The cultivated oyster larvae are then shipped to other locations in Georgia Strait and grown to an edible size.

larger vessels sometimes anchor in this deeper water while other vessels can be seen tied to booms or to shore along the arm's east shore. Summer NW winds can curl around the arm's north shore but are not usually strong – southerlies also are weak here.

If the anchorage near the park is full, nearby alternatives include the east arm where many vessels stern-tie along the shore. Two prime spots include a small bight along the N shore of this arm and, opposite, in the lee of a small islet on the S shore. Talbot Cove and the bight immediately to the west also have shelter and although more open to the northwest, provide good anchorage in settled weather. The cove north of Joyce Point is occupied with an aquaculture operation. Tying to a log boom along the shore south of Cassel Falls, is also acceptable to many boaters – just be prepared to move if a tug arrives.

Teakerne Arm was a busy anchorage in late June and early July 1792 when it was shared by four sailing ships: two under the command of Captain Vancouver and two under the command of the Spanish naval officers Galiano and Valdes. They anchored here off the north shore, a little east of the

arm's entrance, and remained at anchor for over two weeks while survey parties set off in small boats to explore the surrounding waterways.

The weather was wet and gloomy, and Vancouver felt hemmed in by "the dreary rocks and precipices that compose these desolate shores." When he parted company with the Spanish on July 13 and headed toward the open waters off Cape Mudge, his final comment concerning "the station we had just quitted" was "to state the general satisfaction that prevailed on leaving a region so truly desolate and inhospitable." The weather can certainly colour one's perception of an anchorage.

Squirrel Cove, Cortes Island 9

A good anchorage, able to accommodate dozens of boats, Squirrel Cove is well sheltered with good holding in mud – unless you happen to snag your anchor on a sunken log or logging cable in the inner cove. This anchorage has been popular with boaters for years and its location just off Lewis Channel makes it a convenient stopover for those making long legs heading north or south. This is a common layover for northbound vessels planning to catch slack at Dent Rapids, which is about 20 miles away. Although strong winds can send gusts through the anchorage, the holding ground is good, making it a very secure anchorage.

We often anchor with a line ashore to the east of Protection Island, above the knob of land SW of the small bare islet marked '5' on Charts 3555 and 3312. Although Squirrel Cove has a bit of reputation for a cluttered bottom, the result of logging activity years ago, we've stopped here many times and haven't hooked onto anything other than sticky mud. According to published reports, however, the bay east of the little island, as well as the area between it and the larger island to the north, do have logging debris, so a trip line would be prudent in this area. Parts of the shore along the outer bay were also used during logging operations, so be careful there also.

While Captain Vancouver's two ships were anchored across Lewis Channel in Teakerne Arm, a boat party explored Squirrel Cove. At the head of its inner cove the seamen discovered, as described by Archibald Menzies, "a large stream of water rushing down out of the woods." They assumed it was fresh water until they tasted it and found it was salty. The saltwater lagoon they discovered is now a source of recreation for boaters who, depending on the state of the tide, can ride these rapids by dinghy along a straight, boulder-free passage.

Most of the SW part of Squirrel Cove is Klahoose First Nation land and a sign so indicating is conspicuous to starboard upon entering the cove. There is a

Above, aerial view of Squirrel Cove and upper reaches of Von Donop Inlet. Left, Squirrel Cove anchorage. Below, entrance to Gorge Harbour.

good general store (and the Cove Restaurant) located above the government dock, south of the entrance to the cove. Within the cove, also on the SW side, is Marilyn's Salmon Restaurant where traditional native cooked salmon and other seafood dishes are offered to diners who enjoy a great view overlooking the anchorage.

Gorge Harbour, Cortes Island 10

The name of this harbour, surrounded by hills, derives from its narrow steep-sided entrance – called The Gorge – which is less than 200 feet wide in places. Along the west wall of the entrance you can still see the outline of aboriginal rock paintings. Bill Wolferstan concludes that the paintings were completed about 200 years ago and executed by individuals lowered by cedar ropes from the top of the cliff. On the east side of the entrance are huge boulders that formed burial caverns. Although the entrance into the harbour is narrow, it is clear of obstructions. Currents can attain 4 knots in the entrance. Because of these currents, there can be a bad chop south of the Guide Islets in strong south winds. Conditions improve north of the islets.

There are a number of sheltered nooks along the south shore of the harbour, such as the one east of a knob of land that lies south of Tan Island, where you can find a secure spot with a line ashore. We like the area east of Ring Islet in about 20 feet (6 m) of water. Many boats anchor south of the marina or west of Bee Islets. We often go to the extreme west end of the harbour (beyond a lone rock) which is very protected if strong NW winds come up. Holding is good in soft mud and sand.

The marina's facilities include a well-stocked store, restaurant, laundromat and showers. A dirt road winds past a small campground to the main road which is pleasant for hiking or cycling, except when the ferry pulls into Whaletown and a stream of cars temporarily shatters the pastoral atmosphere. The various islets that lie within Gorge Harbour are very pleasant for exploring by dinghy. There is also

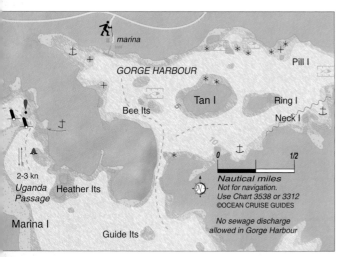

good fishing south of the Marina Reef buoy Q16 and Q20, south of Sutil Point. See charts 3312 or 3538.

Uganda Passage

Uganda Passage, encumbered by rocks and shoals, makes a turn of more than 90 degrees around the end of Shark Spit. However, its tidal streams are weak and the channel is well marked with a starboard-hand buoy and two port-hand buoys, marking the upstream direction for boats proceeding N through the passage. Shark Spit – aptly named for its fin shape jutting from the north end of Marina Island – is a good spot to swim and do some beachcombing for clams, sand dollars and moon shells. A lunch stop lies opposite the tip of **Shark Spit**, behind an islet which forms its southern shore, from where you can watch other boats thread their way through Uganda Passage. See charts 3311 or 3312 for detail.

Von Donop Inlet / Hathayim Marine Park, Cortes I 11

This undeveloped marine park, a joint venture between the Klahoose First Nation band and BC Parks, offers well-sheltered anchorage in several spots along its nearly three-mile length. Thanks to the inlet's narrowness (150 feet / 50 metres at its narrowest) and twisting shape, little wind is able to find its way inside, where the holding ground is good. A mid-channel rock with less than 6 feet (2 m) of water over it lies in the narrowest part of the inlet. Usually marked with kelp and visible at LW, it should be passed by favouring the SW side of the channel, keeping the rock to port. There is a large saltwater lagoon on the east side of the inlet just past this point which can be explored by dinghy, but be aware that currents will run swiftly during mid-tide. Use Charts 3538 or 3312.

Von Donop Inlet (named after Victor Von Donop, a midshipman in the Royal Navy in the 1860s) is normally a very calm anchorage with numerous bights and coves where you can tuck away and think of nothing or everything. There is rarely a stir of wind even when a tempest may be brewing outside. The anchorage's foreshore is a rare blend of Douglas fir, hemlock, red cedar and patches of Sitka spruce, mixed with maple and red alder. It is also home to flying squirrels, river otter and mink, while seals and sea lions can often be spotted near the entrance. In his Desolation Sound cruising guide, Bill Wolferstan reported that many years ago five killer whales entered the

Von Donop Inlet is a good anchorage for exploring by dinghy and kayak.

Aerial view looking north over Von Donop Inlet.

large lagoon at HW and "chose to remain and die here although they had the opportunity to leave on succeeding high tides."

B.C. Parks notes that during spring and summer, visitors can hear the calls of varied thrush and Swainson's thrush, a variety of flycatchers as well as yellow-rumped Townsend's and black-throated grey warblers. Bald eagles are often seen soaring above the inlet.

In our view, the best anchorage in Von Donop is at the head, which opens into a small arrow-shaped basin. We have pulled into the small 2-fathom (4-m) cove on the north side and stayed for several days. On shore, at the head, there are small camping areas and trails leading to Squirrel Cove.

Subtle Islands 12

A sand-and-gravel tombolo joins these two private islands, and the anchorage on their east side, off Plunger Passage, provides shelter from NW winds. A private dock takes up much of the south part of the anchorage. The islands' northern anchorage is the prettier bay and one where we have anchored overnight several times in settled weather. It is, however, open to the northwest. A treed bluff graces the western shoreline and near the entrance to the cove, nestled between two outcroppings, is a secluded pebble beach.

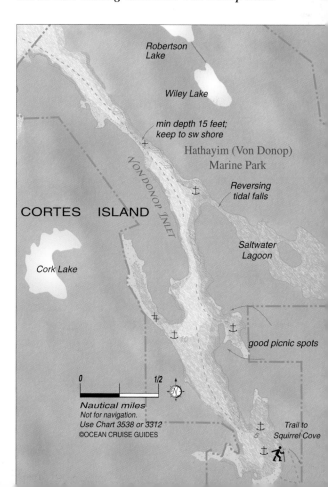

Robertson Lake

Wiley Lake

min depth 15 feet; keep to sw shore

Hathayim (Von Donop) Marine Park

Reversing tidal falls

VON DONOP INLET

CORTES ISLAND

Cork Lake

Saltwater Lagoon

good picnic spots

0   1/2

Nautical miles
Not for navigation.
Use Chart 3538 or 3312
©OCEAN CRUISE GUIDES

Trail to Squirrel Cove

Rebecca Spit, Quadra Island 13 ☂ ↗

Beaches always draw boaters in summer, and beautiful Rebecca Spit Marine Park is no exception. Forming a natural breakwater that shelters Drew Harbour, this park is a striking example of a West Coast spit. It has formed over thousands of years and is comprised of eroded sand and gravel carried by currents from the cliffs at Cape Mudge and deposited along the southeast shore of Quadra Island.

The flood tide flows north along this shoreline, so boaters approaching from the south can ride a favourable current right up to the harbour entrance, where shelter awaits in a bight just inside the spit's northern tip. If that spot is taken, anchorage can be obtained along the mile length of the spit, as close to the shore of the spit as your keel and tide will allow. The band of shallow water is very narrow, after which the depth drops off quickly. (Note that although the depths inside the spit are fairly con-

Above, small boats can anchor near shore. Below, aerial view of Rebecca Spit and Drew Harbour.

stant, there is one bulge of shoal water about a third of the way along the spit.) Tying a line to shore does not work well anywhere along the spit because of an almost constant current and because of the long distance over the beach to the trees.

The shallower area allows boats to anchor in 30 feet (10 m) or less of depth but in summer is often taken by other boats unless you arrive early in the day. We usually anchor outside the shallow band, in 75 feet (23 m) or more, which suits us as there is more room to let out scope. The holding throughout this anchorage is fair at best, with the bottom a mix of hard sand and gravel. The spit provides little protection from S winds and is subject to strong squalls during gales.

Rebecca Spit was named after the British trading schooner *Rebecca* which sailed this coast in the 1860s when sloops and schooners dominated the coasting trade. The crews of these vessels faced various occupational hazards, including attacks by natives which Captain John Walbran, author of *British Columbia Coast Names*, blamed on "the ardent spirits which some of the coasters traded to them, in spite of all warnings." Harbour pirates were another concern and, while lying in Victoria Harbour one March night in 1861, the *Rebecca* was boarded and some "money and goods were stolen."

Before becoming a park in 1959, Rebecca Spit was owned by local residents James and Mary Clandening who generously allowed visitors access to their stretch of beach, offering it as the site of Quadra Island's annual Victoria Day picnic. A 1946 earthquake caused three acres at the end of the spit to sink beneath sea level, and it left two large cracks in the remaining spit. Long marsh grass and the silver sheen of trees killed by saltwater are evidence of the settling that took place. The park no longer allows overnight camping because of concerns about erosion, but the spit remains popular with locals for daytime outings.

In the 18th century, Coast Salish natives occupied southern Quadra Island, and they built trenches and embankments along Rebecca Spit to fortify their ter-

ritory against attack from northern tribes. Despite these efforts, however, the Salish were eventually forced south by the Kwakwaka'wakw. Picnic tables and hiking trails have now replaced prehistoric fortifications on Rebecca Spit where the vistas on a clear summer's evening are magnificent. To the east is a sweeping view across the broad waters of Sutil Channel to the mainland peaks rising above Desolation Sound. To the west are the mountains of Vancouver Island, their rugged slopes outlined by the glowing light of a setting sun.

A marina, hotel and store are located at Heriot Bay while the Taku Resort on the west side of Drew Harbour also has some moorage and dockside facilities including a cafe.

Crescent Channel, Quadra Island 14

Although Crescent Channel's shoreline has become increasingly developed over the years with its numerous bights occupied by floats and private moorings, the anchorage remains relatively peaceful and a relaxing place to spend a day or two. The holding ground is good and the anchorage well protected. The salmon fishing at the north entrance is good.

There are a couple of good spots to anchor in the channel's eastern branch. One option is to anchor off the N end of the largest islet with a line to shore. Another is to anchor on the Quadra Island side, in the second bight and pull your stern in close to the steep, treed shoreline in about 15 feet (5 m). The afternoon sun warms the stone cliffs behind this spot, making a swim off its rock ledges a pleasant prospect. The bay to the west at the head of the channel is sometimes used by aquaculture operations but, if clear, can be used for anchoring. The nearby moss-covered islets are pleasant for exploring, their shorelines forming a lagoon that attracts mergansers and river otters while kingfishers chatter above the pines of Bold Island. See Charts 3538, 3539 or 3312 for detail.

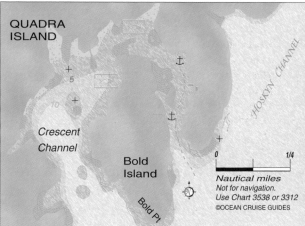

Top, Crescent Channel, looking north. Bottom, stern tied to shore in Crescent Channel.

CHAPTER FIVE

Hole in the Wall

ANCHORAGES OF THE PASSES

Boaters who venture into the mountain-bound channels of the Discovery Islands, beyond Desolation Sound, are entering one of our coast's most scenic cruising areas. Access to this labyrinth of forested islands, squeezed between the B.C. mainland and Vancouver Island, is gained by navigating one or more of the area's numerous tidal passes. Because of the speed of these passes, arriving at slack water is the key to a safe transit.

The main commercial route north is Discovery Passage, which entails transiting Seymour Narrows, where currents can reach 16 knots on an ebb. This is an excellent route and our personal favourite. Many northbound pleasure boaters choose the 'back route' around the top of Sonora Island along Cordero Channel. This route – through the Yuculta Rapids, Gillard Passage and the Dent Rapids – is the most direct route north from Desolation Sound.

Another option for northbound boaters is the 'middle route' up the east side of Quadra Island, through Surge Narrows (or Whiterock Passage and Hole in the Wall) and the Upper and Lower Rapids in Okisollo Channel. One advantage to this route is the chance to stop at Octopus Islands Marine Park, where a cluster of islets provides a beautiful and sheltered anchorage accommodating many vessels.

Okisollo Channel

5

CORDERO CHANNEL

BUTE INLET

Dent Rapids

Gillard
Passage

7

NODALES CHANNEL

Thurston
Bay

Sonora Island

6

Chatham Pt

Okisollo
Channel

Hole in
the Wall

Raza
Island

Kanish
Inlet

4

Maurelle
Island

3

Octopus
Islands

Surge
Narrows

Read
Island

QUADRA
ISLAND

Seymour
Narrows

Cortes
Island

DISCOVERY PASSAGE

Rebecca
Spit

VANCOUVER
ISLAND

2

1

Marina
Island

N

CAMPBELL
RIVER ●

0   5

Nautical miles

©OCEAN CRUISE GUIDES

This is the easiest route for boaters new to these northern passes. Although Surge Narrows and Okisollo Channel can run fast, these passes have less turbulence and the section of strong current is shorter than the long stretch from Yuculta Rapids to the Dents or along Discovery Passage to Seymour Narrows.

THE BACK ROUTE (aka The Dents)

Transiting the three main passes from the Dents to the Yucultas (Ukes) is normally an easier proposition when southbound because the Dents turn between 15 and 25 minutes sooner than the middle

Charts and Publications:

Skippers should opt for the large-scale charts showing detail of all the passes. These charts give important information on direction and speed of currents throughout each pass. Use charts 3537, 3539, 3540 (Campbell River) and 3543 (which has a large-scale inset of Dent Rapids). Also, the CHS book of Charts 3312 covers all passes of this chapter with good detail.

Use Volume One of the CHS Sailing Directions for the B.C. Coast. and Volume 6 of the Canadian Tide and Current Tables.

rapids of Gillard Passage, and the flood stream at this early stage presents few difficulties.

Because of the high level of turbulence in this set of passes (particularly off Whirlpool Point), accurate tidal research and predictions were difficult to obtain and it was only in the late 1980s that the Canadian Hydrographic Service discovered, through the research of Mike Woodward and his colleagues, that currents were actually much faster than originally thought.

Slow or low-powered vessels may find they are battling more current than they can handle and should keep in mind that there are numerous spots to pull into and wait for the next slack, or spend the night and carry on the next day. This includes Big Bay public dock on Stuart Island, the Dent Island Lodge Resort on the small islands east of Dent Island (a reservation for overnight moorage is recommended) or the anchorage in Mermaid Bay.

Yuculta Rapids

If you are northbound, the Yucultas (pronounced uke-la-taws) will be the first challenge. The predominant characteristic of these rapids is the choppy water and turbulence which starts south of Kellsey Point and continues to Gillard Passage. Although this passage is deep and fairly wide, the middle of the pass usually has the least turbulence right up to Whirlpool Point.

Slow vessels arriving at the tail end of a flood can take advantage of a back eddy along the Stuart Island shore up to Kellsey Point. From there, if conditions are safe, cross over to the Sonora Island side

PASS TIP SHEET
Yuculta Rapids, Gillard Passage, Dent Rapids and Arran Rapids use Chart 3543 or 3312
Location: 18 miles N of Squirrel Cove
Reference Station: Gillard Passage for Dents and for Yuculta Rapids.
Maximum Flow: Arran – 14 knots (flood) Gillard – 13 knots (ebb); Dent – 11 knots (flood); Yucultas – 10 knots flood
Slack: less than 10 minutes on large tides.
Nearby Anchorages: Stuart Island public dock at Big Bay, Mermaid Bay, Horn Bay, Shoal Bay.
Direction of Flood: Southeast
Key to Safe Transits: Northbound – Calculate time to travel four mile stretch of passes at your vessel's normal speed to be at Dents as close to slack as possible. Southbound – Arrive at Dent Rapids in the last hour of a flood or at the beginning of a flood.

of the channel (where the northerly ebb current kicks in early) and continue to Gillard Passage.

The Yuculta Rapids are a sort of catch-basin for debris flowing from the other passes. Some of the bits of wood may be submerged below the top layer of fresh water that flows from Bute Inlet. Debris not buoyant enough to be supported by this freshwater layer can sink to the denser salt water 3 to 6 feet (1 to 2 m) down, so keep a sharp eye for deadheads and other wood bobbing just below the surface.

A northbound powerboat proceeds against five knots of current in Gillard Passage.

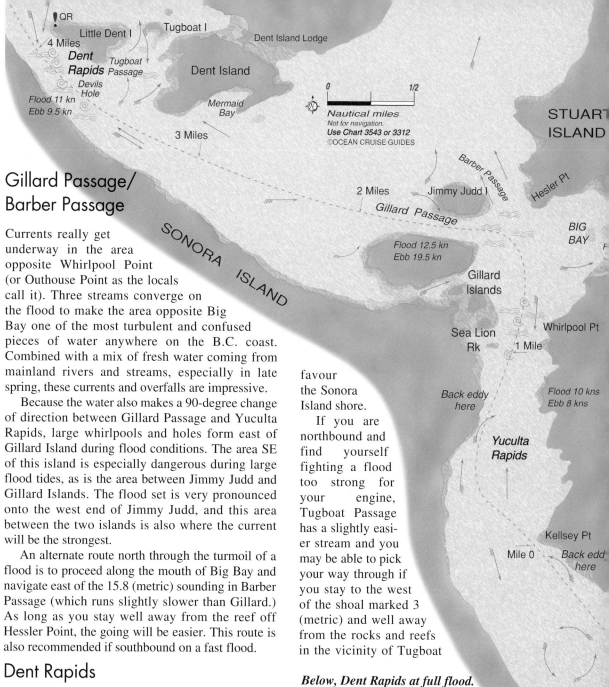

QR
4 Miles
Dent Rapids
Flood 11 kn
Ebb 9.5 kn
Little Dent I
Tugboat Passage
Devils Hole
Tugboat I
Dent Island Lodge
Dent Island
Mermaid Bay
3 Miles

0   1/2
Nautical miles
Not for navigation.
Use Chart 3543 or 3312
©OCEAN CRUISE GUIDES

STUART ISLAND

SONORA ISLAND

Barber Passage
2 Miles
Jimmy Judd I
Gillard Passage
Hesler Pt

BIG BAY

Flood 12.5 kn
Ebb 19.5 kn

Gillard Islands

Sea Lion Rk

Whirlpool Pt
1 Mile

Back eddy here

Flood 10 kns
Ebb 8 kns

Yuculta Rapids

Kellsey Pt
Mile 0
Back edd here

Gillard Passage/ Barber Passage

Currents really get underway in the area opposite Whirlpool Point (or Outhouse Point as the locals call it). Three streams converge on the flood to make the area opposite Big Bay one of the most turbulent and confused pieces of water anywhere on the B.C. coast. Combined with a mix of fresh water coming from mainland rivers and streams, especially in late spring, these currents and overfalls are impressive.

Because the water also makes a 90-degree change of direction between Gillard Passage and Yuculta Rapids, large whirlpools and holes form east of Gillard Island during flood conditions. The area SE of this island is especially dangerous during large flood tides, as is the area between Jimmy Judd and Gillard Islands. The flood set is very pronounced onto the west end of Jimmy Judd, and this area between the two islands is also where the current will be the strongest.

An alternate route north through the turmoil of a flood is to proceed along the mouth of Big Bay and navigate east of the 15.8 (metric) sounding in Barber Passage (which runs slightly slower than Gillard.) As long as you stay well away from the reef off Hessler Point, the going will be easier. This route is also recommended if southbound on a fast flood.

favour the Sonora Island shore.

If you are northbound and find yourself fighting a flood too strong for your engine, Tugboat Passage has a slightly easier stream and you may be able to pick your way through if you stay to the west of the shoal marked 3 (metric) and well away from the rocks and reefs in the vicinity of Tugboat

Dent Rapids

Proceeding north from Jimmy Judd Island, arrive at Little Dent Island near slack or with the beginning of the ebb. Arriving at Devils Hole (a turbulant and aerated section of water) an hour into a strong flood can be, says Woodward, "quite horrendous."

The main problem with the Dent Rapids occurs during the flood as a result of the tremendous wrenching Little Dent Island gives the tidal stream at the NW tip of the island. This forces a major deflection of current over to the Sonora Island shore. In a large tide, the deflection would have the appearance, for tardy southbound boaters, of the edge of a waterfall as it actually drops onto the back eddy east of the QR light. If you are going with the flood,

Below, Dent Rapids at full flood.
Devils Hole is at top centre.

Gillard Passage during flood.

Gillard Passage –
by Mike Woodward

Gillard Passage has traditionally been the route favoured by tugs towing log booms, in preference to the rougher waters of Discovery Passage. However, for decades there were no reliable predictions for Gillard Passage, prompting veteran skippers to develop their own formulas based on predicted times at Seymour Narrows.

Early measurement work from shore by the Canadian Hydrographic Service in Gillard Pass included a 'Mast and Boom' setup that held a small paddlewheel boat out in the current. Later, the use of traditional gas launches resulted in near swampings, preventing surveyors from finding the locations of faster water.

In 1987, as part of a project to obtain modern tidal-stream data for the narrow passes in this general area, high-quality data was collected using boats built to work at Nakwakto Rapids and Sechelt Rapids.

We soon found that the fastest speeds occur well to the east of the narrowest geographic section of the channel. We had heard reports of vessels struggling to make way against predicted currents that were supposed to be considerably less than their actual speed through the water, and we now understood why the predicted speeds were all too low.

In the above photo of the flood tidal stream through Gillard and Barber, note the confluence of the eastern jet of Barber Pass with the jet from Gillard. The turbulence and eddies that result from this interaction should be avoided, and a transit into the main flood through Gillard Passage may best be made along a track from the centre of Yuculta Rapids aiming for, or close to, the eastern tip of Gillard Island.

We spent many long days out in the launches, and one day we decided to pay a visit to a tug that was tied up against its log boom in Mermaid Bay. We were greeted by Lee Hollingsworth and his crew, who invited us aboard for lunch. It turned out that Lee was in his fiftieth year of pulling logs through Gillard Pass and we spent a little extra time in his nice, warm galley. Lee was happy to share his well-honed practical knowledge of the business of getting booms through Gillard in one piece – or not.

Hollingsworth recommends always waiting for slack, staying south of Kellsey Point when northbound or, if southbound, pulling into Denham Bay (the bay just north of Horn Point). And he also warns powerboats not to go through the pass too fast: "There's still lots of deadheads out there." After more than 40 years spent working the passes, Hollingsworth retired from the bridge of a RivTow tug in 1992.

Left – Mike Woodward setting a current meter in Discovery Passage.

"Don't Cut The Tow!"

The 'Dents' present special problems for tug skippers. Because of the tugs' slow speeds, especially when towing booms, two-holing (doing the Dents and Gillard Passage at one go) is not an easy task. Skippers often wait at Mermaid Bay for slack to continue south.

Lee Hollingsworth, a tug skipper for 50 years, has heard lots of stories about the rapids – one of the most humorous from his father who once described an episode from the days of steam tugs when manila towline was used.

"The skip on the southbound tug's getting kinda nervous taking a flood, see. It's a big tide and lots of drift in the water as there was in those days. So he gives his mate an axe and tells him to stand by in case the tow has to be cut. The skip said he would toot the steam whistle as a signal to cut the tow.

"Well, they've just got by the tricky part where the flood sets strong over to Jimmy Judd Island and the skip is relaxing when he sees a friend turning into Gillard Passage from the Ukes. So the friend toots his whistle, which is what they did in those days to passing tugs, and the skip, before he knows what he's doing, toots his whistle too. As soon as it happened he ran out on deck and yelled to the mate "No – don't cut the tow!" but he saw that the mate, who was pretty nervous too, had just finished doing the job. They had to turn around pretty quick in that current and managed to pick up the tow and save it from washing up on Gillard Island."

Island (between Little Dent and Dent Islands). Also, as mentioned, Mermaid Bay and the Dent Island Lodge are good spots to wait out the flood.

On the ebb, the stream at Dent Rapids is much more consistent because there is nothing to deflect the flowing water. If you find yourself riding a faster ebb than planned, stay in the middle of the pass as there is a set to Tugboat Passage and the rocks therein. Once clear of Little Dent, steer well to the N of the shoal patch – the 6/4 sounding (metric) about a half-mile NW of the QR light on Little Dent.

Good view of deflection caused by Little Dent Island in a flood, looking south.

Arran Rapids

Although Arran Rapids (which turn to flood and ebb at the same time as the Dent Rapids) would not normally be used for a direct route north, you might want to use this pass after exploring Bute Inlet or after fishing on the east side of Stuart Island.

These rapids are, in a word, bizarre. The Spanish explorers Valdes and Galiano, while braving these rapids in 1792, were spun around three times and came very close to going down, as it is locally known, 'The Drain.' At 14 knots on the flood, 10 on the ebb, Arran Rapids is an extremely energetic and violent pass. The dangers are caused by air. On a

Tugboat Island

Little Dent Island

Arran Rapids – first transits!

In the summer of 1792, both British and Spanish naval explorers transited these rapids with the help of local natives – the Euclataws – who lived at a nearby village. A survey party commanded by Lieutenant James Johnstone of HMS *Chatham* tried to row through the rapids but had to resort to pulling their boat through with ropes. The Euclataws, watching the action from shore, lent a hand with the ropes.

The Spanish showed up a short time later with their two ships – 50' schooners – and despite warnings from the Euclataws, decided to proceed through the rapids. One of the ships was seized by a whirlpool and was turned right around three times – a surprising experience that caused the crew on both vessels to burst into laughter.

flood tide, salt water rushes toward Arran Point and meets a foil-shaped cove that accelerates and strongly deflects the water halfway across the channel. Because of the turbulence of the water, air is trapped inside and creates a froth which doesn't give props a lot to bite and also doesn't support displacement hulls very well. Conditions in the pass are further complicated by the large amount of fresh water flowing into it in spring and summer months. The flooding saltwater stream, as witnessed by Mike

Woodward who surveyed this pass for CHS, will often just disappear under the quiet and still freshwater from Bute Inlet.

"I've been east of the pass, absolutely still on a layer of green freshwater, watching a 10-knot saltwater stream vanish a few yards away," he recalls.

The pass does not present the same problems on an ebb flow but there can be strong turbulence on the north side of the west entrance as shown on chart 3543. This is a pass that warrants full caution and a close eye to slack water.

THE MIDDLE ROUTE

In many ways the middle route (Surge Narrows to the Okisollo Rapids) is more interesting to use if you plan to continue on to Johnstone Strait. This route connects almost directly with the strait and although currents in these passes can be quite strong, they are not as fearsome as the other two routes because of lighter traffic and less turbulence. The middle route is a good introduction to the northern passes and offers the added bonus of superb scenery and excellent anchorages. The first rapids are Surge Narrows and some 6 miles north are the more turbulent Okisollo Rapids.

Aerial view of Arran Rapids during a flood looking north. Current in the pass reaches 14 knots on large tides.

Surge Narrows (Beazley Passage)

Surge Narrows is the fastest-flowing pass of the middle route and currents here can be turbulent, especially on the south-setting flood. Fortunately there is only one stream. This passage actually begins at Welsford Island at the SE end and extends NW through Beazley Passage, where the current is strongest, and then to Surge Narrows, which is the passage between Antonio Point and Quadra Island.

Beazley Passage is the only safe channel through the Settlers Group of islands, although it does present certain difficulties on both the flood and the ebb. On the flood there is a strong deflection off the SW part of Sturt Island. This generates tremendous turbulence in the shear zone which crosses the pass. Working the back eddy off Sturt Island and crossing the shear zone (as we once vainly attempted) is not an option because it is too easy to lose control in this turbulent area and, because the pass is narrow, you have little room to recover.

The ebb produces less turbulence, but there is the hazard of Tusko Rock, which dries at LW and is located just west of Sturt Island in line with the ebb set from the pass. Boaters should favour the west side of the passage until well clear of Peck Island.

The west side of Peck Island is not recommended because of strong turbulence. "A nightmare," says Woodward. The route north of Sturt Island is not recommended either because of its numerous rocks and reefs, and strong, turbulent currents that can set you onto danger very quickly.

A provincial marine park encompasses most of the Surge Narrows shoreline and several of the Settlers Group islands, including Peck but not Sturt and Goepel, which are private. This particular park is of more interest to kayakers and scuba divers than to boaters – none of the anchorages are recommended because of strong currents and poor holding ground (this area is kelp heaven). The park is best visited by inflatable at slack.

Above, Beazley Passage at flood. Below, looking north during slack at Surge Narrows.

PASS TIP SHEET – SURGE NARROWS
Chart: 3537
Location: 10 miles N of Heriot Bay
Maximum Flows: Flood 12 knots
Slack: 15-20 minutes. The window on this pass during big tides is just a few minutes.
Direction of Flood: South
Nearby Anchorages: N boaters can wait at Hjorth Bay on Read Island or moor at the public wharf opposite the narrows. S boaters can wait at Octopus Islands or at Yeatman Bay.
Key to Safe Transits: Arrive at or close to slack and give Tusko Rock lots of room.

Whiterock Passage

For boaters with experience and confidence in reading one-up range markers, Whiterock Passage is a real treat. It is one of the prettiest channels on the coast, with forested cliffs giving way to low, grassy banks dotted with large deciduous trees.

Whiterock Passage runs between Read and Maurelle Islands, and offers an alternative – albeit longer – route to the Octopus Islands. This narrow, slow-stream channel is a good example of a pass where kelp likes to grow. It has rock outcroppings, reefs and a rock bottom and, like all such passes, will almost always have kelp. Currents in Whiterock Passage rarely exceed 2 knots (flood is north) but the real challenge is the narrowness of the pass and the numerous rocks and ledges. At its narrowest point the width is about 70 feet.

A set of range markers makes the approach to the elbow of the pass easy enough, but the problem comes after making the turn and piloting out of the pass. Because the markers are now behind the boat and disappearing astern, the perspective is reversed. So between twisting around to keep the markers aligned and looking ahead to make sure you are avoiding debris and other boats, you will be busy. But it is excellent piloting practice for further travels up the coast, where you will encounter more of these range markers in passes.

An aerial view of Hole in the Wall looking east.

Hole in the Wall

One of the useful functions of Whiterock Passage is leading your boat to Hole in the Wall and if one good pass deserves another, then this circular route to the Octopus Islands will be a day well spent among some of the most beautiful scenery on the southern B.C. coast.

Of all the passes in this area, Hole in the Wall – which cuts between Sonora and Maurelle Islands – is certainly one of the most dramatic. The water flowing past the steep shorelines is a deep green colour typical of glacial run-off and there are two good lunch stops along the way. Florence Cove is on the channel's south shore, and we've anchored in its west side using a lunch hook. About a mile to the west is a wide bight on the channel's north side where, in 40 feet (12 m) of water, you can drop the hook and enjoy the view up the channel.

Currents in Hole in the Wall are strongest at the western entrance in the vicinity of the light marked 'QR', reaching 12 knots on the flood and 10 knots on the ebb. The area of most significant turbulence will be the shoal area farther west – a spot to avoid on strong tides. We normally set a course south of these shoals. Despite this area of caution, Hole in the Wall is a fairly predictable stream with no obstructions within the pass and is twice as wide as Beazley Passage.

During the north-flowing flood at the west entrance, two well-defined shear zones converge to form a broad area of turbulence, and there is a fairly strong set toward the bluffs on the north side. When the flood is especially strong it creates a lot of air bubbles in the water, both in the shear zones and downstream, which can cause serious cavitation.

The flow on the ebb is weaker and less confined, and the fastest flow dissipates quickly in the more open waters of Okisollo Channel. If you are going with the ebb, the main stream is easy to ride out into the larger channel.

At the east end of the passage, the current at Bassett Point will be about half that found at the west entrance near Springer Point. One hazard to be aware of at the east entrance is floating and submerged debris. There is some stratification between fresh and salt water which can sometimes result in bits of wood floating just below the water's surface.

Okisollo Channel
(Upper and Lower Rapids)

Currents in the Upper Rapids, the first set of rapids encountered when northbound, are considerably stronger (up to 11 knots) than those in the Lower

Rapids, which usually run less than 6 knots. The Upper Rapids passage is also encumbered with reefs and rock outcroppings that generate strong deflection. Seas can be quite turbulent in the area near Bentley Rock during large tides.

On the south-flowing flood, the strongest deflection is just south of two small islets (one of which is marked '10' on Chart 3537) on the E side of the channel below Owen Bay. The safest route through this pass is a course favouring the E side of the channel, giving Bentley Rock a wide berth. During floods it is safe to cross over to Quadra Island once you are past Diamond Bay. The ebb in the Upper Rapids is even more confused, especially in the area downstream of Bentley Rock. Be careful to avoid the strong set to Bentley Rock by crossing to the E side of the channel well upstream. Currents in Okisollo are strongest around this rock and the forces of water here are very hazardous.

Although Okisollo's Upper Rapids can be turbulent, the pass is fairly wide and there are opportunities to pull out and assess the situation if conditions are uncomfortable. Owen Bay is a good anchorage to wait out strong tides. The Lower Rapids are more benign, with currents rarely exceeding 5 knots in the channel S of Gypsy Shoal. The channel N of Okis Islands is free of hazards with less current.

Okisollo Channel enters Discovery Passage about 4 miles south of Chatham Point, which marks the eastern entrance to Johnstone Strait.

PASS TIP SHEET – OKISOLLO RAPIDS
Chart: 3537
Location: Upper Rapids 2 miles north of Octopus Islands Marine Park.
Reference Station: Seymour Narrows.
Maximum Flow: Upper Rapids, max 11 knots. Lower Rapids, 5 knots
Slack: 15 – 20 minutes
Nearby Anchorages: Octopus Islands Marine Park, Owen Bay, Barnes Bay (open to the west).
Key To Safe Transit: Be at Upper Rapids close to slack and stay to east side of channel.

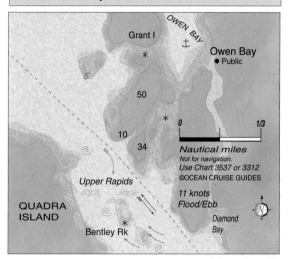

Below, Okisollo Channel's Lower Rapids at the start of a flood. Cameleon Harbour at top right.

Discovery Passage

There's something exciting about making a voyage along Discovery Passage. Hemmed in by the steep slopes of Vancouver Island and the forested shores of Quadra Island, this wide ribbon of cold, swift-flowing water bustles with commercial traffic all summer long. Discovery Passage was once the domain of native peoples who plied its waters by dugout canoe, and it was not until the Klondike Gold Rush in 1898 that steamships started flooding north along this major route of the Inside Passage. The steamships have been replaced by cruise ships, but the flow of traffic in Discovery Passage remains under the control of that great gatekeeper, Seymour Narrows. Even the leviathan liners are very careful about timing their transit for slack water at this pass, which is one of the most formidable on our coast with currents reaching 16 knots.

From May through September cruise ships on the Vancouver-Alaska run regularly use this pass, most heavily on weekends during nightime transits. The captains of these ubiquitous cruise ships have great respect for Seymour Narrows, for their flat-bottomed ships tend to slide stern-out in sharp turns – such as the blind corner in this pass.

"Everything hinges on Seymour Narrows. It tells us how fast to go from Sitka all the way down the Inside Passage," Captain Ympa Ercka of a Holland America Line cruise ship confirmed. Asked about other hair-raising passes or navigational hazards of the coast, Ercka shook his head: "There is only Seymour Narrows. Nothing compares."

For the northbound boater, this passage really starts a few miles south of Cape Mudge, where the first effects of currents from far-off Johnstone Strait are felt north of Mitlenatch Island. Even during calm conditions, the waters here can be choppy and rolly. During strong S winds of 25 knots or more against a flood stream, the seas here can be dangerous and

Left, Cape Mudge lighthouse. Below, a cruise ship steams south in Discovery Passage.

over the years numerous vessels have been lost in this area, usually during winter storms. In summer, southeasterlies are not as common, but seas can still be rough and currents strong in the area 3-to-4 miles south of Wilby Shoals. Also note, during a strong ebb there is a significant set toward Sutil Channel.

If you're bucking a flood tide, the best route for avoiding current is to pass close by the red buoy at Wilby Shoals (stand off a mile to avoid the set) and follow the 20-metre line to the Cape Mudge lighthouse. This will keep you away from the rough water coming out of Discovery Passage and inside the back eddy which starts south of Cape Mudge. Once past the lighthouse, follow the Quadra Island shoreline until you're near Whiskey Point, then either cross over to Campbell River or stay along the Quadra shore to the anchorage of your choice.

Discovery Channel, between Campbell River and Quadra Island, is a busy place so, in addition to the constant current, be prepared for heavy traffic. There are the hourly crossings of the Quadra Island car ferry, the comings and goings of tugs (often with booms or barges), fishboats, numerous pleasure craft and the cruise ships, which usually transit the pass during evening or night-time slack. On weekends there can be four or five lined up from Seymour Narrows to Campbell River. However, Discovery Passage is fairly wide and straight, and you can easily pick a clear spot if you need to cross the channel. Keep your VHF on Channel 16 if you need to clarify a situation with another vessel.

Seymour Narrows at end of flood looking north.

Seymour Narrows

Back in the 1950s, the currents of Seymour Narrows were measured using drift poles (8-foot-long two-by-two's with lead at either end and a flag stick) and a transit mounted on a cairn of Maud Island. CHS surveyors would measure the time the pole needed to travel at given angles on the transit to determine current speed. CHS staff eventually used a 25-foot inflatable dinghy with plenty of horsepower to stay in one position in the pass while a probe, three feet below the surface, measured current.

Hydrographers say the strongest currents at the Narrows are in the vicinity of Ripple Rock (slightly west of mid-channel, directly beneath the hydro lines strung between Vancouver and Maud Islands). On a flood, the strongest turbulence will be along the west wall and in the area south of Ripple Rock. On an ebb, the turbulence – and the set – start between Maud Island and Ripple Rock. The current sets northwest to the west wall.

Northbound vessels should arrive off the Maud Island light within an hour of the ebb finishing or beginning. Once into the narrows, steer toward the tongue of the current stream (east of mid-channel) to avoid the whirlpools and eddies north of Maud Island up to North Bluff. On big tides in low-powered vessels it's prudent to be at the Maud Island light at slack or just a few minutes into the north flowing ebb. If the slack is LW, be sure to arrive at the pass before the end of the ebb because slack here on large tides is not very long – 5 to 10 minutes at most – and you'll want to be past Brown Bay before the south-flowing flood gets underway, which can

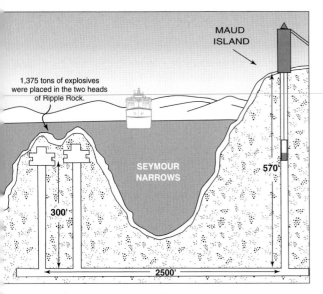

Removing Ripple Rock

Although Captain George Vancouver described Seymour Narrows as a pass that "rushes with some impetuosity" one of his officers said that the pass was "the most nightmarish spectacle his eyes had ever beheld." No doubt this response came from seeing the frightening whirlpools around submerged Ripple Rock. Until the top of this two-headed pinnacle rock was removed in 1958, transiting Seymour Narrows at low tide was extremely hazardous. Ripple Rock used to lie less than 9 feet (3 m) below chart datum where it created dangerous turbulence. Vessels would get caught in the suction around the rock and be pulled under. More than 20 large vessels and over 100 lives were lost before the Public Works of Canada was able to remove this terrible hazard.

In 1955 work commenced on a tunnel – 8 feet wide by 8 feet high – that was dug under the seabed of Seymour Narrows from Maud Island to the base of Ripple Rock, where chambers were carved into its double heads and stuffed with 1,400 tons of Niramex explosive (see illustration). On April 5, 1958, scientists from around the world gathered to watch the largest non-nuclear explosion to date. At 9:31 a.m. the plunger went down and a huge bubble rose in the water, then burst skyward like a fountain that sent chunks of rock flying hundreds of feet into the air. Within minutes the debris had settled. When measurements were taken, it was determined that 35 feet of the rock had been blown off with minimum depth at the south head now being 45 feet (14 m) below low water. The twin heads of Ripple Rock were gone and Seymour Narrows was free of the 'killer' rock.

Above, Ripple Rock being blown up in 1958.
Below, Ripple Rock today, tamer and safer.

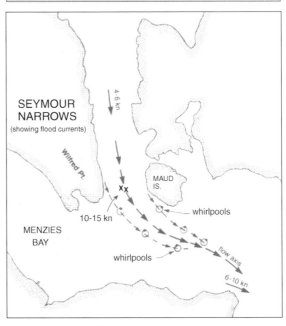

be brutal in a slow-moving boat. On a large flood, Seymour Narrows can reach 16 knots – no place to be in any kind of boat.

Southbound boats should be opposite Brown Bay within the hour of a neap flood ending or beginning. If a large spring flood is underway, it would be wise to be here within a half hour of its end or beginning. Keep well away from the west shore when transiting the narrows. The worst turbulence is often south of Ripple Rock, especially if wind is against current. If you stay on the starboard side of the channel throughout the transit, you'll be out of harm's way in the event you are sharing the narrows with a boom-towing tug or large ship. The good news about Seymour Narrows is that there are no obstructions and just one strong, main stream.

When reading current tables, boaters often assume that the speed of the ebb or flood is like a sine wave, and that being one hour late for slack means the current should be only a fraction of the maximum flow. However, there are surges and slow periods of flow as water backed up at one end of the pass is suddenly released at slack and rushes through the pass to temporarily equalize with the water level on the other side.

"In some passes – and this is quite pronounced in Seymour Narrows – the flow is non-linear," Mike Woodward relates. "So the flow is not comparable to a sine wave – slowly building to maximum flow, but more like a saw-tooth wave. In other words, the current can come on strong very quickly."

Woodward has seen many boats trying to buck a big flood at the Narrows – a hazardous practise for this particular pass. "If you try to use the Maud Island back eddy, which is about 3 knots in a north direction, and your boat has a hull speed of 10 knots, that means you are travelling at 13 knots over ground. When your boat crosses over the flooding jet – which it has to do right near the beacon – it could be hit with 15 knots of current. Suddenly the hull is being forced to go at 28 knots for a brief time

and the bow wave can go over the prow or perhaps cause the vessel to roll. As well, you run the risk of overheating your engine, which could happen just as a large tug and barge are coming on you." Woodward says he has motored up to a number of boaters trying to beat Seymour Narrows and they rarely listen. "They sit for a half-hour or more going nowhere when they could just as easily go around the corner and anchor behind Maud Island and have a cup of tea and save all that fuel."

Campbell River

If any part of B.C.'s coastline can lay claim to being the heart of the Inside Passage, it might well be the waters off Campbell River. A steady stream of vessels, from kayaks to cruise ships, passes by Campbell River throughout the summer, travelling this main artery of the Inside Passage. They are following the route first charted by Captain George Vancouver in 1792 as they pass beneath the white cliffs of Cape Mudge at the southern entrance to Discovery Passage, named for Vancouver's ship.

A full century later, a rush of steamships carrying Klondike-bound prospectors headed north up Discovery Passage, past the mouth of the Campbell River. Passing beneath their keels were huge runs of salmon, which thrive in the cold, swift-flowing waters of Discovery Passage and have earned Campbell River the right to proclaim itself 'Salmon Capital of the World.' Five species of salmon migrate up the Campbell River, but it's the prized

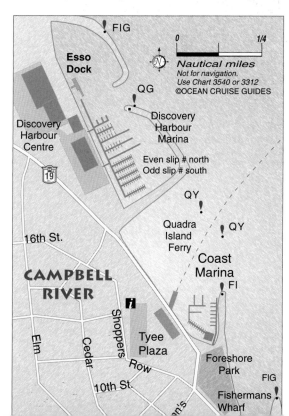

Discovery Harbour Marina in Campbell River provides special entertainment for kids – watching the crabs at Patti Finn's fresh seafood market.

Famous Fishing

Campbell River's fame as a sportfishing destination began with the arrival in 1924 of a boat-builder named Ned Painter who rented and sold his wooden rowboats. This enterprise evolved into a fishing camp he and his wife opened at the mouth of the river, followed by a cottage resort, and, finally, their opening of Painter's Lodge in 1938. This historic resort (which burned in 1985 and was replaced with a modern facility) achieved worldwide fame as a sportfishing retreat and brought many a celebrity to Campbell River, including Bing Crosby and Bob Hope.

This tradition continues today, with multi-million-dollar yachts arriving in Campbell River each summer to await the arrival of their owners. Some come 'north' to spend time fishing local waters, while others simply want to relax in a wilderness setting. Julie Andrews and her husband, movie director Blake Edwards, have often flown by Learjet to Campbell River to board their yacht for a few weeks of cruising. Ms. Andrews has been heard exercising her vocal chords on the stern deck, her beautiful singing voice wafting across the water.

chinook that first caught the world's attention when, in 1896, Sir Richard Musgrave wrote an article for *Field* magazine in which he praised his native guides' simple but skillful method of catching these large fish from dugout canoes.

Campbell River grew into a logging and pulp mill town, where visiting pleasure boaters jostled with commercial fishboats for space at the public docks.

In recent years, however, Campbell River has successfully transformed itself from a blue-collar working town into a base for all kinds of tourism, including sportfishing, kayaking, hiking and, most importantly for us, boating.

Marinas line the shores of the town and smaller marinas thrive on the Quadra Island side of Discovery Passage. The largest by far is the Discovery Harbour Marina (VHF 66A, phone 250-287-2614), owned and operated by the Campbell River Indian Band. The marina is protected by a riprap breakwater which almost completely encloses the facilities and protects the docks from the wash of passing tugs and ships. Fresh, potable water is available at the docks, and power is 20, 30 and 50-amp. Showers and laundry are also available.

It's a short walk from Discovery Harbour Marina to a wide assortment of stores and restaurants. Ocean Pacific Marine Supply, which carries most items a boater might need, is at the top of the ramp

View of Campbell River looking across Discovery Passage to Quathiaski Cove.

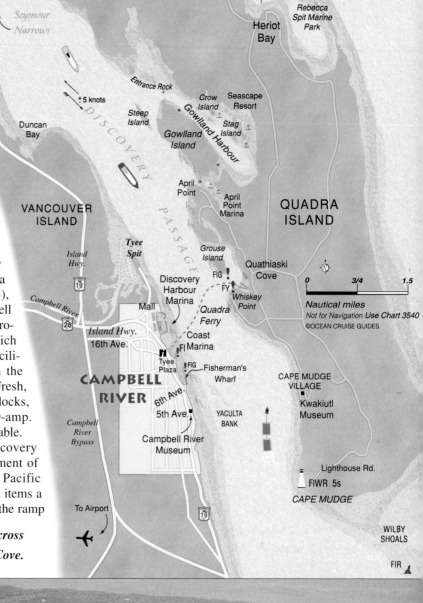

Seymour Narrows

Ferry to Cortes

Rebecca Spit Marine Park

Heriot Bay

Entrance Rock

+5 knots

Crow Island

Seascape Resort

Steep Island

Gowlland Harbour

Stag Island

Duncan Bay

Gowlland Island

April Point

April Point Marina

QUADRA ISLAND

VANCOUVER ISLAND

Tyee Spit

Island Hwy.

Grouse Island

Quathiaski Cove

FIG

Discovery Harbour Marina

FY

Whiskey Point

Campbell River

19

Mall

Quadra Ferry

Nautical miles
Not for Navigation. Use Chart 3540
©OCEAN CRUISE GUIDES

0   3/4   1.5

28

Island Hwy.
16th Ave.

Coast
Fl Marina

CAMPBELL RIVER

Tyee Plaza

FIG

Fisherman's Wharf

CAPE MUDGE VILLAGE

Kwakiutl Museum

6th Ave.

5th Ave.

YACULTA BANK

Campbell River Bypass

Campbell River Museum

Lighthouse Rd.

FlWR 5s

CAPE MUDGE

To Airport

19

WILBY SHOALS

FIR

The anchorage south of April Point is well protected with very good holding ground.

in the main marina building. The Discovery Harbour Centre adjoins the marina and among its 50-some stores are a grocery store and liquor store.

Another excellent marina in Campbell River is the Coast Marina (VHF 66A, phone 250-287-7455). This facility is owned by the Coast Discovery Inn, which allows moorage guests to use the hotel facilities. The marina was rebuilt in 1998, when improved concrete docks and new power and water outlets were installed. This marina has the advantage of being right opposite the downtown area and Tyee Plaza, and is just north of the very pleasant Foreshore Park.

Just south of Coast Marina is the Fisherman's Wharf, which has also made improvements to its facilities to attract pleasure boaters. This marina is a good place to buy fresh fish right on the dock.

There are numerous attractions in and around Campbell River, and the visitor information kiosk in Tyee Plaza has details about local sights and transportation. Elk Falls Provincial Park is just outside Campbell River's city limits on Highway 28 and is named after an impressive 80-foot waterfall that plunges into the Campbell River canyon. Vancouver Island has thousands of caves, many close to Campbell River, such as the Horne Lakes Caves. NorthernVancouver Island is also home to the highest concentration of black bears in the world.

South of the marinas is the Museum at Campbell River, a contemporary facility overlooking Discovery Passage on Oceanside Route 19A near the south entrance to town. The museum's permanent exhibits feature a pioneer settlement, float homes, salmon fishing and First Nations' history. You can also watch a documentary video about the record-setting detonation of Ripple Rock.

Over on Quadra Island, in Cape Mudge Village, the Potlatch Collection at the Kwagiulth Museum and Cultural Centre (phone (250-285-3733) features sacred ceremonial objects such as masks, headdresses, coppers and other regalia used in Kwagiulth (Kwakwaka'wakw) winter ceremonies. There is also a vintage photograph collection, gift shop and, on a nearby beach, over 50 petroglyphs.

THE ANCHORAGES
April Point 1

The bay southeast of April Point is a convenient place to pull into before or after transiting Seymour Narrows, where boaters will find sheltered anchorage and good holding. We often drop anchor beside the April Point Marina, or tie up if the weather is poor and there's a slip available. Entrance to the bay is obstructed by kelp and a rock which has a red spar buoy marking its location. Leave this to starboard.

The April Point Marina is part of the sportfishing lodge and resort located on the point. The resort provides a shuttle service, but in fair weather it's a lovely walk from the docks to the lodge where we have enjoyed an excellent meal. This well-known lodge was built in 1945 by Phil and Phyllis Peterson, an American couple under whose management, and that of their sons Warren and Eric, the lodge developed into a leading sportfishing resort visited by guests from all walks of life, including politicians and entertainment celebrities. In 1998, the Petersons sold their lodge to the Oak Bay Marine Group.

In September, off-season descends and the slips normally filled with mega-yachts throughout the summer start to empty. One misty afternoon in October we pulled into this bay for the night and sat outside in the cockpit, enjoying the peace and pine-scented air until the dampness of early evening drove us below decks. That night we could hear a pod of killer whales in the bay, followed by an owl hooting back, in perfect time, at a foghorn.

Gowlland Harbour 2

Located 5 miles south of Seymour Narrows, Gowlland Harbour is a lovely, land-locked anchorage of wooded islets and hidden passages awaiting exploration by dinghy. Entry is made between Entrance Rock and Vigilant Islets at the harbour entrance – favour the Vigilant Islets side of the channel. To avoid the log booms lining the harbour's western and southern shoreline, there are a number of locations to drop the hook but perhaps the best for shelter is on the east side of Stag Island in 20 feet (6 m). Our CQR has no problem penetrating the hard mud/sand combination here, but we've seen other

GOWLLAND HARBOUR AT A GLANCE

CHARTS: 3540, 3312, 3539
LAT LONG: 50°4.60'N 125°12.89'W
PROS: Fair to good protection with good holding in sand and mud. Excellent sunsets and views of Quadra Island. Marina nearby with showers, laundry. Good spot to clear Seymour Narrows if north-bound and good haven if southbound.
CONS: Northwesterlies can whistle through the harbour. Some anchors have difficulty setting in hard mud-and-sand bottom.
MUST DO: Explore the area by dinghy.

boats have difficulties getting a set. This is the sort of bottom where patience, setting the anchor slowly with generous scope, will usually work.

Tucked close to **Stag Island**, you are sheltered from all but the strongest northwesterlies funnelling into Gowlland Harbour. And funnel they do. In December 2000 a winter 'bomb' tore the Seascape Resort docks from their moorings and sent them a quarter-mile east. With a dozen boats still attached to the docks, the ensemble somehow managed to pass over a reef before finally coming to rest. Miraculously, only a few boats sustained damage. If conditions from the northwest are very strong we've found the area a little further south (at the very tip of Stag Island) is more protected.

Northwest winds from Discovery Passage can push moderate swells right up to Doe Islet and gusts will be keenly felt throughout the small 'animal' islets north of Stag Island. The small bight south of **Vigilant Island** is suitable only as a temporary lunch stop because there is regular wash from tugs working the bay. The bight is also exposed to south-

easterlies and experiences a regular current stream. Several of the 'animal' islets, namely Wren, Crow, Fawn and Mouse, are protected as provincial park reserves, as are the Vigilant Islets, where seals and sea lions regularly haul out. Private homes dot much of the shoreline, but they do not detract from the pleasant setting, and road access to the harbour offers boaters the opportunity to explore some of the nearby parks and trail systems. Closest, about 2 miles (3 km) away, is Blenkin Memorial Park, behind the community centre on West Road.

The boat passage connecting Gowlland Harbour with the April Point anchorage requires local knowledge and no small amount of nerve to safely pilot a keel boat through at HW slack, but it is interesting to explore by dinghy.

Above, well anchored on the east side of Stag Island. Below, aerial view of Gowlland Harbour.

Kanish Bay/Small Inlet, Quadra Island 3

For years, when southbound in Discovery Passage, we would pull into Kanish Bay for the night and depart the next morning in time to catch slack water at Seymour Narrows. We invariably motored to Small Inlet, at the head of Kanish Bay, where we anchored behind the two small islets in the easternmost part in 2 fathoms (4 m). This is a snug spot and although strong north-westerlies can funnel through Kanish Bay with the odd gust whistling past the islets, the holding is good (the bight on the S shore just E of the inlet entrance also provides some shelter from W wind). The **Small Inlet** anchorage also provides access to a lovely forest trail that crosses the neck of land separating Small Inlet from Waiatt Bay and connects with another trail leading to Newton Lake. The only real drawback to Small Inlet is the 4-mile drive from Discovery Passage.

Another more convenient spot to anchor in Kanish Bay is among the **Chained Islands**, just inside Bodega Point. There are several approaches to this small cove, situated south of the islet marked '4' on metric chart 3312. We follow the thread of deep water that runs between the island marked '58' and the islet lying off Bodega Point, keeping close to the larger island to port, and then swing in a wide arc around the islet marked '4', dropping the hook between the islet and the Quadra Island shore in about 40 feet (12 m). Although somewhat open to strong NW winds, which come in muted gusts, this anchorage is otherwise well protected and the holding is very good in sticky mud. Farther into the cove is a small derelict dock which is unsafe for tying up.

Left, beautiful anchorage in Chained Islands.

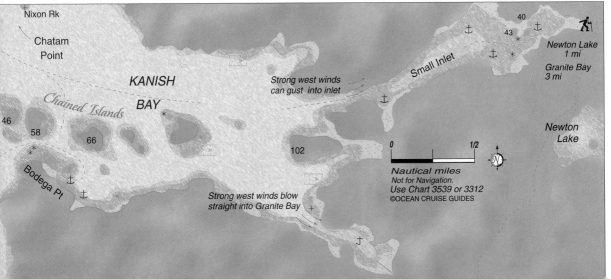

Nixon Rk

Chatam
Point

KANISH

Chained Islands

BAY

46

58

66

Bodega Pt

Strong west winds
can gust into inlet

Small Inlet

Strong west winds blow
straight into Granite Bay

102

40

43

Newton Lake
1 mi

Granite Bay
3 mi

Newton
Lake

0   1/2

Nautical miles
Not for Navigation.
Use Chart 3539 or 3312
©OCEAN CRUISE GUIDES

The islet marked '4' is a small grassy knoll which affords a tranquil morning view of the anchorage.

Granite Bay once the site of a logging and fishing community with a population of some 500 in the early part of the last century. Reclaimed by nature for many years, the bay's shoreline is now dotted with houses. As a result, numerous moored vessels are at the head of the bay, diminishing its appeal as an anchorage. NW winds howl through here keenly.

Kanish Bay was once inhabited by Coast Salish natives who shared their northern frontier with a confederation of Kwakwaka'wakw (Kwakiutl) tribes called the Lekwiltok, later dubbed the 'Vikings of Vancouver Island' for their skill as mariners. About two centuries ago, not long after Captain Vancouver made his historic voyage through local waters, the Kwakwaka'wakw of Salmon River, near Sayward, began moving southward to occupy strategic sites along the channels that weave through the Discovery

KANISH BAY AT A GLANCE

CHARTS: 3539, 3312
LAT LONG: entrance, 50°15.51'N 125°22.03'W
PROS: Selection of good to excellent anchorages with fair to good holding in various mud bottoms. Small Inlet offers best protection. Good hikes from Small Inlet to Waiatt Bay and Newton Lake. Good swimming there and off islet near entrance to Granite Bay. Chained Islands anchorage convenient for northbound yachts.
CONS: Northwesterlies can penetrate most bays. Granite Bay gets strong westerly gusts.
MUST DO: Explore the bays, go swimming!

Above, trail signpost at head of Small Inlet.
Below, aerial showing the head of Small Inlet.

Islands. The Coast Salish villages that had long thrived in Kanish Bay, producing vast middens to depths of 25 feet, were eventually abandoned after repeated raids. These uprooted people resettled in Burrard Inlet and the Gulf Islands.

Octopus Islands/Waiatt Bay 4 🚶

If it weren't for the tidal passes to the south, the Octopus Islands and adjacent Waiatt Bay would no doubt be as busy as Desolation Sound each summer. This park, at the mouth of Waiatt Bay, contains several scenic anchorages separated by small islands

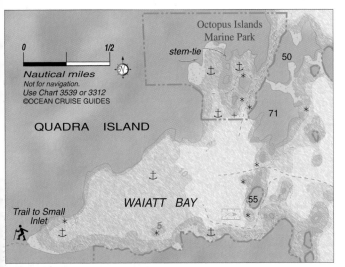

and islets. Its boundaries were extended in 1996 to include the south shore of Waiatt Bay, but the two largest of the Octopus Islands (marked '50' and '71') remain private. An undeveloped park, it's a boater's haven with protected coves, picturesque islets and scenic vistas. Wildlife abounds here, and while poking about in our dinghy we have spotted deer, loons, clam-digging raccoons and a mother merganser with her chicks.

The easiest entry into the anchorage is through the narrow channel that traces the Quadra Island shoreline south from Bodega Anchorage (which is really a tug or commercial waiting area for tide turns at the passes). Entry can also be made south of the Octopus Islands but this is a bit trickier because of islets, shoals and drying reefs clogging the entrance. With someone at the bow, however,

OCTOPUS ISLANDS AT A GLANCE
CHARTS: 3539, 3312
LAT LONG: 50°16.56'N 125°13.94'W
PROS: Marine park, one of the best. Good protection with very good holding in mud, sand and shell bottoms. Lots to do here.
CONS: Main part of anchorage can be busy. Access can be a little tricky for first-timers.
MUST DO: Relax at one of the finest anchorages of the B.C. coast. Explore islets and reefs by dinghy. Swim at Newton Lake.

and proceeding slowly, this entrance is fairly straightforward. When northbound, coming from Surge Narrows, we go above the small islet N of island '55'. The reef is easy to see and the channel has over 20 feet (6 m) at LW. Another approach to the anchorage is to pass close alongside island '55' and either turn tightly around the island or proceed to the Quadra Island shore before turning west.

Inside Waiatt Bay, you have a myriad of choices. Most people like to anchor in the Octopus Islands and set a stern line because of the limited swinging room. When the marine park is too busy, we sometimes anchor at the head of Waiatt Bay, where there is a lovely trail that winds for a half-mile past streams, ferns and evergreens to Small Inlet on the other side of Quadra Island. The trail also branches off to Newton Lake where you can enjoy a refreshing swim. This latter trail ascends some fairly steep terrain but is groomed and signposted.

Waiatt Bay is well protected from most winds. Westerlies will sometimes scoot through the main bay but the holding, in mud and sand, is very good.

Frederick Arm / Estero Basin 5

The head of Frederick Arm is a unique destination for boaters, offering stunning scenery and access to a large uncharted basin. Where the charts end, (3539 or 3312) at the top of the arm, a partly hidden gut leads to the magnificent Estero Basin.

Before dropping anchor in Frederick Arm, we take soundings off the basin's entrance, where depths are uneven and the sandy bottom shoals

Above and opposite, Octopus Islands Marine Park. Below, uncharted Estero Basin.

Top, view up the pass to Estero Basin. Above, the lure of uncharted waters draws all kinds.

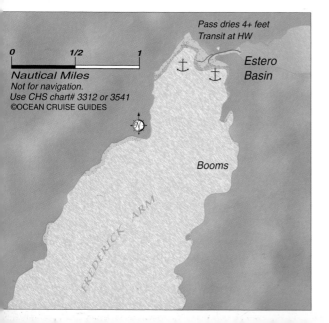

quickly. We have dropped the hook in the arm's NE corner in 65 feet of water, reversed into 50 feet, and later swung into 25. In settled conditions, we've stayed overnight here but if conditions are unstable you can stern tie in the small bight along the east shore of Frederick Arm, or motor the 6 miles to Shoal Bay or a little further to Bickley Bay.

The waters of land-locked Estero Basin spill across a drying flat into the inlet, and few boats enter Estero Basin because of this shallow entrance channel. Back in August 1934, Frederick Arm was visited by coastal pioneers Francis and Amy Barrow, who travelled the Inside Passage in their boat *Toketie* each summer to locate and record petroglyphs for the provincial archives. They had tied to a boom at Estero Basin's mouth where they planned to have lunch before entering, as "the tide was running out very fast." However, as they explained in their logbook entry, a man living at the mouth "called over to us to say that they were going to float a lot of boomsticks through the narrows and as we might have got pinched where we were lying, and as the tide had slacked up a bit, we decided to go through. We bumped quite a few rocks and bent all the blades of the propeller, but I don't think much harm has been done."

When we entered Estero Basin by dinghy one summer afternoon, a family of four was riding rubber air mattresses in the rapids, known locally as 'the Gut'. The father called out to us to take our bathing suits because the swimming was great. We should have heeded his advice because, after making little headway against a rushing ebb current, the three of us (our dog Tuck included) climbed out of the dinghy and proceeded on foot. While Bill hauled the dinghy through the Gut, Anne and Tuck walked along the adjacent sand-and-gravel flats. Once through the narrowest part of the channel, we climbed back in and motored the short distance into the basin where we found a flat rock ledge on the north side and sat there awhile, enjoying the stillness, the sun and the solitude.

Estero Basin, which is about 4 miles long and remains uncharted, was named in 1792 by the explorers Galiano and Valdes who explored this basin by small boat after anchoring their ships in Frederick Arm. Estero means *estuary* or *lagoon* in Spanish, but this basin is more like a huge gorge carved out of the mountains, its deep water enclosed by a precipitous shoreline of forested slopes and sheer cliffs.

Opposite, anchored at the head of Frederick Sound near the entrance to Estero Basin.

Pass dries 4+ feet
Transit at HW

Estero Basin

0   1/2   1

Nautical Miles
Not for navigation.
Use CHS chart# 3312 or 3541
©OCEAN CRUISE GUIDES

Booms

FREDERICK ARM

Aerial view of Handfield Bay looking north.

Handfield Bay, 6

Thurston Bay Marine Park

Thurston Bay Marine Park is comprised of two sections – one encompasses the northern part of Thurston Bay and its surrounding shores, the other takes in Handfield Bay and much of the land lying between this bay and Thurston Bay. **Handfield Bay** is our favourite of the two anchorages, both for shelter and setting. This lovely anchorage is at a popular crossroads just north of the major passes and presents a truly bucolic picture with its islets, pale green water and deciduous trees thriving amongst the evergreens. There is good swimming near the islets at the head of the bay (the water is warmish) and plenty to explore by dinghy. The anchorage is a great spot to

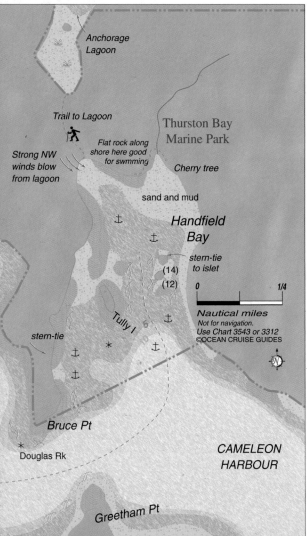

Anchorage Lagoon

Trail to Lagoon

Strong NW winds blow from lagoon

Flat rock along shore here good for swimming

Thurston Bay Marine Park

Cherry tree

sand and mud

Handfield Bay

stern-tie to islet

(14)

(12)

0   1/4

Nautical miles
Not for navigation.
Use Chart 3543 or 3312
©OCEAN CRUISE GUIDES

Tully I

stern-tie

N

Bruce Pt

Douglas Rk

CAMELEON HARBOUR

Greetham Pt

HANDFIELD BAY AT A GLANCE
CHARTS: 3543, 3312
LAT LONG: 50°20.79'N 125°18.95'W
PROS: Marine park. Generally good protection with good-to-excellent holding in sticky mud with sand. Beautiful setting with lots of dinghy exploring. Some hiking available.
CONS: Northwesterlies can whistle through NE side of Handfield Bay and through Cameleon Harbour. Some anchors have difficulty setting in the hard mud-and-sand bottom.
MUST DO: Picnic on Tully Island.

rest after the arduous journey north through the passes and is well worth spending a few days at.

Handfield Bay's entrance is the narrow gap presented by the sharp end of Bruce Point and the reef off Greetham Point. Swing wide when entering to avoid Douglas Rock, which lies a little further west than indicated on the chart. Once inside, we like to anchor north of the two wooded islets in about 10 feet (3 m) and tie a stern line to a tall cedar on the northernmost islet. This is a good spot in settled conditions or if strong winds are expected from the south, with the islet providing a wind break. The holding is excellent in a bottom of mud, sand and shell. During strong northwesterlies however, gusts from the lagoon can really blast through the entire bay and into Cameleon Harbour. A better spot in such conditions is south of Tully Island with a line ashore to Bruce Point peninsula.

A black bear used to appear regularly on shore at the head of the bay, picking the fallen fruit from the large cherry tree, and would retreat into the bush at the sight of humans approaching by dinghy.

Tully Island is mostly dried grass in summer and is a very peaceful spot to have a picnic lunch. We have enjoyed many a sunny afternoon here amid the clusters of pink wild onion that bloom each spring.

The park is undeveloped except for an overgrown trail linking Handfield Bay with **Anchorage Lagoon** at the south end of Thurston Bay. The lagoon is a one- or two-boat spot and the entrance is very shallow (less than 2 feet) with boulders. The anchorage has a minimum depth of about 12 feet (3.7 m). Northwesterlies gust through this anchorage but a line to the north shore helps.

The north end of **Thurston Bay** is fun to explore by dinghy where, behind some islets, a stream feeds into the head of the bay. Near the stream is an overgrown trail which leads inland past an old forestry station to Florence Lake (1.5 miles/2.5 km NE). Cut throat trout fishing is reportedly good there.

The anchorage in Thurston Bay is deep and exposed to both westerlies and south winds. The SE end of **Cameleon Harbour** has a beautiful view to the west, but gets hit when Johnstone Strait kicks up a westerly gale. The holding in sticky mud is good.

Above, Handfield Bay anchorage viewed from its head. Below, stern tied to islet '14'.

Hemming Bay 7

If you've had it with westerlies, a good spot to get out of the wind is Hemming Bay. This anchorage will make you forget what it's like out in Johnstone Strait once you're tucked beside the islets near the head of the bay.

There are numerous spots to anchor along the bay's north and northwest shores that provide good shelter. A good spot is north of the island marked '44' (Charts 3543 and 3312) and its satellite islet, with a view through the narrow entrance into a pretty saltwater lagoon. This is well sheltered from most winds although strong westerlies sometimes gust out of the mouth of the lagoon. Anchor here in about 40 feet in good holding in sticky mud. The very head of the bay, in front of the low shoreline with a cabin, gives better protection in NW gales. Vessels can also anchor SE of island '44' or in SW of the island marked '3' being very careful to avoid the rocks.

A small islet southeast of '44' is a great spot to relax and enjoy a picnic or go for a swim off one of the granite ledges leading into the water. For those wanting to test the waters of Hemming Lake, there are two access points. One is from the north shore of the saltwater lagoon, along a small drainage creek. Follow the creek and cross the old logging road until you're walking parallel with a lagoon filled with old logs. Continue for about a quarter mile to the lake proper where you will find a rock outcropping to swim from. Another access point is from the north arm of the bay, where an old logging road leads west to the creek. (The small waterfall and creek at the west end of the saltwater lagoon connect with the lake, but the path and road along the creek are private property.)

The saltwater lagoon is a beautiful spot to drift around in a dinghy and watch birdlife. Numerous heron make this bay their home and loud squawking from these modern pterodactyls is the greeting meted out to interlopers.

Of note when entering Hemming Bay north of the Lee Islands: there appears to be less water than charted south of Jackson Point, with depths of less than 13 feet (4 m). If taking this pass, proceed with caution. Kelp can be expected across the pass.

Below, saltwater lagoon at head of Hemming Bay.
Opposite, enjoying the islets in Hemming Bay.

Map

To Hemming Lake
Lagoon
Logging road
Private
Private
Lagoon
44
0   1/4
N
Nautical miles
Not for navigation.
Use Chart 3543 or 3312
©OCEAN CRUISE GUIDES
Pinhorn It
Jackson Pt
Menace Rk
Depth less than 10 ft ((3 m)
HEMMING BAY
Lee Islands

CHAPTER SIX

JOHNSTONE STRAIT

It took Captain Vancouver four days to transit the entire length of Johnstone Strait in the summer of 1792. His two ships rounded Chatham Point in a northwesterly and began tacking their way along this 54-mile-long channel, taking soundings near shore. When the current turned against them, they anchored in various bights to await a change in the tide. Upon reaching the western entrance to Johnstone Strait, near Telegraph Cove, Vancouver noted that they had "beat to windward every foot of the channel."

Modern mariners are well-advised to approach Johnstone Strait with the same determination as Vancouver. Of course, we have the advantage of engine power, but it takes a pretty big engine to buck contrary winds and current in Johnstone Strait. Northwesterlies funnel down the strait, which lies in a northwest-southeast direction. With an almost constant north-flowing ebb, a steep chop is common, especially at the junctions of Mayne Passage and Sunderland Channel. In summer, to avoid the predominant afternoon westerlies, most northbound boaters travel the strait in the morning, before the wind kicks up.

Johnstone Strait carries much of the freshwater runoff that flows from mainland rivers to the Pacific

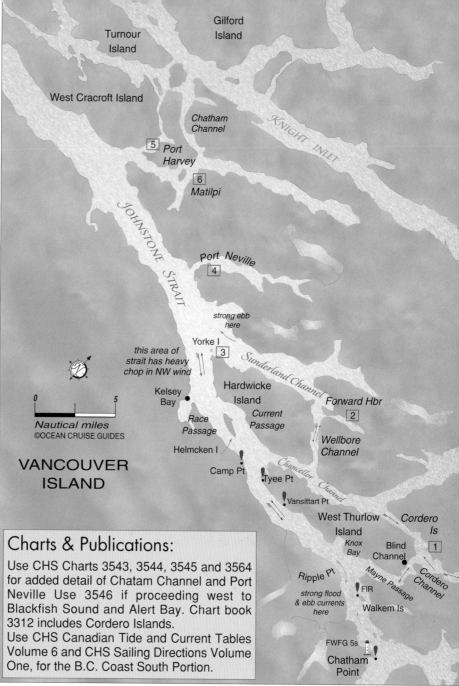

Turnour Island

Gilford Island

West Cracroft Island

Chatham Channel

KNIGHT INLET

5 Port Harvey

6 Matilpi

JOHNSTONE STRAIT

Port Neville
4

strong ebb here

this area of strait has heavy chop in NW wind

Yorke I
3

Sunderland Channel

Kelsey Bay

Hardwicke Island

Current Passage

Forward Hbr
2

0 Nautical miles 5
©OCEAN CRUISE GUIDES

Race Passage

Helmcken I

Wellbore Channel

VANCOUVER ISLAND

Camp Pt

Chancellor Channel

Tyee Pt

Vansittart Pt

West Thurlow Island

Cordero Is
1

Knox Bay

Blind Channel

Cordero Channel

Ripple Pt

strong flood & ebb currents here

FIR

Mayne Passage

Walkem Is

FWFG 5s

Chatham Point

Charts & Publications:

Use CHS Charts 3543, 3544, 3545 and 3564 for added detail of Chatam Channel and Port Neville Use 3546 if proceeding west to Blackfish Sound and Alert Bay. Chart book 3312 includes Cordero Islands.
Use CHS Canadian Tide and Current Tables Volume 6 and CHS Sailing Directions Volume One, for the B.C. Coast South Portion.

Ocean. As a result, currents are complex in this strait, its deep waters in continual motion and always cold, causing frequent fog in summer when warm air comes into contact with its frigid surface. At the height of summer, the deep and swift-flowing waters of Johnstone Strait are the coldest on our coast, with surface temperatures rarely exceeding 10° C (50° F). Even the surface waters of Queen Charlotte Sound are warmer during summertime heating than those in Johnstone Strait.

Because of the large runoff, ebb currents dominate Johnstone Strait. Although flood currents flow east and ebb currents flow west in Johnstone Strait, their speed and times of turn can vary considerably from one side of the channel to the other, with surface waters temporarily flowing in opposite directions, depending on the state of the tide. Generally, flood currents flow strongest on the Vancouver Island side, and ebb currents are strongest along the mainland side of the strait. However, there can be many days when tides are small and there is no appreciable flood current on the surface. As noted in the Sailing Directions, "if the prediction for lower HW at Alert Bay is less than 3.7 m, there generally will be no flood current for that period" west of Yorke Island. The Sailing Directions includes an excellent series of charts that show currents in Johnstone Strait at various stages of tide.

Estuarine currents, fed by freshwater runoff which flows seaward on top of heavier saltwater, contribute to this pattern. Slow-moving boats are advised to keep well to starboard when travelling in either direction, taking advantage of the estuarine current when heading westward and staying out of its path when heading eastward.

Getting used to the constant flow of current is an important aspect of cruising the Johnstone Strait area. The exact timing and predictions by the Canadian Hydrographic Service of the currents in the various channels and for some passes remain largely guesswork taken from years of CHS and fishing fleet observations.

Above, Chatham Point Lighthouse. Below, a westward view over Otter Cove to Johnstone Strait.

The biggest hurdle when northbound is getting from Chatham Point to Port Harvey. Many boaters opt to stay on the 'back route' as long as possible, taking Cordero Channel to Chancellor Channel, then turning off at Wellbore Channel and entering Johnstone Strait via Sunderland Channel, avoiding Current and Race Passages. Anchorages and harbours to stop at along the way include the Cordero Islands, Blind Channel and Forward Harbour.

For boaters who choose the main route along Johnstone Strait, there are numerous bights and bays on both sides of the strait that offer temporary shelter while you wait for a change in the tide.

TIDES AND CURRENTS
Chatham Point to Edith Point

Rock Bay Provincial Marine Park encompasses the two bays on either side of Chatham Point. Otter Cove offers sheltered anchorage at its head, with entry between Rocky Islets and Limestone Island.

The area around Chatham Point can be deceptively calm while a mile or two west of the lighthouse a strong westerly can be blowing. We have experienced all kinds of localized weather – 40-knot winds, fog, lightning storms and sudden downpours – between Chatham Point and Edith Point, the latter a good place to bail out if the Strait is too rough.

When battling a westerly we sometimes take cover from the wind behind the Walkem Islands and work our way through them to get to Mayne Passage. However, this can be a little dangerous in large tides – we have sometimes found ourselves

barely moving against strong winds and 3 knots of current in the midst of these islands and reefs. One option is to pull into the cove between the large island marked '98' and the smaller island marked '64' (Chart 3543) and wait for conditions to improve. There is current and lots of kelp here so you'll have to find a clear spot to drop the hook, but this anchorage serves as a place to regroup.

The safest route in this area is out in the main part of the strait but be prepared for tough conditions if winds are strong. The area E of Walkem Islands to Ripple Point has strong current (up to 5 knots) and tide rips but currents ease west of Edith Point.

In Mayne Passage, west winds will calm down east of Mayne Point and, while gusts persist for a mile or two into the passage, there is rarely much of a swell or chop. The flood sets north in this channel and can reach 5 knots.

Edith Point to Race and Current Passages

From Edith Point, currents in Johnstone Strait are not obvious until near Vansittart Point. From here to Race and Current Passages, the streams can be contrary to that expected, with contrary back eddies playing a role in the strait. Strong current becomes evident in the area near Tyee Point, with large patches of whirlpools and upwelling between Ripple Shoal and Speaker Rock.

Between a rock and a hard place: Johnstone Strait in a westerly near Walkem Islands.

If you're early for slack at Current Passage, Knox Bay serves as a temporary anchorage, as do several bights on the south shore of Johnstone Strait, including one opposite the western end of West Thurlow Island. We anchored here one May in 30 feet (10 m) off a gravel beach backed by the Prince of Wales Range, then hiked up the hillside for a picnic lunch overlooking the strait. Afterward we realized this was where Vancouver's two ships anchored in July 1792 after making little progress against a fresh westerly gale. Fortunately we had no headwinds to contend with when we raised anchor later that afternoon and continued our voyage along the restless waters of Johnstone Strait.

Race and Current Passages

These passes mark the last obstacle encountered by boaters westbound in Johnstone Strait on their way to anchorages further north. Helmcken Island forms a natural obstacle for traffic separation: westbound vessels use Current Passage, eastbound vessels use Race Passage. Although current speeds in the two channels rarely exceed 6 knots, conditions can be turbulent, especially around Ripple Shoal and Earl Ledge – both of which have a strong set onto them.

Also, the hazards of commercial traffic – especially at night or in foggy conditions – should not be underestimated. Tugs with tows that are unable to turn into Current Passage may continue westbound into Race Passage. Fog will hang in this pass long after it has burned off in the strait.

Trying to arrive here at slack is also a challenge. Part of the difficulty in predicting the turn and speed

of current is the daily wind variation of Johnstone Strait. Tide and current tables may not be accurate on days when a strong wind is affecting current, and predictions can be out by an hour or more. If strong westerlies are predicted, you should try to get through the passages as early in the day as possible.

Anchorages on the N side of **Helmcken Island** include an open bay east of the island's small peninsula, which is suitable only for waiting out wind or tide for a few hours because the holding ground is

poor and the anchorage is open to vessel wash and SE winds. Billygoat Bay, the larger bay south and east, is indented well into the island and more sheltered, serving well as an overnight anchorage, but the mud is soft and the holding is only fair. If you spend the night, set the hook carefully so it buries deep. The Sailing Directions goes as far as to recommend mooring lines to shore. The safer entrance to this anchorage is between islands '43' and '42' (Chart 3544). This is the island with a prominent white storage tank and red-and-white radio mast.

Westbound boaters approaching Current Passage have two areas of concern. The first is at Tyee Point and Ripple Shoal, where currents can be strong and heavy tide rips can be expected when a tide is flooding against a SE wind. The other area requiring alertness is near Earl Ledge at the west entrance of Current Passage, where there is a pronounced set onto this ledge during ebbs. If proceeding on an ebb during strong W winds, you may be better off avoiding this set of passes and instead using Wellbore Channel.

Sector lights on both Hardwicke and Helmcken Islands mark the preferred route to pass east of Ripple Shoal and then north of (above) Ripple Shoal when westbound. Keeping an eye for overtaking commercial traffic, you can proceed along Current Passage on a course favouring the south side of the channel, which is especially important when leaving the passage.

At the west end of Helmcken Island, you should be able to discern conditions in the remainder of the passage and into Johnstone Strait. If a west wind is producing a heavy line of whitecaps from Vancouver Island across to Hardwicke Point, it may

The prevailing westerlies in Johnstone Strait leave many trees permanently bent to the east.

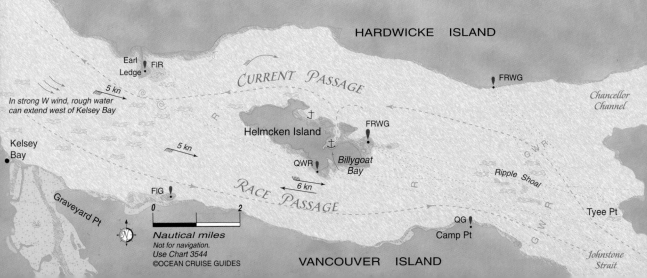

be wise for smaller vessels to anchor for a few hours in one of the two bays on the north side of Helmcken Island. Ebb current against a westerly wind can produce a brutal 3- to 4-foot chop, heavy tide rips and standing waves from Kelsey Bay to Hickey Point. Winds usually die down in late afternoon, providing better conditions to round this point.

However, if you proceed and get caught in these tide rips, stay well away from Earl Ledge and when past the ledge (50°25'N, 125°55'W, marked with a flashing red light), favour Hardwicke Island as conditions are usually worse on the Vancouver Island side of the channel. Vessels can pull into Kelsey Bay where moorage is available; however, there can be considerable chop in the vicinity of the breakwater, and in strong SE winds there is a set onto the wharfs. Winds from Brasseau Bay to Hickey Point are known to accelerate strongly and can be double the strength of those in the middle of the strait. We were knocked down here once under sail.

Eastbound boaters should try to be east of Kelsey Bay before noon and be wary of entering these passes when strong west winds blow against an ebb current. If such conditions exist, it is prudent to bypass these passes altogether and proceed along Sunderland Channel to either Forward Harbour or Blind Channel. Eastbound boaters can get a jump on the passes by spending the night in Port Harvey or Port Neville and getting away early enough to clear the rapids before westerlies pick up.

When approaching Race Passage, we normally stay fairly close to Hardwicke Island until we are about a mile from Earl Ledge, then begin to cross over into Race Passage, staying fairly close to the Vancouver Island side past Camp Point, where the currents are strongest. If you are battling an ebb, there is little relief until well beyond Vansittart Point on West Thurlow Island.

Travelling east, at least in a sailboat, can be exhilarating when a flood tide and westerly wind are in the same direction, although the area around Race Passage is still, for most recreational vessels, quite a challenge in such conditions.

Johnstone Strait West: Hardwicke Point to Cracroft Point

North of Race Passage, boaters can find several bays on the mainland side of Johnstone Strait to escape strong W winds. These include Blenkinsop Bay and the small bay just east of Tuna Point, which offer easy access, good holding and shelter from westerlies. These two bays make acceptable overnight stops if westerlies are predicted to persist through the evening but they are open to the southeast, making Port Neville or Port Harvey better bets if such winds are expected.

Taking Johnstone Strait beyond Port Harvey is the direct route to Blackfish Sound and the towns of

Johnstone Strait, looking east to Mayne Passage and the Walkem Islands.

Alert Bay and Port McNeill. Although there are no well-protected anchorages in the 15-mile stretch to Blackney and Baronet Passages, there are a few bights and hooks on the N (Cracroft Island) side of the strait to anchor in settled or strong W conditions.

Keep an ear to the weather if overnighting along the strait and consider either **Boat Bay** or **Forward Bay** if conditions are favourable. These two anchorages are open to the east but both have islets providing some protection from the wash of passing vessels in the strait. Both anchorages will also provide good shelter if a W breeze comes on early in the morning. We have been caught in Forward Bay when the wind unexpectedly turned SE with force during the night and we anxiously waited for hours in our heaving boat for dawn before raising anchor and finding refuge in another bight along the strait. If the day is cloudy and a southeasterly is expected, **Growler Cove** is reported to be a good, although there you could be sharing this spot with fishboats.

Early-morning travellers heading west from Forward Harbour usually enjoy a good ebb ride from the south end of Sunderland Channel right to the entrance of Havannah Channel.

Greene Point Rapids during a flood with current about five knots. Looking east to Mayne Passage.

Greene Point Rapids

Greene Point Rapids is far less daunting than the major passes to the south. Maximum current is 7 knots with a fairly straight and wide stream. The depths are well marked on the chart, the only danger being the reef extending east from the small island with the QR light. There is a set onto this reef, so stay well clear. There can also be a set onto the rock at the east end of Edsell Islets on the flood, although the pass (thick with kelp) between the island marked '27' (Chart 3543) and West Thurlow Island is a suitable shortcut for small craft going to Mayne Passage (known also as Blind Channel).

Currents in this area's interconnecting channels are strongest in the middle, and slightly slower along shorelines. Charts indicate the flood direction in most of the channels. Mayne Passage floods north.

PASS TIP SHEET – GREENE POINT RAPIDS
Location: 1/2 mile west of Cordero Islands.
Direction of flood: East
Reference Station: Seymour Narrows
Maximum Flow: 7 knots
Slack: 15-30 minutes
Nearby Anchorages: Westbound boaters can wait at Cordero Islands, eastbound vessels in the open bay northwest of the pass.

Sometimes a bay or large bight will produce a back eddy, providing a short burst of positive current. The channels around East and West Thurlow islands are greatly influenced by freshwater runoff from nearby mountains and by Johnstone Strait.

Strong summer westerlies from Johnstone Strait are common, and will push water into the back channels, delaying and diminishing the onset of the ebb. It is worth noting that over a period of hours, wind can push water at a rate of up to 3 per cent of the air speed; thus a 30-knot wind can produce, for example, a 1-knot current. If winds die off in early evening during the onset of the ebb, the current may come on very strong in these channels. Occasionally the effects of a flood may be non-existent as it slides under an outgoing layer of fresh water.

Ebbs along Cordero and Chancellor Channels are helped by the freshwater outflow from the coastal mountains. Currents often reach 2 to 3 knots, and up to 5 knots in places during strong spring tides.

The distance from Dent Rapids to Forward Harbour is 25 miles and the scenery is sublime. Fjord-like channels intersect with inlets and other channels, and the milky-emerald water mirrors the forested mountainsides. There is a magnificent view just west of Lyall Islet, looking north up Loughborough Inlet where its numerous steep points disappear into the mauve haze.

However, if a westerly is blowing, the calm water ends at Lyall Islet because Chancellor Channel will be a bear. During strong westerlies, which can start early in this channel, there can be a white line extending from West Thurlow Island across to Lyall Island. If so, the winds will be at least 20 knots. In such conditions, the distance from Lyall Island to the entrance to Wellbore Channel will seem interminable. Still, it makes arrival at Forward Harbour or Port Neville all the more satisfying because there are no more big passes to face.

Wellbore Channel/ Whirlpool Rapids

Wellbore Channel is a straightforward channel about 4 miles in length from D'Arcy Point to Althorp Point off Sunderland Channel. The current sets up near D'Arcy Point and builds to considerable strength at Whirlpool Rapids. However, the channel is deep and free of obstructions.

Heading up Wellbore Channel against a westerly. Current can be 7 knots at Whirlpool Rapids at north end of this channel.

Although there can be impressive whirlpools at the rapids, especially opposite the light on the small island near the north end, turbulence or overfalls are not excessive at most stages of tide. As you clear the small island, the worst of the current is over and turbulence rarely extends beyond the entrance to Forward Harbour.

The current is reported to be 7 knots at maximum. The shores of the pass, particularly on the east side, can be quite thick with bull kelp, so if you're bucking a tide along the edge of the channel, take care to avoid catching a prop on kelp which may lie just below the surface.

Wellbore Channel is a preferred route to Johnstone Strait when wind-against-current conditions are creating heavy tide-rips in Current and Race Passages. The former was the route followed by British and Spanish explorers in the summer of 1792. The Spanish, whose two ships were smaller than those under the command of Captain Vancouver, anchored opposite the entrance to Forward Harbour in late July. Three weeks earlier, Lieutenant James Johnstone had explored Wellbore Channel by longboat. He knew that an opening to the ocean lay ahead after he and his men were swamped while camping on shore one night, soggy proof that the flood tide was no longer flowing from the south, but from the north.

Blind Channel Resort, West Thurlow Island

The Blind Channel Resort, with its first-rate facilities, has been owned and operated by the Richter family since 1969. Younger members of the extended family arrive each summer to help out, and one of them is often waiting by an empty slip to take your bowline, because currents in Mayne Passage can make docking a challenge. On shore, the facilities include a general store stocked with fresh produce and bread baked on the premises, as well as a liquor store, post office, showers, laundromat and an excellent licensed restaurant. Regular visitors to Blind Channel will be sad to hear that Annemarie Richter passed away in 2003.

Adjacent to the marina resort are the Blind Channel hiking trails. These lie within a tree farm license and were first cleared in the late '80s, when Fletcher Challenge began logging the eastern end of the island. At that time, Edgar and Annemarie Richter voiced their concerns to a forester employed by Fletcher Challenge. The Richters told him that visitors to their marina liked hiking into the nearby woods to view a huge, 800-year-old cedar, 16 feet in diameter, which had been left standing when the area was hand-logged at the turn of the century.

The forester listened, then approached his managers with a proposal (which was approved) to create a buffer strip next to the Richters' property and build hiking trails to acquaint the public with the multiple uses of a forest. A crew of men soon began clearing the first of what are now called the Blind Channel Hiking Trails, which are mapped and explained in a company pamphlet available at the marina's general store. Wooden footbridges span streams and a bench provides a resting spot for hikers beside the Big Cedar. On a hot summer day the trails are a refreshing respite from the blazing sun as soft light filters through the forest's canopy of second-growth timber. (For a history of Blind Channel, see Part One's 'A Storied Coastline'.)

Nearby anchorages, in addition to the Cordero Islands, include a decent spot almost directly across from Blind Channel in **Charles Bay** which can accommodate two or three boats. The best part of the bay, to get out of the current, is north of small Eclipse Island in about 15 feet (4.5 m) minimum depth. The bottom is soft mud and the holding good.

Top left, Blind Channel floats. Bottom left, a cedar snag left standing by turn-of-the century hand loggers on the Blind Channel forest trails.

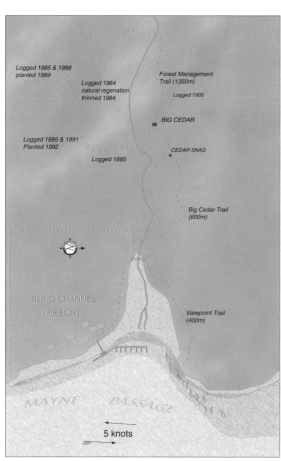

Logged 1885 & 1988
planted 1989

Logged 1964
natural regenation
thinned 1984

Forest Management
Trail (1350m)

Logged 1905

BIG CEDAR

Logged 1885 & 1991
Planted 1992

CEDAR SNAG

Logged 1885

Big Cedar Trail
(600m)

BLIND CHANNEL
RESORT

Viewpoint Trail
(400m)

MAYNE PASSAGE

5 knots

THE ANCHORAGES
Cordero Islands 1

Many times we have traversed Cordero Channel, intent on getting through Greene Point Rapids, and motored right past the Cordero Islands without a second glance. Then, one sunny afternoon in July, we were westbound along Cordero Channel and for once, lulled by the languid weather, we were in no hurry to get anywhere. Under a balmy blue sky we slid past steep shores thickly treed with evergreens and gazed up at distant peaks, pockets of snow clinging to their crowns. Noticing a boat anchored in the nearby cluster of islands, we decided to stop for a closer look at what we were missing.

The anchorage is ringed by islands and garnished with bull kelp which you have to thread through before entering. Protection from wind is good in most conditions. Southerlies usually get lost when they show up at the intersection just below Cordero Islands, and most northwest breezes, blowing down Chancellor Channel, are diverted into Loughborough Inlet. Northwesterly gales, though, will gust through the anchorage.

Aerial view of Mayne Passage showing Blind Channel marina at left and Cordero Islands top.

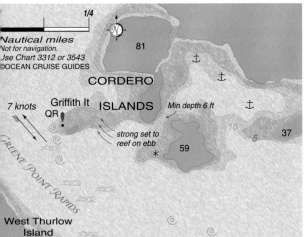

Cordero Islands anchorage offers a peaceful and pretty setting with good protection.

The Cordero Islands anchorage is a beautiful setting. The islands make a fun day of exploration by dinghy, their foreshores consisting of smooth flat stone, pinkish in tone and nice to sit on during a sunny afternoon. A house stands on the mainland shore, backed by tall cedars and fronted by a dock, but its presence is unobtrusive.

The anchorage offers views of busy Cordero Channel and, as this is a major junction for recreational vessels, there is a passing parade of boats during the turn of tide. There is often a lot of birdlife hovering over the Greene Point Rapids – loons, eagles and herons all frequent this anchorage. The salmon fishing is good south of the islands, while bottom fish, such as ling cod, can sometimes be caught in the kelp along the arm west of the rapids.

Forward Harbour ☐2

For northbound boaters, there are few decent anchorages beyond the Cordero Islands until you get past Whirlpool Rapids and set the hook in Forward Harbour, some 15 miles distant. Currents dimish quickly at the entrance, opposite Horace Point, and the channel into the anchorage is clear.

This scenic and spacious harbour affords sheltered anchorage off a fine pebble beach in **Douglas Bay**, and is especially peaceful when a westerly is howling just a few hundred yards away in Sunderland Channel. The anchorage can sometimes be busy with a dozen or more boats anchored near

Our experience with the holding has been good in a bottom of mud and sand, although kelp is abundant along the edges of the cove and sometimes big wads will come up with the anchoring gear. The anchorage has some current but nothing like that which will be on the outside of the surrounding islands. One spot to avoid when anchoring is in front of the gap between the islands marked '81' and '59' on chart 3312. When the tide turns to ebb, there's a strong current pulling into the gap and this is an area to avoid if rowing about in a dinghy. We've used this pass as a shortcut leaving this anchorage, but it should be noted that this pass has less depth than shown on charts 3543 and 3312, with a minimum depth of less than 6 feet (2 m) at LW and not the 18 feet shown on the chart. On strong ebbs the set to the reef between Griffiths Island is considerable.

the beach and north shoreline. We usually find our-selves anchoring in 55 feet (17 m) or more. There is current throughout the anchorage so it makes sense to give other vessels lots of room. The holding is very good in thick mud. Although shelter from the west is good, strong east winds can be a problem and may force you to move to the head of the bay to find shelter. Another option is to tie off, if booms are lying along the south shore. Our experience in Douglas Bay has been that easterlies are about half the strength of what's blowing out in Johnstone Strait. Small vessels sometimes anchor in the nook of the channel leading into Forward Harbour and this appears to be a quiet spot during SE winds. Some logging has taken place on the NE slopes of the harbour but the snowcapped mountain at its head remains a beautiful vista.

A lovely forest trail leads from the pebble beach at Douglas Bay across a neck of land to the shores of Bessborough Bay on the other side. Black bears are sometimes spotted in the vicinity, so be sure to make plenty of noise when hiking this trail.

Above, looking toward head of Forward Harbour.
Below, enjoying the pebble beach in Douglas Bay.

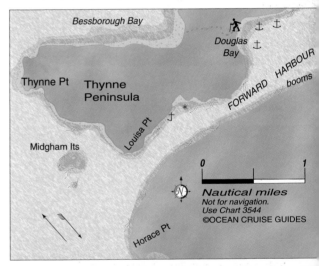

FORWARD HARBOUR AT A GLANCE
CHARTS: 3544
LAT LONG: 50°28.37'N 125°46.04'W
PROS: Good protection from west winds with good holding in sticky mud. Lots of room, deep harbour. Good hiking, nice pebble beach.
CONS: Can be busy. The harbour has current, so be careful how you pick your anchoring spot.
MUST DO: Hike across peninsula to Bessborough Bay.

*Above, underground tunnels on Yorke Island fed
ammunition to the main guns, below.*

Yorke Island 3

This uninhabited island at the junction of Johnstone
Strait and Sunderland Channel makes an unique day
stop for anyone interested in World War II history,
for it was here that the Canadian government built a
gun emplacement to protect the country's west coast
from enemy invasion. Morning is generally the best
time to pull into the kelp-strewn bight at the island's
southeast end, before the prevailing northwesterly in
Johnstone Strait has time to intensify and make
departure a difficult exercise.

When anchoring in this bight, we try to find an
area free of kelp and ensure the anchor is well set
before leaving the vessel. Although this bight provides surprisingly good protection from northwesterlies, it is open to the south and there is usually
some current flowing. See Chart 3544.

After securing our dinghy on the pocket beach
facing the bight, we scramble up the hillside past the
crumbling officer's quarters and hike along what is
left of a road that continues uphill in a northerly
direction, then turns west. The terrain is moss-covered ground dotted with colourful clumps of fox-
glove and thin stands of forest. At a steady pace, it
takes about 20 minutes to reach the deserted bunker
and gun emplacement situated on a cliff overlooking
Johnstone Strait on the island's western edge.

Construction of this military outpost began in
1937 when Yorke Island was placed under the
reserve of the Department of National Defence. The

Yorke Island anchorage has plenty of kelp and current. Keep an eye on the wind while on shore.

site was chosen for its strategic location: any enemy ships approaching Vancouver from the north would have to pass this island sentinel where two turret guns and a searchlight were waiting. Lead shielding protected the 6-inch guns, which swivelled inside well installations and could fire seven 100-lb rounds per minute. The ammunition bunker, connected by a tunnel and pathway to the guns, was camouflaged with cement and rock to make the structure appear part of the cliff.

Yorke Island never came under attack and the last firing practice took place on August 10, 1945, by which time 62 buildings stood on the island, including the officers' quarters, barracks, canteen and drill hall overlooking the old wharf at the island's south-east end. During the war, both naval and fishing vessels were employed to monitor ship movements in the passes and straits leading from Yorke Island.

Port Neville 4

Port Neville marks the end of the major obstacles encountered by northbound boaters. In fact, the main pilotage challenges of the entire Inside Passage, from Vancouver to Skagway, are the series of passes that start at Seymour Narrows or Yuculta Rapids and end at Race Passage or Whirlpool Rapids. There are other difficult areas and other passes, certainly, but the main route of the Inside Passage lies open once you reach Port Neville. Completing the transits of these passes is an accomplishment, and once you're in the beautiful cruising grounds north of Port Neville, you'll be in no hurry to return to the busier waters of the Strait of Georgia. In fact, you may not want to go back at all.

Port Neville is a convenient port, offering easy access off Johnstone Strait and secure anchorage or moorage at the public float. Popular with both pleasure boats and fishboats, the small float at the inlet's mouth is often full and boats regularly raft, especially during commercial fishery openings. There is no water or electric power at the docks and the old store at the head of the dock now houses a small museum.

The long sandy beach that stretches below the pilings is a good place to take a cruising dog for a walk or let the children roam. If the float is crowded, we anchor along the west shore opposite the Port Neville docks. Although kelp and current can be a hindrance, the holding ground is good once the hook has been firmly set. Current can flow up to 3 knots at the entrance to the inlet but is a bit less inside.

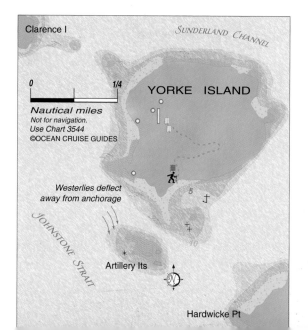

Clarence I

SUNDERLAND CHANNEL

0   1/4

Nautical miles
Not for navigation.
Use Chart 3544
©OCEAN CRUISE GUIDES

YORKE ISLAND

Westerlies deflect
away from anchorage

JOHNSTONE STRAIT

5

10

Artillery Its

Hardwicke Pt

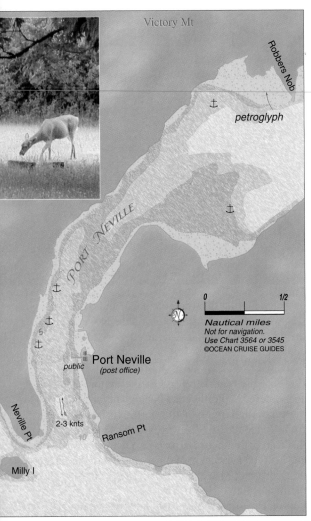

Victory Mt

Robbers Nob

⊥

petroglyph

⊥

PORT NEVILLE

⊥

⊥

5

⊥

public

Port Neville
(post office)

Neville Pt

2-3 knts

Ransom Pt

10

Milly I

0   1/2

Nautical miles
Not for navigation.
Use Chart 3564 or 3545
©OCEAN CRUISE GUIDES

This long, sheltered inlet was the site of several Kwakwakw'waka villages long before its forested shores of prime timber began attracting hand loggers in the late 1800s. The local natives found the narrows were strategically useful for warding off invaders and the Fulmore River, which drains into the head of the inlet, was a source of salmon.

When a 32-year-old Norwegian named Sven Hans Hansen arrived at Port Neville in 1891, several hand loggers already lived in and around the inlet, but Hansen soon became the community leader. His homestead, where he had planted a garden and orchard, became a local gathering place and in 1895 he became the first postmaster for Port Neville. With no wharf yet built, Hans had to transfer all steamship-delivered mail and freight by rowboat. Few non-native women lived upcoast, so after his first wife died, Hansen voyaged back to Norway and returned with his 18-year-old bride Kathinka. Together they raised a family while living off the land. Their growing family soon needed more living space, so in 1923 Hans built the two-storey house that still stands at the top of the wharf.

The Hansen home became a full-scale store and in 1928, with construction of a wharf, Port Neville became a regular port of call for the Union Steamships. Meanwhile, local logging operations were making Port Neville a thriving settlement, with

Above, wildlife can often be spotted near the Port Neville dock. Below, the Port Neville store was built in 1923 and is being restored as a museum.

float homes and logging camps hugging the inlet's shoreline, its waters busy with tugs and barges. A sawmill was built as well as a steam railway for hauling logs from the woods. Also, farmland was cultivated at the head of the inlet. The children living in Port Neville enjoyed birthday picnics at Robbers Nob, complete with ice cream shipped by steamer in wooden barrels surrounded with ice.

Hans passed away in 1939 at the age of 80. His son Olaf remained at Port Neville, settling with his bride Lilly into a log home where he lived until his death in 1997 at the age of 87. Lorna Chesluk, a granddaughter of Hans, lives in the log house where she remains postmistress of Port Neville. Mail can be sent care of general delivery. Although the local population has dwindled and few people now live around the inlet, it is still used for the booming and storage of logs. There are regular reports of bear activity in the inlet and deer can often be seen along the shore.

There is good anchorage south of Hanatsa Point in Baresides Bay, although closer to shore logging debris litters the bottom. During the hippie movement in the 1960s, a commune (now abandoned) was established at Robbers Nob. Petroglyphs can be viewed on foreshore rocks on the west side of the knob along level sandstone near the HW mark.

Forested Milly Island was for years a landmark for northbound vessels until it was extensively logged and a house built on it in the mid-1990s. Much of Hardy Peak, just south of Port Neville, has also been logged and the large spar tree used for the logging operation still stands.

Above, petroglyph at Robbers Knob. Below, a view up Port Neville inlet.

PORT NEVILLE AT A GLANCE
CHARTS: 3564, 3545
LAT LONG: 50°29.18N 126°5.30'W
PROS: Good overnight or extended stop for transient vessels with a public dock and good anchoring opportunities. Inlet well worth exploring. Some wildlife (bear, deer).
CONS: Dock can often be full. Anchoring requires care to ensure set due to kelp. Current throughout inlet.
MUST DO: Visit the log store and Robbers Nob.

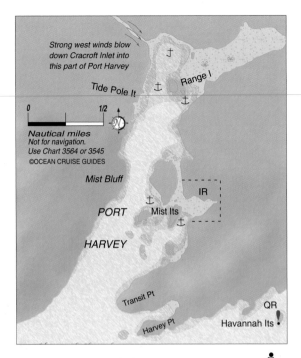

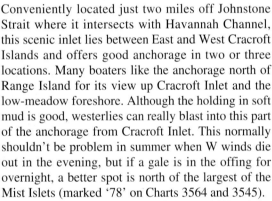

Port Harvey 5

Conveniently located just two miles off Johnstone Strait where it intersects with Havannah Channel, this scenic inlet lies between East and West Cracroft Islands and offers good anchorage in two or three locations. Many boaters like the anchorage north of Range Island for its view up Cracroft Inlet and the low-meadow foreshore. Although the holding in soft mud is good, westerlies can really blast into this part of the anchorage from Cracroft Inlet. This normally shouldn't be problem in summer when W winds die out in the evening, but if a gale is in the offing for overnight, a better spot is north of the largest of the Mist Islets (marked '78' on Charts 3564 and 3545).

A favourite spot of ours is in the middle of the moss-covered **Mist Islets**, between islets '49' and '78' in about 20 feet (6 m) of water. With a stern line bringing us close to shore, we can pull out of the chop from Johnstone Strait and away from the distant howl of westerly winds.

Houses and a dock are located at the head of the inlet, as is a lovely shell midden backed by low bush. The Kwakwaka'wakw (Kwakiutl) natives who once lived here used the drying gorge connecting Port Harvey with Cracroft Inlet as a canoe route.

Log booms are often moored along the west shore, and tugs come and go through the lower half of the bay. Port Harvey was once a hand-logging centre called Cracroft and lively times were known here when the settlement boasted a store, hotel and beer parlor that catered to local loggers.

Matilpi 6

Located opposite the midden of an ancient Kwakwaka'wakw settlement, this anchorage lies between the mainland and the northernmost of the two Indian Islands. Matilpi is an easy distance from Port Neville (about 15 miles) and close to Chatham Channel. The anchorage is marked by a lovely shell midden which fringes the mainland shore, and the two islets providing shelter from Havannah Channel. After anchoring behind the Indian Islands in 30 feet (10 m), we often go ashore and enjoy the shell beach which is good for swimming although you have to watch for bits of old glass while being mindful that black bears sometimes wander the shoreline at LW.

Holding ground in Matilpi, in mud and shell, is good and protection is also good from most winds. We've also anchored with good results between the islands when the main anchorage has been filled.

Apart from the midden, nothing remains of the Kwakwaka'wakw village that stood here before it was abandoned in the last century when its residents joined the band at Karlukwees on nearby Turnour Island. There's a haunted feel to the place, which only adds to its beauty. Although the village may be gone, the animals depicted in Kwakwaka'wakw crests remain. We've seen red-throated loons swim past the islets and we've listened to a raven cluck vociferously at its neighbours in the forest. On one visit, we watched a black bear thrash its way onto the beach to check out the berry bushes and another time a mink poked its nose out of the brush to take a quick look at us. When night draws in and the forest becomes dark and still, the midden lying along the water's edge remains ghostly white.

Nearby anchorages include Burial Cove, which can be busy with local traffic and not a great anchorage because of poor protection from south winds. A better bet, if Matilpi is busy, is in the lee of **Triangle Island** in about 30 feet (10 m). **Warren Islands** are worth exploring if you're waiting for a tide change but are too exposed to E winds for overnight. Detail on Chatham Channel can be found in Chapter Seven. Chart 3564 has excellent detail on Havannah Channel and this anchorage.

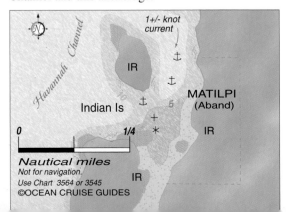

Matilpi anchorage

BLACKFISH SOUND

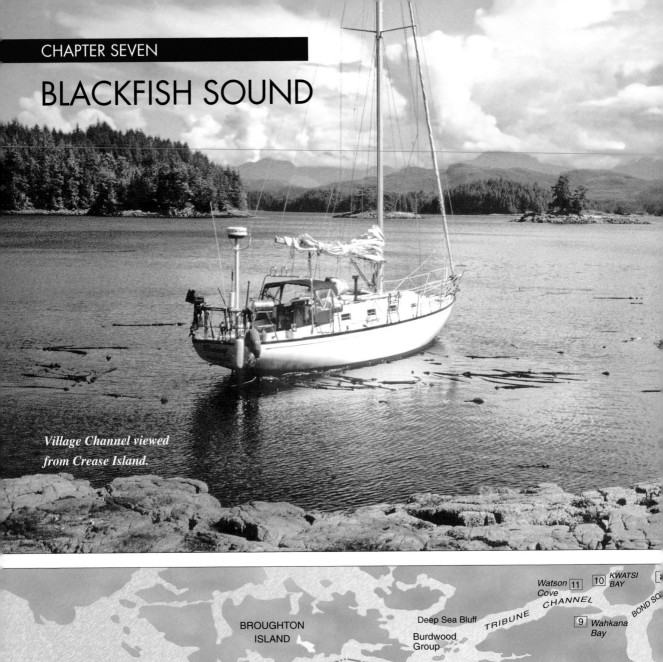

Village Channel viewed from Crease Island.

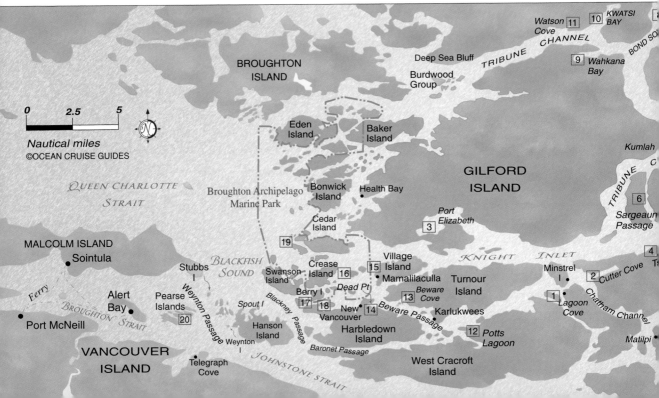

Watson Cove [11] [10] KWATSI BAY

Deep Sea Bluff

Burdwood Group

TRIBUNE CHANNEL

[9] Wahkana Bay

BOND SO

BROUGHTON ISLAND

Eden Island

Baker Island

GILFORD ISLAND

Kumlah

TRIBUNE C

0   2.5   5

Nautical miles
©OCEAN CRUISE GUIDES

QUEEN CHARLOTTE STRAIT

Broughton Archipelago Marine Park

Bonwick Island

Health Bay

Cedar Island

Port Elizabeth

[3]

[6] Sargeaun Passage

MALCOLM ISLAND
• Sointula

BLACKFISH SOUND

[19]

Swanson Island

Crease Island

[16]

Village Island

[15]

• Mamalilaculla

Turnour Island

Minstrel •

KNIGHT INLET

[4] T

[2] Cutter Cove

Stubbs I

Pearse Islands

Alert Bay

Spout I

Berry I

Dead Pt

Beware Cove

[13]

Karlukwees

[1] Lagoon Cove

Chatham Channel

Port McNeill •

Ferry

BROUGHTON STRAIT

[20]

Weynton Passage

Blackney Passage

[17] [18]

New Vancouver

[14]

Beware passage

[12] Potts Lagoon

Matilpi •

VANCOUVER ISLAND

Telegraph Cove

Hanson Island

Weynton

Harbledown Island

Baronet Passage

JOHNSTONE STRAIT

West Cracroft Island

T he fragrant islands and green waters of Blackfish Sound await boaters sailing clear of Johnstone Strait. In this area you will find a heady mix of stunning scenery, prolific wildlife and a palpable atmosphere of the past. Heavy cedars draped with shawls of cat-tail moss stand along shorelines, where they seem to be forever waiting. And the tree-top utterings of ravens sound as unsettling today as when they were first heard thousands of years ago by the local Kwakiutl. Many boaters agree there's something about Blackfish Sound that takes hold of you and never lets go.

Getting to Blackfish Sound and Queen Charlotte Strait, though, can seem like *The Seven Voyages of Sinbad*, what with westerly winds, the currents in Johnstone Strait and the prevalence of fog in mid-to-late summer. And then there are the passes still to be transited.

Blackney Passage & Weynton Passage

These passes receive considerable current – at least 6 knots – and can have impressive rips, especially in wind-against-current conditions. They are used extensively by commercial traffic, including cruise ships, and are major routes for killer whales.

Bill Mackay, a pioneer of the local whale watching industry (who today runs Mackay Whale Watching out of Port McNeill), has seen killer whales work against a large flood (which sets southeast) in Weynton Passage, by swimming close to Weynton Island and threading through the Plumper Islands.

At first glance, both Weynton and Blackney appear to be straightforward passes that are fairly wide and without major obstructions. However, because of their orientation to Queen Charlotte and Johnstone Straits, difficulties can arise for small craft during windy conditions. Weynton Passage, especially, can be deceptive. Although it is fairly wide and bound by numerous islands, the current is not errant and diffused (as you might assume) but is surprisingly strong, especially between Stubbs Island and the top end of the Plumper Islands. On a couple of occasions we have felt as if we were towing Stubbs Island for hours. More than anything, be wary of a strong wind against current.

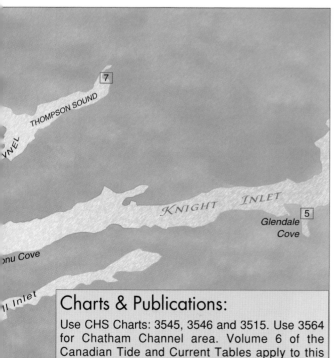

Charts & Publications:

Use CHS Charts: 3545, 3546 and 3515. Use 3564 for Chatham Channel area. Volume 6 of the Canadian Tide and Current Tables apply to this area. It is also very important to have the CHS Sailing Directions Volume One on board also.

"A big flood against a southeaster is bad. You'll see haystacks from Stubbs Island to Donegal Head (on Malcolm Island)," Mackay says. Of concern in these conditions is a pronounced set onto Stephenson Islets where the worst turbulence can occur. Stubbs Island, as John Chappell warns in *Cruising Beyond Desolation Sound*, is to be avoided – locals call this island ' Sinkhole' and the Sailing Directions advise of heavy tide-rips in the vicinity. There is also a strong set onto Donegal Head during an ebb.

Weynton Passage underwent extensive monitoring by Mike Woodward of CHS. In 1981 he installed a current meter southeast of Stubbs Island on top of the 18-metre shoal on the southeast side and gathered months of current data, which was incorporated in the 1986 Tide & Current Tables.

Blackney Passage is assigned as a secondary station on Johnstone Strait and is also somewhat difficult to predict. The maximum current is reported to

be 5 knots but Bill Mackay says he has seen up to 10 knots in sheer zones near Cracroft Point. Tide rips can be strong off this point during flood-against-wind conditions. Because this is a busy pass, be very careful when approaching in reduced visibility and stay well to your side of the channel.

Blackfish Sound, from the north side of Hanson Island to a line between Bold Head on Swanson Island and Donegal Head on Malcolm Island, can also be a challenge for small craft during large tides and strong winds. Currents can be 3- to 5-knots and because of the sound's openness to wind from Queen Charlotte Strait, the seas here can build to 4 to 5 feet and form dangerous tide rips – especially over Egeria Shoal. If you are caught in such conditions, look for a haven. The north side of Hanson Island is quite foul, and during strong westerlies the only bay providing easy access and protection from most winds lies south of Spout Islet. The southwest end of this bay provides good shelter from wind and swell off the sound. Other options include the anchorage behind Mound Island or, in south winds, Farewell Harbour.

There is still much that is unkown about the currents around Malcolm Island and Alert Bay. Currents for Alert Bay and Pulteney Point are referenced for Johnstone Strait which, as any gillnetter will confirm, is as predictable as next week's weather. There's a lack of research into the currents in this entire area, so the tide predictions of Weynton Passage are not always an accurate indicator for the nearby channels.

PASS TIP SHEET
Blackney Pass: (Licka Point) 50°34'N, 126°41'W, five knots
Weynton Pass: 50°35'N, 126°49'W, 6 knots
Blackfish Sound: 50°35'N, 126°42'W, 3 knots
Slack: 10-25 minutes. **Flood:** East
Nearby Anchorages: – W, Growler Cove, E, Sprout Island or north side of Hanson Island.

Blackney Passage is a busy commercial route but only poses a problem when wind is against current.

Killer Whales and You

Blackfish Sound, the body of water that lends its name to the general area, is one of the best places on our coast to view killer whales – once known as 'blackfish'. Their species name is *orcinus orca*, and these sociable marine mammals frequent the swift-flowing waters of Johnstone Strait and the nearby passes where salmon often collect waiting for a tide change. Here the orca feed on salmon, and often stay long periods in Robson Bight to rub against rounded pebbles in the bight's rocky shallows. In 1982 this bight was protected as an ecological reserve to prevent vessels from entering and disturbing the killer whales. When noted marine mammalogist Michael Bigg died in 1990, the reserve was renamed the Robson Bight/Michael Bigg Ecological Reserve to honour his pioneering research on killer whales along the B.C. coast.

The nearby boardwalk community of Telegraph Cove, founded in 1912 as a one-room telegraph station, has become a popular base for whale-watching tours in Johnstone Strait, while serious students of whale behaviour set up camp on West Cracroft Island, at Swaine Point, directly opposite Robson Bight. The whales often travel between Johnstone Strait and Blackfish Sound via Blackney Passage, and the Pacific Killer Whale Foundation monitors underwater whale vocalizations from Hanson Island.

The best time to sight orcas in Johnstone Strait is from July to October, when sightings are frequent. Keep in mind a few guidelines as set out by the Department of Fisheries and Oceans:

1) Do not split groups of whales.
2) Do not disturb whales while they are resting on the surface.
3) Do not chase whales.
4) Slow down and move carefully when within 1,000 feet (300 m).
5) Do not come any closer than 300 feet (100 m).

We generally maintain a distance of 1,000 feet (300 m) if we spot a pod. Occasionally a pod will surface close to your vessel and if this occurs, maintain your speed and direction until the pod moves away.

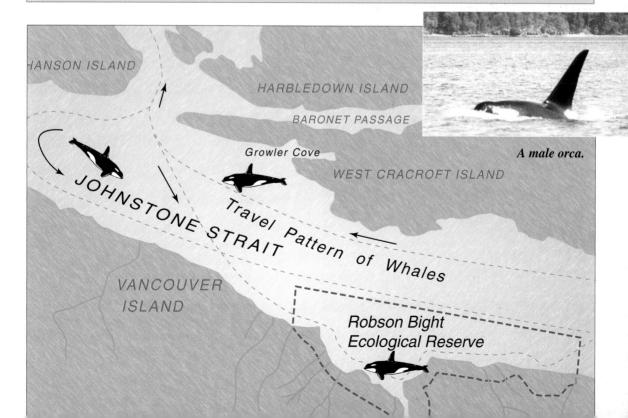

HANSON ISLAND

HARBLEDOWN ISLAND

BARONET PASSAGE

Growler Cove

WEST CRACROFT ISLAND

A male orca.

JOHNSTONE STRAIT

Travel Pattern of Whales

VANCOUVER ISLAND

Robson Bight Ecological Reserve

Above, fin whale exhibit in museum. Below, view across Telegraph Cove to Johnstone Strait.

Telegraph Cove

This cove is home to a number of companies offering tours for travellers wanting to see whales, bears and other wildlife. If such tours are of interest, you can temporarily tie up at the main front-facing dock (below the red building) and inquire about whale-watching at Stubbs Island Charters at the top of the dock or about bear watching at Tide Rip Tours.

Telegraph Cove is an authentic boardwalk community that harks back to the days when the Union Steamships ruled Broughton Archipelago. This small community has good restaurants, souvenir and craft shops, and a general store. A tour along the boardwalk presents great views of this cove with its amenities and of Johnstone Strait. One of the best reasons to visit Telegraph Cove is the whale museum that displays skeletons of numerous species of whale. The museum has a killer whale interpretive centre and also features a 66-foot-long (20 m) fin whale skeleton discovered on top of the bow bulb of the *MS Galaxy* cruise ship in the summer of 1999. Boaters wanting to have lunch and spend a few hours enjoying this unique port can usually tie up at the front dock but be sure to either call ahead or check with the Stubbs Island office.

Vessels wanting to stay overnight should call ahead to either Telegraph Cove Marina at (250) 928-3163 or to Telegraph Cove Resorts at (250) 928-3131. Limited moorage is available for boats 30 to 50 feet. Water is available as well as power, laundry and showers. Although there is a gas dock, there is no diesel available here. Stubbs Island Charters (250) 928-3185, run by Jim and Mary Borrowman, has regular whale-watching tours departing from Telegraph Cove aboard their vessel *Lukwa*.

Other channels and passes:

Baronet Passage

Baronet Passage is not often used by recreational boaters but it does offer a different approach to Potts Lagoon and Clio Channel. Currents are in the 3 to 4 knot range at springs in the vicinity of Walden Island and about 2 knots at most other times. Amazingly, the flood sets west in this pass – as it does in Clio Channel. Baronet Passage is a secondary station referenced on Seymour Narrows. There is no suitable anchorage in this 7-mile passage, but there are several bights for lunch stops.

This is a good channel in which to catch spring salmon, and the experts advise fishing close to shore during LW slack and fishing through the rising tide. The waters off Cracroft Point at the western entrance to Baronet Passage are a gathering point for salmon during an ebb tide, as they wait for the next flood to push them eastward. Parson Bay is also reputed to be a hot spot at times in summer months.

When the west-flowing flood current reaches the western end of Baronet Passage, it meets a south-flowing flood in Blackney Passage. Currents here attain 5 knots and create heavy races off Cracroft Point and can be very turbulent in strong winds.

Whitebeach Passage

Whitebeach Passage is a narrow pass that connects Blackfish Sound with Indian Channel and the Carey Group of islands. A summer village thrived on Compton Island back in the 1940s when houses overlooked the white beach which was often lined with dugout canoes and is today used by kayakers. Currents in the pass rarely exceed 2 knots and vessels should favour the N side of the pass at the narrowest part to avoid the drying outcrop and shoal water. Bull kelp thrives along both sides of the pass.

Indian and Village Channels

Indian Channel and Village Channel are the main thoroughfares, and the safest routes, of the Carey and Indian groups of islands. Because of currents, numerous reefs and unmarked rocks throughout this area, you should stick with the main channels and anchorages. Currents in these channels are surprisingly swift and can run up to 3 knots (flood flows east). The Sailing Directions warn, in bold type, that these channels are sprinkled with unmarked rocks and shoals, so keep your depth sounder on all the time and navigate very carefully in this area.

Eastbound in Chatham Channel.

Chatham Channel

Chatham Channel is a narrow gorge-like channel with a constricted kelp-laden pass at its east end. The pass itself is pretty and home to much bird life, including herons and eagles. The main piloting challenge is the 2-mile stretch from Root Point westward where currents can be up to 5 knots but are usually not turbulent. Range markers at each end of the narrows greatly assist with staying in the middle of the channel. Although the flood sets east, the times of maximum current can change depending on freshet outflow from Knight Inlet (especially in May and June) or after large rains, which can delay the onset of the flood. Just west of the pass is a large scar on the mountainside from a 1975 slide.

Chatham Channel received its name from the extraordinary pilotage and survey of this shallow narrows by Lieutenant Broughton while in command of the 90-ton *Chatham* in 1792. Broughton guided his ship along Havannah Channel, then proceeded into Chatham Channel and made a similar survey of Tribune Channel.

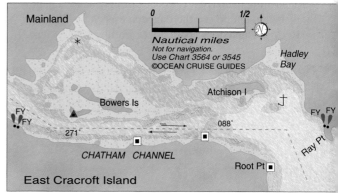

Be especially careful if you're bucking a flood near the day beacon on the small island just south of Bowers Island (the route north of Bowers Island should not be attempted because of shoal water.) Another tricky spot is close to the west end of the pass, at its narrowest point where the current is strongest, with accompanying upwellings and whirlpools. These difficulties are compounded by large masses of bull kelp which grow almost entirely across the channel in this area during the summer. Fog is also common and will persist in this pass after it has burned off elsewhere.

Boaters have many choices at the junction of Chatham and Clio Channels with Knight Inlet. You can turn southwest into Clio Channel to explore Potts Lagoon and Beware Passage, go west to Village Island and the Carey Group, head north up Tribune Channel, or turn east into Knight Inlet to see the bears at Glendale Cove.

Beware Passage

This pass has earned its name from the proliferation of rocks, reefs and bull kelp throughout its length. Transiting the pass at LW slack offers the advantage of being able to see the dangers, especially Beware Rock – which dries about 5 feet. Fortunately, current is not an issue as the stream is only 2- to 3-knots at springs. The flood current flows east.

This pass should not be attempted if visibility is poor – you must be able to see at least half a mile to ensure your position on one of the two most common routes through the pass. Chart 3545 provides excellent detail of the routes and their hazards. As mentioned, Beware Rock, lying in the middle of the pass at the west end, is the major navigational challenge and, as is the case in all rock-strewn passes, the rule is to go dead slow throughout the transit.

If transiting the pass at HW, the safest approach is along the bottom route (going below Care Rock). If westbound, this route is along the channel between Kamano Island and an islet marked '15'. Steer 266° to the open water north of the island marked '44' near Harbledown Island and pick your way along the channel between two small islets to the north and Harbledown Island to the south. The last dangers involve getting past the drying reefs of Beware Rock and another rock to the south that dries 3 feet. This will be more difficult at HW if these rocks cannot be seen, but using the small islet marked '12' south of Care Island and the east end of Dead Point as a reference for a danger bearing will assure a safe transit. This bearing is about 270° when westbound – GPS is a helpful back-up to pinpoint position. We often use the route above Care Rock at LW, turning north from Kamano Island and then turning west, staying close to Care Island. We like the fact this channel is deep and, during summer months, the location of most reefs can be identified by the presence of bull kelp.

The numerous islets in Beware Passage are a pretty sight in spring with wildflowers along the shores. We've sighted dolphins in this passage. Near the passage's eastern entrance, on the shores of Turnour Island, is the overgrown site of Karlukwees village and is where an old government wharf stands in disrepair. It's a beautiful scene and sad to see this once-busy village abandoned. We've seen six boats rafted to the old dilapidated pilings of this old wharf, which seems like tempting fate. The foreshore consists of a clamshell midden, and some petroglyphs can be found in the vicinity. Visiting beyond the foreshore should not be done without permission of the local band office. Anchorages in Beware Pass include Beware Cove and Dead Point Bay (see page 250 to 251).

Yvonne Maximchuk, of Echo Bay, painted this view of Karlukwees from early photographs.

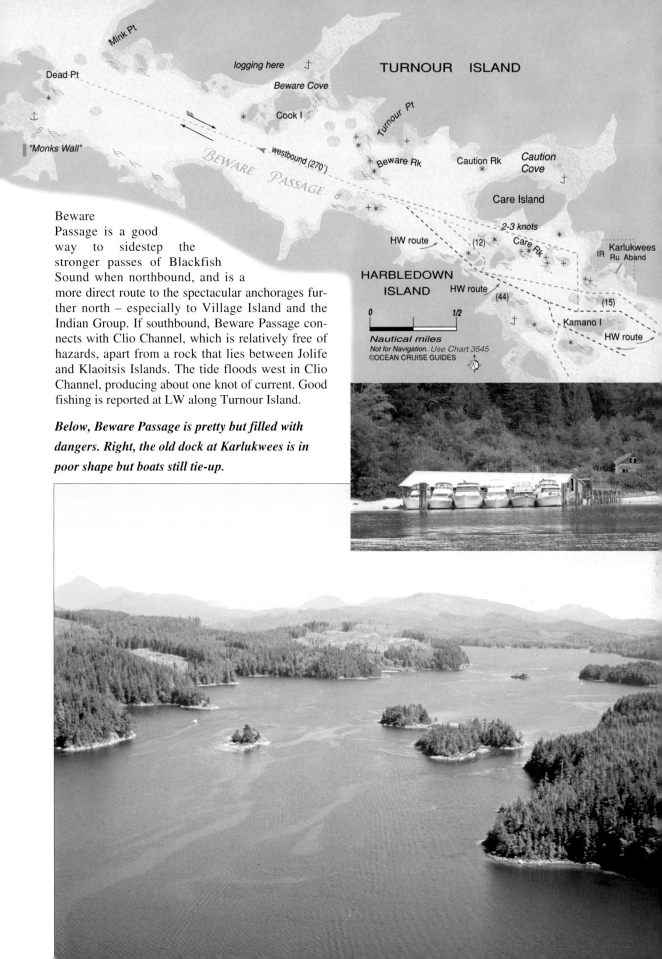

TURNOUR ISLAND

Mink Pt

Dead Pt

⚓

5

*

*

"Monks Wall"

logging here ⚓

Beware Cove

Cook I

Turnour Pt

westbound (270')

BEWARE PASSAGE 5 10

++

**

+ Beware Rk

*

+ +

**

Caution Rk

*

Caution
Cove

⚓

Care Island

2-3 knots

HW route

(12) *

Care Rk

* + +
* * + + +

Karlukwees
IR Ru Aband

++

**HARBLEDOWN
ISLAND**   HW route

(44)

0 ——————— 1/2

Nautical miles
Not for Navigation. Use Chart 3545
©OCEAN CRUISE GUIDES

⚓

(15)

Kamano I

HW route

*

HW route

Beware
Passage is a good
way to sidestep the
stronger passes of Blackfish
Sound when northbound, and is a
more direct route to the spectacular anchorages further north – especially to Village Island and the
Indian Group. If southbound, Beware Passage connects with Clio Channel, which is relatively free of
hazards, apart from a rock that lies between Jolife
and Klaoitsis Islands. The tide floods west in Clio
Channel, producing about one knot of current. Good
fishing is reported at LW along Turnour Island.

*Below, Beware Passage is pretty but filled with
dangers. Right, the old dock at Karlukwees is in
poor shape but boats still tie-up.*

THE ANCHORAGES:

Lagoon Cove 1

Near the western entrance of Chatham Channel are several anchorages and marinas, including the Minstrel Island docks and the popular Lagoon Cove Marina operated by Bill and Jean Barber. The Barbers cruised this area for years before transforming Lagoon Cove into a successful marine resort with a sociable atmosphere. For boaters wanting to drop the hook, there is good anchorage south of the marina in about 60 feet (19 m) of water; however, it is open to strong NW winds.

Above, Lagoon Cove Marina and anchorage.
Below, a calm evening at Cutter Cove.

Cutter Cove 2

This anchorage has received a bit of a bad reputation because the holding is fair at best, the winds blow through almost uninhibited, and the bottom is littered with rocks. Yet, it remains one of the busiest anchorages in Blackfish Sound due to its proximity to great cruising, fishing and the popular marina nearby at Lagoon Cove.

John Chappell (*Cruising Beyond Desolation Sound*) had this anchorage right 25 years ago when he said if a westerly is predicted, anchor on the north side of the cove, and if an easterly is predicted, go to the south side. But the holding ground takes some getting used to – it feels like soft mud or ooze on top of rock or the other way around. Whatever anchoring tackle you employ, be alert if the wind comes up strongly in the night – if your vessel isn't dragging, someone else's may be. The cove is fairly level for the first two thirds of its length and shelves near the head. We like to anchor near the old snag just past the bluff on the north side in about 30 feet (9 m).

We've been here several times with never a problem. Granted, we've not been here in a howling wind but that is the luck of the draw when cruising. We've enjoyed the peaceful views, the sunsets and exploring the head of the bay. Still, Cutter Cove has that bad rep!

Port Elizabeth 3

Situated in lower Knight Inlet, Port Elizabeth lies on the north side, between Minstrel Island and Village Island. Fair protection can be gained from west winds in Duck Cove, north of the island marked '47' on Chart 3545. During easterlies and southerlies, we've anchored in the SE corner of the harbour and found it secure, although gusts come over the low shoreline. The setting in Port Elizabeth is uninteresting (there are log dump sites in the harbour and an aquaculture operation) but the anchorage is useful to get out the weather in Knight Inlet. There is a good lunch stop at the entrance to Port Elizabeth, off Gifford Point, where two islets and a clamshell beach look appealing.

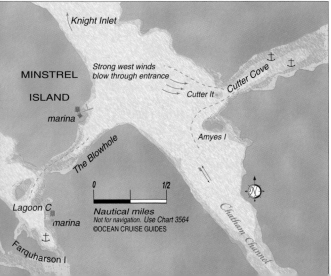

0   3
Nautical miles
Not for navigation.
Use Chart 3515
©OCEAN CRUISE GUIDES

Sargeaunt Passage

Steep Hd

KNIGHT   INLET

Hoeya Hd
beach

Sail Cove
2,380 ft (721 m)

1 kn

Tomakstum I

Siwash Bay

Glendale Cove

Prominent Pt

Rough Pt

Martin Lake

Protection Pt

Tsakonu Cove

KNIGHT INLET

The longest inlet on the British Columbia coast, Knight Inlet (named by Lieut. Broughton) cleaves its way for nearly 70 miles into the Coast Mountains. No wider than one-and-a-half miles, the inlet winds past snow-clad summits and numerous waterfalls before reaching the glacier-fed rivers at its head. There, the massive peak of Mount Waddington rises more than 13,000 feet. Exploring this wild and remote channel can be formidable in any vessel.

The entrance to Knight Inlet lies between Warr Bluff (Village Island) and Slope Point. From its entrance to Glendale Cove, the inlet is quite open to the west, and afternoon summer winds funnel into this area with force – often 20 to 25 knots. Currents from Village Island to Steep Head at Sargeaunt Passage can be 3 knots on an ebb and against a strong westerly will produce a rough 4- to 5-foot chop. The Sailing Directions caution that wind has a considerable effect on the rate of tidal currents and an increase of 2 knots of current can be expected when strong winds are blowing with the tidal stream. The turn of current occurs 1 to 2 hours after high or low water at Alert Bay.

Pacific white-sided dolphins are often sighted in Knight Inlet in the reach up to Glendale Cove.

East of Tribune Channel, the current is about one knot, but conditions can be quite rough from Protection Point to Sallie Point when westerlies are blowing against an ebb. On big ebbs, a bad tide rip is reported south of Hoeya Head which can produce a dangerous swell during strong west winds. Late afternoon inflow winds are common in summer in many stretches of water right to the inlet's head. Pacific white-sided dolphins are common in Knight Inlet, so don't be surprised to find a troupe tagging along on your journey up the inlet. The only chart available for this area is 3515.

Tsakonu Cove 4

Farther east up Knight Inlet, Tsakonu Cove lies below Sargeaunt Passage and is a pretty spot offering overnight anchorage during settled weather, but is completely open to the east. Strong W winds can come over from Cutter Cove and some anchors may drag in the mud-and-pebble bottom, as Muriel Wylie Blanchet noted in *The Curve of Time*. Despite recent logging activity at the head of the cove, this anchorage still has a wild and remote feel and is a beautiful spot at night when the moon is full. Further up the inlet, Hoeya Sound is open to the west and too deep for small boats to anchor. (There's a nice beach east of Hoeya Head.) There is really no decent anchorage until Glendale Cove, 18 miles from Tsakonu Cove.

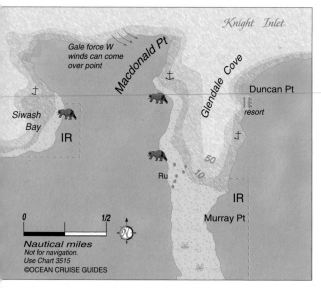

Above, a grizzly known as "Sargeaunt" lurks in grass by shoreline. Below, a view of Glendale Cove anchorage looking north.

Glendale Cove 5

After the long trip up Knight Inlet, this pretty cove offers a welcome respite from westerlies in the lee of the bight south of Macdonald Point. Anchor in about 50 to 70 feet (15 to 20 m) as close to the west shore and the beach as possible. The anchorage shelves more than indicated on the chart. Although the bottom is sticky mud, make sure you are well anchored before shutting off the engine. If you are spending extended time here, a line to the west shore is a good idea if strong west winds are expected. Even in the summer, westerlies can reach 30 knots in this area and may blast right over the headland. If conditions are severe, consider retreating to one of the bights along the west shore north of Naena Point or behind Adeane Point. Glendale Cove is also open to NE winds, although these are not common in summer months. If strong SE winds are called for, the east shore of **Siwash Bay**, just around the corner, provides better shelter.

Grizzly bears can be seen in the cove from spring until mid-July, at which time they move up the hillsides to feed on berries. By late August they return

---

GLENDALE COVE AT A GLANCE:
CHARTS: 3515
LAT LONG: 50˚41.05'N 125˚44.20'W
PROS: Beautiful remote location, stunning views and wildlife make this a special destination. Anchorage has good holding, protection only fair.
CONS: Long drive in and out of inlet. Sudden wind change can result in moving vessel.
MUST DO: Spot a grizzly! Go to Cascade Falls.

to the south end of the estuary and Glendale Creek to feed on spawning salmon. Black bears can be seen throughout the summer months near the lodge and in Siwash Bay. Glendale Cove attracts both grizzly and black bears because of the salmon stream and the LW buffet available on the beach and estuary. For early-summer visitors, mornings are a good time to venture by dinghy, slowly making your way, to the west side of the cove where you'll soon spot a bear. Grizzlies are often seen along the beach near Macdonald Point, so be careful if venturing on shore. If you want to observe bears throughout the day, anchor opposite the pilings of the old pier and you'll have a great view from the safety of your boat. Usually two or three bears can be seen along the beach. The bottom shelves steeply here so be careful how your vessel is swinging.

For wildlife buffs, it is hard to beat this anchorage. Glendale Cove and area have become world-renowned for sighting bears, seals, porpoises, killer whales and eagles. People from around the world come to this beautiful and remote cove to view the concentrated population of grizzly bears. Knight Inlet Lodge, located just south of Duncan Point, exists for the sole purpose of offering such sightings. Although it has no moorage, supplies or restaurant facilities for visiting boaters, the lodge employees are very friendly in offering information about the cove and bear watching.

The viewing of bears that feed in Glendale Creek each fall is regulated by a local conservancy group. The Knight Inlet Lodge (as well as tour companies located in Telegraph Cove) use viewing stands along the creek for their clients. Boaters who are keen to actually spend a few days at the lodge with guides can contact the lodge at by phone at (250) 337-1953. If you arrive by boat in early September and want to join a group visiting a bear-viewing stand, check with the lodge for a time. They discourage people from venturing to the viewing stands on their own.

Also in Glendale Cove are reports of naturally occuring obsidian (volcanic) glass being found at the head of the bay. The obsidian reported here is generally deep black and of good knappable (breakable) quality. This is one of only three locations of obsidian glass on the B.C. coast, the other sites being in Dean Channel and the Queen Charlottes.

In settled conditions Knight Inlet is well worth exploring and most boats can travel much of the inlet in a day and return to Glendale Cove. Also, there are a few overnight anchorages farther into the inlet, or you might consider using a fisherman's mooring (see sidebar). Keep in mind conditions in the inlet can change rapidly.

Kwalate Creek is six miles north of Glendale Cove.

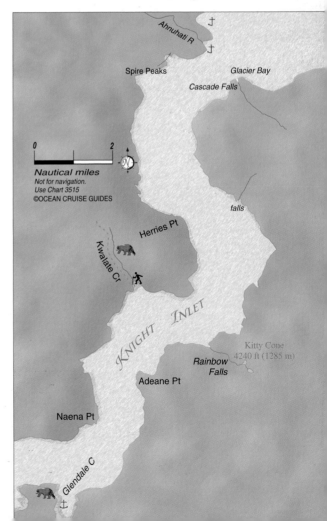

Six miles north of Glendale Cove is a trail accessed at the mouth of **Kwalate Creek**. The trail follows this boisterous creek for a few miles, then turns up to follow the hillside to a viewpoint. Be aware that bears can be along the creek in summer. Keep an eye for fresh tracks or scat indicating recent bear traffic – an airhorn is a must. Fishing at the creek mouth is good in summer months. Although good as a lunch stop, the creek mouth is open to inflow winds and anchoring overnight is not secure.

Fisherman's Mooring

Fishing vessels travelling in Knight Inlet sometimes employ a mooring tactic which works well in small bights when there is nowhere else to drop the hook. The method is to find a suitable spot such as an indentation in the shoreline with deep water. For overnight mooring, avoid slopes where there is evidence of recent slides. Point your bow into the wind and tie lines fore and aft to each shore so that you are lying parallel with the inlet. You can add a third line amidships to pull yourself as close to shore as you like. Pick a bight that has enough lee to provide shelter from the wind and, ideally, where the shore is deflecting any waves.

Left, our boat Sway with a fisherman's mooring at Spire Peaks while we explore the area by dinghy. The slope behind appears unstable and this bight would not be suitable for overnight. Below, the view from Ahnuhati River to Cascade Falls.

For real adventure cruising, the upper reaches of Knight Inlet offer spectacular views of glaciers, hanging waterfalls and frequent wildlife sightings. There are anchorage possibilities opposite **Glacier Bay** (15 miles from Glendale Cove) and at **Wahshihlas Bay** (25 miles distant) where log booms are sometimes tied up. Although the sighting of wildlife at the head of Knight Inlet is an exciting prospect – bear, moose and wolves frequent the river flats – the area is quite open and evening williwaws can occur if a north wind pipes up. The Klinaklini and Franklin River meet opposite Dutchman Head.

One of two beautiful waterfalls in the vicinity is **Rainbows Falls**, about 5 miles from Glendale Cove on the east side of the inlet. The mist from the falls, falling hundreds of feet, produces a beautiful rainbow in the afternoon and early evening. Perhaps the most dramatic of waterfalls along the southern B.C. coast is **Cascade Falls**, about 14 miles from Glendale Cove. This waterfall drops an amazing volume of water from about a 100 feet, generating a constant cool breeze. Opposite this waterfall are **Spire Peaks**, one of the most impressive ridges along Knight Inlet.

Around the corner from these peaks is an anchoring possibility at the mouth of the **Ahnuhati River**. Another is the bay north of Ahnuhati Point. The mouth of the Ahnuhati River was once the site of a native village, but no evidence of this remains today. In his book *Full Moon, Flood Tide*, Bill Proctor talks about cannonballs being found on the beach here and speculates that either the village was bombarded or the cannonballs were traded for furs. The anchorage is along the southwest shore and requires a stern line. Another recommended anchorage is at the mouth of the Sim River in Wahshihlas Bay.

Above, the dramatic sheer cliffs of Spire Peaks. Below, Cascade Falls create a cool mist from the huge volume of water falling from Glacier Peak.

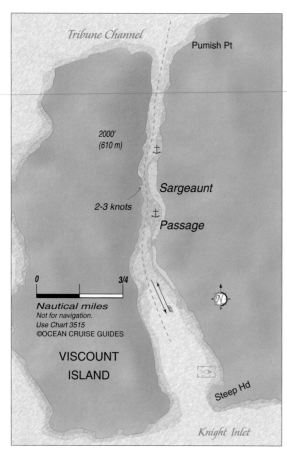

View of western entrance of Tribune Channel.

TRIBUNE CHANNEL
Sargeaunt Passage 6

If you are heading north into Tribune Channel from Chatham Channel or Knight Inlet, Sargeaunt Passage provides a scenic and sheltered route. The pass also provides decent anchorage, well protected with good holding, on either side of the narrows in the upper third of the passage. Because of the high, steep mountainsides, which rise to over 1,800 feet on Viscount Island, the channel can be gloomy in the evening and much cooler than just outside in Tribune Channel. The channel shallows to less than 20 feet (7 m) depth and, as shown on chart 3515, vessels should stay fairly close to Viscount Island when transiting the passage. Current in the pass ranges from 2 to 3 knots depending on the tide.

Winds through this part of the channel seem fluky in the summer, but if a strong southerly is forecast, a sheltered anchorage should be sought out, either in the north end of Sargeaunt Passage or further north in Kwatsi Bay.

Tribune Channel, north of Sargeaunt Passage, is truly spectacular with steep sides and, in spring, beautiful cascading waterfalls. Although there are no secure anchorages until Wahkana Bay and Kwatsi Bay, there are two sounds well worth seeing. The small bay west of Kumlah Island is reported to be good in a westerly (drift collects here). Flood current meets at the entrance to Bond Sound and current in the channel can flow at 1 to 2 knots.

Thompson Sound 7

This beautiful inlet has an extensive mud flat on its north side from the large Kakweiken River and is a fascinating area to explore. Anchorage is possible in settled weather at the head of the sound opposite Sackville Island. Depths are over 100 feet (30 m) well into the anchorage where the bottom shoals rapidly. Favour the SE shore when approaching this pocket of deep water and keep the white X scar in the granite rock hillside off your port bow (11 o'clock). Anchor in 60 to 80 feet (19 to 24 m) with mud and sand providing good holding. If a big westerly is coming up, you should retreat to the anchorage west of Kumlah Island or head for Kwatsi Bay.

An old steam donkey as well as numerous bits of old logging equipment lie rusting along the head of the beach on the east side. A small private cabin and dock are located on the point of land to the southeast of the anchorage. Logging operations sometimes locate at the mouth of McAlister Creek.

On a rising tide, you can explore for some distance (2 miles) up the river and really get a feel for the remote wilderness of this sound. There are bears in this area and you should be extremely careful if setting out on foot into the brush. During late summer, grizzlies will be feeding along this river. There are also numerous species of birds in Thompson Sound, including heron and eagle.

Thompson Sound anchorage between mudflats.

Heading up the wild Kakweiken River.

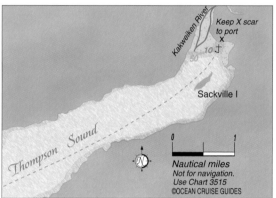

Bond Sound 8

Bond Sound with Ahta Valley in background.

This is another beautiful inlet along Tribune Channel with interesting river valleys; the Ahta River empties here. If exploring the river by dinghy, be sure to arrive at HW as the mud flats are extensive and at LW the boulders in the river will stop most dinghies. There is no real anchorage in the sound but there is a bight near the head along the east side where anchoring with a line ashore will keep you away from inflow winds. Any kind of a westerly blows keenly into Bond Sound.

The Ahta River has undergone extensive cleaning and rejuvenating for salmon stock, thanks to the Mainland Enhancement of Salmonid Species Society (MESSS). According to Bill Proctor, the stream supports all five of the West Coast salmon stocks as well as steelhead and trout. The valley is home to several species of mammals including cougar, bear (black and grizzly), river otter, wolverine and deer.

Wahkana Bay, Gilford Island 9

A sac-like anchorage opposite Bond Sound, this bay provides good anchorage in most conditions. A stream at the SW head of the bay is also the site of extensive work by MESSS to try to bring back coho salmon runs after the creek was severely damaged by logging and a landslide in the 1960s. After years of work cleaning up the stream, salmon are starting to return and with them the kingfishers and eagles. A partial trail along the stream leads to a small lake and makes for a good hike, but be careful not to knock debris into the creek. Black bear inhabit Gilford Island, so taking along an airhorn is a good idea.

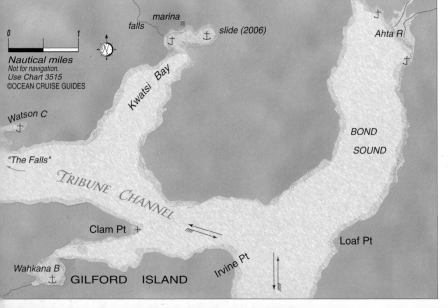

Wahkana Bay and local salmon stream (inset).
Right, scenic anchorage at head of Kwatsi Bay.

The anchorage itself is quite deep, showing about 100 feet (35 m) on chart 3515 but there are shallower areas along the south and east shore where depths are between 35 and 65 feet (10 and 20 m). This is the preferred part of the bay to duck out of the west winds which can gust through from Viner Sound. The drop-off is quite steep and the shelving is narrow so it may be a good idea to tie a line to shore. Holding in sand and mud is good. This is usually a very quiet bay, rich with birdlife.

Kwatsi Bay, Tribune Channel 10

Near the bend where Tribune Channel turns west is a good marina and anchorage at the head of Kwatsi Bay, a 2-mile detour off the main channel. The marina – owned and operated by Max Knierim and Anca Fraser – has a parallel mooring dock able to handle 8 to 10 medium-sized vessels. This marina (once the site of a shingle mill) has potable water and showers on the dock but no power. A small store sells local products (including honey and some excellent jams) and souvenirs. On alternating nights there are happy-hour gatherings or potluck dinners on the dock at which visiting boaters share anchorage stories and ideas on the world. Kids love this marina, where they are welcomed by Max and Anca's two children, Marieke and Russell. It's a short dinghy ride from the marina to a trail leading up to a beautiful tum-

Kwatsi Bay Marina is an oasis within an oasis.
Inset, Russell Knierim catches a red snapper.

bling waterfall. Good fishing, especially for snapper and cod, is also nearby along the shores of the bay close to its entrance at Tribune Channel.

One of the main attractions at Kwatsi Bay is the beautiful scenery at the head of the bay – a stunning vista of clouds and trees and soaring smooth granite. The steep rock sides of the bay give the feeling you are floating in a lake very high in the mountains

where the air smells pine-fresh and clean. Westerly winds diminish at the entrance to Kwatsi Bay, and the inner bay, especially on the east side, is quite protected and peaceful.

The recommended anchorage is this eastern side of the bay in about 100 feet in good holding. (A slide in the fall of 2005 dumped debris in the extreme NE corner of the bay.) The sheer sides may produce williwaws, but the nights we've anchored here have been absolutely still. According to Max and Anca, northeasterlies produce the strongest winds in the bay but these are rare in summer. The west part of the bay is reputed to have an uneven and rocky bottom but provides the best shelter if a hard westerly is kicking up.

Paradise Found

Jim Roby has been cruising the Inside Passage since the 1970s but can't seem to get much further than Kwatsi Bay. For the past four years he's spent the summer at the marina dock and is a familiar figure helping arriving boaters with their lines.

"This is such a peaceful anchorage and the people here are great," he says. A member of the Ed Monk Wooden Boat Club, he keeps *Anchor*, his 50-foot Monk McQueen, built in 1969, on Lake Union while he spends winters in Arizona.

Jim has never cruised beyond Cape Caution and he says the area around Kwatsi Bay is paradise. "The Broughton's are the best. Why go further when there is all this great cruising right here?" he says. Who can argue with that?

Watson Cove 11

This is a deep anchorage with good shelter from SE winds but it is quite exposed to west winds. However, the cove is a good lunch stop as there are two waterfalls nearby. The most spectacular one is about half a mile west of the cove and consists of large cascading falls sliding down hundreds of feet of granite before reaching the sea. According to Bill Proctor the locals call it simply 'The Falls' as there is no other one in the area that's quite this large. He says the nearby fish farm workers refer to it as 'Glacier Falls' and tourists call it 'Lacy Falls,' so take your pick. Another, much smaller waterfall is at the head of Watson Cove, hidden among the thick forest and rock outcropping on the north side. On the south side, also at the head of the bay and about a hundred-yard walk from the shore, is a huge cedar measuring about 15 feet across. Aquaculture operations have recently moved away, although at the time of writing a holding pen remained in the cove.

Beyond Watson Cove to the west, just beyond Rainy Point, is a large scar in the hillside from a slide in 2000. Deep Sea Bluff marks the western terminus of Tribune Channel. Just beyond lies the Burdwood Group and Broughton Archipelago, another great cruising area covered in Chapter Eight.

Potts Lagoon 12

Lagoons are tempting to visit, but many along our coast are very dangerous to enter. Those that can cause trouble are typified by a large elliptical basin with a small neck opening. One lagoon, however, that offers safe anchorage for boats heading to or from Blackfish Sound is Potts Lagoon.

With its fairly wide and deep entrance leading into a relatively small basin, Potts Lagoon presents no threat to boats seeking shelter. Good, all-weather

Above, "The Falls" outside of Watson Cove.
Below, Potts Lagoon provides good shelter.

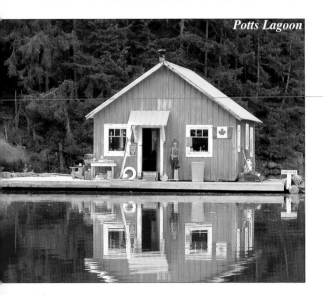

Potts Lagoon

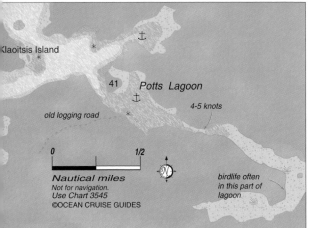

Klaoitsis Island

41   Potts Lagoon

old logging road

4-5 knots

0   1/2

Nautical miles
Not for navigation.
Use Chart 3545
©OCEAN CRUISE GUIDES

birdlife often
in this part of
lagoon

saw a flock of sandhill cranes circle overhead and, while making quite a racket, eventually land at the far end of the lagoon on a marsh flat. In summer months black bears feed among the berry bushes near the old logging camp on the southwest side of the anchorage, so be careful and take an air horn and a stout stick if you decide to hike along the logging road. Also, if exploring the lagoon, keep an eye on the state of the tide, for the lagoon nearly dries at LW and there can be a 4- to 5-knot stream at the neck during spring tides.

Several floathomes are moored along the SW side of the anchorage. The first person to homestead in Potts Lagoon was a man named Murray Potts, who lived at the head of the lagoon where he kept cows at his creekside farm and had a horse for plowing. Potts lived in his namesake lagoon until 1946, when he left to accept the job of Indian Agent at Alert Bay.

Beware Cove, Turnour Island 13

This cove is a good spot to wait for a tide change or to find overnight anchorage in settled weather. Two or three boats can anchor north of the two small islets on the south side of the cove and this is really where the best protection is found. Most northwesterlies die out just outside of Cook Island, but the anchorage is fairly open to south winds. The holding is in soft mud and sand, and there is a lot of kelp along the edges of the anchorage so be sure you are well set before turning in for the night.

The safest approach to Beware Cove is along the west entrance on the north side of Cook Island. We found the pass south and east of Cook Island has less

anchorage can be found inside the entrance, behind the small island marked '41' on Chart 3545. This scenic anchorage is well protected and safe in all winds – although westerlies can occasionally sneak around the small island. Another option is to anchor in the cove outside the entrance.

If the weather is fine, plan on spending an extra day or two at Potts Lagoon. The upper reaches of the lagoon, reached via a narrow set of rapids, are very interesting to explore by dinghy. One September we

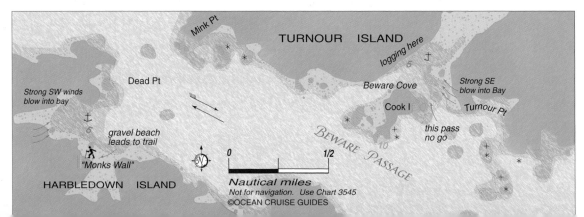

Mink Pt

TURNOUR   ISLAND

logging here

Dead Pt

Strong SW winds
blow into bay

Beware Cove

Strong SE
blow into Bay

Cook I

Turnour Pt

gravel beach
leads to trail

this pass
no go

"Monks Wall"

BEWARE PASSAGE

HARBLEDOWN   ISLAND

0   1/2

Nautical miles
Not for navigation. Use Chart 3545
©OCEAN CRUISE GUIDES

Beware Cove has fair protection from the west but gets hit by wind from the south.

depth than shown on the chart, with a least depth of about 10 feet (3 m). It is almost choked with kelp. John Chappell noted in his book that the original Kwakiutl name of the cove was "bad smell coming up from beach" in reference to the large expanse of tidal flat that takes up the east end of the cove.

Dead Point Bay

At Beware Passage's western entrance is an unnamed bay southwest of Dead Point, which has a straightforward entrance and good holding ground in sand and mud. This is a fair-weather anchorage, providing shelter from northwesterlies but not from southwesterlies, which apparently blow with force over the low hills. We've used this anchorage when southbound from Village Island and have always enjoyed the beautiful sunsets. See Chart 3545.

A shallow cove indents the bay's southern shore and hidden in the brush along its west side (see map) is a stone wall that was built by William and Mary Anne Galley in the late 1800s when they homesteaded here with their three sons. They built this rock wall on the site of an abandoned Catholic Mission (established in 1864), but the structure came to be known as Monks' Wall because of an unverified report that Buddhist monks had built a temple on Harbledown Island.

Another early settler was a Kanaka named George Kamano who cleared 20 acres at the head of the cove and planted fruit trees. He and his wife raised a large family, and one of their daughters, Maria, married Jim Joliffe. They homesteaded on land next to the Kamano farm where they also cultivated a fruit orchard.

Above, Dead Point Bay offers shelter in settled conditions. Below, pioneers built Monks' Wall.

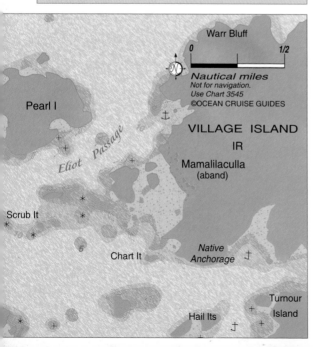

Mamalilaculla, Village Island 15

For years boaters have anchored off Village Island to visit the abandoned Kwakiutl village of Mamalilaculla. The anchorage providing access to the village lies on the west side of the island, where a reef and string of islets extends from the anchorage's northern point and creates a natural breakwater to NW winds and sea. The swinging room is limited but the holding ground is good and the anchorage is fairly sheltered, except during strong northwesterlies. There are now a couple of floats for boaters to tie up to, but the plank walkway beside the old government dock has been removed.

Native Anchorage on the SW side of Village Island is another spot to consider if the weather is settled – it has a pretty view to the south. Over half of the bay is a drying mudflat so you should anchor as close to the entrance of the bay as possible. Holding is good in sand, shell and mud, but this bay is open to the south and east, and provides only limited protection from westerlies. East winds can funnel along Canoe Passage into the anchorage.

If staying overnight, we usually anchor on the west side of the island, north of the jetty. When heading ashore, we beach the dinghy near the old wharf and scramble up the hillside trail. At the top, the path leads past a dilapidated wooden building

where a missionary nurse named Kathleen O'Brien once ran a school and a small tuberculosis sanatorium for the local children. She came to Village Island in 1920 and was named to the Order of the British Empire for her years of missionary work before she retired to England in 1945.

Just beyond the abandoned schoolhouse is the village site, situated atop a low bluff overlooking a shallow cove dotted with islets. At the base of the bluff, along the water's edge, is an extensive midden. During our first visit to the village in the fall of 1989 the village's last totem pole was still standing, but by the following spring it had toppled toward the sea. That was also the year Tom Sewid began acting as a guardian for the traditional territory of the Mamalaleqala. Under his direction, members of the Qwe'Qwa'Sot' Enox Band based in Campbell River started maintaining the village site and providing tours to visitors for a small fee. Mark Puglas, whose grandparents once lived on Village Island, was our guide when we took a tour in 1993.

On a more recent visit in summer 2003, we tied to the temporary floats that had been installed by Village Island Tours adjacent to the old wharf. We were greeted by Tom Sewid, who donned traditional regalia and stood in front of the existing long house frame to deliver his eloquent speech about his ancestors and their beliefs, which are passed down orally from generation to generation in the form of myths.

Above, fallen totem with sea wolf at village's east side. Below, Tom Sewid, a guardian of the village. Opposite, view of Mamalilaculla, looking east.

Anchorage near Mamalilaculla. The dock, as shown here in 2005, is no longer in use.

The role of storyteller comes naturally to Tom, whose grandfather was Chief James Aul Sewid, author of *Guests Never Leave Hungry* and recipient of the Order of Canada for his work at improving the lives of his people. Today, visitors may be greeted by other native guardians as Tom's time is split with his wildlife tour company. On our most recent visit, in summer 2005, the floats had been removed.

Village Island was the scene of a famous potlatch that took place in the winter of 1921, an event that resulted in a mass arrest and confiscation of regalia, including masks and rattles. In 1884, the Canadian government had placed a ban on potlatches. This decision was based on a lack of understanding of nature culture and an attempt to assimilate the Kwakwaka'wakw people, as well as a growing alarm at the destruction of property (as a display of wealth and power) that was taking place at these gatherings. Yet, these celebrations were central to their culture and were still being held in secret. At Mamalilaculla a long house was built with no crests engraved on the house posts, so that different clans in the area could come and hold secret potlatches here. The large potlatch gathering of December 1921 resulted in 49 people being charged and 26 eventually sent to jail for several months. Hence the village came to be known as Mamalillaculla, which means 'village of the last potlatch', although its true name is Meem Quam Leese – 'the village with the rocks and islands in front.'

In the early 1960s the village was still thriving, but by the end of the decade everyone had left. A wooden sea wolf lying in the grass had once protected a home's entrance. The sea wolf crest is also found on a toppled totem pole, which had landed on its back with the sea wolf pointed seaward. The orca and eagle on the very top of the pole are gone because (according to legend) the whale swam out to sea and the eagle flew into the sky. Set back from the fallen pole are the massive corner posts and cross beams of the village's long house. Up to 300 men were required to lift these log beams. Cedar siding and roofing were then added, but these could be removed and towed by canoe to a summer fishing village in Knight Inlet.

Goat Island anchorage, Crease Island /Carey Group 16

The Carey Group contains several one-boat anchorages, including one on the east side of Leone Island and another along the SE shore of **Madrona Island**. The best overnight anchorage in Village Channel, however, is a small bay on the SE side of Crease

CREASE ISLAND

0   1/3

Nautical miles
Not for navigation.
Use Chart 3546
©OCEAN CRUISE GUIDES

Raleigh Pt

Fern I

10   5

Goat I

VILLAGE CHANNEL

Carey Group

1-3 kn

Madrona i

Leone I

Chief's
Bathtub

Island opposite **Goat Island** (sometimes called Goat Island Anchorage) which can accommodate a dozen boats. Sheltered from moderate westerlies, the anchorage offers good holding in mud, although there is some kelp along the rim of the anchorage and patches of eel grass throughout. Set your anchor well, for evening W winds can gust through this bay. The approach to the anchorage is on either side of Goat Island – the north side is better because it is clear of underwater obstacles. Some current is noticeable throughout the anchorage.

A scenic lunch spot can be found on the northeast side of Crease Island, off the shoreline's granite ledge, with a splendid view of Village Channel and its avenue of islands.

Crease Island was named in 1905 by the Geographic Board of Canada to honour Sir Henry Pering Pellew Crease, the father of the Bar of British Columbia. Born in Cornwall, England, the son of a naval captain, Crease emigrated to the Crown colony of Vancouver Island in 1858 where, as a judge, he travelled to distant parts of the province. On one occasion, while in northern British Columbia, Judge Crease was seriously injured but continued trying cases from a stretcher. When his condition worsened, his native bearers were tempted to desert him but, according to John Walbran in *British Columbia Coast Names*, Crease "made them carry him down the steep trails not 'feet foremost like a dead man,' as he said, 'but head foremost', by which means he persuaded them to bring him out."

The Crease Island anchorage makes a very good base from which to explore the area's numerous islands. There is plenty to see and do nearby, between visiting the various native sites and enjoying the good fishing in Knight Inlet.

If you are looking for a lunch spot in the immediate area, there is a pretty anchorage just east of **Leone Island** in about 20 feet (6 m) of water. Although there is a fish farm a few hundred yards south, the view to the east is good. Also, decent anchorage in settled weather can be found on the northeast side of **Alder Island** but it is somewhat exposed to the daytime westerlies.

CREASE ISLAND AT A GLANCE

CHARTS: 3546
LAT LONG: 50°39.91'N 126°38.61'W
PROS: Good holding, fair protection from most winds. Close to native sites, lots of nearby beachcombing and dinghy exploring. (Native sites include: Karlukwees, Mamalilaculla, Chief's Bathtub). Beautiful passes and intricate waterways make this an excellent spot for a few days' stay.
CONS: Wind out of NW can gust over low hillsides. Open to easterlies. Some aquaculture.
MUST DO: Explore area by dinghy.

Aerial view of 'Goat Island Anchorage' at Crease Island. This anchorage can accommodate a dozen vessels and is safe in most summer conditions.

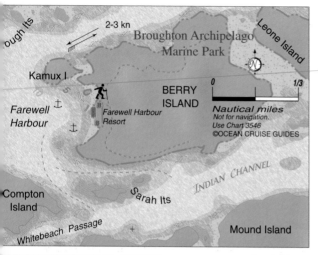

Farewell Harbour 17

The islands and islets clustered around Blackfish Sound form a gunkholer's paradise. Several of these islands lie within the convoluted boundary of Broughton Archipelago Marine Park. One of these is Berry Island, with a popular anchorage called Farewell Harbour on its west side. The harbour got its name from officers of the surveying vessel *Beaver* in 1870 because it was the last place surveyed as the ship departed the area.

Although the holding ground is quite good, in sand and sticky mud, the harbour experiences healthy current during large tides and the anchorage can be uncomfortable when strong westerlies blast over West Passage. This is, however, a good place to be in easterlies in the lee of Berry Island. The best spot to anchor, away from most of the current, is between Kamux Island and the reef due south which is marked by kelp. Depths in this part of the anchorage are about 30 feet (10 m).

The entrance through West Passage should not be attempted during a strong westerly and a large flood tide because of the very dangerous reefs, especially Punt Rock. The better approach during such conditions is from the south between Compton and Sarah Islands. Currents during springs in West Passage are easily in the 4-knot range so be careful here.

Luxury yachts drop anchor here during the summer months and on shore is a sportfishing lodge, called the Farewell Harbour Resort, built in 1982 on a private acreage before the rest of the island became

Above, view of Chief's Bathtub and pictograph on Berry Island. Below, Farewell Harbour.

part of the marine park. There is a path from the resort connecting with the park's hiking trails. The resort owner, Paul Weaver, normally allows boaters to tie their dinghy at his marina dock while they walk the park trails. Boaters should check first at the front desk, however, for permission.

The fishing is good around Berry Island and halibut can be caught right in Farewell Harbour. On the north side of Berry Island, just below the HW mark, is an eroded depression in the side of a cliff known as the Chief's Bathtub, for it fills with water at high tide. This rock formation and its adjacent pictographs can be viewed from Village Channel.

Mound Island 18

A popular alternative to Farewell Harbour is the large anchorage south of Mound Island. Clear of aquaculture operations, the bay is quiet with a nice view of the mountains to the east. This is a good anchorage from which to explore the many nearby middens, such as the one at the SW end of Mound Island. Holding in mud with sand and shell is good. Anchor within the 30 feet (10 m) line, keeping a healthy distance from the rocks along both shores.

There is another anchorage for one or two boats farther east along the north shore of **Harbledown Island**, behind a small islet in front of a mud-and-shell beach. This is a pretty spot with a great view across Indian Channel to the islands of the Carey Group. Farther east still is **New Vancouver** where First Nations people have built a new dock and a long house dedicated in 2003.

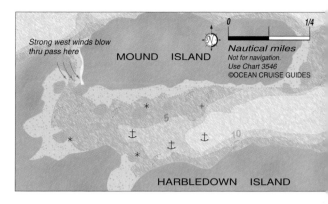

Cedar Island 19

This beautiful anchorage is located in a cluster of islets to the west of Cedar Island at the north end of Providence Passage. The entrance is narrow but hazard-free, allowing most mid-sized vessels entry.

This tiny anchorage is an excellent lunch stop or overnight anchorage in settled weather. The main drawback, especially for sailboats, is the lack of depth – 4 feet (1.2 m) – during zero tides. With our boat drawing over 5 feet, this anchorage is usually a temporary stop. Although fairly open to west winds, the islets divert the swell coming from Queen Charlotte Strait. The anchorage east of Cedar Island is deeper but gets some current, and strong west winds can come in unwelcome gusts through the gut facing Providence Passage.

Aerial view of Mound Island anchorage, looking east to New Vancouver on Harbledown Island.

The foreshores of the surrounding islets consist of smooth stone, their slopes blanketed with mosses and gentle crowns covered with salal, cedar and spruce. Nearby are a number of interesting islands to explore by dinghy including White Cliff Islets – a popular nesting area for oystercatchers. Pick your weather carefully if visiting these islets.

In 1912, a man named George Nelson began camping on Cedar Island so he could fish the 'Merry-Go-Round' in Providence Pass. This was a popular spot for the local fishermen who trolled with handlines from rowboats along the kelp beds where, as Bill Proctor explains in his book *Full Moon, Flood Tide*, "the big springs like to lie." He recounts how the Merry-Go-Round was discovered by a Japanese troller in 1918 when a flood tide pushed him into the pass where he caught dozens of coho in one day. He promptly told his pals about this hot spot, and the next day about 20 boats joined him, drifting around in a big circle and catching coho.

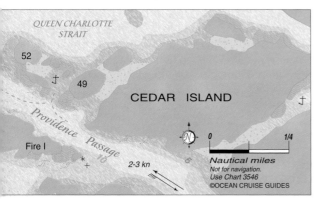

Cormorant Channel Marine Park (Pearse Islands) 20

This beautiful undeveloped marine park consists of a number of islands of the Pearse and Plumper archipelagos, situated at the northwestern end of Johnstone Strait between Hanson Island and Cormorant Island. In addition to the eastern portion of the Pearse Islands and most of the Plumper Islands, the park takes in Stephenson Islet and Stubbs Island. Safe overnight anchorage in most conditions can be gained in the Pearse Islands.

Running through the middle of the park is impressive Weynton Passage, which carries a large part of the water flowing from Johnstone Strait to the Pacific Ocean. Currents in Weynton Passage can reach 6 knots. (See page 231 for more detail.)

The Cormorant Channel area (from Johnstone Strait north to Queen Charlotte Strait) is part of the core habitat of the northern resident killer whale population. It is one of the best places on this coast to witness these magnificent creatures in their natural habitat. Both Weynton Passage and, more often, Blackney Passage are excellent viewing spots.

Salmon fishing in the area is very good and the waters adjacent to this marine park are rich in wildlife. Both the Pearse and Plumper Islands are renowned for their world-class scuba diving, enhanced by the superb visibility of the water – you can often see the set of your anchor at these islands.

Cedar Island anchorage is a sublime hideaway.

Currents are ever-present in these islands (in the 1- to 3-knot range, setting your vessel either NW or SE) but there are some pretty spots with enough swinging room to ease a boater's concern. The best anchorage is inside the long narrows between the largest island marked '104' and a smaller island marked '75' on Chart 3546. Although the entrance from the south is tight with lots of kelp streaming along the edges of the shoreline, it is clear of obstructions with a depth of about 20 feet (6 m). Entrance from the north is also hazard-free and is wider. We like to anchor about halfway along, opposite a small gut, in about 25 feet with good holding in sand and mud. Although this anchorage is oriented in a NW-SE line, winds from these directions usually enter only in diminished gusts. The anchorage is also free of swell from the outside straits.

Locals sometimes use these narrows as a pass, so have an anchor light on in the evening. Also during the night, bull kelp carried along with current may foul your rode and although this doesn't normally present a problem, you may hear the kelp bulbs continuously thumping against the hull. Current may also start spinning your prop; to avoid it fouling on kelp, leave the engine in gear. This anchorage is a good base for exploring the entire group of islands which are home to an abundance of birdlife and seal-

Right, a small cul-de-sac anchorage looking south to Johnstone Strait. Below, an aerial view (looking east) of the main anchorage at Pearse Islands.

ife. If venturing by dinghy to the outer islands, be very careful of currents and winds.

Just SE of this anchorage is a small one-boat nook and although it is a tight spot and open to the southeast, it is quite safe in west winds or settled conditions, and provides southbound boaters a quick access to Johnstone Strait. We've anchored at the widest spot, opposite a small bight in the island marked '72'. The anchorage provides a great view south to the strait and a peaceful setting. At the head of this cove lies a drying reef which, although a barrier to boats, does not prevent the movement of water between this anchorage and the larger anchorage. The steady flow of water will normally keep your bow pointed in or out of the anchorage.

Another anchorage possibility lies south of the island marked '44' but in settled conditions only.

PEARSE ISLANDS AT A GLANCE
CHARTS: 3546
LAT LONG: 50˚35.05'N 126˚52.23'W
PROS: Good protection from most winds with good holding. Excellent visibility in water. Quiet anchorage.
CONS: Ebb and flow of current will swing your vessel around but strength of current under two knots. Entrances tricky in poor visibility.
MUST DO: Explore islands by dinghy.

This cove is quite open to the north and seems to get the most current of all these islands.

The Pearse Islands are ringed by reefs and shoal water, especially on the north and east sides, requiring the full concentration of boaters entering these islands. Because of their proximity to a large pass, strong currents and breaking seas are a common hazard. If arriving from the SE on an ebb, be careful of the set to Stephenson Islands and give this area a wide berth. Arriving from the north can be even more challenging as both the Pearse Reefs and Stubbs Island can generate dangerous waves during big tides and wind. **Close reading of the Sailing Directions is essential for cruising in these waters.**

In the late 1800s, steamboats would take on wood fuel at the Pearse Islands where a camp of mostly Chinese workers would cut and split Douglas fir. Although the steamers burned mostly coal to fire their boilers, they sometimes used wood. The Pearse Islands and Alert Bay were among the last places the northbound steamers could get Douglas fir, which burns hotter and slower than other wood.

Compared to the Pearse Islands, the Plumper Islands get more current, owing to their parallel orientation to Weynton Passage, and really have no safe anchorages. One anchorage that is popular with divers, is between the two most northerly islands marked '70' and '69'. Currents during HW come over the tombolo with some strength. Navigating through these islands is dangerous because of the ever-present current.

Alert Bay

An important village of the 'Namgis people occupied the terraced shoreline at the mouth of the Nimpkish River when Captain Vancouver anchored nearby in the summer of 1792. The British naval captain was waiting "uncomfortably idle" while two of his officers – Broughton and Puget – surveyed the islands lying at the eastern end of Queen Charlotte Strait. With time on his hands, Vancouver headed ashore to the village where he paid a visit to the home of Chief Cheslakee. The chief's hospitality was reciprocated on board the ship *Discovery* but things turned momentarily sour when Vancouver found his guest trying to steal one of his logbooks – an item of idle curiousity to the chief but of irreplaceable value to the captain.

In 1870, the 'Namgis moved their main village across Broughton Strait to Alert Bay on Cormorant Island (named for the British naval survey ships *Alert* and *Cormorant*) where some white settlers had established a store and saltery. A sawmill was soon built, as well as a hospital, residential school and salmon cannery. Natives from other villages also moved to Alert Bay and it became a major port for the commercial fishery. The fishing village remains a cultural and commercial centre of the Kwakwaka'wakw (Kwakiutl).

Alert Bay is a bustling port with an excellent small-boat harbour protected by a stone breakwater. Overnight and temporary moorage is available, with visiting boats allowed 4 hours free moorage – just time enough to take on water and provisions (the local grocery store provides transportation back to the docks), then set off on a walking tour of this interesting town rich in native culture. A Visitor Information Centre is located on the waterfront, and across the street is the Old Customs House, built in

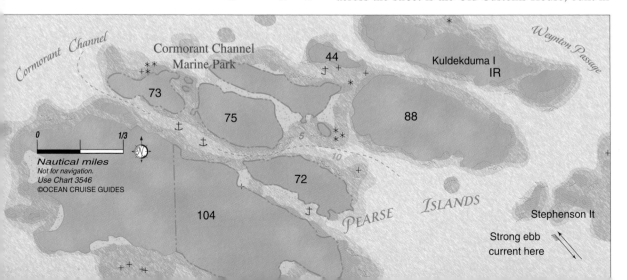

1917, its upper floor now a charming restaurant. The last operating fuel dock in Alert Bay was closed in 2005 and, at present, Port McNeill is now the closest location for fuel.

A short distance past the InfoCentre along the waterfront is the 'Namgis Burial Grounds where the first of its 17 totem poles was raised in the late 19th century. A pamphlet identifying each pole is available at the Infocentre. Of note is Pole #9, carved in 1970 by Henry Hunt and Tony Hunt with assistance from John Livingston and Lawrence Bell (Haida) at the Royal British Columbia Museum in Victoria. This pole is a memorial to Mungo Martin of Fort Rupert, a high-ranking chief, renowned carver and respected leader who was the first to openly host a potlatch when its prohibition ended. The two shorter poles at the front of the grounds, representing Thunderbird and Giant Halibut, were carved in 1995 to commemorate the opening of a new road in front of the cemetery and the resolution of a land claim the 'Namgis First Nation had with the Department of Highways. The burial grounds are sacred and visitors are asked to honour the 'No Trespassing' sign by viewing the totem poles from the roadside.

A hike up the hillside behind the town will take you to Gator Gardens Ecological Park, a natural swamp fed by an underground spring which supplies the island's water system. When the early white settlers built a dam halfway up the hill to store water for their cannery, the surrounding area was flooded and the trees died, their tall trunks and craggy limbs now devoid of vegetation. These dead trees, which can be viewed from a boardwalk, make ideal perches for bald eagles and ravens. Nature trails wind through the surrounding forest.

There are more sights to see on the other side of town, past the boat harbour. Follow the main road along the waterfront and you will pass the Historical Anglican Church – constructed in 1892 under the supervision of Reverend James Hall who relocated his mission from Fort Rupert to Alert Bay in 1880. The church's stained glass window depicts scenes of that era, including the mission ship *Columbia* and a 'Namgis canoe.

A short distance farther along the road is the U'mista Cultural Centre, a modern museum built in the traditional plank-and-beam style. Housed inside is a collection of elaborate masks, rattles and whistles that were used at potlatch celebrations of feasting, dancing and gift-giving. Many of these items were seized by the Canadian government following

Native public art greets visitors to Alert Bay's small boat harbour.

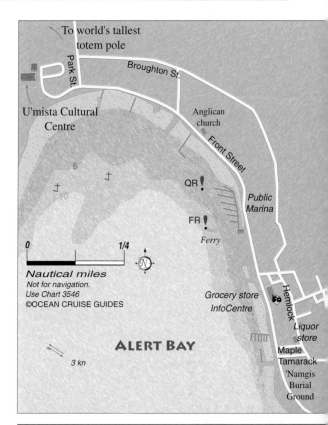

a mass arrest at Village Island in 1921, then returned in 1979 for display in the U'mista Cultural Centre.

A 10-minute hike up the hillside behind the museum, along residential streets, will take you to the Big House, originally built in 1963 and modeled on the traditional residences of the Kwakiutl people. A fire destroyed the building in August 1997 and a new Big House was built in May 1999. A community centre, it is primarily used for potlatches. Nearby is the world's tallest totem pole, which stands 173' high. Raised in 1973, the pole displays the crests of various tribes and is crowned with Sun Man, crest of the Quatsino. This pole has become a point of interest for passing cruise ships which glide slowly past Cormorant Island before entering Johnstone Strait.

Port McNeill

This prosperous logging town is an ideal port in which to reprovision, do laundry, and take on fuel and water. Inland are the rivers, lakes and forests of the Nimpkish Valley, while local waters offer excellent fishing, especially near the entrance of Mitchell Bay on Malcolm Island and along the east side of Cormorant Island.

Port McNeill is a busy port during the summer boating season, but if you call the harbourmaster on Channel 66A, an empty slip can usually be found (try to arrive before noon). Some boats anchor off (across the bay, SW of **Ledge Point**) but we usually tie up and stay for a day or two. The municipal docks (with showers) are well run and maintained, and the town's facilities are all close by. A new

Top, 'Namgis Burial Grounds. Left, Anglican Church. Below, U'mista Cultural Centre.

Above, a BC ferry pulls away from Port McNeill where the small boat harbour (also shown below) accommodates visiting boats.

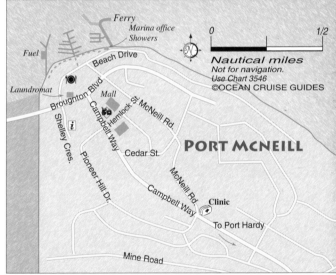

laundromat is on Broughton Blvd. across the street from the Tourist Information Centre. Two large grocery stores are located in plazas on Campbell Way just a few minutes from the marina. A medical clinic is located farther up the hill on the same street. There are a number of restaurants along Beach Drive.

The hub of town is the harbour, with its ferry dock, public marina, fuel dock, log-loading facility and local fleet of floatplanes. At the seaward end of the municipal pier we have seen people catch coho by throwing a line in the water. A fish-cleaning station near the ramp is well utilized.

Although there are small boat facilities in both Sointula and Alert Bay, visiting by ferry as a foot passenger is another option. While in Port McNeill it's easy to hop aboard the inter-island ferry which runs all day between the three ports.

Sointula – a Finnish word meaning harmony – was founded at the turn of the last century by pioneer farmers from Finland who wanted to create a utopia of co-operative rural living in a scenic seaside setting. They were granted government land and today visitors can stroll the town's tidy streets and visit the local museum, shops and restaurants. An interesting nautical pub called The Bilge is located right beside the ferry dock.

CHAPTER EIGHT

BROUGHTON ARCHIPELAGO

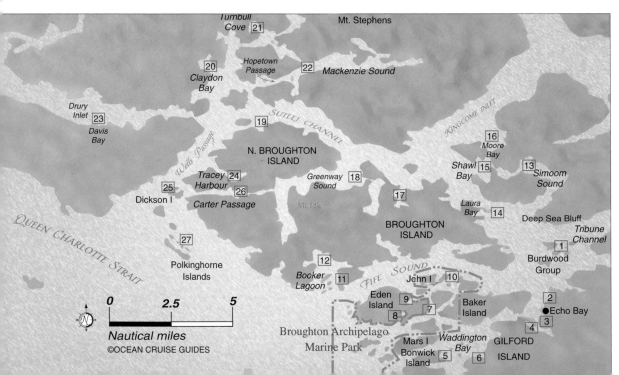

Turnbull Cove 21

Mt. Stephens

20

Hopetown Passage 22

Claydon Bay

Mackenzie Sound

Drury Inlet 23

SUTLEJ CHANNEL

19

Davis Bay

KINGCOME INLET

16

Moore Bay

N. BROUGHTON ISLAND

Wells Passage

Shawl Bay 15

13

Simoom Sound

Tracey Harbour 24

Greenway Sound 18

26

17

Laura Bay 14

25

Carter Passage

Mt Ick

Deep Sea Bluff

Dickson I

BROUGHTON ISLAND

Tribune Channel

1

Burdwood Group

QUEEN CHARLOTTE STRAIT

27

Polkinghorne Islands

12

FIFE SOUND

2

● Echo Bay

Booker Lagoon

11

John I 10

3

Eden Island

9

Baker Island

4

8

7

Broughton Archipelago Marine Park

Mars I Bonwick Island

5

Waddington Bay

GILFORD ISLAND

6

0   2.5   5

Nautical miles

©OCEAN CRUISE GUIDES

In rainy weather, the remote islands of Broughton Archipelago seem shrouded in the past, when hand loggers worked the coast and small settlements clustered around sawmills. This sense of bygone days prevails while anchored beside a deserted midden or motoring past the rotting remains of a wharf where people once awaited a Union Steamship, its whistle piercing the foggy silence to announce the arrival of mail and supplies.

When the sun breaks through the mist and such musings dissipate, a mariner's contemplations may turn to the present reality: interesting passes, pristine anchorages and the sublime scenery of Broughton Archipelago where low islands front a backdrop of snow-capped mountains. Marina resorts are tucked into various bays and coves, and their operators appreciate every visitor. Boaters arriving for fuel or supplies often succumb to the charm of these upcoast mini-communities, pausing to exchange

Charts & Publications:

Use CHS Charts: 3546, 3547, 3515. Canadian Tide and Current Tables Volume 6 applies to this area. Also be sure to have the CHS Sailing Directions Volume One for the British Columbia south coast.

yarns with fellow cruisers and spend a few days before setting off for new anchorages.

Broughton Archipelago is a term loosely used to describe the area in and around the extensive marine park named for it. This undeveloped park's meandering boundary encompasses some 300 islands and islets lying between Fife Sound and Blackfish Sound. (Anchorages south of Bonwick Island are covered in Ch. 7, Blackfish Sound.) The Broughton area in general has dozens of intriguing anchorages, some quite busy at the height of summer but others offering the seclusion and remoteness boaters expect along the east side of Queen Charlotte Strait.

Logging camps still exist in some of the area's inlets, but aquaculture and fish farms are now a more common sight, their presence hotly opposed by many of the area's residents because the proliferation of sea lice on penned fish is viewed as a threat to the region's wild salmon stocks. Clamshell middens are plentiful throughout this traditional territory of the Kwakwaka'wakw (Kwakuitl). Villages once dotted the shores of these islands, which are interconnected with narrow, maze-like passages.

Summer weather among the islands is dominated by Queen Charlotte Strait, with morning cloud or fog usually clearing by mid-day as the prevailing summer northwesterly sets in and blows through the channels. This sea breeze usually dies out in the evening, while at night a land breeze often funnels down the mainland inlets. Fog is a common occurrence from late July right through September, but it usually burns off by noon.

Tides and Currents

Booker Lagoon Passage, Carter Passage and Hopetown Passage are shallow passes with streams in the 4- to 8-knot range and should be attempted only at HW slack. Hopetown Passage is perhaps best transited by dinghy – the drying reef at the east entrance has snared more than a few boats. The passes are described in detail in The Anchorages section of this chapter.

Stuart Narrows, located at the entrance to Drury Inlet, has fairly strong currents with an ebb of 7 knots and a flood of 6 knots, referenced to Alert Bay. The normal route through the pass is south of

Rising over 400 feet, Deep Sea Bluff marks the west entrance of Tribune Channel.

Welde Rock, favouring the S side of the passage. Current streams are fairly smooth without much turbulence. However, large whirlpools can form downstream of Welde Rock and, as a result, the pass should be navigated near slack. Current is found in many of the small passages and channels, but usually reaches no more than 2 knots. Indian Passage, Old Passage and Cramer Passage have slightly stronger streams (up to 3 knots).

Deep Sea Bluff

This well-known landmark was named by Captain Vancouver when he and his officers explored and charted these waters in 1792. As Vancouver noted in his journals, while his ship *Discovery* lay at anchor off Hanson Island in late July, any investigation of the area's multitude of islands was unnecessary until he determined "how far the *Chatham* had been able to succeed in fixing the continuation of the continental shore." Under the command of Lieutenant Broughton, the Chatham had exited Johnstone Strait via Havannah Channel, picked her way along narrow and shallow Chatham Channel, then followed the twists and turns of Tribune Channel to its western entrance. By the time Broughton arrived at Deep Sea Bluff, he and his men had safely piloted their ship through a watery labyrinth in an impressive test of seamanship. Broughton then entered Queen Charlotte Strait via Fife Sound and made a beeline south to rendezvous with the *Discovery*, passing to port an "extensive cluster of islands, rocky islets and rocks" which Vancouver, in commemoration of his lieutenant's discovery, named Broughton's Archipelago, a reference that was revived two centuries later with the establishment of Broughton Archipelago Marine Park.

THE ANCHORAGES
Burdwood Group 1

This group of small islands and islets lies at the entrance to Tribune Channel where it intersects with Fife Sound and Penphrase Passage. For about 5,000 years, native fishing camps were located on these islands. Today summertime kayakers often set up camp at these former sites, one of which is marked by a beautiful midden where the clear water shimmers turquoise-green over a clean white crescent of crushed clamshells. This stunning midden lies at the east end of the islet north of the island marked '110' on Chart 3515.

Access is fairly clear into the Burdwood Group from either Tribune Channel (keeping island '85' off the port) or Hornet Passage (keeping island '85' to starboard). Gunkholing around these islands is a sheer delight with plenty of wildlife reported both on the islands (deer, cougar and wolves often swim to the islands) and in the surrounding waters. We've seen killer whales and humpback whales within a mile and a half of these islands. Many species of birds make the Burdwood Group their home, including eagles and numerous sea ducks.

Above, the Burdwood Group is a good lunch stop with a beautiful midden beach, right.

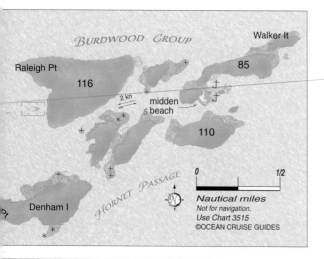

Above, the east side of Scott Cove is a good bet in SE winds. Below, the beautiful Burdwood Group.

Although there is no obvious protected overnight anchorage, there are one or two locations to drop the hook for the day south of island '85'. Several small islets are adjacent to the island with the midden and these provide some protection from W winds. We anchor either just NE of the midden in about 70 feet (21 m) or between the two islets that line up with the midden in about 30 feet (9 m). Current can flow through the islands at a knot or more. You can anchor right in the middle of the islets and this might be the safest bet for overnight, if you don't mind the 120-foot depth. West and S winds can pipe through here, but in settled weather this anchorage would be fine. Although we have stayed overnight here, we usually treat the islands as a day stop, enjoying the beautiful beach for swimming and exploring the area before retreating to a more secure spot for the night.

The closest overnight anchorage is **Scott Cove**, either the westernmost bay or, in settled weather, the bight behind an islet. Most of this cove is being used for forestry and salmon hatchery operations. Another option is Pierre's Bay Lodge & Marina, in the next bay over, which attracts boaters to its restaurant and bakery. The small pretty cove at the head of **Viner Sound** is another option, although strong westerlies find their way into this anchorage.

BURDWOOD GROUP AT A GLANCE
CHARTS: 3515
LAT LONG: 50˚47.79'N 126˚27.39'W
PROS: A beautiful oasis with clean midden beach.
CONS: Anchorage area quite deep.
MUST DO: Have a picnic on the beautiful midden.

Echo Bay, Gilford Island ![2]

Echo Bay's anchorage and marinas, looking NW.

Echo Bay, on the northwest side of Gilford Island, is a year-round floathome community with two marinas just inside its entrance and a scenic anchorage at its head where the open uplands of Echo Bay Marine Park provide access to good trails. The anchorage is sheltered from all winds and the holding ground is good, but swinging room is limited. The marine park's small wharf is used by the school boat, and on shore is a shell beach edged by a seawall that was built by the BC Forest Service in 1958 to stop the bank from eroding. A schoolyard is located above the open uplands of the park, and behind the school is a lovely stream called Ranger Creek. Old logging trails lead deep into the woods. One of these trails leads east to a lake and others lead south to 'Proctor Bay' and Shoal Harbour. Use Chart 3515.

Like most isolated villages, Echo Bay clings tenaciously to a way of life that began at the turn of the last century when hand loggers moved from cove to cove working their claims. Camps consisted of two or three families, their individual floathomes rafted together and moored to shore with long logs holding them off the beach at low tide. The children attended a floating school that also moved about, following the greatest concentration of students.

The white-shell beach and flattened area at the head of Echo Bay was once the largest First Nations village in the area. Now it is home to one of the last one-room schools in Canada. Children come to school by boat, but in every other way it is a normal school complete with computers and teeter-totters. Between 1920 and 1960, about 40 families of log-gers and fishermen lived in and around Echo Bay. In 1910 Louie McCay bought land around Echo Bay, clearing room for a garden where the park is now, and built a store on a large float, as well as a fuel float and fish-buying camp. In the 1930s a shingle mill was built where the community hall now stands, and a camp and cookhouse were built where the one-room school, constructed in 1961, now stands. Children living in floathomes in Echo Bay would haul themselves to the school dock on a pulley float.

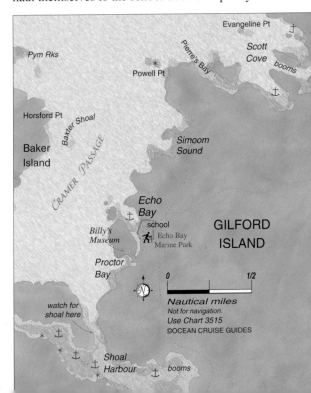

Above, the well-maintained floats at Echo Bay Resort. Below, Windsong Sea Village. Bottom, Echo Bay's colourful floathomes.

Summer is the make-or-break season for most resort operators in this area, and Echo Bay's two marinas welcome visiting boaters who can tie up and enjoy one of the B.C. coast's prettiest floathome settings. Both marinas are located at the entrance to this small bay, with Windsong Sea Village lying along the north shore at the foot of a rock bluff. Sounds echo clearly off its face, giving the bay its name. The evening sun lingers here, bathing the floathomes and moored vessels in sunlight. Open from mid-June to mid-September, the marina also houses a tiny art gallery.

Directly opposite, on the bay's south shore, is the Echo Bay Resort, established in 1934. In addition to 1,100 feet of dock space with 15- or 30-amp power, the resort includes a small hotel built in the mid-1920s. The grocery store here is one of the largest in the area and is well stocked. Fuel, water and block ice are available, as are fishing licences, bait and tackle. Other facilities include a post office, laundromat and showers. The concrete float holding the grocery store was once part of the Lake Washington Floating Bridge near Seattle.

Just north of Echo Bay is the abandoned settlement of Little Simoom Sound, where a floating village (originally located in Simoom Sound) once served loggers and various logging outfits in the area. Today there are a few floathomes and guided tour operators located in Little Simoom Sound. The old Simoom Sound Post Office building was towed to Echo Bay and is part of the Echo Bay Resort.

'Proctor Bay' [3]

A neck of land separates Echo Bay from the bay directly south, known locally as Proctor Bay. This small bay is home to three well-known writers and environmentalists. Boaters anchored in Echo Bay can follow the short trail through the woods to arrive at the museum and homestead of Bill Proctor. If you arrive by boat, you can tie to Proctor's dock on the north side of the bay, or you can anchor off in about 60 feet (20 m). Bill Proctor, who grew up on Swanson Island, has long been known as a fighter for the preservation of wild salmon stocks and lately has received an even wider audience with the publication of his bestselling book *Full Moon, Flood Tide*. Co-written with artist Yvonne Maximchuk, the book is filled with fascinating recollections of life in this area over the past century along with tips on local anchorages and wildlife viewing.

A lifelong resident of this area and an avid collector, Proctor built a museum on his property in 1999 to house all of the artifacts he has acquired over the years – his own memorabilia and that of various individuals who have homesteaded and worked in the area at fishing, hand logging and trapping. His museum charges no admission fee but accepts donations for local salmon enhancement. Over 3,000 vistors come to see his museum each summer.

Across the bay from the Proctor homestead is the home of marine biologist Alexandra Morton, renowned for her work studying orcas and the complexity of the language of these whales. Morton has also been instrumental in researching the impact of fish farms on wild salmon stocks and works with various organizations to restore salmon-bearing creeks in the Broughton Archipelago.

Local author and artist Yvonne Maximchuk lives at the SW end of Proctor Bay where she operates an artist retreat from her home. Maximchuk paints canvases of local scenes, past and present, and created the cover and inside art for *Full Moon, Flood Tide*. Yvonne is also well known for her superb pottery and ceramic work. Her art is displayed in Victoria, Campbell River and Port McNeill. Yvonne's husband Albert is a prawner (and potter) who has fished Broughton Archipelago for many years.

Shoal Harbour 4

This is a well-protected and pretty anchorage that provides shelter from west winds but not from easterlies, which funnel strongly throughout the harbour. Used for years as a logging base with booms along

Above, Bill Proctor in his gift shop. Below, artist Yvonne Maximchuk with her husband Albert. Bottom, Shoal Harbour, looking southeast.

the SE side, Shoal Harbour's eastern arm continues to be busy with forestry operations.

Good anchorage is available in the western arm but depths can be a little shallow – about 7 to 10 feet (2-3 m) feet at very low tides. The area west of the small islet, outside this arm, offers more depth and plenty of swinging room. Anchorage south of this islet is also good but be aware that there could be a satellite cable running from shore out to the islet. If you see a satellite dish on the small islet, stay clear. Farther into the harbour, there is an anchorage east of an islet located on the north side. Anchor in soft mud with good holding. Use Chart 3515.

Waddington Bay 5

Waddington Bay, at the NE end of Bonwick Island, is an all-weather anchorage that provides relatively good protection from most winds brewing out in Queen Charlotte Strait. Not only is it sheltered with good holding in sticky mud, but the cluster of islets at its entrance is perfect for birdwatching, picnicking or simply exploring by dinghy, while the nearby

channels offer good fishing. A maze of small islands – the Fox Group – clogs the entrance but careful attention to Chart 3546 and a slow approach will get you safely inside.

Entry from the north and northeast is made between the two islands marked '46' and '52'. If you're approaching from the south, the conservative entry is to keep islands '66' and '41' to port, then proceed in between the two above-mentioned islands. An alternative approach is to proceed west of island '66' and thread your way slowly through the reefs which are fairly easy to spot.

Most boats anchor in the main part of the bay, east of the small islet guarding the inner and more shallow part of Waddington Bay. Afternoon wester-lies can be expected throughout the bay and some-times the gusts are strong. A good way to escape these west winds is to tie a stern line on the east shore of the small island and, with your anchor well

Above, the anchorage west of central islet in Shoal Harbour. Below, aerial view of Waddington Bay.

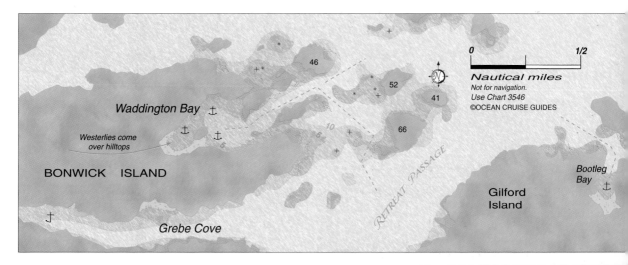

Waddington Bay

Westerlies come over hilltops

BONWICK ISLAND

Grebe Cove

RETREAT PASSAGE

Gilford Island

Bootleg Bay

0   1/2
Nautical miles
Not for navigation.
Use Chart 3546
©OCEAN CRUISE GUIDES

WADDINGTON BAY AT A GLANCE:

CHARTS: 3546, 3515
LAT LONG: 50°43.03'N 126°36.87'W
PROS: The central anchorage in Broughton Archipelago, with numerous anchorages and marinas nearby. Fairly well protected with good holding. Good fishing, crabbing and birdwatching nearby.
CONS: Occasionally busy, can receive gusty summer west winds. As in most northern anchorages, there is limited hiking.
MUST DO: Explore nearby islets and reefs.

set, pull yourself snug up to the island. Yours will be the only barbecue that isn't flaming out. We usually anchor in the small inner bay in a minimum depth of about 12 feet (4 m). This is more protected from SE winds, but westerlies still pipe through smartly. Fortunately the holding is very good in thick mud. On shore are a few short trails.

Grebe Cove, next door, has decent anchorage near the head. Few boats venture into this long narrow anchorage, so it is usually quiet. It gets some west winds coming over from Sedgley Cove and is exposed to the east, as the Sailing Directions warns. Holding, though, is good. Carrie Bay, further south, has a better reputation for protection from W winds, but its shoreline is not as interesting.

'Bootleg Bay' 6

An alternative to Waddington Bay is the unnamed, L-shaped cove that lies about a mile due east on Gilford Island. Known locally as Bootleg Bay, this anchorage has a fairly clear entrance but has lots of kelp along this stretch of the shoreline. The anchorage is small and holds only one or two boats; but it is serene and not often visited by recreational vessels. It is also well protected, with a forested shore blocking most wind, although southeasterlies sometimes

Bootleg Bay offers cozy anchorage.

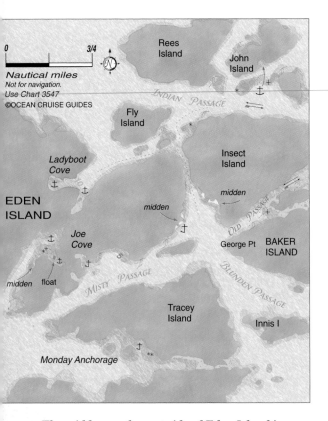

The midden on the east side of Eden Island is a perfect picnicking spot with great views.

gust through. In summer mosquitoes like it also, so have nets in place at night. Holding is good in soft mud in 12 feet (4 m) at the end of the leg; beyond this the bay dries. We usually tie a line to a tree at the small knob on the west shore where there is a clearing for campers and some short trails. This is a very good alternative if Waddington Bay is full for the night. A fellow named Johnny Card lived and hand logged in this bay from the mid- to late-1920s and this anchorage is still sometimes referred to by locals as Johnny Card's Bay.

Old Passage / 7
Misty Passage / Indian Passage

At the southwest corner of Insect Island is an intersection of channels which just begs for exploration. This is a beautiful area and was the location of at least four native villages in the past. The intersection takes in five islands, including Baker, Tracey and Eden Islands. The only anchorage lies at the northwest end of Blunden Passage, where it intersects with the three other channels. Two middens, marking old village sites, overlook this marine crossroads, one gracing the southeast shore of Eden Island, the other lying opposite on Insect Island.

We've motored or drifted through these passes many times en route to the many nearby anchorages and have always thought the anchorage noted above would make a good spot to stay overnight, even though summer westerlies tend to gust through the intersection. Our friends Fred and Rita Vitringa of Quadra Island anchored their 35-foot sailboat many times over the years off the Eden Island beach during summer months and were well tucked out of west winds. We explored this anchorage by dinghy one summer while our boat was anchored at John Island, and not a single boat or kayak passed by as we lazed on the beaches for several hours.

Nearby is another beautiful channel – Old Passage – which is a pretty route to take if you're going from the Burdwood Group to Joe Cove, or taking Insect Island Pass to Ladyboot Cove. Standing along the shorelines are cedars canted over the water and draped with cat-tail moss. With the current pulling your vessel and the breeze lifting the moss like an exotic veil, the visual effect is quite transporting. However, between the kelp, currents and strong afternoon winds that blow throughout the pass, the small basin here is not a relaxing place to anchor. Minimum depth in the pass is 10 feet (3 m) at the west end. The northern section of Blunden Passage, between Insect Island and Eden Island, is one of the most sublime passages anywhere.

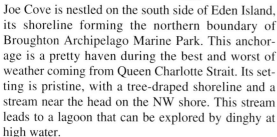

Joe Cove, Eden Island [8]

Joe Cove is nestled on the south side of Eden Island, its shoreline forming the northern boundary of Broughton Archipelago Marine Park. This anchorage is a pretty haven during the best and worst of weather coming from Queen Charlotte Strait. Its setting is pristine, with a tree-draped shoreline and a stream near the head on the NW shore. This stream leads to a lagoon that can be explored by dinghy at high water.

There are several spots to anchor in sheltered Joe Cove and the holding throughout in thick mud is very good. At the head is a small basin with room for three or four boats. This anchorage is fairly sheltered from W winds, which diminish by the time they reach this part of the cove.

Many mid-size and smaller vessels like the narrow east arm, where a float is located. Boats can either tie up or anchor off with a line tied to the float, or simply anchor off with a line to shore. This inner anchorage provides complete protection from all winds, although occasional W gusts are felt. The rocks lying west of the islet at the entrance to this pocket anchorage are shown on Chart 3547 and the

Top, the float at Joe Cove is a convenient tie-up for visitors. Above, a nearby midden beach.

Aerial view of Joe Cove showing small cove with float. Vessels can also anchor and stern tie here.

usual entry is between these rocks and the islet – staying closer to this islet. Minimum depth in this channel is about 15 feet. Entry is also possible close along Eden Island and the very small islet (really just a large rock). Favour the Eden shore with channel minimum depth of about 10 feet (3 m).

Bill Proctor, who grew up in this area, recounts in *Full Moon, Flood Tide* that a native trapper from Alert Bay named Joe Jack used to spend his winters in Joe Cove, where he and his wife lived in a shake

JOE COVE AT A GLANCE:
CHARTS: 3547
LAT LONG: 50°45'N 126°39.71'W
PROS: A sublime anchorage. Good midden beaches nearby. Eagles perch on nearby trees. Good holding throughout. Inner bay very protected.
CONS: Main bay a little open to westerlies, inner bay is shallow.
MUST DO: Explore area by dinghy.

shack. They also dug clams for a living, something their ancestors did in great numbers as evidenced by the numerous clamshell middens in the immediate area. One of these pocket beaches lies at the mouth of Joe Cove, overlooking the entrance channel.

Southwest of Joe Cove is a sac-like bay, also on Eden Island, known locally as **Mud Bay**, which offers good protection from W winds although it is quite open to SE winds. This wide bay would be especially useful for larger yachts. **Monday Anchorage** is another possibility although the entire bay receives unimpeded west winds. There is some shelter behind the east islet on the N shore. **Sunday Harbour** is also open to west winds, which reach every corner.

'Ladyboot Cove', aka 9 'Tombstone Bay' or 'East of Eden'

This bay, unnamed on the charts but locally known by the names listed above, lies on the NE side of Eden Island. The heel of the boot, which is the small cove with a drying foreshore, has room for two or three boats and is sheltered from northwesterlies and light southwesterlies but provides little protection from strong E winds. The smaller inner bay to the west (the toe of the boot) offers better shelter from most winds, except strong easterlies, in depths of over 20 feet (6 m) with a mud-and-shell bottom. The holding ground here is quite good and if an easterly is forecast, you can tuck yourself up to the north shore in the lee of the small hook of land and get out

The Andersons of Port McNeill on Irish Rebel spend a relaxing weekend at Ladyboot Cove.

John Island anchorage is a good one-boat bight shared only with a large colony of sea stars.

of some of the gusts. Depths here at LW are about 10 feet (3 m). There was once a small settlement and logging operation on this side of the cove.

This is a popular cove with locals, and rafts of small boats from Port McNeill often appear here on weekends. Good fishing is reported just outside the cove, along the Eden Island shoreline and off the north tip of Fly Island. Another good fishing spot is from the Walkem Cone bluffs to Gordon Point on Broughton Island.

Due north of Ladyboot Cove is another small cove, known locally as **Little Tombstone Bay**, where a loner named Matt Rose once lived and operated a small sawmill. He built a boat grid right beside his sawmill so he could use his boat engine to power the mill, constantly moving the engine from boat to mill and back again. This is quite a tight little cove – requiring a line ashore – but it is well protected from most winds and the holding is good.

Misty Passage, between Eden Island and Tracey Island, gets one or 2 knots of current and is a safe pass, although a westerly blowing against an east-flowing ebb can produce a surprisingly stiff chop, at least for dinghies. There is a small bight halfway along the pass, with a drying lagoon directly north, which makes for a pleasant lunch stop and is tucked out of most of the afternoon W wind.

John Island 10

If Ladyboot Cove is full, this bight on the SE side of John Island is an idyllic, one-boat anchorage and will provide excellent overnight shelter in almost all conditions. Part of the Benjamin Group of islands, which lie within the boundaries of Broughton Archipelago Marine Park, this sheltered spot can be entered off Indian Passage through a small collection of islands with about 20 feet (6 m) of water or via the deeper channel a little further to the west.

The small cove has lots of kelp around the sides of the entrance but there is usually a large clear area in the middle to get the hook down. We anchor in 20 feet (6 m on Chart 3547) in mud and shell, and point *Sway*'s bow southwest with the stern tied to the east side of the bight. Westerlies may gust through Indian Pass, but this bight is out of almost all wind. The NE side of the cove shelves quickly but the visibility is good and the shoal water can be easily seen. At low water the shoreline and tidal pools make for an interesting morning's exploration. This cove seems to be a sea star city with dozens of these colourful creatures easily visible in the shallows.

Evening sunlight pours into this secluded spot, nestled amongst low-lying islands. The small island opposite was once used for raising goats by a man named Louie McCay. He and his family lived in a cabin he built in 1925 near Twin Lagoon on Broughton Island, a short boat trip across Fife Sound. The narrow bay on Davis Island is open to west wind and chop.

Cullen Harbour, [11] Broughton Island

When travelling from Fife Sound to anchorages north, boaters are faced with a dilemma. Do you turn east through Raleigh Passage and explore Simoom Sound, Penphrase Passage and Kingcome Inlet, or

---

CULLEN HARBOUR AT A GLANCE

CHARTS: 3547
LAT LONG: 50°46.38'N 126°44.59'W
PROS: Unusual anchorage on the edge of Queen Charlotte Strait with lots of room. Secure from wind with good holding.
CONS: Gets some swell from strait and some current from Booker Passage.
MUST DO: Explore islets and Booker Passage.

Above, stone man at entrance to Booker Passage.

Below, view of Cullen Harbour, looking north.

turn west and find an anchorage near Queen Charlotte Strait for further explorations north? Either way is a win for cruisers and, if westbound, Cullen Harbour on Broughton Island is an excellent anchorage for overnighting.

The entrance to Cullen Harbour from the south is between Gordon Point and Nelly Islet, staying in the middle of the channel until you are past Ben Rock and the peninsula on the opposite shore. We sometimes enter the anchorage from the west, coming close along Olden Island (the reef shown at the SW end of this island extends a little further south than shown on the chart with a rock at 50°46.08'N and 126°45.17'W). The passage east of Long Island has numerous obstacles and hazards, and kelp grows nearly across the passage.

There is plenty of room in Cullen Harbour, and boats often anchor in a line along the east side to the small islet that marks the entrance to Booker

Lagoon. Boats also anchor just east of Long Island, where protection from W winds is better. Westerlies (which normally die out in early evening) can enter the harbour during gusts, and S gusts can also find their way well into the harbour. During HW, remnants of swell from Queen Charlotte Strait will be felt, especially along the S side of the harbour. Holding is very good in the mud-and-sand mix and most of the current from Booker Lagoon will be avoided inside the 30-foot (10 m) line. If you are staying for a few days, there are many small islets and passes to explore by dinghy, but beware of strong currents in Booker Lagoon (see pass info below) and swells from Queen Charlotte Strait breaking on the outer reefs.

Several shell middens mark the site of former native villages, and a retired sea captain once homesteaded in this harbour. Good fishing is reported along the outer shoreline SW of Wicklow Point.

Booker Passage
Booker Lagoon 12

Top, view of pass looking east. Above, facing 5 knots of ebb current at Booker Passage.

Just beyond Cullen Harbour is one of the most beautiful lagoons of the Inside Passage. However, entering this lagoon must be timed correctly as the lagoon is guarded by a very swift little pass. We tried to enter it on one occasion 15 minutes after LW at Alert Bay and were greeted with 5 knots of current ebbing out of the lagoon. Maximum current in the passage is at least 7 to 8 knots – some local fishermen say it is more like 10 to 12 knots. At full flood or ebb on big tides, the pass is a cauldron of white and turquoise water with whirlpools for hundreds of yards leading to and from the narrows.

In our observations of the pass, slack times on large tides are about 25 minutes after HW at Alert Bay and 35 minutes after LW. Slack period is about 10 minutes. During neap tides, the period of slack is about 25 minutes and during these smaller tides it should be safe to transit this pass up to one hour after Alert Bay. There is good depth, about 20 feet (6 m), throughout the pass.

If you are **westbound**, be sure to give the reef at the E end of Long Island a wide berth. Kelp will be present along the length of this reef and there may be a stone man showing the HW side of the reef. We aim for the centre of the small bight on Broughton Island and make our turn once we have rounded the kelp and have a clear view up the pass. Be careful to stay right in the middle of this pass as it is very narrow (perhaps 50 or 60 feet at HW) and there are rock outcroppings off Long Island and along the N shore. At the passage's W entrance, favour the island

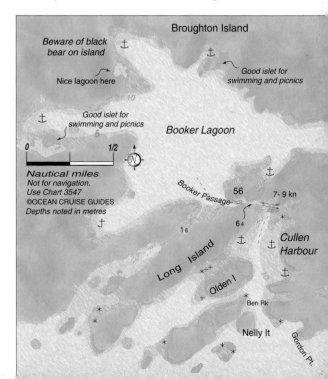

The anchorage on the north side of Booker Lagoon is well sheltered with a lovely islet for exploring and swimming.

marked '56' to avoid the marked rock to the south.

If **eastbound**, the pass can be hard to pick out from across the bay, but the small islet north of Long Island indicates the entrance. We come near the island marked '56' and check that no other boat has entered the pass. If there is another vessel in the pass, it is best to turn around as this is a one-boat pass. (The passage west of Long Island might be attempted at HW slack, but the entire entrance area to the south is kelp-infested, as is the pass itself, which is quite shallow.)

Inside the lagoon, you are presented with a myriad of anchoring possiblities – especially now that all aquaculture operations (although they are still shown on recent editions of Chart 3547) have been removed. During normal summer weather with daytime westerlies, the two NW bays offer good shelter and have nearby scenic islets. Drying lagoons with nearby middens are adjacent to these anchorages and make for interesting areas to explore by dinghy. Bears are reported in the area so be sure to take along an air horn if hiking into the bush.

The small cove due north of the pass is also quite good and although west winds do curl around the steep rock shoreline, the gusts are not strong by the time they make it into the anchorage. This cove is also well protected in south winds. There is a pretty islet in this anchorage which is ideal for picnics or for swimming from the granite shoreline. Seals and kingfishers also seem to like this cove and will likely be the only sounds you hear while anchored here.

Above, Booker Lagoon, with westernmost anchorage in foreground. Right and bottom, a small drying lagoon and nearby western anchorage.

The remains of a log dump can be seen on the north side of the anchorage; logging took place in this area up to the late 1960s. There is reported to be an old logging road here.

The bay at the extreme E end offers good protection during SE winds, and during settled conditions it is a good spot to enjoy the sunsets. There is another small cove S of this, with the island marked '56' to the west, which also provides shelter in SE winds.

The holding ground is good throughout the lagoon – soft mud in the bays to the east, and sticky mud and sand in the western bays. There may be discarded logging gear near the shore of the north and west bays. The head of the south arm is also an anchoring possibility, but it seems to get more breeze when a westerly is blowing.

BOOKER LAGOON AT A GLANCE
CHARTS: 3547
LAT LONG: 50°47.19'N 126°45.47'W
PROS: A beautiful destination with many safe overnight anchorages. Lots of things to do here – swim, hike, explore and picnic. Good fishing and prawning nearby.
CONS: Access is through a tricky pass.
MUST DO: Explore lagoons and islets.

Above, entrance to Simoom Sound. Left, a hump-back whale feeds in Penphrase Passage.

Simoom Sound [13]

This large, dog-leg inlet is where Captain Vancouver anchored his two ships in the summer of 1792 while survey parties set out in boats to examine the continental shoreline west of Deep Sea Bluff. By ship's boat Vancouver explored Simoom Sound to O'Brien Bay its head, where he walked across the narrow isthmus that separates it from Shawl Bay. Standing on the edge of the lagoon there, Vancouver could see the entrance to Sutlej Channel.

Simoom Sound's two popular anchorages, offering good protection from the west, are **McIntosh Bay** and **O'Brien Bay**. For the latter, anchor in

about 50 feet (15 m) in soft mud at the extreme NW end of the bay. If you tuck behind the knob of land extending from the N shore, you will gain good protection from an E wind. We've also found good protection from SE winds in McIntosh Bay, in the the cove north of Hannant Point in about 25 feet (8 m). Be careful to avoid this spot's numerous rocks and shoal water, especially to the south.

In the last century, Simoom Sound was home to a major logging camp which evolved into a floating village complete with store, community hall, post office and school. A large empty float served as a tennis court/baseball diamond. From 1908 to 1936, a man named Jack Dunseith ran a post office out of his general store, which sat on floats inside the entrance. According to some reports, Dunseith also ran a floating casino and saloon. In 1936, the entire village was moved to Little Simoom Sound (the small bay N of Echo Bay) where Dunseith's daughter Irene and son-in-law Dan Sutherland ran the store and post office for nearly forty years. In 1973 the store and fuel dock was moved to Echo Bay where it remains and the post office still retains its Simoom Sound name.

Laura Bay, Broughton Island [14]

The small inner bay of this anchorage has become a favourite with boaters over the years for, although it has limited room, it offers a pretty setting with excellent shelter in most winds. The main part of the bay is open to SE winds which die out near the western point of Trivett Island, although gusts from this direction do enter the inner bay.

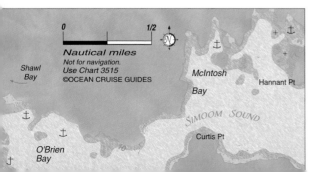

0   1/2

Nautical miles
Not for navigation.
Use Chart 3515
©OCEAN CRUISE GUIDES

Shawl
Bay

McIntosh

Bay

Hannant Pt

SIMOOM SOUND

Curtis Pt

O'Brien
Bay

*Above, aerial view of Laura Bay's inner anchorage where stern-ties are often necessary (right).
Bottom right, Shawl Bay Marina.*

Vessels tuck in behind the small island north of this point and normally tie a stern line to the peninsula jutting out from Broughton Island. The only chart available for this anchorage is 3515 which has little detail of this anchorage. There is shoal water and a rock awash NE of the small island. Further E, a drying tombolo connects Trivett and Broughton Islands. Anchoring NE of the small island provides only about 10 feet (3 m) of water and this depth carries almost to the E end of the small peninsula. NW of the small island the depth is about 18 feet (6 m). Holding is good in thick mud and sand.

Shawl Bay 15

Tucked in a bight on the bay's SE shore, the Shawl Bay Marina is a popular stop for boaters, where overnight moorage includes a pancake breakfast. Brown family members, who have owned the marina for several decades, serve visitors breakfast on a large float sheltered by a pavilion roof. The general store is stocked with dry and canned goods, as well as freshly baked bread and cinnamon buns.

A narrow neck of water, with a minimum reported depth of about 2 feet, connects the north end of Shawl Bay with Moore Bay. With depths of about 10 feet (3 m) and little current, this passage can be piloted by most keel boats at mid-tide. Shoals extend partially into the pass at two locations from Gregory Island, and kelp thrives along the edges.

Just outside of Shawl Bay we have twice seen a humpback whale, which locals say has been visiting this area for some years.

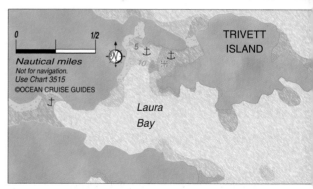

Nautical miles
Not for navigation.
Use Chart 3515
©OCEAN CRUISE GUIDES

0   1/2

TRIVETT ISLAND

Laura Bay

Above, Thief Island anchorage in Moore Bay and, below, view of Kingcome Inlet from anchorage.

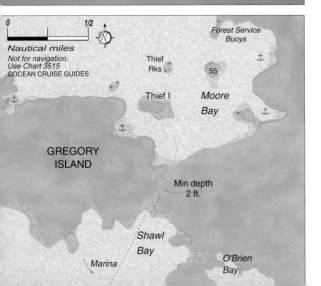

MOORE BAY AT A GLANCE:
CHARTS: 3515
LAT LONG: 50°45'N 126°40'W
PROS: Wide bay with lots of anchoring sites, good views to Kingcome Inlet, lots to explore by dinghy. Swimming in E side of bay or by gravel beach.
CONS: Quite deep in spots. E side of bay is open to west wind.
MUST DO: Swim near forest service dock. Visit Shawl Bay.

Moore Bay 16

Lying at the entrance to stunning Kingcome Inlet, this large bay offers several good anchorages and great views of the surrounding mountains and inlets. One of the most protected anchorages lies at the NE end of arrowhead-shaped **Gregory Island**, SW of Thief Island, where you can anchor in the crux of a bay in 35 feet (10 m). This is well sheltered from westerlies and only a persistent E wind will be a problem. The anchorage has a rocky bottom, however, and some anchors will have to be coaxed in before setting. We have found that once our CQR has dug in, the holding is quite good. There is a superb view of the entrance to Kingcome Inlet from this small bay. Thief Island, to the NE, is quite pretty with a granite shelf on its S side. Rock cod of decent size can be caught near Thief Rocks, about a half-mile north of the anchorage. At low water, there are numerous tidal pools along these reefs to explore.

Farther west along Gregory Island is another cove located behind a peninsular arm, which provides decent shelter from W winds but is open to the east.

The head of the cove is shoal and the foreshore is low and uninviting.

Good shelter from easterlies can be found on the E side of Moore Bay where there are two spots to spend the night. The first, opposite the Thief Island anchorage, lies behind a small island in about 45 feet (14 m) of depth with a gravel-and-mud beach to the E. The other location, and more sheltered from E winds, is in the bay's NE corner where two BC Forest Service mooring buoys are located near a small dock. On shore is a stream, a few trails and a small campsite overlooking the anchorage. Sunsets are spectacular here and the swimming is very good in cool, clean water.

The two anchorages at the west entrance of Kingcome Inlet – **Reid Bay** and the narrower bay below it W of **Magin Islets** – are both exposed to E winds. In settled weather we've stayed overnight at the head of the smaller bay, anchoring in about 40 feet (13 m). This bay commands a beautiful up-inlet view of snow clinging to the rocky peaks of mainland mountains, but the steep sides of the anchorage are a little gloomy and nearby Moore Bay is a better overnight stop.

Kingcome Inlet

Kingcome Inlet is widely known for its fjord-like beauty and stunning vistas of snowcapped mountains. *I Heard The Owl Call My Name*, a famous novel by Margaret Craven, was set in remote Kingcome Village. The village, unconnected by road to the outside, is located about a mile up the Kingcome River at the head of the inlet and is the

A forest service dinghy dock provides access to shore in the northeast part of scenic Moore Bay.

Gregory Island

A fellow named Blondy Carlson once tended a garden on Gregory Island. He kept his floathouse tied in Shawl Bay where he had another garden at the head of the lagoon. Blondy, like many of the area's settlers, was a jack of all trades who worked a trapline at the head of Wakeman Sound. He was also a hand logger who, according to Bill Proctor in his book *Full Moon, Flood Tide*, had a habit of "borrowing" trees from land that wasn't part of his claim. In one instance, Blondy had just finished borrowing a large cedar off the bluff above Steep Point in Penphrase Passage when a Forest Service boat came along. When a tree slides down a steep slope into the water, it will often shoot clear back out of the water and land with an impressive splash. This is what Blondy's tree apparently did, prompting the forestry boat's crew to stop and wait for Blondy as he scrambled down the bluff so they could ask him what he was up to. When Blondy said he needed a firewood log, the forester responded that most people burn fir. Blondy, displaying the resourcefulness required in such a situation, told them he needed kindling.

ancestral village of the Tsawataineuk, "People with Eulachon". This long, silvery fish, also called oolichan, was valued as a food source and for its oil, which could be used as a condiment, preservative and medicine.

The distance is 17 miles from the mouth of Kingcome Inlet to its head, where **Anchorage Cove**

Above, the view looking east up Kingcome Inlet.
Below right, Stopford Bay, Cypress Harbour.

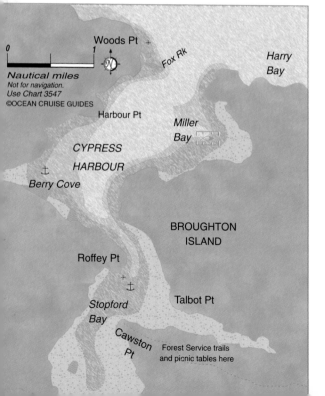

provides anchorage but no shelter from north and west winds. The river is navigable only by small craft, and if you wish to visit the native village, you may want to check with the Browns at Shawl Bay beforehand to find out if visitors are welcome.

Captain Vancouver's crew surveyed Kingcome Inlet by longboat in 1792, but it was named by Captain Pender in 1865 for Rear Admiral John Kingcome, who was commander in chief on this station. In 1895 the Halliday brothers settled along the river flats at the head of the inlet where they established one of British Columbia's most isolated cattle ranches, which stayed in the family until the 1990s. William Halliday also was an Indian agent for the federal government and played a controversial role implementing the official ban on potlatching which was enforced with zeal in the 1920s when several arrests were made.

In 1958 the Edmonton-born Anglican missionary Eric Powell moved to the native village in Kingcome Inlet, where his experiences formed the basis of Craven's bestselling novel. Powell moved away in 1961, serving as a minister in various coastal communities. He died in Victoria in 1997.

Cypress Harbour [17]

Several anchorages lie within this harbour although **Miller Bay**, just inside the entrance, is currently occupied by what appears to be a derelict fish farm. Anchorage is also available south of Harbour Point in **Berry Cove**. This spot provides good protection from westerlies but not from east winds. Anchor in 25 feet (8 m) in soft mud. Aquaculture may be taking place in this part of the bay at times.

The best spot we've found for shelter is the inner anchorage of **Stopford Bay**, reached via a narrow

entrance with kelp on either side. This anchorage is a quiet place to spend a day or two but is shallow. Chart 3547 indicates a rock with 6 feet (2 m) or less of depth at LW is located about 100 yards south of Roffey Point. We've anchored southeast of this rock in 14 feet (4 m) with good holding in soft mud. If you are anchoring during large tides, a line ashore might be a good idea to prevent the possiblity of swinging over the rock.

Inland of Cawston Point is an old logging camp which was considered an eyesore by John Chappell back in the 1970s but is now a pleasant campsite maintained by the BC Forest Service with picnic tables, fire pits and an old logging road which leads to a low marsh where cranberries grow. Good fishing is reported south of Moore Point into Harry Bay.

Great blue herons also like this anchorage. It's a beautiful sight to see these birds lifting on their huge wings high above the treetops, their primordial squawk echoing throughout the forested lands.

Greenway Sound, 18

Most boaters pulling into Greenway Sound are heading to the marina in the bay east of Greenway Point. For large vessels especially, this is an excellent facility with its wide U-shaped docks and 30 amp power. Run for years by Thomas and Ann Taylor of LaConner, the Greenway Sound Resort has a licensed restaurant, store, showers and laundry.

In addition to the facilites at the marina, boaters are also drawn to the nearby BC Forest Service trail leading up to Broughton Lake and Beaver Dam Lake. The trail, which runs beside a creek, starts at a dinghy dock S of the resort at the base of Mount Ick. Hikers can take a turn-off to the right and climb to the viewpoint above Broughton Lake or continue walking farther alongside the lake to an old "cordouroy" road made of logs, which leads to Beaver Dam Lake. The trail is about 2 miles each way.

For boaters wanting a quiet gunkhole, there are two good spots at the mouth of Greenway Sound near the SE shore. A fish farm lies at the entrance to Greenway Sound, between Walker Point and Cecil Islet, but this is unseen from the anchorages to the

Above, Cypress Harbour, showing Stopford Bay with Berry Cove in background. Below, a small nook inside the entrance of Greenway Sound.

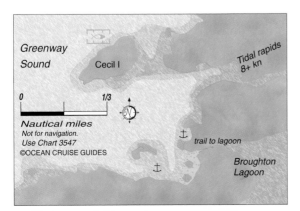

Greenway Sound

Cecil I

Tidal rapids 8+ kn

0   1/3

Nautical miles
Not for navigation.
Use Chart 3547
©OCEAN CRUISE GUIDES

trail to lagoon

Broughton Lagoon

Sullivan Bay is a good place to reprovision, take on fuel and soak up the ambiance.

south. The innermost anchorage is protected by a small, unnamed islet. The other anchorage is a bight immediately to the north, where a smooth cliff face of rock and shrubs form a grotto-like backdrop. We have been stern-tied in this spot, in about 25 feet (8 m) of depth, when a stiff W breeze was blowing and current was pouring out of Broughton Lagoon, yet the anchorage stayed calm. This anchorage also enjoys the warmth of a western exposure and becomes awash in evening sunlight.

Broughton Lagoon can be explored on foot along a trail leading from the S anchorage. The lagoon can also be explored by dinghy or small powerboat, but you should be very careful at the entrance to ensure you have arrived at slack, reported to be about 2 hours after Alert Bay. Wait at the E end of the small bay N of the lagoon entrance to ensure arrival at slack because the current here is in the 8- to 10-knot range. According to locals, there is anchorage at the extreme southwest side of the lagoon.

Sullivan Bay, 19
North Broughton Island

Sullivan Bay is a classic example of an upcoast resort. Historically located at an important crossroads for the logging and fishing industries, today its position at the intersection of Wells Passage and Sutlej Channel makes it a good place to reprovision before setting out to new anchorages.

In 1945, the floating village at Claydon Bay was towed to Sullivan Bay, where the string of buildings included a store and post office servicing what was, until the mid-50s, the busiest floatplane base on the coast. Several of the original buildings remain as part of the Sullivan Bay Marine Resort, such as the "Town Hall" which contains a ping-pong table, board games and easy chairs.

Operated for the last three decades by Pat Finnerty and Lynn Whitehead, this full-service marina has a well-stocked grocery and liquor store, fuel dock and potable water. A potluck dinner and other social events are held regularly. Many boaters use Sullivan Bay as a base for the area's renowned sportfishing. Others simply enjoy the lovely setting while strolling the floats, chatting with fellow visitors or lounging in deck chairs.

Claydon Bay 20

This is a popular anchorage close to Sullivan Bay and especially useful if the marina is full for the night. Claydon Bay was an old Union Steamship stop and logging camp where several float camps, now long abandoned, once occupied the bay. In the early 1940s there were 19 families living here in floathouses, as well as dozens of single men living in bunkhouses. Remains of the logging roads and wharfs are still visible in the north arm of the anchorage. Enter the anchorage along the SW shore and, if proceeding into the north arm, keep the islets to your starboard side. See chart 3547.

The two arms of the bay provide decent shelter in most winds with very good holding in a mud bottom. The entire anchorage is susceptible to strong summer westerlies which gust over the surrounding low hills. SE winds also gust strongly into the main part of the bay. The N bay has the better sunsets and is a good spot for a quick swim off the boat – water temperatures in this bay are quite warm. Deer flies can be persistent and come in swarms – which seems to be the case throughout Mackenzie Sound.

The NE arm of Claydon Bay has the best sunsets.
Holding is good throughout the anchorage.

Turnbull Cove 21

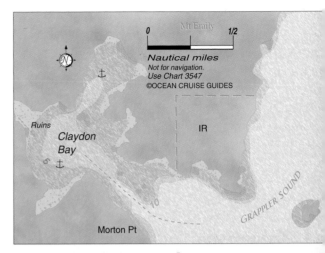

This roomy anchorage provides good shelter from all winds except strong southeasterlies. It was once busy with log booms and floathomes, and the last old-time logger to live here (from 1960 to 1985) was Owen Lane, who operated a logging camp at Huaskin Lake. The old steam donkey displayed on the Port McNeill waterfront was used by Lane to pull logs out of Huaskin Lake. In July 2005, a fairly large slide pushed some debris to the shoreline on the north side of the cove W of the two small points. Boaters should be careful if anchoring here as the slope could still be unstable and the bottom foul with debris. The west side of the cove provides the best shelter and holding is good in thick mud. The SD cautions "SE gales circle the cove at full force."

A Forest Service trail leads from the NE side of the cove (there is a sign at the trailhead) over a high hill to Huaskin Lake, where there is a swimming float and a cleared area with picnic tables. The hike is about three-quarters of a mile and takes about 30 minutes. Large and scenic, Huaskin Lake stretches in numerous directions but visitors reaching the lake from Turnbull Cove are looking north up the E arm of the lake, which extends about 4 miles north to within 2 miles of Seymour Inlet. Part of the lake also splits off to the west where it travels over 7 miles and almost touches Actaeon Sound off Drury Inlet.

West of Turnbull Cove, beside Watson Point, is an abandoned sawmill operated from 1930 to 1965 by Charles and Ivy Kilbourne. North of Watson Point is a large bay with Embley Lagoon on the E side, an inviting lagoon to explore at HW. East of Turnbull Cove is the entrance to the 5-mile long Nepah Lagoon. This lagoon is reported to be quite pretty. We haven't ventured inside, but the entrance at Roaringhole Rapids looks like it lives up to its name. With a shoal depth of 3 feet (1 m) and a huge lagoon behind it, this would be a dangerous pass at anything other than HW slack. Chart 3547, however, shows excellent detail of the entrance with a detailed note on slack times for the pass – 2 hours after HW at Alert Bay for HW slack. The chart doesn't note the current, but it would no doubt be well above 7 knots. The only useable anchorage within the lagoon is in Yuki Bay along the northeast shore.

The holding – and the fishing – are good in Turnbull Cove.

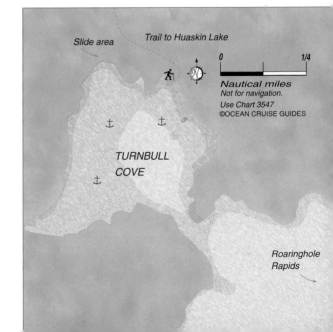

TURNBULL COVE AT A GLANCE
CHARTS: 3547
LAT LONG: 50°57.60'N 126°50.11'W
PROS: Remote, peaceful anchorage. Excellent hiking and fishing nearby.
CONS: Can become a wind bowl in S winds.
MUST DO: Hike to Huaskin Lake.

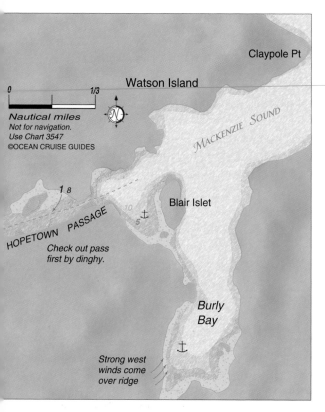

Claypole Pt

Watson Island

MACKENZIE SOUND

0   1/3

Nautical miles
Not for navigation.
Use Chart 3547
©OCEAN CRUISE GUIDES

1 8

Blair Islet

HOPETOWN PASSAGE

10
5

Check out pass
first by dinghy.

Burly
Bay

Strong west
winds come
over ridge

A boat waits for slack at Hopetown Passage, with
Claypole Point and Mt. Stephens in background.

Mackenzie Sound 22

Mackenzie Sound, a watery chasm carved into the mountains, is best entered via **Kenneth Passage**. Captain Vancouver observed that "this channel is excessively dangerous, owing to the number of rocky islets, sunken rocks, and, by the tides setting through it with great rapidity and irregularity." Currents in Kenneth Passage are strongest opposite the island marked '70' and Jessie Point, and are perhaps 3 to 4 knots at large tides. Chart 3547 clearly shows all dangers. Wide languid whirlpools extend from this area well into **Steamboat Bay**, which is a pretty anchorage for a lunch stop but receives a bit too much current to our liking for an overnight stay. Proceeding through the pass, the safer route is N of the island marked '79' where the water stays deep.

There are few hazards in the deep waters of Mackenzie Sound, its entrance marked by the sheer cliffs of Claypole Point, but there are few good anchorages as well. Three miles east of Claypole Point is the entrance, encumbered with rocks, to **Nimmo Bay**. A scenic anchorage lies near the E end of Little Nimmo Bay with reported good holding. A fishing lodge is located on the bay's north shore.

At the head of Mackenzie Sound is a small anchorage, useable in calm weather, along the N shore. A creek leads to Mackenzie Lake from this anchorage, but keep in mind that grizzly bears are often sighted in this area.

Turning back to the west, **Burly Bay** has a dramatic granite hill on its E side and affords a great view to Claypole Point and the mountains beyond. However, with the steep hills on either side and a low foreshore in the middle, strong W and S winds would enter the bay easily. Blair Islet Bay, SW of Blair Islet, is better protected and also has a pretty view to Hopetown Passage. Some current from Hopetown Passage comes into this anchorage.

Hopetown Passage is a good shortcut for vessels wanting to get quickly from Mackenzie Sound to Sullivan Bay. While tracing the mainland shore northbound in the ship's boats, Captain Vancouver and his men transited this passage, noting afterward that it was admissable only for boats. The Sailing Directions further qualifies this pass as suitable only for shallow-draft boats at HW. It is quite shoal at the E end with a large drying rock covering all but the north side of the pass. Numerous vessels have struck this rock over the years and this is a pass a skipper should reconnoiter first at LW in a dinghy before taking the mother ship through. We transited this pass at an Alert Bay HW of 13.6 feet (4 m) and had about 8 feet (3 m) of water at the shallowest point.

We made it through by favouring the Watson Island shore, and perhaps we were lucky. Currents can be swift here also, and are likely in the range of 4 knots. If westbound, be sure to arrive at the very tail end of a flood to be safe.

Overlooking Hopetown Passage is Hoy Bay, where the Kwawwaineuk band still has a small settlement on the E side of the bay. A shell midden graces the foreshore and a totem pole stands in front of a house overlooking the beach. On a point of land due west of the settlement there is a tiny graveyard. The W side of the bay is often used as a log dump and sorting area.

Drury Inlet   **23**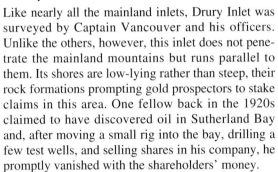

Like nearly all the mainland inlets, Drury Inlet was surveyed by Captain Vancouver and his officers. Unlike the others, however, this inlet does not penetrate the mainland mountains but runs parallel to them. Its shores are low-lying rather than steep, their rock formations prompting gold prospectors to stake claims in this area. One fellow back in the 1920s claimed to have discovered oil in Sutherland Bay and, after moving a small rig into the bay, drilling a few test wells, and selling shares in his company, he promptly vanished with the shareholders' money.

Vancouver and his men proceeded through **Stuart Narrows** and traced the mainland shore for several miles before "landing to dine about the time of high water." They "soon perceived a rapid ebb tide coming from the westward" and correctly surmised that this was yet another inlet they had entered. Tidal currents in Stuart Narrows, at the entrance to Drury Inlet, can reach 7 knots on a ebb

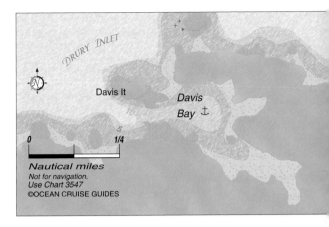

and 6 knots on a flood, but are generally weaker, attaining about 2 knots on a 6-foot (2 m) tide.

Captain Vancouver returned to the ships at anchor in Simoom Sound, leaving Second Lieutenant Puget and Master Whidbey in charge of the launch and cutter to continue the survey of this 11-mile-long inlet. When they reached its head, they followed Actress Passage into Actaeon Sound, past overfalls and sunken rocks, before reaching the tidal rapids at the entrance to Tsibass Lagoon. Whidbey ascended the falls here at LW to find a small lake branching in various directions through a "low, swampy, woodland country."

Extensive logging has taken place in this area since Vancouver's survey, but Drury Inlet remains for the most part a sparsely inhabited inlet offering numerous anchorages, including **Richmond Bay**

Davis Bay provides good shelter in a pretty setting.

and **Jennis Bay**, where old logging-camp sites remain on shore. The best anchorage, except in strong easterlies, is at the head of **Sutherland Bay** where the bottom is mud and trails lead inland toward Blunden Harbour. **Davis Bay** is a pretty anchorage offering good shelter and holding in the middle of the bay in about 24 feet (8 m). Entry is made S of Davis Islet, keeping close to the smaller islet off its SE side. Use Chart 3547.

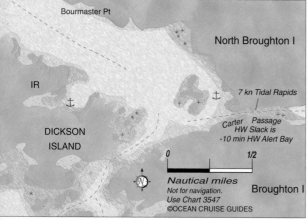

Tracey Harbour 24

This long and well-protected inlet is a favourite with boaters wanting a base for a few days of fishing in Wells Passage. It is a bit of a drive (2 miles) from Wells Passage to the anchorage at **Napier Bay** but the steep hillsides knock down most winds from the strait. At the NE side of the bay, within the entrance to a small cove, the holding is good but the view of the logging operation on the S side of the bay is the trade off. The bay south of Carter Point is prettier and offers good protection from most wind but the bottom is poor with possibly a combination of ooze and rock or a thin layer of mud on rock.

Dickson Island 25

An unattractive but very convenient anchorage lies on the NE side of Dickson Island, an uninhabited Indian Reserve. The shoreline surrounding this cove was extensively logged in the late 1980s and has grown back somewhat since to provide a better buffer from W winds. The topography of the island and nearby islands provide good protection from southeasterlies, but the anchorage is open to the NE which is a rare wind in summer. Most boaters tie a stern line to the south shore since there is limited swinging room. We often go well into the anchorage and tie a stern line to the small island inside the cove, anchoring in about 20 feet (6 m) in soft mud.

We've stayed at this anchorage many times as a stopover before heading north to Blunden Harbour or Miles Inlet, and have found the protection good. A short dinghy ride away in Wells Passage off Bourmaster Point there is excellent fishing. In the

Above left, a minke whale feeds near Dickson Island while birds dive for the crumbs. Below, Dickson Island anchorage isn't pretty but it works.

Above, Tracey Harbour is secure in most winds.
Right, the anchorage at Dickson Island. Bottom,
conning the entrance to Carter Passage.

first half of the last century, the cove was used by floating logging camps as well as a fish-buying camp run by a man named Tommy Badger who bought salmon from the trollers working Wells Pass.

If you want to make this area a base for a few days, there are many other good anchorages nearby, including Tracey Harbour and, one of our favourites, Carter Passage. Also, there is a good anchorage on the N side of the entrance to **Carter Passage**, just below the steep hillside and E of the collection of reefs. Although the anchorage looks open to the west, winds from this direction are forced up the hill, leaving behind nascent gusts. In a SE wind, this spot is very well protected. Some current from Carter Passage wanders into this anchorage but, otherwise, this is a very quiet spot.

Carter Passage Anchorage   26

Over the years, this anchorage has remained a quiet retreat for boaters wanting to enjoy simple peace and quiet. Its remoteness has been helped by the fact the anchorage can only be accessed for a few minutes each day owing to the impressive tidal rapids at its west entrance.

The anchorage is not accessible from the east, except in a dinghy during a high tide of at least 10 feet at Alert Bay. The deeper part of this pass is along the N side but be aware there are numerous large boulders in this pass and that slack water is very short – often 15 minutes or less.

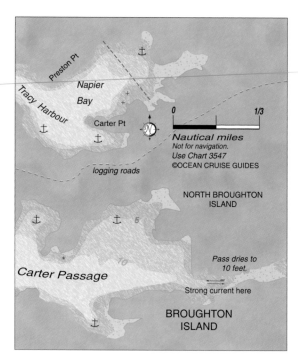

Above, good anchorage can be had in a bight on the north shore at the entrance to Carter Passage. Below, anchorage within the passage is sublime.

Transiting the western entrance of Carter Passage is not difficult at slack HW as the entrance is fairly straight and there are no major obstructions – the two rocks within the pass shown on the chart are well off to the S at the eastern end of the pass. Bull kelp thrives in large patches along the sides of the

channel, leaving the middle clear. Minimum depth, as indicated on Chart 3547, is indeed 10 feet (3 m) and, since this is a narrow pass, transiting on a HW slack is the safest approach. Current in the pass is reported in the Sailing Directions at 7 knots, and it is all of that. High water slack is very close to Alert Bay HW, perhaps minus 10 or 15 minutes. Low water slack, however, is about one hour after Alert Bay LW. As you transit the pass, be sure to favour the N shore to avoid the aforementioned rocks.

Once you are east of the pass, any leftover current quickly dissipates and you can look ahead to the enjoyable prospect of not one but three excellent anchorages. The two bays along the N side have lots of room and good depth with a flat sticky mud bottom. We prefer the larger second bay as the small peninsula along its west shore deflects W wind coming into the bay. Anchoring depth in this bay is about 40 feet (13 m) and, as noted, holding is superb. There may be another boat or two around but because of the space you don't notice. This is the type of anchorage where solitude can be drunk in great gulps and the only sound breaking the silence is the occasional dignified rattle of a kingfisher.

CARTER PASSGE AT A GLANCE
CHARTS: 3547
LAT LONG: 50˚50.17'N 126˚54.51'W
PROS: Serene, well protected and good holding. Remote and peaceful.
CONS: Entrance is through a set of rapids.
MUST DO: Lots to explore by dinghy or do nothing.

Polkinghorne Islands 27 🏊 🛶

Boaters leaving Carter Passage or Dickson Island for Queen Charlotte Strait can follow the ethereal passage E of Dickson Island. On a sunny afternoon, threading your way among the numerous small islets is dreamlike. The view is of cat-tail moss hanging from silver snags and little bays with verdant grass crowding the shoreline. This little passage also has current coming from Carter Passage and during large tides it will exceed 2 knots. This passage can be maze-like, so it's important to verify your correct position throughout the transit. Because of the rocks extending W of Drew Islet, we tend to come close to Percy Island before turning south.

Just beyond this beautiful collection of islands is another cluster at the Polkinghorne Islands. Named for a commander in the British navy, these islands merit a day of exploration by dinghy among the array of small islets and reefs. The bare rocks in the middle of the islets create striking scenes against the sky over Queen Charlotte Strait. Herons and seals abound throughout the islands. Although the water is cool, there are a couple of good spots to swim opposite the large lagoon in the middle of the biggest island. See Chart 3547.

We have anchored for lunch stops in the bay to the south, in depths of about 40 feet (13 m), and found the bottom to be rocky with only fair holding. The bay to the N may be better; we've seen larger vessels anchored and tied to shore there. Westerlies gust through the entire anchorage but are weaker than winds blowing out in the strait. The anchorage is quite exposed to SE winds.

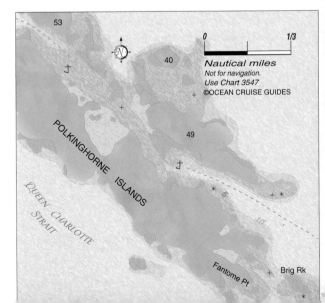

Polkinghorne Islands are an excellent day stop with numerous islets to explore. Staying overnight is possible only in very settled conditions.

53

40

Nautical miles
Not for navigation.
Use Chart 3547
©OCEAN CRUISE GUIDES

0   1/3

49

POLKINGHORNE ISLANDS

QUEEN CHARLOTTE STRAIT

6

10

Fantome Pt   Brig Rk

CHAPTER NINE

QUEEN CHARLOTTE STRAIT

Murray Labyrinth

etween currents, wind and waves, the natural elements are always at play in Queen Charlotte Strait. Remnant ocean swells roll in from Queen Charlotte Sound and sweep onto exposed shorelines or shudder into spray against rocky islets. This heavy swell is frequent in the northwest part of Queen Charlotte Strait, where it's open to the Pacific Ocean, and crossing the strait (about 14 miles wide) will give you a taste of open ocean cruising. Combined swell and wave heights in the strait are often over 12 feet (4 m) when a westerly is blowing against an ebbing tide

Tides and Currents

Tide differences in Queen Charlotte Strait are referenced on Alert Bay, with the flood stream setting ESE and the ebb WNW. Currents in adjacent waters of the strait can be surprisingly strong, with streams often 2 knots or more in the vicinity of island groups. In early summer, melting snow along the mainland shore tends to accentuate the ebb current on the northeast side of the strait while afternoon northwest winds can increase the strength of flood current along the Vancouver Island side of the 50-mile long strait.

The large passes, Nakwakto Rapids and Nahwitti Bar, are covered later in this chapter. Other channels and passes requiring vigilance include Bolivar Passage, which can experience up to 4 knots of current, especially at the south end near Alex Rock and Davey Rock. Browning and Christie Passages are also in the 3- to 4-knot range of current. The S end of Shelter Passage during a southeasterly will be turbulent, especially during a south-flowing flood.

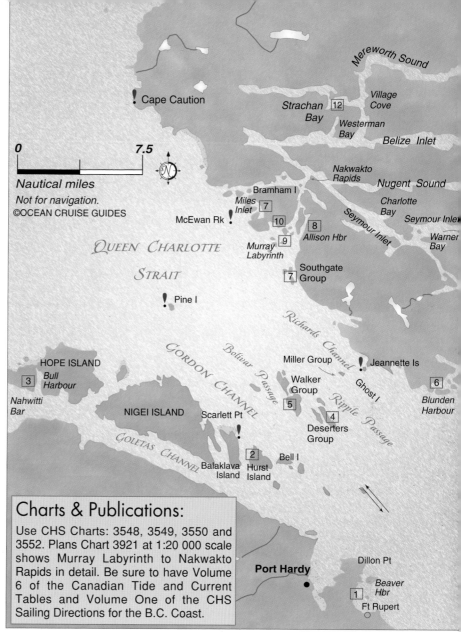

Mereworth Sound

Cape Caution

Strachan Bay · 12 · Village Cove

Westerman Bay

Belize Inlet

0   7.5

Nautical miles
Not for navigation.
©OCEAN CRUISE GUIDES

Nakwakto Rapids   Nugent Sound

Bramham I
Miles Inlet · 7 ·

McEwan Rk ·

Charlotte Bay

Seymour Inlet   Seymour Inlet

· 10 ·

· 8 ·
Allison Hbr

· 9 ·

Murray Labyrinth

QUEEN CHARLOTTE STRAIT

Warner Bay

Southgate · 7 · Group

Pine I

Richards Channel

Miller Group

Jeannette Is

Bolivar Passage

HOPE ISLAND

· 3 · Bull Harbour

Nahwitti Bar

NIGEI ISLAND

GORDON CHANNEL

Scarlett Pt

Walker Group

Ghost I

Ripple Passage

· 5 ·

Deserters Group

· 6 ·

Blunden Harbour

· 4 ·

GOLETAS CHANNEL

Balaklava Island

· 2 ·
Hurst Island

Bell I

Port Hardy

Dillon Pt

Beaver · 1 · Hbr

Ft Rupert

Charts & Publications:
Use CHS Charts: 3548, 3549, 3550 and
3552. Plans Chart 3921 at 1:20 000 scale
shows Murray Labyrinth to Nakwakto
Rapids in detail. Be sure to have Volume
6 of the Canadian Tide and Current
Tables and Volume One of the CHS
Sailing Directions for the B.C. Coast.

Ripple Passage is in the 2-knot range but current is felt for some distance on either side of the Walker and Deserters Groups of islands.

Pine Island

Pine Island stands like a lonely sentinel at the strait's western entrance, where it bears the full brunt of Queen Charlotte Sound's winter storms. Until 1907, when a lighthouse was built here, Pine Island's only visitors were the seabirds who nest here, including the rhinoceros auklet. This nocturnal seabird tends to make awkward landings when flying back from sea after dark, sometimes running into a tree and landing with thud on the ground – which is where this species burrows to make a nest.

The early lighthouse keepers stationed on Pine Island had to endure long winters of isolation, listen-ing to the incessant pounding of surf on the island's rocky foreshore. Sometimes they were marooned for days on end when the seas were too rough for a boat to land safely. Then, in the winter of 1967, on a black February night, hurricane-force winds drove a 50-foot wave onto Pine Island.

This rogue wave demolished outbuildings and washed away fuel tanks, surging right up to the front steps of the lightkeepers' house. Mr. and Mrs. Brown, their two daughters and the assistant light-keeper all scrambled to higher ground where they huddled around a campfire for the rest of the night. Afterwards, demoralized by the wreckage to which their years of hard work had been reduced in a mat-ter of seconds, the Browns left for another posting and the Pine Island light station was rebuilt to stronger standards on higher ground.

Above, Pine Island lighthouse. Below, sea fog is a frequent challenge in Queen Charlotte Strait.

Wind and Fog

On early summer mornings, Queen Charlotte Strait can be surprisingly calm. By late morning, a sea breeze typically develops and, combined with the prevailing summer northwesterly, often produces a heavy swell at the strait's W entrance. These winds regularly increase to 20 or 30 knots before dying out by evening, to be replaced by a weaker land breeze. Northwesterlies are stronger on the W side of the strait (the area around Port Hardy always seems, in our experience, to be blowing 25 to 30 knots).

Pilotage can be a challenge in the shoal-infested waters of Queen Charlotte Strait, especially in late summer when sea fog is a frequent hazard. August is the worst month for fog in Queen Charlotte Strait, and Captain Vancouver noted in his journals that "since the commencement of the month of August (1792), the foggy weather had totally precluded our making any celestial observations." Shoals and drying rocks are especially numerous on the north side of Queen Charlotte Strait, and when Captain Vancouver's two ships were sailing northbound in these waters, the mainland was unshrouded but the islands ahead were obscured by a thick fog. They were transiting Richards Channel, between the Millar Group and the mainland, when *Discovery* "suddenly grounded on a bed of sunken rocks."

A signal was immediately sent to the *Chatham*, under the command of Lieut. Broughton, and her crew promptly dropped anchor and launched their boats to assist the *Discovery*. Her port bow was hard on the rocks while her stern remained afloat. The crew carried out a stream anchor to heave the ship off, but the tide was falling rapidly, causing the ship to swing forward. Drinking water was drained overboard and wood fuel tossed in an attempt to lighten the ship's ballast. Meanwhile, the local natives paddled out in canoes to take a closer look at the stricken vessel. The ship was heeled "very considerably" on its starboard side and, as the tide ebbed, the crew removed upper spars to shore the ship. At low water, the starboard main chains came within 3 inches of the water's surface but, fortunately, the seas were calm and the ship refloated at two o'clock in the morning. Today, a light on the southern Jeannette Island marks the channel's north side, which should be favoured to avoid the drying reefs that lie opposite, off Ghost Island. Tidal currents can reach 3 knots in Richards Channel and heavy overfalls develop if there's a strong wind against tide.

Vancouver's initial survey of these waters was continued in the 1800s by the Royal Navy. After gold was discovered on the Yukon's Klondike River in 1896, steamship traffic along the Inside Passage increased dramatically as prospectors rushed north. Lighthouses were built at strategic points along the main route, including Scarlett Point (1905) and Pulteney Point (1907). The steamships of a century ago have given way to cruise liners that service the Vancouver-Alaska run, following the main route of Gordon Channel.

Port Hardy

A major service centre for pleasure boaters, Port Hardy is also the terminus for BC Ferries' *Queen of the North*, which offers day cruises to Prince Rupert, and *Queen of Chilliwack*, which provides service to several North Coast communities.

The town's public **Seagate Wharf** has a T-shaped float attached on the north side during summer months and accommodates about a half a dozen vessels. This wharf extends from the foot of Granville Street in the heart of town and is a good place to tie up for a few hours to reprovision. If the public dock is full, there are four mooring buoys nearby for recreational craft. Although west winds seem to die just outside of the wharf area, it is open to swell from Hardy Bay.

Above, Port Hardy's waterfront park and public wharf. Below, aerial view, looking north.

A better place to tie up overnight is at the **Quarterdeck Marina**, located due south of the town centre near the head of Hardy Bay (see map). Services at the Quarterdeck Marina include power, water, showers, a laundromat and restaurant. The marina also has a haulout and well-stocked marine store. An airport is located 5 miles (8 km) away, and taxis are available. The public commercial docks to the north can also accommodate visiting boats, but you may have to raft with another vessel.

The town is named in honour of Sir Thomas Hardy who was right-hand man to Lord Horatio Nelson, Britain's greatest naval hero. No naval battles have been staged in the waters off Port Hardy but Britain's Hudson's Bay Company did establish Fort Rupert at nearby Beaver Harbour in 1849 after coal was discovered there.

Permanent settlement of Port Hardy didn't begin until the turn of the last century when it grew slowly along with the local industries of fishing, logging and mining. Today, the population of Port Hardy is about 5,000. Visitors to Port Hardy can enjoy a stroll past Fisherman's Wharf and along Market Street with its selection of shops. The local museum features an exhibit on the excavation site at nearby Bear Cove, which was first occupied more than 8,000 years ago and is the location of the BC Ferries terminal for Port Hardy. The museum also has on video Edward Curtis's epic film *Land of the War Canoe*, which premiered in New York in 1914.

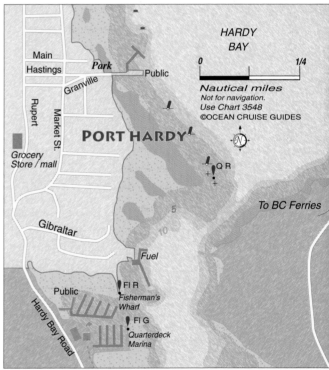

THE ANCHORAGES

Beaver Harbour 1

This historic harbour, just around the corner from Port Hardy, provides a good haven for boaters looking to escape a tough westerly. The harbour is ringed with small islands and offers several anchorages that are sheltered from most winds. Strong W winds diminish in the lee of Round Island and easy entry can be made south of Deer Island.

Good anchorages include the SW lee of Cattle Islands, south of the fish farm. Anchor here in 15 to 30 feet (5 to 10 m) in mud. There is a small but nice bight on the S shore of Peel Island which provides very good holding and protection from W winds but is open to south winds. A few hundred yards to the

west is Patrician Cove, good also in west winds but open to the south. Basket Eaters' Cove, half a mile to the north, provides good shelter in all winds but from the northeast.

The Spanish explorers Valdes and Galiano anchored their ships *Sutil* and *Mexicana* off Thomas Point in August 1792. They spent a windy, rainy night at this location, taking water over the bow as their schooners pitched in high seas. Next morning the wind eased and, finding their cables damaged, they weighed anchor and left. Had they been able to sail their vessels into the harbour, they would have enjoyed a quieter night at anchor.

Fort Rupert, built by the Hudson's Bay Company in 1849, once stood on Beaver Harbour's south shore, its construction overseen by Captain William McNeill, commander of the HBC steamship *Beaver*. The fort was built to protect the company's coal mining interests in the area after coal was discovered along the beach at the mouth of Suquash Creek, near the western entrance to Broughton Strait. About 10,000 tons of coal were shipped out of Beaver Harbour. The coal was transported in canoes to Beaver Harbour by the local natives, who had abandoned their main villages along the Cluxewe River to establish a new village beside Fort Rupert.

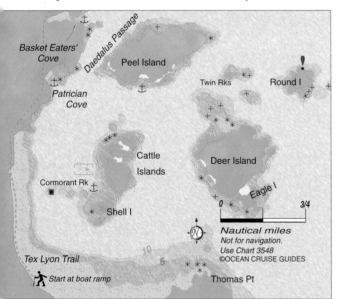

BEAVER HARBOUR AT A GLANCE:
CHARTS: 3548
LAT LONG: 50°42.76'N 127°24.66'W
PROS: Shelter can be found from most winds. Good haven from westerlies. Usually quiet with good beaches and hikes nearby.
CONS: Aquaculture SW of Cattle Islands.
MUST DO: Walk a leg of the Tex Lyon Trail.

Aerial view of Beaver Harbour showing lee provided by Peel Island during NW winds.

When the HBC abandoned Fort Rupert in 1882, its factor, Scottish-born Robert Hunt, stayed to run the company store with his wife Mary Ebbetts, a Tlingit noblewoman from Alaska. They had 11 children and it's said that most of the area's longtime residents are related to the Hunts. The artist Henry Hunt was born at Fort Rupert in 1923, and worked as a logger and fisherman before apprenticing with his father-in-law Mungo Martin at the Royal British Columbia Museum in Victoria. Hunt eventually succeeded his father-in-law as chief carver. His sons Tony and Richard, born in Alert Bay, also became leading artists. Henry Hunt died in Victoria in 1985.

Little remains of the old fort in Beaver Harbour. More enduring are the petroglyphs carved on the sandstone foreshore. Across the water is Deer Island, where Edward Curtis filmed *Land of the War Canoe* (originally called *In the Land of the Head Hunters*). A self-taught photographer from Seattle, Curtis devoted his life to photographing and filming the aboriginal people of North America.

The 4.5-mile (7-km) **Tex Lyon Trail** traces the shoreline from the boat launch at the SW corner of Beaver Harbour to Dillon Point. The trail starts out easily with a 20-minute hike from the boat launch to the rock bluff opposite Cattle Island, then becomes a more challenging 4-hour hike from the bluff to Dillon Point. Allow 8 hours for the entire round-trip hike, and wear proper attire and footwear.

God's Pocket Marine Park 2

Situated at the south entrance to Goletas Channel, this marine park encompasses Hurst Island, Bell Island and numerous smaller islands and islets. God's Pocket is a local name for the small cove on Hurst Island's W side. This spot provides good shelter and has long been a favoured anchorage for recreational boaters heading north. A small resort here provides overnight moorage, showers, and laundry facilities. Harlequin Bay, on the east side of Hurst Island, is protected from S and W winds.

The small channel between **Bell Island** and Heard Island provides some shelter as an anchorage, with a view of cruise ships in Gordon Channel, but a fish farm takes up most of the west side. The cove formed by two islets off Bell's south shore is protected from swell and S wind but west winds whistle through the cove with surprising strength.

Goletas Channel extends for 23 miles between Vancouver Island and a chain of islands through which several navigable channels lead to Gordon Channel. Northwest and SE winds funnel up and down Goletas Channel, causing local winds along the island points to accelerate with force.

Below, God's Pocket is a haven from all winds.

Bottom, aerial view of God's Pocket, looking SE.

Bull Harbour 3

Lying off the NE tip of Vancouver Island, Hope Island is a jumping-off point for boaters heading around the top of Vancouver Island to cruise its west coast. Bull Harbour, entered off Goletas Channel, provides protected anchorage at the N end of Hope Island. The harbour was called Ga'ya by the Nahwitty people who had a village-fortress on the rocks at Cape Sutil. In more recent times, a Canadian Coast Guard station was located in Bull Harbour but it was closed in the early 1990s.

While anchored in Bull Harbour, take the opportunity to hike the road leading from the old government dock to the abandoned Coast Guard Station at Roller Bay. At Roller Bay you can stand on the exposed edge of Hope Island and watch the waves crash onto the shore. The beach consists of pebbles

the size of cannonballs. Logs, bleached white by sun and saltwater, have been tossed onto shore where they lie in disarray. The vista is an unobstructed view of Queen Charlotte Sound, where swells roll relentlessly across Cook Bank and release their energy onto shore. It's an exhilarating experience to view such a sight.

Nahwitti Bar

Located at the W end of Hope Island and extending across the entrance of Goletas Channel, this bar is known for its steep waves when an ebbing current is against strong west winds or big ocean swells. When these incessant swells, coming from depths of 30 fathoms, roll into the channel, where the depths off Mexicana Point are 6 to 7 fathoms, the change in depth can result in breaking waves. The bar can be especially dangerous in late afternoon during an ebb if a westerly and large swells are in play.

However, Nahwitti Bar can be traversed safely with a bit of planning. Prudent boaters should try to cross the bar in the early morning, before wind and swell have had a chance to build. This tactic may be preferable to waiting for slack in late morning or afternoon, as the leftover waves may continue breaking for some time. The route to the south, over the Tatnall Reefs close to Vancouver Island, is sometimes used by vessels to avoid the Nahwitti Bar; however, skippers should be very cautious using this passage. This entire stretch of coast becomes a lee shore when a late-morning westerly builds, as is common in summer.

Roller Bay earns it name with a thunderous surf that's constantly moving debris on the beach.

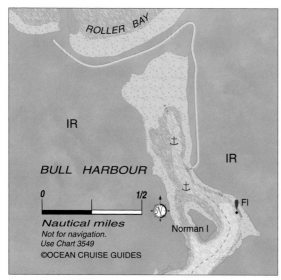

Deserters Group 4

The Deserters Group contains a sheltered, storm-proof anchorage – often used by local boaters – situated near the south end of Wishart Island with Deserters Island as its east shore. Easiest entry is from the south, favouring the Deserters Island shoreline to avoid a set of drying rock ledges off Wishart Island that are located at the point where the entrance channel opens up to the anchorage. A person at the bow would be a good idea if this is your first visit to the anchorage. Once inside, we usually anchor closer to the Deserters Island shoreline where minimum depth is shown on charts to be about 10 feet (3 m). With openings at either end of the cove, the current (up to about 2 knots) flowing through the anchorage will keep your boat lying parallel to the east shore. The other spot to anchor in this tight cove, which is actually a passage between the two islands, lies closer to Wishart Island and the south entrance, being careful to avoid the shoal water. Holding is very good in firm mud. Although muted gusts may make their way into this cove, the shelter from all wind is otherwise excellent.

There is much to explore by dinghy in this small archipelago, including the fascinating and narrow, twisting passage that leads north from the anchorage, along which a couple of derelict fishboats sit beached on a small midden. At HW, vessels drawing

Above and below, Deserters Group anchorage provides good shelter with good holding.

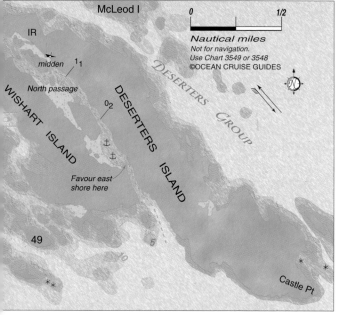

McLeod I

IR

midden 1 1

North passage

WISHART ISLAND

DESERTERS GROUP

DESERTERS ISLAND

Favour east
shore here

49

5

10

Castle Pt

0　　　　　　　　1/2

Nautical miles
Not for navigation.
Use Chart 3549 or 3548
©OCEAN CRUISE GUIDES

N

> **DESERTERS AND WALKER GROUPS**
> **AT A GLANCE**
> **CHARTS:** 3549
> **LAT LONG:** Dsrtr Grp: 50°52.65'N 127°28.63'W
> **PROS:** Two beautiful archipelagos side by side with dozens of islets. Fair to good shelter from most winds, fair to good holding ground. Lots to explore, fishing nearby. A cruiser's paradise.
> **CONS:** Reefs and currents throughout. Lots of kelp. Challenging piloting to access some areas.
> **MUST DO:** Fish off Castle Point, hop in the dinghy for a tour through Deserters Pass.

6 feet or less can use the north channel to access or leave this anchorage. This must be carefully done and the pass should be toured at LW in a dinghy if deciding to take your boat through. (See map.) It's a fascinating little pass with lots to see. The salmon fishing is good off Castle Point.

'Shelter Anchorage', Walker Group 5

Situated about 25 miles N of Pulteney Point, this small but intriguing archipelago contains a use-able anchorage in the channel between Kent and Staples Islands, known locally as Shelter Anchorage. Chart 3549 provides good detail of the few hazards in the immediate vicinity and the anchorage can be gained with either an E or W approach. The best spot offering protected shelter is on the north side of the channel, just south of

Above left, ready to go fishing near Castle Point. Below, the north passage out of the Deserters Group anchorage is a pretty channel.

the small islet (where a commercial buoy is moored). We usually tie our stern off to the islet with our bow set in a SW direction, then pull ourselves as close to the islet as possible to get out of the NW winds which gust through the anchorage. South winds are muted by Staples Island. The holding, in about 15 to 25 feet (5 to 8 m), is just fair in soft mud and stone with kelp patches throughout. We've seen 40-foot powerboats (using Bruce and CQR anchors) repeatedly re-anchor during persistent 25-knot gusts, each time hauling up large clumps of kelp, but eventually getting their anchors to hold. If there's no room at the islet to stern-tie, the west shore of Kent Island offers shelter from W winds. Bull kelp thrives throughout the anchorage's entrances, which have currents up to 2 knots.

Top, aerial view of Kent Island lagoon. Right, beautiful beach at east end of lagoon. Below, aerial view of Shelter Anchorage, looking north.

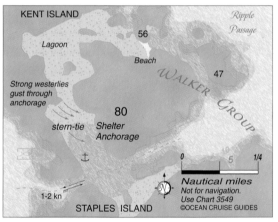

One July morning we arrived at this anchorage from Bolivar Passage in dripping fog with a building SE wind. To our surprise, after we entered from the mist outside, the anchorage was sunny, empty and quite sheltered. With dozens of small islands in the area and two lagoons, there is plenty to explore by dinghy. A beautiful fine sand beach lies between the islands marked '80' and '56' on Chart 3549. This beach, which reveals itself at mid-LW, is entirely surrounded by small islets and is sheltered from most wind and swell. The bay in front (east) of the beach is too shallow for most boats to anchor. The lagoon between Shelter Anchorage and the beach is beautiful for exploring and can be safely navigated

Above, exploring the emerald waters of Kent Island lagoon. Below, Blunden Harbour, looking north.

at a half-tide or better. Less than this, it dries in parts, making passage by dinghy difficult.

You can explore the east sides of Kent and Staples Islands and discover a number of small islets and sand beaches. Be careful in a dinghy if a wind is blowing though, as there can be quite a chop along the outside of the islands.

Blunden Harbour 6

This historic harbour is large and sheltered, with an impressive selection of small islets and passes you can explore by dinghy. The key to finding the harbour's entrance, which lies between Shelf Head and Edgell Point, is to identify Siwiti Rock (named for the hereditary chief of the Nakwakto tribe), which has less than 6 feet (2 m) of water over it and is usually marked by kelp and a breaking swell. Barren Rock, further E, also stands out and helps in navigation. Burgess Island melds too completely into Robinson Island to be of much help when approaching from the south.

Once you are between Edgell and Robinson Islands, sheltered anchorage (especially from W winds) can be obtained in a bight immediately E of Bartlett Point (with a line ashore) or by proceeding to the inner harbour where secure anchorage can be found almost anywhere in depths between 12 feet (3.7 m) and 20 feet (6 m) over a thick mud bottom. Entrance to the inner anchorage is restricted by a drying reef and rock that lie S of the Augustine Islands and by another drying reef off Bartlett Point, but with Chart 3548 pilotage is straightforward.

The inner anchorage is expansive, with several areas to anchor. Westerly winds often penetrate the harbour and a good spot out of the breeze is just inside the narrow opening between Robinson Island and the mainland shore, with a stern line to the W shore. The anchorages just east of Grave Islet and Byrnes Island are also prized for providing protection during westerlies. Wherever you anchor, the inner part of Blunden Harbour is one of the more secure anchorages in Queen Charlotte Strait with very good holding in thick mud and lots of room to let out scope.

Many boaters like to spend days anchored here because there is so much to see and explore. This is an anchorage where you can almost get lost in the maze of islets lying east of Augustine Islands in the passage leading to beautiful Bradley Lagoon. The current can be quite strong (at least 4 to 5 knots during big tides) at the shallow neck entering the lagoon, but the passage is quite safe if transited within an hour of HW slack. The lagoon itself is huge and uncharted, which makes for an exciting day of exploration by dinghy.

The other main attraction at Blunden Harbour is the shell midden marking the former site of a Kwakiutl village that once stood on the N shore, behind the Augustine Islands. This village was depicted in a famous 1930

A beautiful white midden beach lies along the north shore of Blunden Harbour.

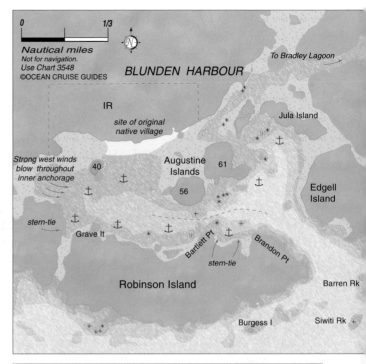

BLUNDEN HARBOUR AT A GLANCE:

CHARTS: 3548 (has excellent 1:15 000 scale inset)
LAT LONG: 50°54.31'N 127°17.34'W
PROS: An important and historic location for First Nations people. Fair to good protection from most wind. Excellent holding throughout most of harbour. Lots of channels and islets to investigate by dinghy.
MUST DO: Walk beautiful midden at north end of anchorage. Explore Bradley Lagoon.

Top, the tall ship Pacific Grace anchors east of Augustine Islands. Middle, the passage into Bradley Lagoon. Bottom, currents in the passage can be strong (4 to 5 knots) on large tides.

painting by Emily Carr entitled *Blunden Harbour*. It depicts a boardwalk backed by plank houses and graced with welcoming figures overlooking a tide-covered beach. The several hundred inhabitants of the village, seeking better access to halibut and deep-sea fishing, had moved to Blunden Harbour in the mid-19th century from various villages around Smith and Seymour Inlets.

In 1918, a sawmill and steamship landing called Port Progress were established near the harbour entrance. Abandoned in the early 1930s, the settlement's store and post office were derelict by the time Muriel Wylie Blanchet, author of *The Curve of Time*, pulled into Blunden Harbour one summer in the 1940s and tied to a half-sunken float near the entrance.

The native village, on the north side of the habour, also appeared unoccupied with its main buildings under lock and key. In front of the village there stood a "beautifully spiralled totem pole, on top of which sat a comfortable-looking carved eagle with outstretched wings" overlooking the white shell beach. Steps led to the village platform where two communal houses, supported by carved interior houseposts, were padlocked. Blanchet and her children entered one of the long houses "by the two loose boards, round at the side, that are always left for departing spirits."

Today, few traces remain of the original village, its residents eventually relocating in the 1960s to the Tsulquate reserve at Port Hardy. Some fallen posts protrude from the grassy bank above the shell midden, but the scene depicted by Emily Carr is no more. Time and nature have reclaimed her canvas.

Southgate Group 7

This group of islands has long been used by south-bound tugs waiting for settled weather after departing Seymour Inlet with a log boom. Small vessels will find sheltered anchorage between Knight Island and the mainland, approaching between Southgate Island and Knight Island, or along the far more challenging channel from the south, between Tinson Islands and Arm Islands. Depending on the direction of the wind, shelter can be found either E of Knight island in 24 feet (7.6 m) or east of Southgate Island in about 40 feet (12.8 m). We have temporarily anchored east of Knight Island in mud and sand, and found the holding very good.

Allison Harbour 8

Numerous bights along the east shore of Allison Harbour provide good anchorage, as does the head, with a mud bottom. A former port of call for the

Union Steamships, this harbour – named after Allison Logging Co. – was once a supply centre for nearby logging camps and the site of a sawmill.

In foggy conditions, common in summer months in this area, the entrance to Allison Harbour is much easier to negotiate than the one into nearby Murray Labyrinth. From Harris Island (easy to identify with its tall white mast) stay to a course keeping the Southgate Group island marked '56' on Chart 3921 (and 3550) close to starboard and aim for Eno Island and City Point. From this point, passage into the harbour is clear of hazards.

In thick fog we keep the harbour's E shoreline within sight. About half a mile in there is a small cove S of an islet where good anchorage can be obtained in 30 feet (10 m) of water. This anchorage used to be a landing site for logs towed out of Seymour Inlet, and cables once used for binding booms can still be seen rusting on shore. West winds die out near the entrance to the harbour, making this anchorage secure in all winds.

A wooded islet is connected to the anchorage's north shore by a tombolo. In the early 1990s, a one-room cabin owned by Port Hardy residents stood tucked in the islet's trees, with a salal-lined path leading from it down to the water's edge. It was a charming feature amid the surrounding wilderness.

At the head of Allison Harbour there is a much larger area to anchor which is also quite secure and quiet in almost all wind conditions. Anchor in 24 feet (8 m) on a flat mud bottom. The lagoon farther north of this spot makes for an inviting day of dinghy exploring.

Murray Labyrinth 9

Located 12 miles south of Cape Caution, Murray Labyrinth is a pristine anchorage and a rewarding destination for mariners who learn to navigate intricate shorelines. This particular cove is encircled by islets, rocks and reefs, but safe entry is possible from two directions. The preferred entrance is from the SW, shown clearly on Chart 3921 with detail of the dog-leg entrance channel that cuts between the islets. The other more daunting entrance from the north has ample depth in a narrow channel but is best reconnoitered by dinghy at LW first.

The entrance from the south follows a 12 foot (4 m) trench clear of kelp in a NE direction to two islands where the first 45 degree turn to port is made. The S island marked '34' has a reef close to its N side which has lots of kelp over it and juts out slightly into the channel. Once past this reef, make another 45 degree turn to port and follow the clear water until past an islet on the starboard side and,

Sway anchored in small cove on east side of Allison Harbour. Most of the harbour is well sheltered.

allowing for the reef on its north side, make a slow 90 degree turn into the cove. Once inside, the best spot to anchor is on the SE side, away from a rock that lies in the middle of the anchorage. The entire cove is quite sheltered, with only the odd weak gust disturbing the serenity of the islands. We have been anchored here when Egg Island was reporting a SE gale and all that ever moved within Murray Labyrinth were the tree tops. Holding is very good in sticky mud and sand. There is little current running through the anchorage or the entrance channels.

This has been a favourite anchorage of ours for many years and we linger here for as long as possible. The area immediately south of Cape Caution is often very quiet as most boaters are focused on getting around the cape and often overlook these beautiful islands at the entrance to Seymour Inlet.

It is also a utopia for those who enjoy puttering about in the dinghy, with miles of shoreline, numerous little passages and dozens of islets to explore. Beyond Murray Labyrinth to the west, lie the

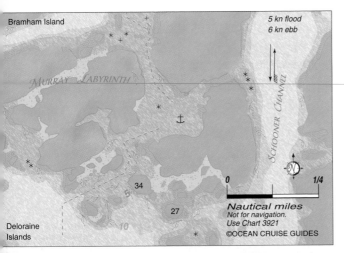

Bramham Island

5 kn flood
6 kn ebb

MURRAY LABYRINTH

SCHOONER CHANNEL

34

27

Deloraine
Islands

10

0   1/4

Nautical miles
Not for navigation.
Use Chart 3921
©OCEAN CRUISE GUIDES

> ### MURRAY LABYRINTH AT A GLANCE:
> **CHARTS:** 3921, 3550
> **LAT LONG:** 51°2.80'N 127°31.93'W
> **PROS:** Pristine. Peaceful. Far from the madding crowd feel. A week here goes by all too fast.
> **MUST DO:** Nothing stenuous. Explore the islets.

Deloraine Islands with their tiny coves and rocky islets upon which grow an assortment of ferns and mosses and where bonaparte gulls carve out pieces of blue sky. In the other direction you can explore Allison Harbour and Schooner Channel right to the entrance of the feared Nakwakto Rapids. Local wildlife we have noted in our log in this area include killer whales (actually seen a little further north around the corner from Skull Cove), seals, kingfishers, red-throated loons and various sea ducks.

Skull Cove, Bramham I 10

The only part of this anchorage which seems to be out of the wind is the SW corner near the spot marked 4.3 m on Chart 3921. Locals and fish-boats can often be seen on this side of the anchorage, which also has a great view out to the strait. The north part of Skull Cove, just northwest of the two islets in the middle of the cove, really seems to get the wind – especially when it's out of the south. Although we have found the holding

Left, aerial view of Murray Labyrinth and Skull Cove, looking south. Below, Murray Labyrinth.

to be fairly good, gusts throughout this part of the anchorage may cause a sleepless night. In settled weather, though, this is an intriguing cove in which to spend a few days exploring. The inner bay, east of the three islets, is quite pretty but has only enough depth for small shoal-draft vessels.

Miles Inlet, Bramham I 11

Located 10 miles south of Cape Caution on the north side of Queen Charlotte Strait, T-shaped Miles Inlet offers superb protection from angry winds and seas. The inlet has a straightforward approach, making it an ideal haven if sea fog has started rolling in from Queen Charlotte Sound.

Pale-colored McEwan Rock lies about one mile west of the entrance to Miles Inlet and is marked with a light. The entrance channel, between Bramham Point and McEwan Point, is long, straight and free of hazards, narrowing to 150 feet before reaching the head where the inlet branches into two arms. You can anchor at this junction with a clear view down the entrance channel to Queen Charlotte Strait. Neither westerlies nor southeasterlies seem to make much impact on the anchorage. We have also anchored in the NW arm, in about 25 feet (8 m) of water, its far end bounded by a lagoon with swift currents at its bottleneck entrance. The lagoon beyond with numerous islets and birdlife makes for an interesting day of exploring by dinghy.

Our favourite spot to drop the hook is in the south arm opposite the entrance to another lagoon. There will be about 10 feet (3 m) at LW in this part of the anchorage with good holding in soft mud. This is a nice area to row about in the

Above, Sway anchored in the serene south arm of Miles Inlet. Below, exploring two lagoons at south end.

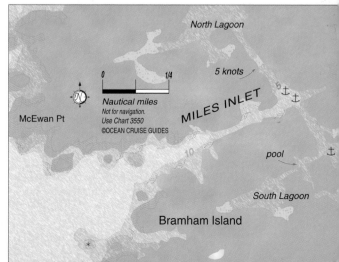

North Lagoon

5 knots

MILES INLET

0   1/4

Nautical miles
Not for navigation.
Use Chart 3550
©OCEAN CRUISE GUIDES

McEwan Pt

10

pool

South Lagoon

Bramham Island

McEwan Rock, near entrance of Miles Inlet.

dinghy or for swimming – there is an area, almost like a pool, in front of a small reversing falls leading to the lagoon. Yet another lagoon, leading south from the pool area, is accessible by foot at mid-tide.

Nakwakto Rapids

Seymour and Belize Inlets form an almost-land-locked, 85-mile-long basin of water joined to Queen Charlotte Strait by one confined opening called Nakwakto Rapids – the world's fastest tidal rapids. Less than a sixth of a mile wide, this dramatic bottle-neck creates currents that are extremely turbulent and unpredictable when squeezed through its small, twisting and shallow opening. The flow through the pass, which attains 16 knots on an ebb, is complicated by a number of other factors – water forced to turn more than 130 degrees, obstacles such as Turret Rock, and extremely steep shelving at both the west and east entrances. Use Chart 3921 for the rapids.

An ebb current from the eastern inlets is travelling along a 250 foot trench when it hits a shoaling wall at the pass with depths of only 50 feet off Johnson and Harvell Points. A similar wall exists just off Kitching Point and Butress Island where shoal water creates a venturi effect in the flow just 100 yards or so from an abyss 280 feet deep.

Tremendous turbulence is generated by these dramatic changes along the bottom, resulting in large whirlpools and upwellings.

The greatest turbulence, however, is caused by Turret Rock. During a strong ebb, this treed islet appears in aerial photos like a large tug plowing up a bow wave at full steam. The reef to the southwest of Turret Rock must be avoided in all conditions. This reef is an important factor in making ebb currents faster than floods; the other ingredient is fresh water runoff from the 85 miles of inlets. The turmoil generated by this reef includes an overfall which first rises 3 feet, then drops 5 feet.

In *The Curve of Time*, Muriel Wylie Blanchet relates how – on her way to the pass – she and her children met a fishing inspector in Allison Harbour who had just survived a traumatic experience in the Nakwakto Rapids. Entering the pass 20 minutes after slack water, his 40-foot boat was seized by the current and rammed against a shelving cliff.

Over the years tugboat operators developed their own equations for determining slack at the rapids but, fortunately for us, this complex pass was surveyed by Mike Woodward of the Canadian Hydropgraphic Service in 1983-84 and his findings were first incorporated into daily predictions of the Tide and Current Tables in 1987.

However, with only a 6-minute window at Nakwakto, it's prudent to arrive a half hour early and watch, from a safe distance, for signs of slack. Meteorological conditions will sometimes alter tides slightly, and slack water may not always be exactly at the time estimated in the tables. Slack water here doesn't coincide with HW and LW, but occurs mid-way in the cycle when the water level inside the

Seymour basin briefly equals that in the Strait. Maximum currents develop near HW and LW when water level differences are greatest. Temporary anchorages at which to wait for slack include Treadwell Bay, just to the west of Nakwakto Rapids, and the entrance to Cougar Inlet at the north end of Schooner Channel.

Butress Island directs most of the current during an ebb into Slingsby Channel, and this results in Schooner Channel receiving much less current. Vessels exiting Slingsby Channel with an ebb during strong west winds will encounter large seas from the Outer Narrows to Lascelles Point. Currents in these narrows can be 9 knots on an ebb (and this is 5 miles from the main set of rapids), and waves over 15 feet (5 m) are not uncommon here. Mariners should be very wary about approaching the narrows during these conditions. If such sea conditions are anticipated, a good option is to take Schooner Channel to Allison Harbour or to Miles Inlet, and avoid the Outer Narrows completely. The channel between Fox Islands and Bramham Island is a possible pull-out lane, but there is lots of kelp in this pass and the currents, with whirlpools, are strong. The basin between the two Fox Islands is almost completely choked with kelp and is not a suitable anchorage.

Schooner Channel is very narrow, but free of swell and waves. Tidal streams can attain 5 knots on the flood and 6 on the ebb, so it can be a little hair-raising if your boat is caught in a carrying current. Be sure to monitor your position as you transit the passage because of the numerous protruding reefs, including a rock that lies in the middle of the channel near Murray Labyrinth. However, Schooner Channel is very pretty, its narrowness and overhanging trees evocative of a small river.

Seymour Basin 12

Top, racing the tide to post our boat name on Turret Rock. Above, the same rock at full ebb.

Once you've made it through the Nakwakto Rapids, there are over 85 miles of protected waterways to explore in Seymour and Belize Inlets. Although logging has taken place here for decades, a detailed survey of the area didn't take place until the early 1980s. Chart 3552 now provides mariners with detailed survey information for cruising this maze of long, narrow inlets.

Protected anchorage near the Nakwakto Rapids can be found about 3 miles into Nugent Sound, NW of a mid-channel islet in about 20 feet (6.5 m). Another nearby anchorage is **Charlotte Bay**, about 5 miles SE of the rapids. Back in the days of hand logging, camp boats would converge on Charlotte Bay for summertime gatherings where its flat beach, was the perfect picnic site.

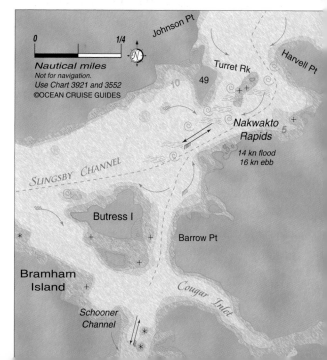

Nakwakto Rapids during ebb

Above, early morning in Strachan Bay. Right, Warner Bay. Bottom, sailing in Seymour Inlet.

Seymour Inlet extends east for 38 miles before terminating at a glacier-covered plateau, which is a source of Squamish winds in winter. During cold spells, when parts of the Seymour Basin freeze over, people once living at the logging camps would haul their rowboats to the ice-free narrows by sled to get to a port for supplies. The first hand loggers began arriving in "cedar country" in 1885, drawn to the area's abundant shoreside stands of timber where a tall conifer could be felled and slid straight into the water. From the 1920s to the 1960s, as many as 50 camps operated in the Seymour Basin, including a large one run by A.P. Allison at **Warner Bay** in Seymour Inlet some 18 miles from Nakwakto Rapids. Allison took over the claim in 1926 and used a wheel generator for electricity while the sawmill produced boat lumber and shake bolts.

We have anchored near the mouth of Warner Bay, on its east side, where we tied a line ashore to keep us well away from a log boom. A lovely lagoon lies at the bay's head, which we explored by dinghy, and we also hiked along the logging road.

In Belize Inlet, just north of Seymour Inlet, anchorage can be found in **Westerman Bay** near its west end, or farther along in **Mereworth Sound** and **Alison Sound**. **Village Cove**, at the entrance to Mereworth Sound, is sheltered by two wooded islets. In adjacent **Strachan Bay** there is a lovely, secluded cove lying in the bay's SW corner. A creek leading into Pack Lake lies opposite in the bay's NW corner. Moored nearby is the float home of old-timer Charlie Chilson who grew up in the Seymour Basin and worked a timber claim above Pack Lake.

The weather was splendid when we anchored in Strachan Bay's southwest cove in 45 feet of depth one September evening. Next morning, under a cloudless sky, the anchorage was, to quote Emily Carr, "in the brilliant sparkle of the morning when everything that was not superlatively blue was superlatively green."

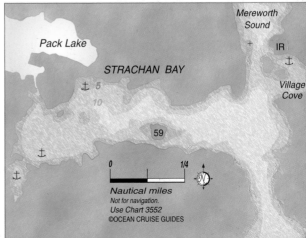

Mereworth Sound

Pack Lake

IR

STRACHAN BAY

Village Cove

5

10

59

0   1/4

Nautical miles
Not for navigation.
Use Chart 3552
©OCEAN CRUISE GUIDES

INDEX

Sunset Cove, Jedediah Is.

Photo Credits

pg VI, Ian Douglas
pg 8, by permission of Canadian Hydrographic Service
pg 11 top, Mike Woodward
pg 16, 17, Vancouver Archives
pg 18, top, bottom, Cummins Diesel
pg 20, Garmin Corp
pg. 22, Poet's Cove Resort
pg 29, top, Yvonne Maximchuk
pg 29, bottom painting by Alan Nakano of 'Haida Travellers' by permission of the artist
pg 30, painting by John Horton of 'I Name This Place Desolation Sound' by permission of the artist
pg 33, top, painting by John Horton of 'Repairs to Discovery' by permission of the artist
pg 31, top, Cartesia
pg 33 middle, Tourism Vancouver
pg 34, Alan Nakano
pg 35 bottom, Campbell River Museum
pg 36, top, Campbell River Museum
pg 36 bottom, painting by Alan Nakano of 'The Buyer and the Fisherman'
pg 39 top, Campbell River Museum
pg 40, bottom Ian Douglas
pg 42, 43, Ian Douglas
pg 45 top, painting by EJ Hughes, 'Indian Houses at Alert Bay' 1951, by permission of the artist and the National Gallery of Canada

pg 45 middle, painting by Emily Carr, 'Kwakiutl House', 1912, oil on card, Collection of the Vancouver Art Gallery, Emily Carr Trust, Photo: Trevor Mills
pg 52 top, Michael DeFreitas
pg 53, Corbis
pg 55, orca ill. by Alan Nakano
pg 56, humpback whale ill. by Alan Nakano
pg 58, 59 bottom right, Russ Heinl,
pg 68, Russ Heinl
pg 71, top Chris Cheadle
pg 74, Russ Heinl
pg 78, Buchart Gardens
pg 84 top, 86, 87, 89 Michael DeFreitas
pg 96, Russ Heinl
pg 98, bottom, 99, bottom, Michael DeFreitas
pg 103, bottom, Michael DeFreitas
pg 104, Russ Heinl
pg 105, top, 110, Michael DeFreitas
pg 117, 128 Russ Heinl
pg 131, Ian Douglas
pg 139, Fraser River Port Authority
pg 156, Chris Cheadle
pg 159, top, middle, bottom Phil Hersee
pg 170, Phil Hersee
pg 171, Chris Cheadle
pg 176, Ian Douglas
pg 179 top, 181, 182 bottom, 183 top, Russ Heinl
pg 180 bottom, Ian Douglas
pg 184, Russ Heinl
pg 187, bottom, 188, Mike Woodward
pg 189, 190, 191 bottom, 192, 193, 195, 201 bottom, Russ Heinl
pg 191 top, 196 bottom, Mike Woodward
pg 203 bottom, 204, 208, Ian Douglas
pg 214, 218, 221, Russ Heinl
pg 236, painting by Yvonne Maximchuk of 'Karlukwees' by permission of the artist
pg 248, top inset, Arno Andreas
pg 264, Russ Heinl
pg 310 middle, Province of British Columbia
pg 313 middle, Mike Woodward
pg 314, Chris Cheadle

All other photography by Anne Vipond & Bill Kelly.